Supply Chains in Reverse Logistics

Currently, it is obvious that new types of production (Industry 4.0) are accompanying new ways of distribution, which advance logistics, physical distribution science, and even supply chain management. The changing environment of the logistics activities carried out is also important for the development of the supply chain. Care for ecology, the recent pandemic, and the situation in Ukraine are other reasons to adapt logistics to the needs of an individual customer/recipient. It would be impossible without developing an appropriate strategy and applying appropriate tools for managing supply chains in the national and international dimensions. This book helps specifically with that.

When analyzing the needs and structure of modern supply chains, in the context of their safety and risk reduction, it is impossible to ignore the problem of digitization, which allows for logistic analysis of the company, determining optimal routes, designing logistic systems, optimizing storage processes and costs, and predicting possible threats (crisis situations) and their effects (losses). IT support, automatic data exchange, e-logistics, telematics, traceability, and chatbots between various departments of the company along the upper and lower parts of the supply chain improve the flow of material and accompanying information through automation, robotization, proactivity, and document digitization. These new trends make it possible to define logistics as modern logistics using new achievements of science and technology.

Modern logistics must also consider ecological aspects in line with assumptions about protecting the environment and improving our climate. Efficiently organized reverse logistics is not without significance for ecology. It is supported by renewable energy, electric vehicles, proper education in the field of a closed economy, cleaner production, waste minimization, the use of passive infrastructure, and proper waste management that allows us to positively influence environmental protection and human health. To meet the needs of creating modern supply chains, the authors developed this powerful book in which they analyze and present current and future solutions that influence the development of these issues in modern reverse logistics.

Supply Chains in Reverse Logistics

The Process Approach for Sustainability and Environmental Protection

Robert Stanisławski and Andrzej Szymonik

Designed cover image: Shutterstock

First published 2024
by Routledge
605 Third Avenue, New York, NY 10158

and by Routledge
4 Park Square, Milton Park, Abingdon, Oxon, OX14 4RN

Routledge is an imprint of the Taylor & Francis Group, an informa business

ISBN: 978-1-032-44529-8 (hbk)
ISBN: 978-1-032-44528-1 (pbk)
ISBN: 978-1-003-37261-5 (ebk)

DOI: 10.4324/9781003372615

Typeset in Garamond
by codeMantra

Contents

About the Author

Robert Stanisławski

Robert Stanisławski is a graduate of the University of Lodz. In 1999, he defended his doctoral dissertation in the field of logistics. The degree of a Postdoctoral Research Associate (dr hab.) in the field of Management Science, he obtained in 2018.

Currently, Robert Stanisławski has been a Professor (PhD) at the Department of Supply Chain Management (Institute of Management) in Faculty of Management and Organisation at the Technical University of Lodz since 2004.

His scientific publications include over 150 articles (authorship and co-authorship) at the national and international editions and many monographs which were edited by him in Polish as well as English version. Last monograph was devoted to supply chain security and published by Routledge publisher in 2022.

His research interests are related to innovation and the implementation of new solutions under "open innovation" by enterprises of all sizes. In addition, he is interested in issues related to logistics and the new technological solutions used within it (Logistics 4.0 and 5.0). The main areas of his research include: innovation, innovativeness and open innovation among economic organizations of all sizes, logistics, eurologistics or ecologistics at various stages of application in relation to economic organizations – modern systems in logistics and production (Internet of Things, Big Data, cloud computing, SCADA, etc.), use of RPA (Robotic Process Automation) and the development of centers of competence and excellence (CoE) among various organizations (economic and public), organizations' management on the international market – instruments in international exchange.

Andrzej Szymonik

Andrzej Szymonik (PhD, Professor) is a Graduate of the Military Communications Academy (currently known as CSŁiI) in Zegrze and the Military Communications Academy in Sankt Petersburg. In 2001, he defended his doctoral dissertation at the Technical University of Czestochowa. In 2008, the Faculty of Management of University of Warsaw granted him the degree of a Postdoctoral Research Associate (dr hab.) in the field of Management Science. In 2018, he received the title of professor in the field of Social Sciences at the University of Natural Sciences and Humanities in Siedlce.

During the years 1972–2010, he served in the army and reached the rank of general of the brigade; he was the commander of the Command Support Brigade and the Head of the Science and Military Education Department in the Polish Ministry of National Defence. Currently, he works as a professor at the Lodz University of Technology, Faculty of Organization and Management.

His achievements include 19 original monographs (details at www.gen-prof.pl), 31 original scientific publications in national and international journals, 85 co-authored scientific publications and participation in collective studies. Last monograph was devoted to supply chain security and published by Routledge publisher in 2022.

He is interested in: security of logistics systems, use of the tools of the fourth industrial revolution in modern logistics, developing models to increase the efficiency and effectiveness of logistics processes in a changing environment and growing customer needs, design for logistics in Industry 4.0, comprehensive logistics management (Total Logistics Management).

Introduction

In the 21st century, new types of production (Industry 4.0) are accompanied by new ways of distribution. This means the expansive development of logistics, i.e. the science of physical distribution, and in practical terms, also the concept and philosophy of supply chain management. The supply chain functioning is also largely impacted by the rapidly changing environment and climate change resulting from the degradation of the natural environment. The former include the negative impact of the Covid-19 pandemic on societies, the situation in Ukraine, fuel and financial crisis, as well as high inflation in most countries in the world. Among the latter, the increasing social awareness in the field of care for ecology and the need to eliminate the destructive impact of man on the natural environment should be mentioned. In the context of logistics, this forces its adaptation to the needs of an individual customer (recipient), which is impossible without developing and using an appropriate strategy and tools for managing supply chains in the national and international dimensions.

When analyzing the needs and structure of modern supply chains in the context of their security and risk reduction, it is impossible to ignore digitization, which enables the logistic analysis of the company, the determination of optimal routes, the design of logistic systems, the optimization of storage processes and costs, and the prediction of possible threats (crises) and their effects (losses). Practical examples of the use of tools supporting the functioning of supply chains include IT support, automatic data exchange, telematics, traceability, chatbots between various departments of the company along the upper and lower parts of the supply chain, improving the flow of the material stream and accompanying information, robotization, proactivity, and digitization of documents.

DOI: 10.4324/9781003372615-1

Reverse logistics is of particular importance for the proper functioning (from the point of view of the average person) of the supply chain. Its concept includes a greater usage of renewable energy, supplying it to production processes and transport. Positive effects in terms of environmental protection and health of all citizens (on a global scale) in the world should be expected thanks to specific actions such as proper education in the field of closed economy, clean production, waste minimization, use of passive infrastructure, and rationalization of waste management.

This monograph presents issues related to "modern logistics" in the context of ecology, i.e. environmental protection through the use of renewable energy to a greater extent. In practical terms, this means reducing the negative impact of humans on the ecosystem, which should have a positive impact on the quality of life on our planet. This monograph analyzes and presents current and future solutions that will affect the development of modern reverse logistics (ecology).

This monograph consists of seven chapters. **Chapter 1** contains information that presents the latest trends in modern logistics, which performs its tasks in very difficult periods caused by Covid-19, events in Ukraine, or increasing logistics costs (inflation, fuel problems). There are new solutions on the market for the 21st century, like Industry 4.0, which are already functioning or are being implemented. Ten trends were described, including Internet of Things (IoT), artificial intelligence (AI), robotics, last mile delivery logistics, automated warehouse, blockchain, cloud computing, big data, autonomous vehicles, and flexible logistics.

Much attention in this chapter is devoted to quality in logistics. Business people know very well that quality management in logistics is of key importance for their survival and development. Quality assurance and its control and management are interconnected in terms of benefits related to process improvement, increased productivity, and the level of customer satisfaction/loyalty. Cost minimization and good quality of logistics services are key factors in the success and position of the company in the market.

The last section describes the SMAC (Social, Mobile, Analytics, Cloud) architecture, which allows one to develop logistics and be "closer to the customer" with minimum financial outlays and maximum range. The ever-increasing amount of data that is provided by mobile devices, social platforms, web browsers, and loyalty programs creates a new business model based on customer-generated information. Proper processing of this information is a prerequisite for achieving business success.

Chapter 2 focuses on supply chain management. At the outset, the essence of supply chain management was presented, considering not only the traditional flow of material stream but also reverse logistics. The added value of this subsection is the presented 11 conclusions and postulates that characterize the object and subject of the supply chain as well as modern tools and instruments used to improve it. The next, second subsection characterizes a flow of material stream that is balanced in the context of the flow from the supplier to the recipient. Caring for society, natural environment, and economy should be implemented and assessed in a systemic manner so that there are as many winners and the least harm possible. The further content of this chapter is related to the packaging management, in which it is emphasized that a well-designed packaging in practice is one that is friendly to business and environmental protection, meets the expectations of customers as well as current legal standards and the latest technical solutions. The last subsection is related to the identification of threats that may appear in the implementation of processes within the supply chain. After presenting topology and classification, it focuses on the seven threats of the 21st century that affect the flow of goods and associated information.

Chapter 3 consists of six sections. The first is closely related to the natural environment safety system (NESS), in which the executive subsystem (forces and resources temporarily subordinated to, e.g. fire brigade, police, army that perform rescue tasks) and management subsystem (performs all management functions, i.e. planning, organizing, motivating, controlling, making decisions, and coordinating the way of ensuring the safety of the natural environment by the executive subsystem), as well as the natural environment, which is the object of impact and threat (any phenomenon undesirable from the point of view of the undisturbed operation of the SNN (NESS)) were distinguished and described. The ecological threats and their sources were identified. The following subsections were related to reverse logistics. Traditional and reverse logistics have been compared. The place and role of reverse logistics in the supply chain were shown, considering the processes carried out in it. Much attention was also dedicated to problems related to the reverse logistics such as:

- closed economy (the use of resources and materials is not linear, but circular, renewable energy is used);
- cleaner production (minimization, reduction at source, pollution prevention, cleaner production, eco-efficiency);
- waste minimization (actions applied to an object, material, substance before it becomes waste);
- passive building infrastructure, which is a building with extremely low energy requirements for interior heating.

Chapter 4 is devoted to the analysis of the basic processes and activities in logistics. Without more precise identification, evaluation, redefinition, and optimization of processes, it is difficult to achieve the 7R goal, i.e. the right product, the right quantity, the right condition, the right place, the right time, the right consumer (customer), and the right cost. The analysis of the presented processes such as flow of the material stream, information and decision-making processes, intralogistics in warehouse management, infrastructure of logistic flows, waste management, logistic customer service, logistic costs allows one:

- to improve the management of product flow and storage processes, which in effect contributes to satisfying the material needs of people participating in logistic processes;
- to increase the efficiency of the flow of materials and products, contributing to the reduction of flow costs and, consequently, the costs of the entire logistic processes;
- facilitate the implementation of modern and innovative solutions described in the first chapter of the monograph.

In this chapter, attention should be paid to the material related to waste management, which will minimize the negative impact of waste on human health and the environment, as well as lead to the optimization of processes in the area of reverse logistics.

Chapter 5 concerns IT systems supporting the functioning of logistics. It describes selected systems that facilitate planning, implementation, control, and monitoring of logistics processes. These include the following systems: effective consumer service, customer relationship management, supply chain management, distribution resource planning, warehouse management, transport management, fixed assets management, and enterprise resource planning.

Much attention in this chapter is devoted to transport telematics, knowledge about transport, integration of information technology and telecommunications in applications for the purposes of traffic management and control in transport systems, and stimulation of technical and organizational activities enabling the increase of efficiency and safety of the operation of these systems. Individual telematics solutions cooperate with each other, often under the control of a superior factor. In the third section, traceability is described, which makes it possible to trace the path of a product, from the moment it is created from raw materials, until it is delivered to the last customer in the supply chain and allows one to monitor the parameters identifying these goods and all locations covered by the flow.

The importance of this chapter is probably influenced by the content related to e-logistics and chatbots, which gained special importance during Covid-19. Closed shopping malls and the search for a reduction in personnel costs are the factors that meet the needs of e-commerce.

Chapter 6 contains materials related to the use of renewable energy sources in logistics. It is an up-to-date and important topic in the reality of the current global energy crisis and environmental problems. There is no doubt that a helpful solution that will partially neutralize the aforementioned problem is the wide use of renewable energy, including its use in logistics. The content of this chapter has been divided into three parts. The first one describes selected renewable energy sources which are obtained from wind, liquid biofuel, biogas, heat pumps, solar radiation, water, sun, and geothermal energy. The second part contains materials on energy storage, which contributes to the independence of the grid based on renewable energy. Much attention is devoted to the four technologies of energy storage, i.e. mechanical, electrochemical, chemical, and thermal. The last part is about the practical use of renewable energy for logistics. The focus is on issues related to electric passenger cars and trucks and organizing environmentally friendly transport for the last mile logistics.

Chapter 7 is entirely empirical and was created on the basis of own research conducted in 2022 on a group of enterprises that own and/or manage warehouses. This applies to all types of entities whose activity is related to warehouse management in micro, small, medium and large enterprises, in accordance with the European Union classification. This chapter is divided into several parts. The first one describes the research methodology, in which a simplified model of the research procedure is presented, covering the essential elements such as: identification of research gaps, formulation of the research goal, description of methodological rigors, description of the method of selecting the research sample, and method of selecting research methods and tools.

The second part of this chapter characterizes the research sample. The characterization was based on the size of enterprises, location, range of influence, type of services provided, type of warehouses, or the level of modernity of warehouses. The third part describes the most commonly used sources of renewable energy that warehouses use to protect the environment. The next element concerns the identification of various solutions that entities take to save energy, and thus also protect the environment. The last element is the assessment of the BMS (Building Management System), which allows one to manage the building in the area of energy saving and its better use.

The fourth part identifies and assesses the importance of practices and actions for environmental protection in warehouse management, taking into account such elements as: ESG (Environmental, Social and Corporate Governance) practices, or a comparison of "hard" and "soft" actions taken (in warehouses) to protect the environment.

In the fifth part, an assessment of the resources available to warehouses in terms of environmental protection was carried out. This was done in the context of the expansive development of Logistics 4.0 and Industry 4.0. In connection with this assessment, an analysis was also carried out in terms of determinants, barriers and benefits that warehouses (the surveyed enterprises) derive from the implementation of pro-ecological solutions.

In the last part of this chapter, an assessment of plans for the future among the surveyed entities in the context of implementing pro-ecological solutions, including the concept of Industry 4.0, was carried out. This chapter ends with conclusions and recommendations on the discussed issues.

The book is intended primarily for students of such fields of study as logistics, transport, management, production and logistics management, economics, security, as well as managers and directors managing logistics departments in production companies or warehouses. The particular usefulness of this monograph results from its pro-ecological element, in which attention is focused on aspects related to renewable sources and environmental protection. Much attention is devoted to the topic of "modern logistics" and its importance for eliminating negative impact on the environment.

The monograph is a useful tool for people who want to understand the principles of functioning of supply chains in the context of the development of Industry 4.0. and environmental protection. This book is also a map with the most important elements of creating a modern model of supply chain security management. It is certainly a one-of-a-kind guide that explains in a simple way the rules for the functioning of the supply chain in a turbulent environment and reverse logistics management, in the context of its importance for the protection of available natural resources and the development of future generations.

Chapter 1

Modern Logistics

1.1 Logistics and Industry 4.0

Digitization, globalization, and customer requirements mean that logistics companies compete in search of new solutions to deliver the ordered goods as soon as possible. It is possible if the warehouse and transportation processes are optimal along the global supply chains aimed at customer satisfaction. Automation of logistics processes, increased productivity and efficiency in the workflow, transparency, and traceability of the supply chain are key to enabling flexible and dynamic relationships among different actors.

The logistics industry carries out its tasks in a very difficult period, marked by the Covid-19 pandemic, events in Ukraine, or rising logistics costs (inflation, fuel crisis). Yet, despite these difficult times, today's logistics companies can deliver almost anything to the customer's door, from a single cosmetic to heavy, oversized items.[1]

When analyzing the literature on the subject, it should be noted that many solutions meeting the needs of the 21st century already exist or are being introduced to the market. Below are some of them (Figure 1.1).

First. Internet of Things (IoT) in Industry 4.0 involves adding digital sensors and network technologies to devices and systems that monitor and transmit data online without human intervention. The IoT is based on the following:

- network machines (connected to computer networks);
- cyber-physical system (CPS) components connected to intelligent and highly flexible applications.

DOI: 10.4324/9781003372615-2

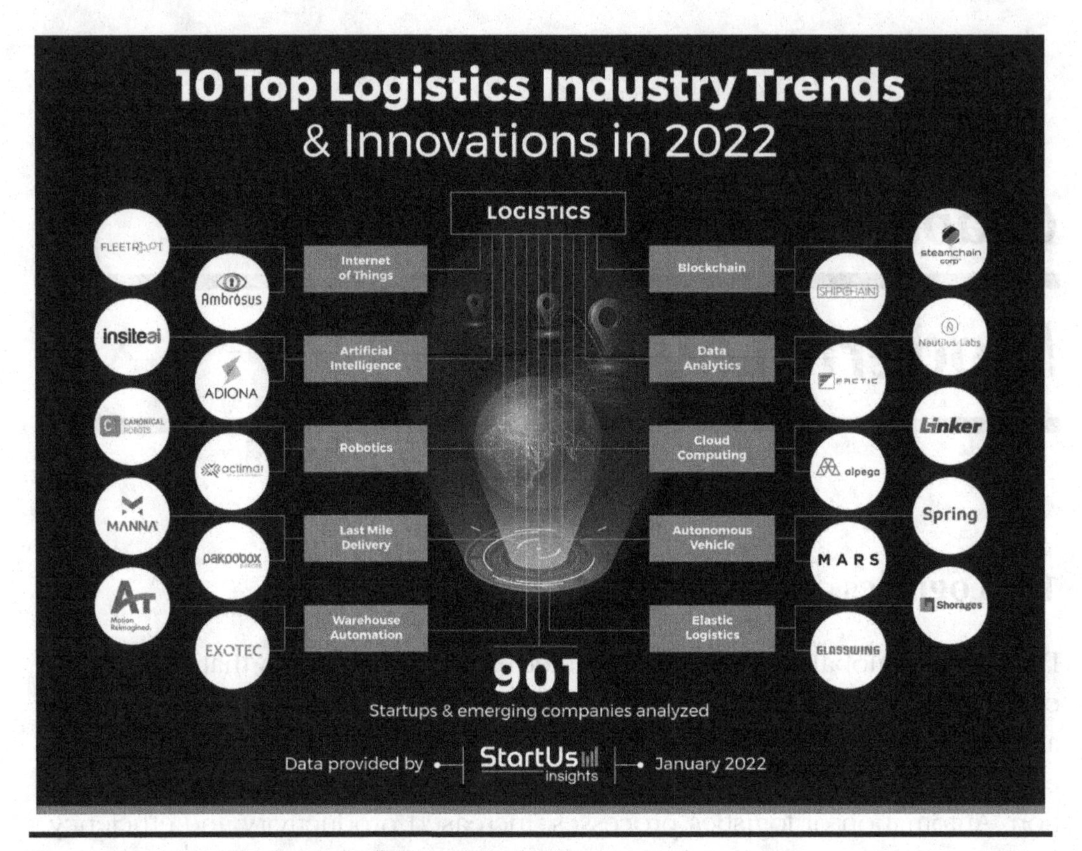

Figure 1.1 Top 10 trends in the logistics industry.

Source: **Based on *Top 10 Logistics Industry Trends & Innovations in 2022,* https://www-startus-insights-com.translate.goog/innovators-guide/top-10-logistics-industry-trends-innovations-in -2021/?, 4/20/2022.**

CPSs are inextricably linked with embedded systems, which are part of complete devices performing dedicated functions that often have real-time processing limitations. They combine such embedded systems with digital networks, facilitating independent data processing. The assignment of an IP address enables them to control and monitor these systems online.

Physical objects become "intelligent", connect with each other, and lead to innovative changes, including logistics. The interactions of various systems and devices that enable the following are already observed (5 Top Internet of Things Startups Impacting Logistics & Supply Chain, 2022):

- Tracking the location, traffic speed, and route of shipments in real time. This helps companies to efficiently plan supply chain operations such as order fulfillment, goods pick-up, and processing. IoT-based solutions enable companies to closely monitor the movement and condition of goods in the supply chain.

- Maintaining optimal temperature during transporting goods that must be transported in special conditions. This mainly applies to foods and pharmaceuticals. Appropriate cooling of temperature-sensitive goods during storage and transportation helps companies comply with global regulations and minimize waste.
- Managing inventory along the supply chain and dealing with fluctuations in supply and demand. Automated inventory control systems increase efficiency and increase productivity in logistics. IoT solutions use radio frequency identification (RFID), sensors, cameras, and the global positioning system (GPS) to track inventory throughout the supply chain.
- Monitoring real-time vehicle diagnostics in the area of periodic inspections and fleet performance optimization. IoT sensors use system data to detect failures before they occur and maintain vehicle health.
- Monitoring driver performance thanks to the data from IoT devices. The Driver Monitoring and Alerting System (DMAS) provides companies with a full insight into assets and keeps drivers safe on the road.

Second. Artificial intelligence (AI), thanks to the rapid development of machine learning, computing power, and big data analytics, has also found application in logistics. AI algorithms combined with machine learning support companies in actively dealing with fluctuations in demand. For example, AI-powered forecasting solutions enable managers to plan supply chain processes and find ways to reduce operating costs. AI has many uses in the freight management sector. With data analysis software, you can optimize routes based on weather or traffic patterns and manage vehicle operation (Top 10 Logistics Industry Trends & Innovations in 2022, 2022).

Third. The logistics industry continues to increase its use of robotics – machines capable of performing tasks that humans could perform. Using robotics in logistics processes increases the speed and accuracy of supply chain operations and reduces human error. Robots can work 24 hours a day, complete tasks faster than humans, tolerate hostile environments, and perform repetitive and dangerous processes (Top 5 Out Of 600 Robotics Startups In Logistics, 2022). In practice, robots are used in logistics, among others, for:

- loading and unloading goods, unloading containers, palletizing, and delivering logistic loads directly to a packing station or warehouse;
- collaborating with people, offering help, and increasing the efficiency of logistics operations (robots support the processes carried out on assembly lines, collecting, placing, and packing goods in a short time, while eliminating potential human errors);
- sorting products, loading elements into machines, quality control, and packaging.

Robotics for logistics is developing rapidly, as exemplified by the Singapore-based startup GreyOrange, which offers advanced robotics based on AI. It is based on intelligent software that allows users to control devices to cooperate effectively. By reducing the time from order to delivery, this flexible automation solves customers' business challenges of fast and error-free order fulfillment (Disrupting and redefining fulfillment, 2022).

Fourth. Last-mile logistics, while "only" delivering an order from a warehouse or distribution center to the end user, is one of the most important components of the supply chain and a key competitive advantage.[2] The last stage of delivering goods to the recipient is essential for building a positive customer experience. It becomes all the more necessary to ensure timely and efficient delivery. The dynamic development of the e-commerce sector caused by the pandemic, a significant increase in orders, or the increasingly frequent shortening of the delivery time for purchases, do not make this task easier (Ostatnia mila w logistyce to już nie tylko dostawa, 2022). Long routes, traffic jams, lack of parking spaces, high costs (the last mile is 41% of the cost of the supply chain) (Problem ostatniej mili. Czym jest i jak go rozwiązać?, 2022) – these are just some of the problems faced by logisticians who make last mile deliveries.

Many inconveniences are eliminated by new technologies, which include:

- drones that can reach remote areas, thus reducing delivery time and costs.
- smart lockers that provide customers with flexibility in picking up packages and making returns, as well as allow the storage of goods that require special temperature, humidity, and security conditions.

Fifth. An automated warehouse is a facility in which most of the logistics processes are fully automatic, that is, with no or minimal human involvement. This applies to such operations as accepting goods from outside, transporting and storing (warehousing) inside, and picking and forwarding them for further shipment. Specialized machines and devices are responsible for this area, including racks, elevators, conveyor systems, and software. The role of people working in this type of warehouse is definitely "secondary". It is usually limited to supervising the machines and performing tasks the machines cannot handle (Sojka, 2022). Warehouse automation is carried out with the pick-and-place technology (consisting in picking elements and placing them in a designated place) by[3]:

- automated guided vehicles (AGVs);
- robotic retrieval;
- automatic storage and retrieval system (ASRS);
- put-wall picking.

Sixth. Blockchain is a shared, immutable ledger that simplifies recording transactions and tracking resources across a business network. A resource can be tangible (products, warehouses, cars, cash, land) or intangible (intellectual property, patents, copyrights). Almost anything of value can be tracked and bought/sold on a blockchain network, thus reducing the risks and costs for all parties involved (*Czym jest technologia blockchain?*, 2022). A blockchain consists of many interconnected blocks that store new data from transactions. The completed transaction and the related details are stored in a block that receives its unique hash.[4] The moment a new block is added to the blockchain, it becomes publicly available.

The potential of blockchain technology as a decentralized form of documentation is unlimited but has advantages and disadvantages. Its advantages include (*Technologia Blockchain – czym jest?*, 2022):

- High accuracy – blockchain transactions are validated by a network of thousands or even millions of computers. Human interference in the data verification process is eliminated, thanks to which the record is free of human errors. Even if a computer made a computational error, it would only be in one copy of the blockchain;
- Cost reduction – blockchain reduces transaction costs by eliminating the need for third-party verification;
- Decentralization (dispersion) – this is one of the most important blockchain features, as it does not store data in one location. Instead, blockchains are copied and distributed over a network of computers. They each update their copy whenever a new block is added to the chain. Decentralization makes the data stored difficult to manipulate.

- Transaction efficiency, privacy, and security – financial institutions provide their services only on weekdays, while blockchain operates 24 hours a day, 7 days a week. Traditional transactions (e.g., via a bank) may take up to several days, while in the network of blocks, they take place under entirely different conditions, making them much more efficient. Blockchain is particularly appreciated in cross-border transactions, which take much longer using the traditional method due to different time zones. Another advantage is that after recording the transaction, its authenticity must be verified by the blockchain network, in which each block has a unique hash;
- Greater transparency – storing data in open-source blockchains also makes manipulation difficult. It is unlikely that a change in the blockchain of the millions of computers on the network would be unnoticed. This technology enables end-to-end tracing by all members of the blockchain. It provides faster dispute resolution than traditional supply chain systems;
- Blockchain technology can reduce the time wasted in sending e-mails and making phone calls to determine the cause of non-compliance;

On the other hand, blockchain has the following disadvantages (*Technologia Blockchain – czym jest?*, 2022):

- Susceptibility to hacker attacks – although difficult to carry out, hacker attacks are possible;
- Consistently high computing power of the blockchain is associated with high costs;
- A small number of qualified specialists to implement and use blockchain;
- The need to share a common and replicated database in each element of the supply chain with the appropriate additional investment;
- The requirement for transparency, security, and privacy of all information made available;
- Unconvincing tangible economic benefits for the blockchain participants.

More and more often, blockchain is used in practice in the management of logistics processes in the supply chain. It should be noted that this is a complicated and difficult process for several reasons (The Supply Chain and Blockchain, 2022):

- The development and implementation life cycle is very long and uncertain. Organizations need to become familiar with and master blockchain technology, which is still in its infancy when it comes to industrial applications;
- Having the skills and qualified specialists still comes at a very high cost due to long-term training needs. In addition, it requires the willingness and cooperation of the involved actors of the participants and the reaching of an agreement to build a new common system that will provide "added value" for all participants of these systems;
- Each participant's data storage and processing systems must be able to process all transactions, not just their own. This requires more resources, which is associated with additional costs;
- In current solutions, transaction logs are not protected, which allows participants to access information without restrictions. Future applications will have to address this issue. It is very likely that some order fulfillment details should be stored in external systems (for security reasons);
- Current blockchain applications are developed on independent platforms and private networks, which makes them incompatible with other applications. This creates an additional need for collaboration among participants to maintain identification, consensus, and authorization systems and to ensure trust and privacy;
- The blockchain benefits are achieved only after reaching a critical mass of participants. This requires the development of a very diverse user community involved in technology adoption, which is difficult to achieve when there are well-established systems and industry regulations, and any changes result in high costs of implementing new technologies

Despite many difficulties, blockchain is starting to be tested and used in logistics. One of the first examples of its practical applications is tracking the activities performed in the supply chain, such as: identifying logistic entities performing them or determining the place and time of each logistics process (Blockchain in logistics and transportation: Transformation Ahead, 2022). Each actor in the supply chain can identify the following:

- Input and output products as well as knowledge, supported by appropriate documentation, in the scope of picking various batches of products within the enterprise to create individual products or new batches in accordance with orders;

- Companies from which components for production were obtained;
- Logistics, transportation, and forwarding companies.

An example of a food supply chain model based on a blockchain network is presented in Figure 1.2.

The collected data can also be used to evaluate the performance of each activity and monitor the integrity of the product quality during distribution. This reduces workload and ensures traceability while increasing productivity, reducing costs, and increasing confidence that products are genuine and maintain their quality.

Another potential use of blockchain in the trucking industry is performance monitoring. One of the factors determining the cost of freight is the size of the cargo. IoT sensors can successfully determine the weight and volume of the cargo and thus charge for the carriage of goods.

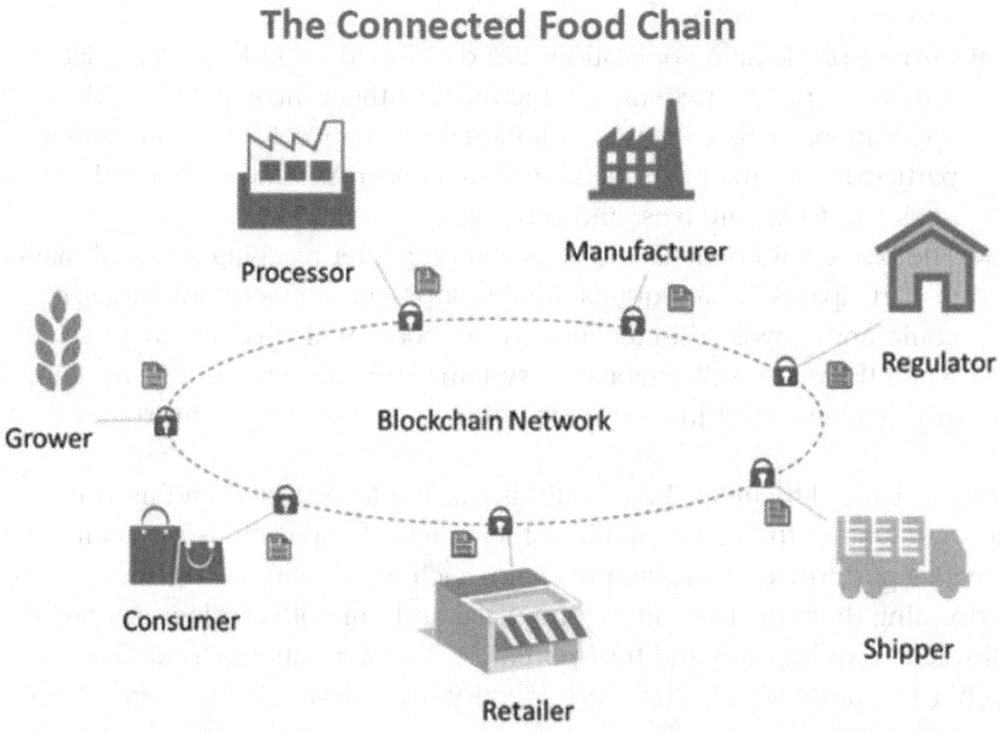

Figure 1.2 A food supply chain model based on a blockchain network.

Source: **Based on S. Prabhat, D. Albright, Food Safety: Traceability and Transparency by Way of Blockchain, https://www.foodlogistics.com/safety/blog/21070106/food-safety-traceability-and-transparency-by-way-of-blockchain, 4/20/2022.**

Vehicle history information is another potential use of blockchain technology as a truck enters the aftermarket. The obtained data is considered immutable and transparent, and the parties to the transaction do not have to establish mutual trust beforehand.

Seventh. Cloud computing involves computing services offered by external entities, available on request at any time and scaling as needed (Rosenberg & Mateos, 2011). The term "cloud computing" refers to shared software and/or information that users access through a network. Instead of storing information on their physical servers or hard drives, users rely on servers maintained by cloud software vendors. From the user's perspective, all information is stored and easily accessible online 24/7 and from various devices such as desktops, laptops, tablets, and smartphones (Sahiner, 2022).

Supply chain management is increasingly embracing cloud computing capabilities among different stakeholders, which can include different departments within one organization or a wider chain of countless sub-suppliers, integrated services, and companies (Figure 1.3).

Cloud computing can be divided by several criteria. The first division concerns cloud designing, creating, and managing. These criteria result in the following clouds (Leończuk, 2012):

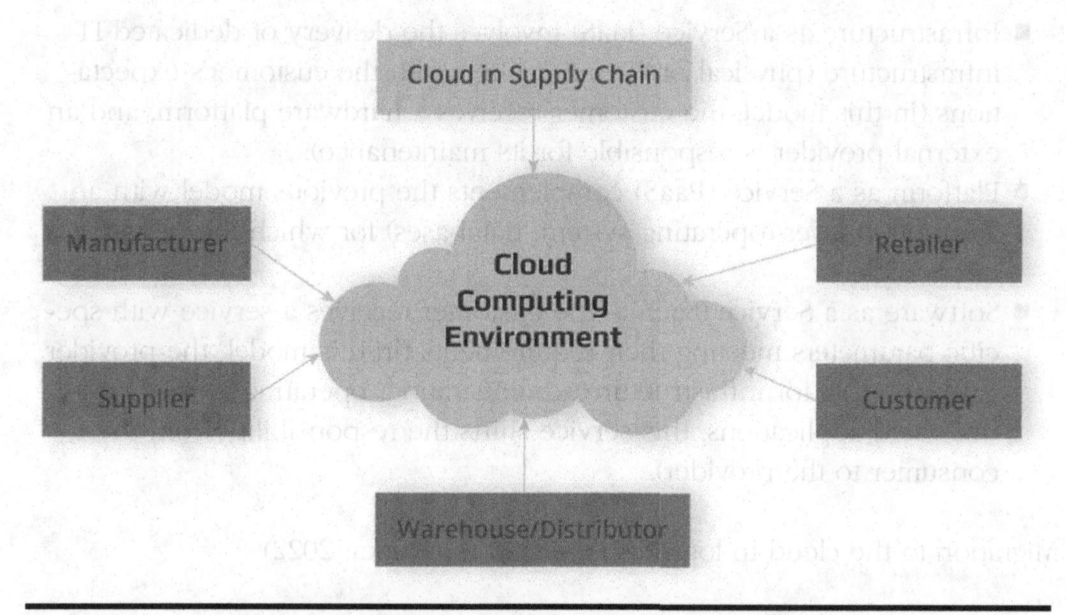

Figure 1.3 Cloud stakeholders in the supply chain.

Source: **Based on W. Dutka, Logistics and Supply Chain in the Cloud: Capabilities and Migration Strategies, https://intellias-com.translate.goog/logistics-and-supply-chain-in-the-cloud-capabilities-and-migration-strategies /? 5/3/2022.**

- public, intended for a mass audience – their main advantage is universal availability, which means they can be used by any person with Internet access (free e-mail services are a typical example of public clouds);
- private, that is, dedicated IT resources or off-the-shelf solutions, intended for one economic entity (dedicated resources should be understood here as the latest IT technologies and highly qualified staff of engineers);
- hybrid, combining elements of both models.

The decision between private and public entities requires logistics companies to decide on the scope of adapting their cloud infrastructure and the logistics solutions they want to implement. Public cloud solutions that limit customization for ultimate efficiency, usability, and adaptability are the antidote to complexity (direct the industry toward a future where it can benefit from technological innovation without battling complexity at the same time).

Other division criteria of cloud computing solutions are the access to and use of resources and the transfer of responsibility for hardware, licensing, and connectivity to an external provider. Thus, the following models can be distinguished (Jaką chmurę obliczeniową wybrać?, 2022):

- Infrastructure as a Service (IaaS) involves the delivery of dedicated IT infrastructure (physical or virtual) in line with the customer's expectations (in this model, the customer receives a hardware platform, and an external provider is responsible for its maintenance);
- Platform as a Service (PaaS) complements the previous model with an application layer (operating system, databases) for which the provider is responsible.
- Software as a Service (SaaS) – the customer receives a service with specific parameters meeting their requirements (in this model, the provider is responsible for infrastructure administration, operating system, and dedicated applications; this service shifts the responsibility from the consumer to the provider).

Migration to the cloud in logistics is related to (Dutka, 2022):

- Planning and preparation. Companies should choose the most beneficial cloud integration strategy. Two basic methods available are shallow or "lift-and-shift" migration of local applications and solutions without server changes (thanks to the "lift-and-shift", the application moves to the cloud without additional configuration). While deep integration with the cloud requires additional changes to the application during its migration to take advantage of full cloud capabilities (e.g., a monolithic application can be split into several microservice applications for greater flexibility and easier access for customers);

- Choosing a cloud environment – you can choose a single or hybrid cloud, local solution, and multicloud approach. Depending on the choice, the cloud environment may consist of IaaS, PaaS, or SaaS;
- Migrating and viewing applications and services. You can use an Internet connection to migrate your application to the cloud for small database migrations. It is best to consider physically moving the servers to a cloud provider for large ones.

The following features are best suited for cloud data migration:

- cloud supply chain planning (typically requires migrating ERP systems with all data);
- sourcing and procurement (this segment benefits from quick implementation and lower costs);
- cloud manufacturing.

The tangible benefits of using cloud computing in logistics include the following (Five Business Benefits Of Using Cloud Logistics, 2022):

- reduction of costs related to the use of information technology in logistics – the costs are distributed among many users;
- easy and quick access to innovative solutions proven in the management of logistics processes through the use of traceability and automatic identification applications, for instance;
- reduction of costs related to training people responsible for IT processes in logistics;
- real-time access to inventory;
- precise control of logistics costs along the supply chain;
- rational access to computing power and memory, we order as much as we need;
- easier access to IT systems in the event of a change in the company's place of business;
- the potential of integrating cloud computing with mobile information technologies;

- convenience of switching to new software and IT equipment due to easy access to IT specialists;
- not dealing with the installation, updating of programs, or the purchase of licenses for their use (this is the responsibility of the service provider);
- not dealing with the operation (repair) of the IT system;
- archiving of documentation;
- online content analysis and filtering carried out in the cloud, outside the company's computer;
- transparency and traceability of logistics processes;
- more reliable protection of data and equipment against cyberattacks – service providers use the latest solutions.

Of course, external services carry certain risks and inconveniences, including the following (Hoey, 2022; Szymonik, 2015):

- no direct control over the IT system (hardware and software);
- the risk of information being lost or stolen by the cloud computing provider;
- sharing the company's strategic data (e.g., list of markets, list of contractors) with competitors;
- introducing new solutions that include applications and services unnecessary from the user's point of view;
- increasing prices for services by the owner of the cloud;
- difficult integration with suppliers – not all may have compatible IT systems, for example, ERP.

Eighth. The flow of goods around the world generates huge data sets (big data), which contain the following information (Gilb, 2022):

- origin and destination, weight, content, size, and location (tracking millions of shipments);
- transportation companies' data related to road traffic, weather, vehicle diagnostics, location, etc.;
- anticipation and prevention of bottlenecks in the supply chain.

Warehouse managers use the created data sets[5] to monitor and evaluate how customer behavior changes and what is often expected from manufacturers and delivery (courier) companies. In addition, warehouse managers have a detailed view of the loading, transportation, unloading, and delivery process. This allows them to better plan routes and schedule deliveries to increase safety and reduce fuel expenses (Lahoti, 2022).

The benefits of using big data in business include the following (Pros and Cons of Big Data: Solutions To Empower Your Business, 2022):

- Real-time fleet tracking. Thanks to big data analysis technology, RFID tags, GPS devices, and barcodes, logistics companies can track vehicles in real time. These systems can capture traffic, road network, and fleet data, allowing logisticians to optimize routes and plan and execute delivery schedules. It also provides customers with real-time delivery status updates, and in the event of a delay, customers receive automatic notifications;
- Effective warehouse management because the managers have real-time information about stock levels, deliveries, loading, transportation, and unloading processes and can make rational decisions;
- Efficient management of last-mile deliveries thanks to data related to deliveries and customers. Logistics service providers can better modify the internal process to achieve good quality, efficiency, and transparency;
- Proper equipment operation thanks to real-time data on equipment and means of transportation. Companies can perform predictive analytics based on this real-time information to find patterns, performance deterioration, irregularities, and future failures. As a result, they can maintain their equipment, improve vehicle performance, and avoid costly downtime.

Ninth. In recent times, there has been more and more writing and talking about autonomous vehicles (also known as connected vehicles, driverless vehicles, and robotic vehicles), which are based on technological innovations and can significantly change the dynamics of logistics. Such vehicles integrate various technologies and can run without human intervention. However, this evolutionary process still requires much research and testing.

Level 1[6] was the earliest autonomy level, namely Cruise Control, introduced in 1958 by Chrysler, followed by several driver assistance systems. Level 2 is found in today's technology, where vehicles steer, accelerate, and brake semi-automatically. In 2014, the Mercedes-Benz Future Truck 2025, the world's first automated truck (Level 3), was presented.

Companies are currently working on Level 4, involving highly automated driving, with the final step being Level 5 – a fully automated or autonomous vehicle where the car makes decisions on its own. Renault and Nissan, together with Google's sister company Waymo, plan to introduce autonomous taxis and delivery services to France and Japan. Honda announced a USD 2.75 billion investment in a collaboration project with General Motors to develop autonomous cars. Toyota and SoftBank agreed to cooperate in developing autonomous cars and new mobility services. UPS also invested in TuSimple, an autonomous driving technology company, and Volkswagen tests the autonomous electric Golf in Hamburg. The above companies report said projects as largely successful (Groims, 2022).

Autonomous vehicles offer many advantages in logistics. These include the following (Groims, 2022):

- Gradual reduction of deficits among drivers due to the use of Levels 4 and 5 autonomous trucks. Moreover, automation creates better working conditions and increases safety, which makes it possible to employ elderly and disabled people as drivers;
- Reduction of personnel costs because each autonomous truck can theoretically run 24 hours a day, 365 days a year. If goods could be transported without a driver, shipping companies' operating costs would drop by up to 40%;
- Savings in transportation thanks to autonomous vehicle design taking into account load size, destination, and working time. Autonomous vehicles are more economical (use less fuel) as they use long-haul convoy techniques and optimize routes through AI-assisted technology.

Autonomous vehicles can also be widely used in underground tunnels to move logistic loads (Figure 1.4). For example, Olten-based Cargo Sous terrain AG presented its vision of connecting production and logistics facilities with Swiss cities for the first time ten years ago.

The first step is automatically loading pallets or modified refrigerated containers for goods onto electric vehicles without a driver in designated "hubs". Next, the containers are to be transported underground in lifts and onto the tracks. Then, the autonomous cargo-carrying vehicles travel to their destination at a constant speed of 30 kilometers per hour. Finally, the goods are removed there and distributed locally (Bradley, 2021).

Tenth. Another area that affects supply chain processes is the so-called elastic logistics (EL), which involves the following (Mecalux, 2021):

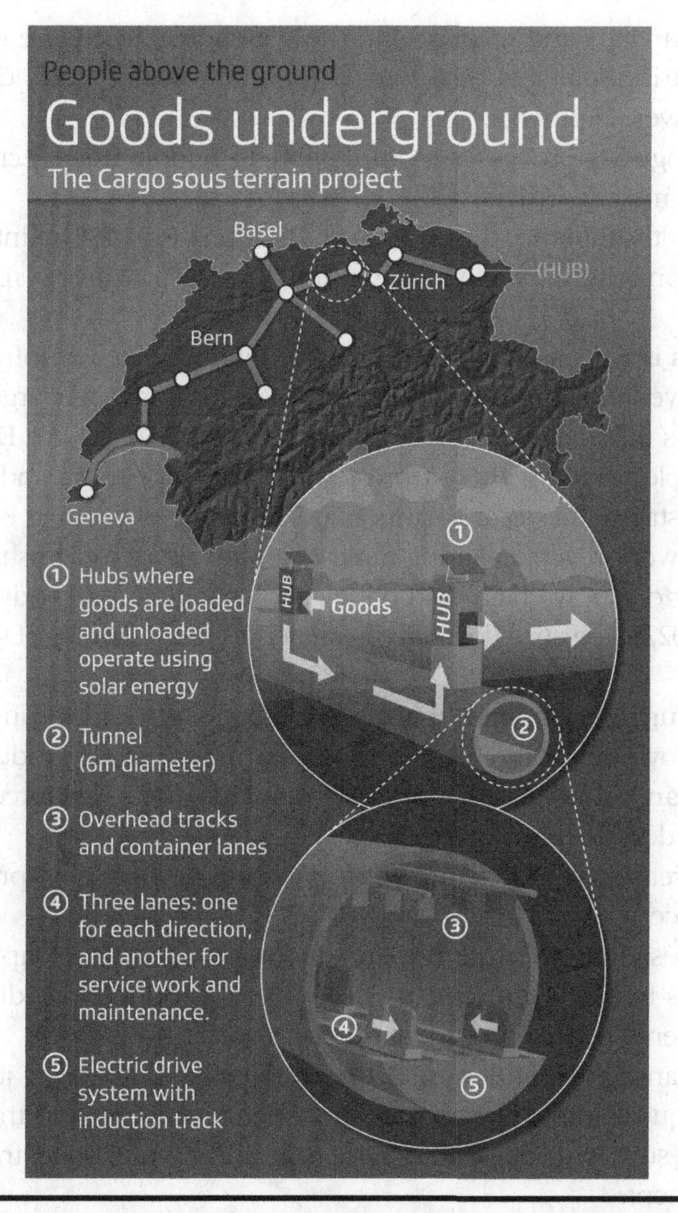

Figure 1.4 Underground tunnel for transporting the material stream underground.

Source: **Based on S., Bradley (2021), Futuristic underground cargo project moves a step closer to reality, available at: https://www-swissinfo-ch.translate.goog/eng/futuristic-underground-cargo-project-moves-a-step-closer-to-reality/46674218?, 06.06.2021.**

- flexible management of fluctuating demand in the supply chain;
- increasing or limiting warehouse resources to handle more orders or manufacture faster;

- scaling activities and resources in the warehouse to ensure their efficiency during seasonal peak orders and reduce their costs during periods of fewer shipments;
- making logistics processes more flexible to handle unexpected increases in the number of orders;
- dealing with unplanned threats and situations (caused by intentional or unintentional human activities, natural hazards, or diseases).

Elastic logistics is not based on renting or owning buildings or infrastructure, does not involve long-term investments, and does not manage large, complex operations that may need to be automated and adapted. An EL model is typically implemented without fixed-term contracts or space and location restrictions. It streamlines omnichannel operations by expanding e-commerce fulfillment network reach, ensuring rapid retail inventory replenishment, and/or responding to supply chain disruptions and changing market dynamics (Halbmaier, 2022). Logistics flexibility is related to the following (Deyglio, 2022):

- manufacturing companies that have a reserve of production capacity, which allows scalability in the event of an increase in product demand;
- effective and quick reconfiguration of workstations (resources), depending on orders or market needs;
- efficient retooling of machines (production lines) for new products in accordance with the customer's wishes;
- rapid redesign and testing of parts and components to adapt them to numerous market requirements from a new product, including customer requirements and environmental impact;
- effective and efficient design of the supply chain, adapting it to customer requirements, market conditions, environment, and transportation;
- adjusting supply to demand, keeping in mind warehouse and inventory management;
- redesigning products and their components in the face of resource scarcity and risk requirements;
- effective response to unplanned situations, threats caused by human activities (intentional and unintentional), and climate;
- quick response to cyberattacks on information systems by all participants in the supply chain.

The so-called circular economy has essential meaning in modern logistics. Each new product has a specific life cycle. In the last phase, it loses its usefulness and becomes waste, which must then be effectively and adequately managed. A helpful tool in these activities is a well-designed supply chain in which waste is moved to be repaired, reused, or processed. In the organization of reverse logistics, in the circular economy, particular attention should be paid to resource-intensive sectors such as electronics, ICT, plastics, textiles, and construction.

1.2 Quality in the Logistics Sector

Customer satisfaction is the goal of any economic system that operates in a turbulent environment. Competition forces us to look for new and retain existing customers by using and implementing the best products or services to satisfy the customer.

Business people know very well that quality management in logistics is key to their survival and development. Quality assurance, control, and management are interrelated in terms of benefits related to process improvement, increased productivity, and increased customer satisfaction/loyalty.

Cost minimization and good quality of logistics services are key factors in the success and position of the company in the market. It should be noted, however, that the quality of logistics services is difficult to quantify because it is a function of data collected based on changing customer perceptions about the measurement process over time. The quality of the logistics service can be defined with reference to two balancing bases, that is, physical distribution and customer service.

The quality of logistics services can be measured by several key factors, which include the following (5 Key Factors to Measure Proven Logistics Service Quality, 2022):

- **Tangibles** in the logistics industry. Currently, almost all customers want to be able to track their goods and services online, paying particular attention to various protection methods and the safety of goods.
- **Reliability** of the logistics service quality is quantified by several criteria, including meeting deadlines, service time availability, and reliability. Customers value the following highly in terms of reliability: speed of services, respecting the specified timeframe, and service performance without complications or damage.
- **Responsiveness (reaction)** of the logistics service quality is measured using conditions that show how logisticians communicate with

customers. To interact with customers satisfactorily, so they are satisfied with the service, a logistician should have experience, be communicative, committed, goal-oriented, and be good at organizing work and tasks.

- **Assurance** that the developed products, services, and systems achieve their intended purpose in a safe, accessible, and reliable manner, and moreover, minimize losses, eliminate alterations, redesign, remanufacturing, or services.
- **Empathy** – the ability to recognize and sympathize with customer requirements. As practice shows, not all logisticians offer customers satisfactory service in terms of tastes and preferences.

The logistics industry uses many systems to help ensure quality[7] and compliance. These include the U.S. Food and Drug Administration (FDA) Current Good Manufacturing Practice (CGMP),[8] FDA GxP,[9] ISO 9000,[10] ISO 13485,[11] ISO 27000,[12] ISO 14000,[13] IATF 16949,[14] Title 21 CFR Part 11,[15] and ISO 28000 (Supply Chain Safety Management System).

The Qualityze EQMS has been developed to monitor quality and compliance in manufacturing, automotive, logistics, and other industries. In the case of the logistics industry, this system is used in many areas, including the following (Why is Quality Assurance Important in the Logistics Sector?, 2022):

- Nonconformance management enables logistics companies to streamline their defect and deviation management processes while allowing them to document all necessary details. It helps them meet regulatory standards by ensuring that the product meets all specified requirements. It is a cloud-based solution that provides greater flexibility, scalability, and security to manage high-quality data, processes, and systems on a centralized platform without any issues;
- Change management is an integral part of logistics quality management. This helps logisticians identify and evaluate organizational changes that can lead to failure in supply chain processes. Monitoring such situations makes it possible to react in advance to phenomena that negatively impact logistics efficiency. At the same time, logisticians can plan activities that neutralize and counteract waste;
- Audit management means impartial evaluation of all aspects of the supply chain system, including document flow, supplier relationships, planning procedures, logistics infrastructure, quality control costs, time

to market, and more. Qualityze Audit Management simplifies the entire audit process cycle, enabling logistics companies to perform all online and offline audits efficiently. It includes a predefined audit checklist that can be configured according to individual business requirements;

- CAPA (Corrective and Preventive Action) management is a key function in logistics and transportation management to maintain service stability and organizational productivity. It identifies actions that can either correct the identified root cause or prevent its occurrence. The purpose of CAPA tracking is to provide a mechanism for minimizing the risk of harm (remedying an existing root cause) or effective continual improvement, which is the primary goal of a quality management system along the entire supply chain (Levy, 2022);
- Document management in logistics involves many challenges, including paper-intensive and high-cost processes. Its basic requirements are flawless and secure communication of information related to the order, including location, supply chain, delivery date, and place. Qualityze Document Management for Logistics helps create, manage, and track digital documents in a centralized repository. This solution helps streamline all document tasks, including document retrieval or checking;
- Supplier quality management requires appropriate tools, which include: quality assessment; quality audit; technical purchasing conditions; supply needs; procedures; receipt of goods; supplier classification. This enables sorting vendors that meet the business requirements and creating a list of approved vendors based on their performance and quality;
- Complaints management that reduces costs and increases customer satisfaction helps gain customers' trust and loyalty. This system covers activities related to the complaint records and data collection for complaint processing; problem and nonconformance identification, conducting corrective actions; considering complaints; records of the reasons why the problem was not detected and its causes; generating supplier charges based on conclusions from the complaint processing process; collecting documents such as photos, films, etc.; support for simple and complex complaint processing;
- Total Productive Maintenance (TPM) [16] in logistics is a system that connects all company employees in maintaining a collision-free flow of the material flow, thanks to keeping the machinery park operational through maintenance, repairs, repairs, and planned inspections and inspections. TPM allows the user to manage, monitor, and track all maintenance schedules. It allows for a proactive and calculated

approach to maintaining equipment life. It simplifies maintenance tasks – corrective maintenance, preventive maintenance, risk-based maintenance, reliability-based maintenance, or condition-based maintenance, giving a competitive advantage;
- Management of material (supply) compliance in procurement, production, and distribution is particularly important from the point of view of broadly understood quality. Today's supply of materials most often takes place along the supply chain in an international, global dimension, which is increasingly complex and exposed to threats related to the growing malicious involvement of third parties. As a result, deliveries may be exposed to corruption, impersonation by other companies, imitation of goods, brand piracy, technical deficiencies, and environmental pollution. Only the supervision of material compliance will result in the elimination of dishonest material suppliers in accordance with the law.
- Calibration management concerns the following:
  - equipment – mainly checking the accuracy by comparing the measurements with the values defined in the standard;
  - logistics processes, such as customer contact management, sales and customer classification, billing and invoicing, service prices, logistics assets,[17] management of offers and service contracts, access to equipment work orders, records, profiles, and manuals.

There is software on the market that supports calibration, for example, Qualer. It enables real-time processing of calibrations and documentation, increasing efficiency and productivity while reducing costs (Calibration Management Software, 2022).

Logistics inspection management is objective proof that the processes are carried out with care for the quality and safety of goods and following business ethics. Companies outsourcing logistics processes have control over their course. Lack of proper supervision can result in loss of customer confidence, lower revenues, delayed shipment, waste generation, and cause a product recall if it does not meet the market quality specifications. Inspection management enables companies to streamline control of:

- first piece;
- before production;
- during production;
- before shipping;
- container loading.

The software helps auditors identify and resolve quality issues before they cause harm to brands or sellers. These intuitive and customizable solutions make logistics inspection processes simpler and more efficient.

Logistics quality assurance requires regularity, transparency, efficiency, and appropriate instruments and tools, which are often costly to purchase and operate. The methods supporting quality assurance in the logistics industry include testing (Why Quality Assurance is Vital in the Logistics Sector?, 2022):

- mobile devices to ensure that users in all areas of the supply chain have access to relevant data and reporting applications through their devices and enjoy a smooth, user-friendly experience that increases productivity;
- cloud storage to provide a very smooth transition and help improve security, latency, and overall performance;
- functionalities to check if all software features work properly in various logistics situations;
- performance to ensure that the company's software applications do not crash or degrade during periods of intense activity to assess logistics processes (performance and functionality testing often go hand in hand).

1.3 SMAC in Logistics

The 21st century poses a number of challenges to logistics, including the following (Bujak et al., 2014):

- increasing focus of logistics activities on customer expectations (personalization),
- creating new values and functionalities for the customer;
- shortening of the product life cycle in connection with the pressure to reduce it in the context of product development and time to reach the end user;
- new concepts and strategies of SCM operation conditioned by growing trends related to time and cost reduction, emerging new technologies (e.g., IoT, cloud computing, autonomous vehicles, robots);
- building strategic alliances;
- shifting the competitive struggle to the entire supply chain;

- initiating and putting into practice a stream of innovation (e.g., big data, mobile devices – tablets, smartphones, cell phones);
- introduction of innovative IT systems enabling full integration of activities within the supply chain, increasing flexibility and reducing operating costs;
- increased transparency in the operations of the entire supply chain (e.g., monitoring);
- growing importance of combined transportation and properly organized (innovative) reloading;
- increased number of parcels combined with e-commerce concepts (visible increase during the recent Covid-19 pandemic);
- growing importance of aspects related to sustainability (circular economy, renewable energy use);
- necessity to provide services in cities – last-mile logistics;
- globalization and liberalization of world trade.

The presented trends necessitate searching for new solutions in logistics. They include SMAC, sometimes referred to as the "third platform". SMAC is an acronym for (Monnappa, 2022; Nadaj SMAC swojemu biznesowi, 2022):

Social (networks) break down barriers to the information flow among people and become platforms, thanks to which the rapid exchange of knowledge is increasingly effective and more often used for business purposes, including logistics. Communication on social media platforms strongly displaces telephone or e-mail communication. Social networks facilitate better customer interaction, thanks to which it becomes possible to react faster to problems and build a knowledge base developed on user preferences and behaviors. Employees associated with the community can exchange experiences and interesting content and speed up problem-solving much easier and faster, including material flow among participants in the supply chain.

It should be emphasized that there are currently over 2 billion active social media users worldwide and over 4.5 billion mobile phone users. No industry or organization can afford to ignore the opportunity these staggering numbers offer to connect directly with consumers (SMAC Net: The Digital Platform of the Future?, 2022).

Mobile devices, such as smartphones and tablets, are used by people not only in everyday life to communicate with each other but also to run a business. In the case of activities within the supply chain, modern mobile communication devices are used to implement such processes as:

- transportation (e.g., route optimization, cargo tracking,
- supplying workstations (e.g., production intralogistics, ongoing inventory monitoring).
- shaping the inventory structure (e.g., order, delivery tracking, completion).
- logistic customer service (e.g., marketing, ordering, delivering, handling complaints, tracking deliveries to the customer).
- warehousing (ordering, storing, issuing).
- logistic costs (e.g., invoicing);
- packaging management.

The increase in the popularity of online shopping, which was visible during the recent pandemic (Covid-19), at the same time forced entrepreneurs to develop their e-commerce marketing channels and provide customers with mobile channels. Under these conditions, presenting the offer on mobile devices is the basis for gaining or maintaining a strong market position and the foundation of good after-sales services.

Analytics is the foundation of a good performance assessment of individual processes in the supply chain. It is a starting point for assessing the effectiveness of the logistics processes, which helps reduce operating costs, improve the quality of service, and, as a result, improve the reputation of enterprises. The analysis should consider all logistic parameters of the enterprise (e.g., selection of suppliers, warehouse management, picking, complaints, customer behavior, number of employees per shift, degree of automation, etc.) to accurately determine the efficiency of individual logistics operations.

Based on the data analyzed by advanced algorithms, logisticians can deduce how to ensure customer loyalty, improve marketing campaigns, improve product development processes, and provide services that match the preferences and requirements of customers. Furthermore, by learning user preferences, logisticians can present content aligned with their expectations. The overriding goal of using analytical tools in running a business is therefore making correct decisions based on the up-to-date and aggregated information.

Cloud computing offers tools that enable efficient information gathering and effective enterprise management, including logistics. Cloud computing tools in logistics:

- break down geographic barriers;
- access data at any time and place;
- avoid costs related to building IT infrastructure;

- offer unlimited storage space;
- ensure constant access to data;
- control logistic processes in real time;
- communicate with all actors in the supply chain;
- communicate with all business partners and customers within a consistent interface and any devices;
- provide cheap and easy data archiving;
- authorize the billing and reporting processes.

The cloud is the factor that holds the other elements of SMAC together.

Notes

1 An oversized item exceeds the following dimensions: width – 2.5 m, length – 16.5 m (semi-trailer) or 18.5 m (trailer), height – 4 m, weight – 42 t.

2 More on last-mile delivery in Subsection 6.3.

3 Put-wall – solutions that optimize the workflow by taking large volumes of orders from conventional or automated warehouse systems and using intelligent manual sorting for fast and accurate fulfillment.

4 Hash is the result of a mathematical operation (called a hash function) on a specific string of characters (e.g., on a password or file). This function converts user-supplied input (such as a password) to a short, fixed-size value. An important property of the hash is that it is irreversible (e.g., the math operation inverse to addition is subtraction and for multiplication – division). A person with a hash cannot use an inverse function of the hash function to find out the sequence of characters (e.g., passwords) for which the hash was generated *(Co to jest hash?*, available at: https://bezpieczny.blog/co-to-jest-hash/, 3/28/2022).

5 Big data refers to datasets that are so large and complex that they require new technologies, such as artificial intelligence, to be processed. The data comes from many different sources. Often it is data of the same type, for example, GPS data from millions of cell phones used to avoid traffic jams. Data can also be mixed. The technology enables very fast data collection (in near real time) and analysis to obtain new conclusions *(Big data: definicja, korzyści, wyzwania (infografika)*, available at: https://www.europarl.europa.eu/news/pl/headlines/society/20210211STO97614/big-data-definicja-korzysci-wyzwania-infografika, 5/5/2022).

6 Autonomy levels: Level 0 – no automation; Level 1 – driver assistance; Level 2 – partial driving automation; Level 3 – conditional driving automation; Level 4 – high diving automation; Level 5 – full driving automation (the vehicle makes decisions on its own).

7 Quality control includes efforts to detect defects, while quality assurance involves efforts to completely prevent these defects.
8 FDA ensures the quality of medicinal products and food processing by carefully monitoring manufacturers' compliance with the Current Good Manufacturing Practice (CGMP) regulations.
9 The term GxP covers a wide range of compliance activities such as Good Manufacturing Practice (GMP), Good Laboratory Practice (GLP), Good Clinical Practice (GCP), and others, along with product-specific requirements that life science organizations must meet.
10 The ISO 9000 family is a set of quality management standards. These include basic standards for quality management systems and standards for supporting technology.
11 ISO 13485 is the internationally recognized standard of the medical devices industry for quality management systems.
12 The ISO 27000 family of standards is a series of best practices helping organizations to improve information security.
13 ISO 14000 is a series of international standards for environmental management.
14 IATF 16949 specifies the requirements for a quality management system process to drive continual improvement, prevent defect, and reduce variability and waste in the automotive industry supply chain.
15 Title 21 CFR Part 11 is the part of Title 21 of the Code of Federal Regulations that establishes the U.S. Food and Drug Administration (FDA) regulations on electronic records and electronic signatures.
16 Total Productive Maintenance (TPM) is one of the elements of lean manufacturing, which ensures maximum availability and efficiency of the manufacturing machinery. The goal of TPM is the best use of the available time of machines to manufacture products, available at: https://queris.pl/baza-wiedzy/tpm-total-productive-maintenance/, 5/22/2022).
17 Assets are material resources controlled by a given economic entity with a reliably determined value, created as a result of past events, aimed at achieving future economic benefits.

Chapter 2

Supply Chain Management

2.1 The Essence of the Supply Chain

The literature on the subject does not offer an unambiguous definition of the supply chain. There are many reasons, including the lack of an unambiguous definition of logistics or logistics system and the supply chain synonyms used in theory and practice, such as logistics networks, logistics chains/channels, distribution chains/channels, supply networks, etc. Nevertheless, the most common term is the supply chain. This is because the essence and importance of the supply chain are reflected in its definitions. Below are some of them:

- Supply chain is a network of manufacturers and service providers that work together to process and move goods – from the raw material to the end user. All these entities are linked by the flows of physical goods, information, and cash (Bozarth & Handfield, 2007);
- Supply chain is the organization and management of information, material, and financial flows to ultimately meet customer needs (Ducrot, 2022);
- Supply chain – as a process – is a sequence of events in the movement of goods, increasing their value (Fertsch, 2006);
- Supply chain is the network of all the people, organizations, resources, activities, and technologies involved in creating and selling a product. The supply chain covers everything from the supply of source materials from supplier to manufacturer to final delivery to the end user (Lutkevich, 2022);

DOI: 10.4324/9781003372615-3

- Supply chain is a network of organizations involved, by linking with suppliers and customers, in various processes and activities that create value in the form of products and services delivered to end users (Christopher, 2000);
- Supply chain is a network of related and interdependent organizations that, working in cooperation with each other, jointly control, direct, and improve the flow of goods and information from suppliers to end users (Christopher, 2000);
- Supply chain consists of mining, manufacturing, trading, and service companies cooperating in various areas, as well as their customers, among whom stream of products, information, and financial resources flow (Witkowski, 2003);
- Supply chain is a physical network that starts with the supplier and ends with the end customer. It covers aspects related to product development, purchasing, production, physical distribution, after-sales services, as well as deliveries by external bidders (Słownik biznesowy, 2022);

Based on the above definitions, certain features that define the supply chain can be identified. They are listed below.

First. In the supply chain, material (raw materials and returns) and information flow both upstream and downstream. Therefore, the following can be distinguished (Figure 2.1) (Bozarth & Handfield, 2007):

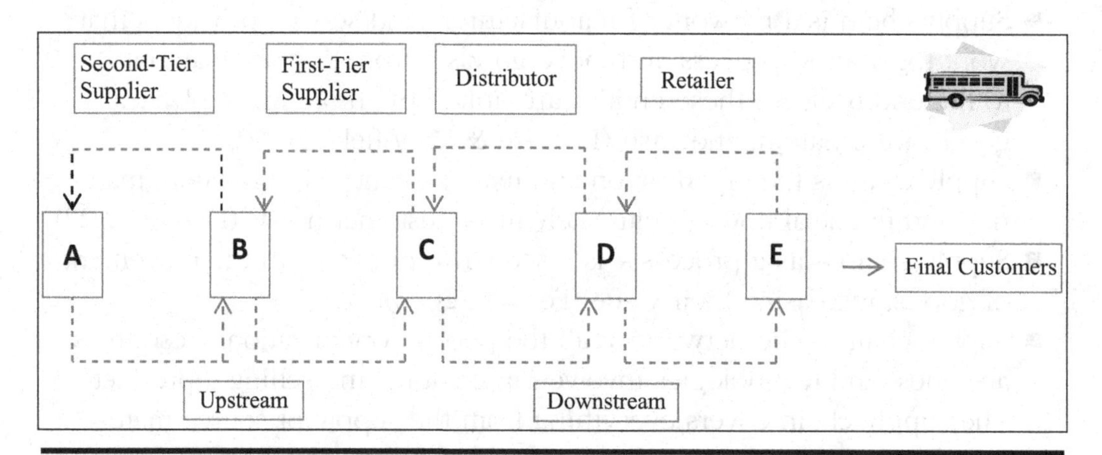

Figure 2.1 Simplified structure of the supply chain.

Source: Based on C.B. Bozarth, R.B. Handfield, *Wprowadzenie do zarządzani operacjami i łańcuchem dostaw,* Helion, Gliwice 2007, p. 35.

- Upstream, that is, the section with activities or companies positioned earlier in the supply chain in relation to other activities or companies;
- Downstream, that is, the section with activities or companies located later in the supply chain in relation to other activities or companies;
- First-tier supplier – an entity that provides products or services directly to a company;
- Second-tier and subsequent supplier – an entity that provides products or services to a first-tier supplier of a company.

The presented supply chain structure simplifies reality because, in practice, we have many suppliers, and the number of customers is even greater. Depending on the position in the supply chain, the analyzed company supplies another company or is supplied by another company to provide a service or manufacture a product and deliver it to the customer, bearing in mind that the product's final price must cover the expenses of all predecessors.

Where: A, B – first- and second-tier suppliers; C – manufacturer; D, E – distributor and retailer

Second. In the supply chain, actors are linked by the physical movement of goods and the transfer of information and funds. An example can be a company selling the latest generation computers with various configurations and prices in Galeria Łódzka. Although this company does not manufacture computers but only sells them, it provides its customers with valuable services – it offers them a convenient location and a wide range of products. This store is just one of the links in the supply chain that covers many economic systems, including:

- manufacturers of integrated circuits, power supply units, cables, batteries, and computer cases;
- companies assembling computers from parts;
- software development companies;
- transportation companies;
- wholesalers, virtual companies, distributors;
- service;
- institutions dealing with the disposal of end-of-life computers;
- companies enabling the transmission of information with the use of modern information technologies;
- financial sector (handling transfers, credits, loans, taxes, etc.);
- enterprises providing basic services such as security, cleaning, etc.

Third. The supply chain is a network of enterprises formed to develop a new product, exchange resources, achieve economies of scale, reduce costs, increase competitiveness, etc. They are divided into horizontal and vertical. The former are networks created by manufacturers of similar or the same goods. The latter are collections of enterprises in the "supplier-customer" relationship.

Fourth. Supply chain management is not the same as "vertical integration." Vertical integration typically involves the vertical acquisition of suppliers and distributors. Until recently, this was considered a welcome strategy, but now more and more companies are focusing on their core skills, that is, the areas of activity they do best and which set them apart from their competitors. The remaining activities are outsourced to external companies.

Fifth. The supply chain is made up of mining, processing, trading, and service companies, which perform various tasks on the way from raw material extraction to end users (Figure 2.2).

The basic steps of the supply chain include:

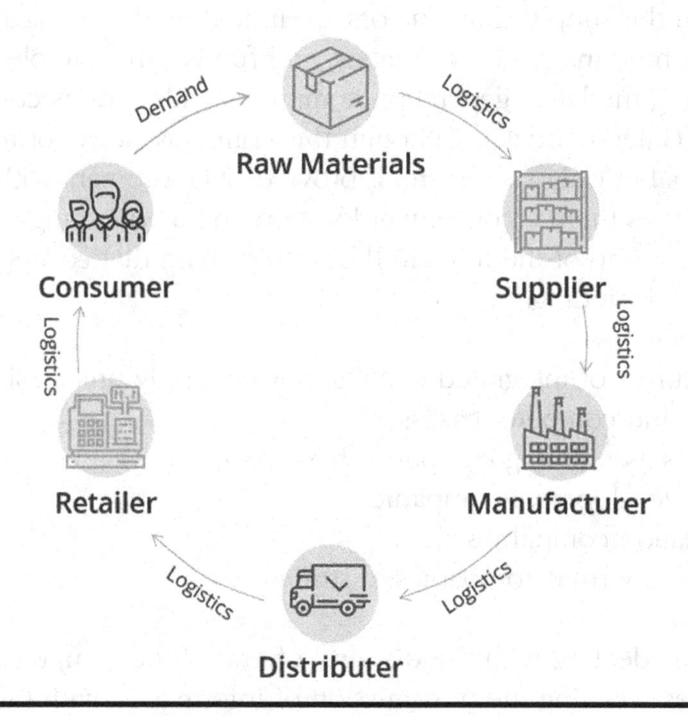

Figure 2.2 Structure (model) of a typical supply chain.

Source: Based on *Supply Chain,* https://corporatefinanceinstitute-com.translate.goog/resources/knowledge/strategy/supply-chain/?, 6/8/2022

- sourcing raw materials;
- delivery of components and parts needed to manufacture the product;
- manufacture of the product in accordance with the documentation;
- delivering products to a distributor or customer;
- customer support and return services.

Sixth. The supply chain is a fast and flexible system linked and guided by the customer selection mechanism, aiming for the highest customer satisfaction and highest profits for the companies in this chain.

Seventh. Integrating and coordinating enterprise logistic systems is nowadays considered the essence of modern logistics management. The main factors influencing the direction and dynamics of changes in logistics are the customer's growing needs and requirements. These requirements most significantly affect the new way of managing the supply chain.

Eighth. The supply chain can be described by indicating the following features: process (object of flow), structure (entity structure), and goals – the functional scope and areas of cooperation of the participating entities (Sołtysik, 2000).

Ninth. The scope of the logistics chain consists of raw materials, auxiliary materials, and cooperating elements purchased on the supply market in accordance with the demand and directed to the production process, as well as finished products transferred for sale.

Tenth. The supply chain is a network of facilities and distribution options that perform three primary functions: purchasing raw materials, converting those materials into products, and distributing those products to customers. Due to their role as shippers and consignees of cargo and the accompanying information and financial streams, their fundamental role in supply chains is unquestionable. The company's services are also important links in the supply chains, including:

- logistics, transportation, and forwarding companies;
- intermediaries providing information, for example, as part of cloud computing[1] (Rosenberg & Mateos, 2022) or big data[2] (Big Data- czym jest i w jaki sposób funkcjonuje, 2022);
- plants engaged in sorting, collecting, disposal, and recycling waste.

Eleventh. For environmental reasons, the supply chain for returnable packaging is becoming increasingly important. Its processes are presented in Figure 2.3. This chain allows to:

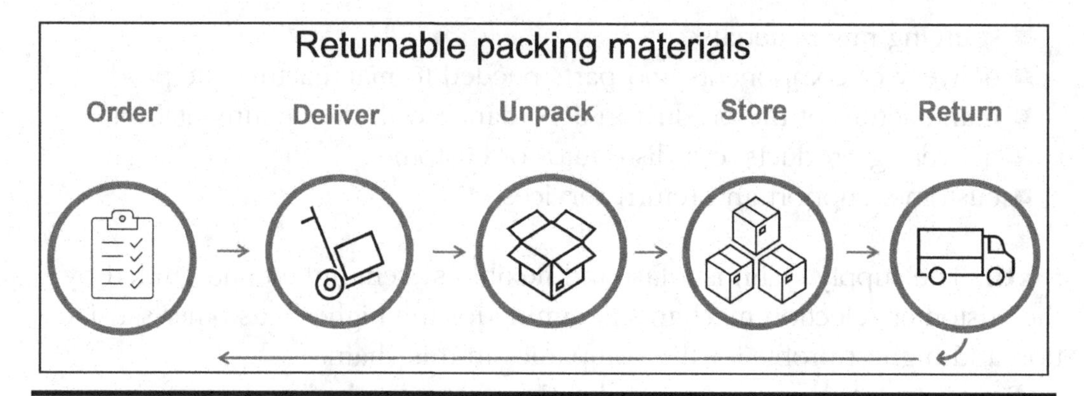

Figure 2.3 Supply chain of returnable packaging.

Source: **Based on *Reduce costs with returnable packaging management in supply chain,* https://www2-novacura-com.translate.goog/blog/reduce-costs-with-returnable-packaging?, 7/20/2022.**

- significantly reduce the amount of packaging on the market;
- make optimal use of returnable packaging;
- introduce pooling;[3]
- conduct packaging transactions.

Each activity must be carried out by effective and efficient supply chain management (SCM), which includes the supervision of materials, information, and finances from supplier to manufacturer, wholesaler, retailer, and then consumer. The three main flows in the supply chain concern products, information, and financial resources. They occur in three main stages: strategy, planning, and operation. SCM involves the coordination and integration of these flows both within and among companies.

There are several popular supply chain business structures (models). The models have two main goals:

- responsiveness (matching all links and participants in the supply chain to the benefit of everyone);
- efficiency (the ratio between the amount obtained and the amount spent in logistics processes along the supply chain).

In practice, there are supply chain models that often overlap (Lutkevich, 2022):

- Continuous flow model – best suited for mature industries with a certain degree of stability (e.g., process manufacturing – oil industry);

- Agile model – best suited for industries with unpredictable demand and custom-made products (e.g., during floods, prolonged droughts);
- Fast chain model – best suited for products with a short life cycle (winter and summer clothing);
- Flexible model – best suited for stabile industries with a few relatively predictable peaks in demand (e.g., influenza vaccines);
- Efficient chain model – best suited for highly competitive markets where pricing plays a major role, such as during energy crises.

Modern supply chains are transparent, acceptable to participants; enable stakeholders to understand the state of the supply chain; minimize inventories; care for customers and employees; minimize losses; implement digital technology; implement automation and robotization; are resistant to disruptions; care about the environment.

The tools and instruments that support the proper functioning of the supply chains include:

- Lean manufacturing, allowing for greater efficiency and shortening the cycle time while using the available resources, which increases flexibility and minimizes waste;
- Traceability, ensuring the safety of products delivered to the market by recording and collecting data about them at every stage of the supply chain;
- Inventory monitoring using IT systems and automatic identification;
- "Logistics 4.0" solutions, which contribute to shortening the time of order fulfillment and digitization of the supply chain, omnichannel, the use of big data to predict customer needs, control and traceability of each stage of the supply chain;
- Reverse logistics to have the lowest possible environmental impact, for example, by reducing electricity consumption, gas emissions, and efficient water use.
- Supply chain sustainability, that is, environmental, social, and economic management that encourages good management practices throughout the life cycle of goods and services.

During the recent pandemic, electronic commerce, also known as e-commerce, has developed. An example of an e-commerce delivery chain is shown in Figure 2.4.

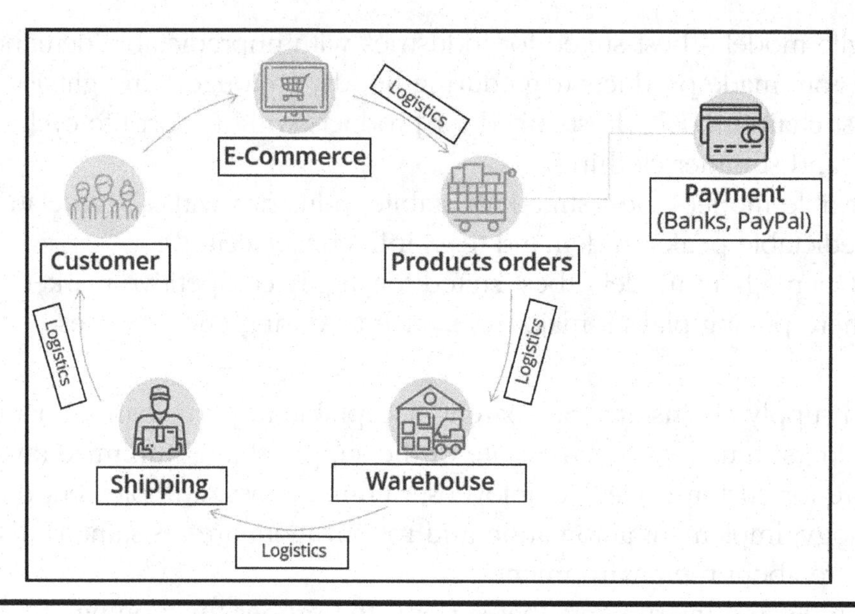

Figure 2.4 Supply chain for e-commerce.

Source: **Based on** ***Supply Chain,*** **https://corporatefinanceinstitute-com.translate.goog/resources/knowledge/strategy/supply-chain/?, 6/8/2022**

The e-commerce company runs a website that sells various products. The customer places an order, for example, via an online checkout basket, and makes an e-payment. After placing the order and paying, the information is delivered to the warehouse, which prepares the product for delivery to the customer by the shipping company.

2.2 Sustainable Supply Chains

A sustainable supply chain has many important features. They include the following:

- minimizing adverse environmental and social impacts during all logistic processes, from manufacturing, storage, delivery to the customer, and waste management;
- providing products and services that meet customer expectations and, at the same time, ensuring the lowest environmental impact in line with corporate social responsibility (CSR);

- environmental, social, and economic management that encourages good practices of conduct and operation throughout the life cycle of a product and service;
- thoughtful management of resources (energy, water, raw materials, etc.) and the use of renewable energy sources.

In the current turbulent environment (Covid-19 pandemic, fuel crisis, climate change, natural disasters, war in Ukraine), the supply chain structures have become increasingly complex and unpredictable, which means that introducing sustainable management in the entire supply chain in economic, social and environmental dimensions is sometimes impossible or very difficult. Nevertheless, despite many difficulties in sustainable supply chain management (SSCM), companies strive for cooperation and coordination within CSR[4] because they are well aware that more and more customers, especially in developed countries, are ready to pay more for environmentally friendly products.

Supply chain sustainability entails the following (Supply Chain Sustainability, 2022):

- Environmental responsibility, which includes protecting the environment against potential damage caused by supply chain activities, such as production, storage, packaging, transportation, returns, complaints, and other processes.
- Financial responsibility, which concerns shareholders, employers/employees, customers, business partners, domestic institutions, and financial institutions.
- Social responsibility, which includes principles, ethics, morals, and philanthropic expectations of society toward a business. This means that every individual in a sustainable supply chain is treated fairly, equally, and in accordance with the requirements of human rights.

Supply chain sustainability is the key to improving productivity and optimizing costs. Moreover, it helps to reduce the impact on the environment, forces continuous improvement in the supply chain, improves partnership relations, creates mutually beneficial business opportunities, promotes a conducive work culture, and helps develop better techniques to reduce risk in the supply chain.

Sustainable supply chain management components include first- and subsequent- (second, third, etc.) tier suppliers or top-tier and lower-tier suppliers. In practice, there are four SSCM types (Figure 2.5) (Villena & Gioia, 2022).

First. Direct approach – companies set and monitor social and environmental goals for their first-tier supplier concerning second-tier suppliers. They constantly monitor risks that harm corporate social responsibility.

Second. Indirect approach – multinational companies (corporations) delegate elements of sustainability management of lower-tier suppliers to their first-tier suppliers. This approach is effective because multinational companies are more effective in their operation, practical examples of which include:

- free supplier training that provides some incentives to implement sustainability practices;
- invitations to participate in exclusive, advantageous, and long-term supply contracts;
- supplier sustainability awards (e.g., providing modern tools for improving logistics processes.

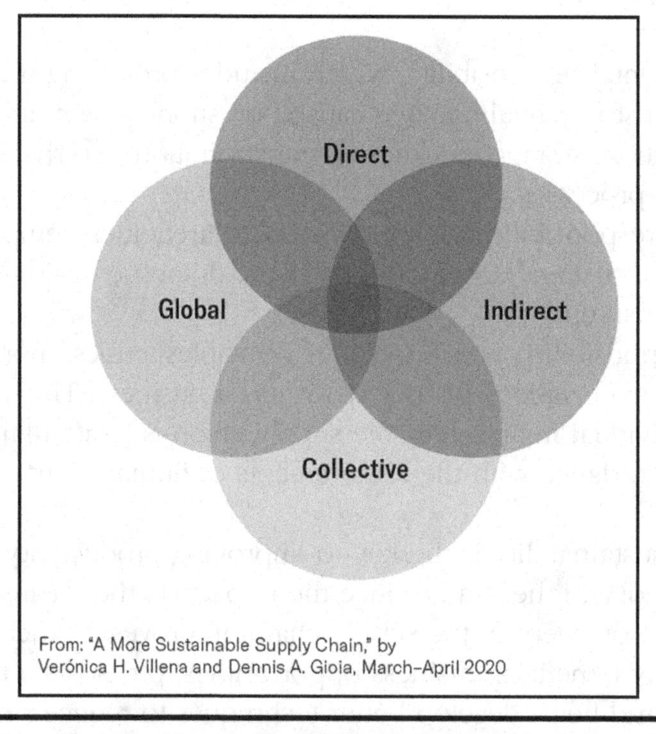

Figure 2.5 Types of sustainable supply chain management by lower-tier suppliers.

Source: Based on V.H. Villena, D.A. Gioia, A More, *Sustainable Supply Chain,* https://hbr-org.translate.goog/2020/03/a-more-sustainable-supply-chain?,6/18/2022

Third. Collective approach – companies focus primarily on developing good sustainability practices and standards, providing assessment tools, and offering training to first- and lower-tier suppliers. An interesting and good solution worth following is the Responsible Business Alliance (RBA) Code of Conduct (Responsible Business Alliance, 2022), which sets standards for working conditions in the electronics industry. It aims to ensure supply chain security, treat employees with respect and dignity, and conduct business in an environmentally responsible and ethical manner. The RBA members include Intel, HP, IBM, Dell, Philips, and Apple. Collaborative initiatives have many advantages, including:

- improved performance of suppliers that can benefit from standardized self-assessment or audit;
- acquiring new reliable suppliers who already have implemented sustainability requirements.

Industry associations have a unique authority over both first- and lower-tier suppliers as most of their members are major players in their sectors. One such example is the electronics manufacturer Flex, a full member of the RBA and a first-tier supplier for many multinational corporations. A second-tier electronics supplier is unlikely to reject Flex's request for a compliance audit as it knows Flex itself has passed this audit and other top-tier electronics suppliers are likely to start issuing similar audit requests to stay competitive.

Fourth. Global approach – multinational cooperation of companies (corporations) with international organizations and non-governmental organizations in sustainability management of lower-tier suppliers. The world's largest initiatives in this area include the United Nations Global Compact[5] (UN Global Compact, 2022), which already has over 12,000 participants, including 8,000 companies from 145 countries. Another good example is the three multinationals: Microsoft, Johnson & Johnson, and Walmart, which participate in the Supply Chain Program of the Carbon Disclosure Project (CDP) (The Carbon Disclosure Project, 2022), a global data-collection platform where suppliers disclose information about their carbon emissions.

A sustainable supply chain combines operational efficiency with strategies to minimize waste in terms of labor, processes, energy, and raw materials. It is a continuous, evolutionary, and profitable process for the planet and the people, which also contributes to business development.

Socially responsible business practices support not only the planet and the people but also business development. Activities that make supply chains sustainable include waste minimization; cleaner production; circular economy; well-organized and effective reverse logistics (including cannibalization[6]); repair, renovation, remanufacturing, and recycling; automatic identification; tracking logistics processes; matching supply to demand; environmental management systems; safe working conditions; compliance with labor law; humane solving of social problems at workplaces and after working hours.

2.3 Sustainable Packaging Logistics

In logistics, a lot of attention is paid to the industry that deals with packaging. Good packaging should be safe for the stored product and provide convenient access to the contents, suitable for transportation and optimal for storage, contain the necessary information about the product, be legible for customers and logisticians, and be aesthetic and environmentally friendly. It is possible to meet all these requirements when you compromise, follow sustainability standards, and use the right tools to design good packaging. In practice, the R&D department, after receiving and analyzing all information, uses advanced computational programs to create a packaging concept, technical drawing, and a 3D model from which a prototype is made. It is then tested and modified if necessary. After necessary modifications and tests, the packaging is ready for mass production. The design and implementation process is presented in Figure 2.6.

In practice, well-designed packaging is business and environment friendly, satisfies customer expectations, fulfills the applicable legal standards, and applies the latest technical solutions. Below are some of them:

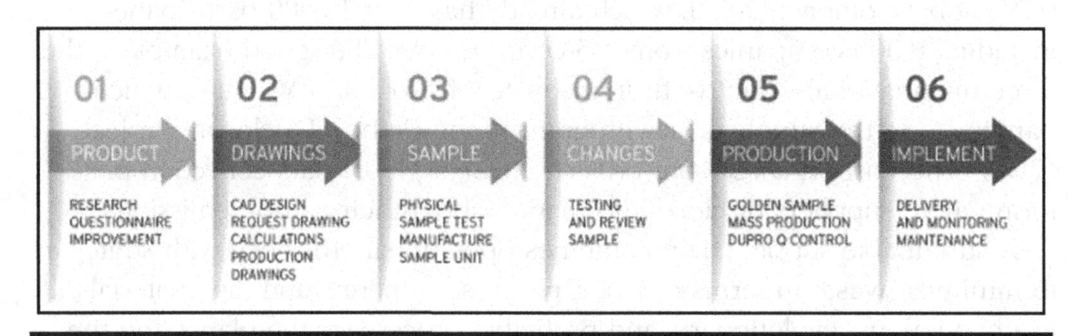

Figure 2.6 The process of designing and implementing a new packaging.

Source: **Based on *What does the design process look like ?*, https://rotom.pl/uslugi/projektowanie-opakowan, 20.07./2022.**

First. Each packaging should be tailored to the customer, who defines their requirements, for example, dimensions, material, durability, and industrial applications. When products are designed according to the company's needs, they become an indispensable part of the production chain. This increases the efficiency of these products and reduces the risk of damage to the goods. This promotes greater work efficiency. Thanks to such advanced logistics services, almost any packaging can be reused, whether made of metal, wood, or plastic. Individually designed packaging means greater ergonomics at work and, thus, better efficiency and safety. Thanks to this, we reduce their negative impact on the environment (Poznaj 4 zasady zrównoważonej logistyki opakowań, 2022).

Second. Each packaging is increasingly created thanks to automated systems with 3D scanning technology to determine the overall dimensions of the item shipped. This information is used to cut the correct size of the cardboard box, and then the item is automatically inserted into the box along with the appropriate documentation, marketing materials, and other personalization elements. This approach minimizes packaging material per piece, saves filling material, and eliminates waste. In high-volume environments, it can also help reduce costs and dramatically increase throughput (Geoffrion, 2022).

Third. Modern tracking and inventory of packaging in transportation, warehouses, and production would not be possible without RFID. It provides accurate, real-time information on where a given package is in the supply chain. This real-time setup enables manufacturers to plan and respond more quickly to changing dynamics in the packaging industry.

Fourth. In sustainable waste management, an important area is a properly created packaging recovery system, which includes (Figure 2.7):

- tracking – information on the status of packaging in the supply chain is collected on an ongoing basis (automatic identification, IT systems, e.g., WMS);
- inventories of recovered and unrecovered packaging and making appropriate decisions;
- checking the packaging quality and, if necessary, repairing and maintaining it;
- reuse of packaging.

The packaging recovery system involves rational activities for businesses and the environment. It has three main goals:

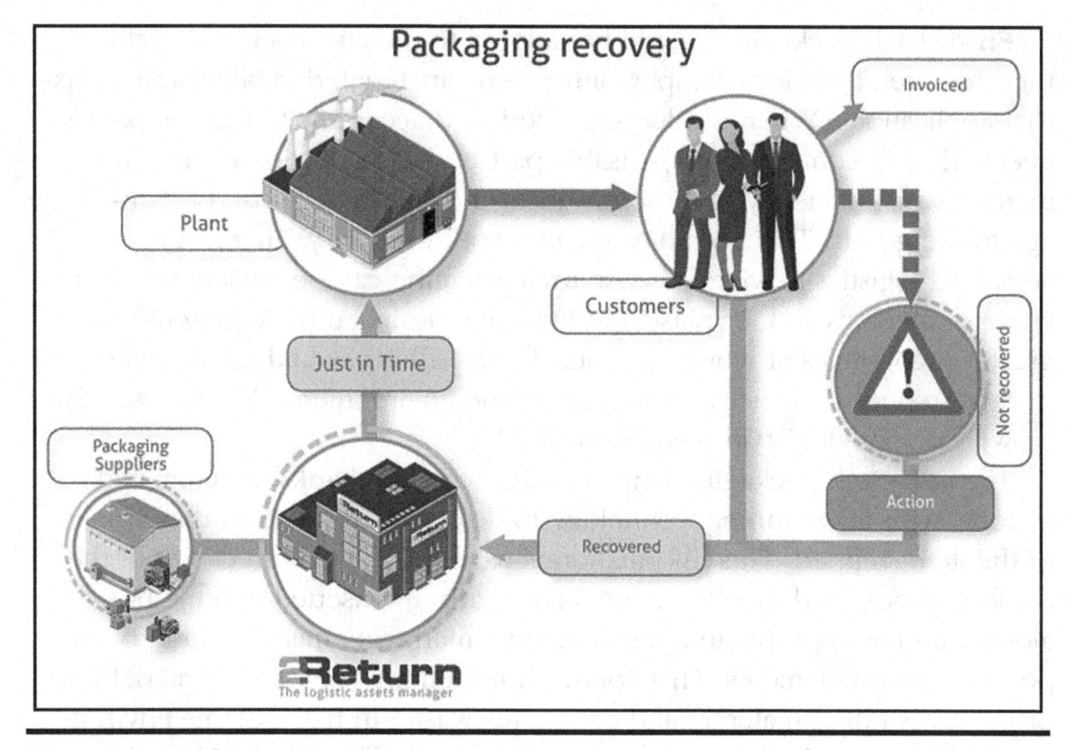

Figure 2.7 Packaging recovery system.

Source: **Based on *Learn the 4 principles of sustainable packaging logistics,* https://rotom.co.uk/services/packing-recover, 07/10/2022.**

- reducing solid waste generated by disposable packaging;
- reducing natural resources used, for example, wood, fuel, water;
- reducing costs of buying new packaging.

The latest logistics systems make return flow management a good business for many companies. Rotom is a good example of such a company. It has offices in countries such as the Netherlands (headquarters), Belgium, France, Germany, Austria, Poland, Spain, Portugal, United Kingdom, and Denmark and specializes in providing the best solutions for transportation and storage. Rotom also collects selected packages from end users and reuses them, checking their technical condition, thus extending the life of plastic pallets, containers, and crates. In addition, it regularly inspects and maintains returnable packaging, thus guaranteeing good quality, which prevents premature disposal of the damaged packaging and increases the safety of employees and transported goods (Poznaj 4 zasady zrównoważonej logistyki opakowań, 2022).

2.4 Threats to the Supply Chain Operation

The current supply chains are highly complex due to internationalization, increased intensity of various flows between enterprises and customers, and changes due to frequent unforeseen circumstances. The supply chain includes activities (processes) that are subject to uncertainty and may concern the location of manufacturing and service companies, warehouses, and distribution centers; internal and external transportation; warehouse management; inventory development and control; customer service; waste management, including packaging; green logistics; information flow (using the latest information technologies).

Each process carried out within the supply chain is exposed to threats that can be defined as undesirable phenomena from the point of view of smooth operation, which include the flow of goods and accompanying information from suppliers to customers. Such phenomena or their accumulation in a specific place and time, having a destructive effect on the supply chain, create a situation that is dangerous for the viability (development) of the flow of material and accompanying information.

Supply chain threats can stem from internal processes and the external environment. The topology and classification of threats are presented in Table 2.1 and Figure 2.8.

Table 2.1 Classification of threats

Origin	• natural (e.g., earthquakes, floods) • biological (e.g., Covid-19 pandemic) • political (e.g., war in Ukraine) • technological (e.g., system failures, cyberattacks)
Impacted area	• management (e.g., lack of full identification of threats and their effects, overestimation of opportunities, misinterpretation of results, lack of tools to optimize and simulate activities) • procurement (e.g., inconsistent supplier selection criteria, selection of the supplier only based on the lowest price, no buffer stock) • manufacturing (e.g., theft of resources, unavailability of qualified personnel, production interruptions, product adulteration) • distribution (e.g., ignoring new products and manufacturers, poor quality of products)

(Continued)

Table 2.1 (Continued)

	• transportation (e.g., disruptions caused by fire, explosion, accident of a means of transportation, washing off the deck, inability to move due to weather conditions) • warehouse management (e.g., thefts, losses due to excessively high stocks, structural failures, power grid and IT system failures) • packaging handling (e.g., destruction of products during transportation due to inappropriate packaging, failure to deliver packaging on time due to bad weather, contamination) • handling customer orders (e.g., disruptions caused by lack of stock and incorrect orders and invoices, inability to locate the product) • green logistics (e.g., failure of a sewage treatment plant, illegal landfills) • IT system (e.g., loss of confidentiality, integrity, passive and active attacks, random errors)
Duration	• short-term, sporadic • long-lasting, increasing • repeated
Physical properties	• material (e.g., introduction of an agent causing the so-called bioterrorism, poor quality of manufacturing processes) • energy (e.g., gas, fuel) • intangible (e.g., financial, political, social crisis) • spreading (e.g., as a result of the supply of poisoned food to retailers) • non-spreading (e.g., due to the naturalization of contaminated sites)
Reception	• local • extensive

Source: Based on A. Szymonik Zarządzanie bezpieczeństwem gospodarczym w systemie bezpieczeństwa narodowego Aspekt logistyczny, *Politechnika Łódzka, Łódź*, 2016, pp. 55–58.

The 21st-century supply chains operate in a turbulent environment dominated by such events as Covid-19, the war in Ukraine, the energy crisis, and inflation. As a result, some unexpected issues emerged (Maihold & Mühlhöfer, 2022):

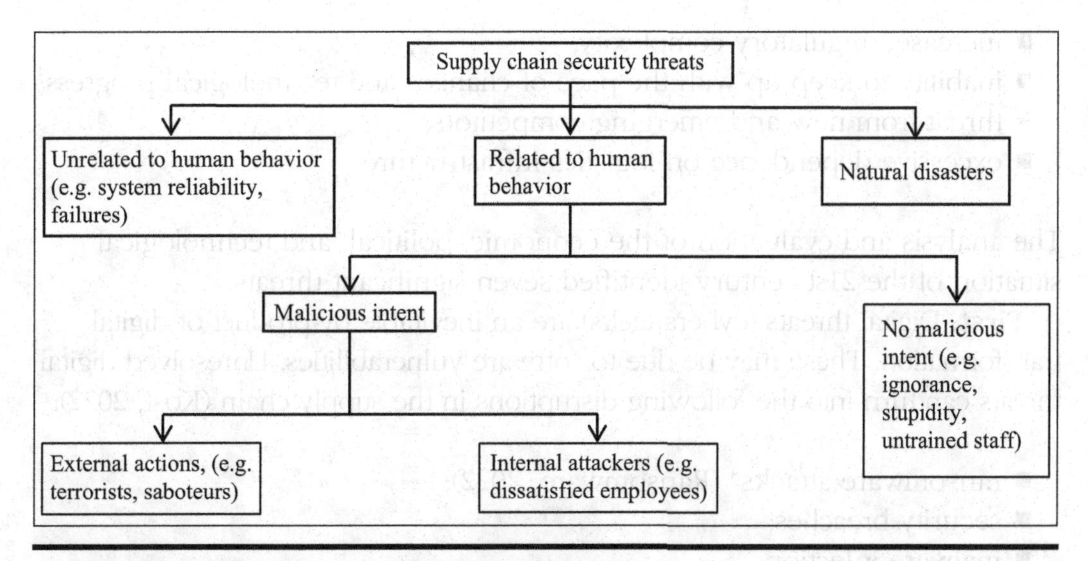

Figure 2.8 Topology of the supply chain threats.

Source: **Based on Kołodziński E. (2015), *Modelowanie systemów bezpieczeństwa,* [in:] Inżynieria systemów bezpieczeństwa, [ed.] P. Sienkiewicz, PWE, Warszawa, p.10.**

- factory closures in China in early 2020;
- economic blockage as a result of a pandemic in many countries around the world;
- major disruptions in global supply and value chains;
- scarcity of resources (raw materials, basic production materials, semiconductors);
- labor shortages;
- increased demand for tradable goods;
- disruption of logistics networks;
- cyberattacks;
- increasing costs of logistics processes;
- transition from just-in-time (JIT) to just-in-case (JIC) management.
- rising fuel prices for the transportation of goods by land, sea, or air

The main threats to global supply chains currently include (Adonisa, 2022):

- increased security risks from cybercrime and data privacy breaches;
- failures of critical IT systems;
- dependence on external suppliers;
- third-party vulnerability and digital supply chain resilience;
- competition/antitrust law control related to M&A[7] (M&A, 2022);

- increased regulatory complexity;
- inability to keep up with the pace of changes and technological progress;
- threat from new and emerging competitors;
- excessive dependence on logistics infrastructure.

The analysis and evaluation of the economic, political, and technological situation of the 21st century identified seven significant threats.

First. Digital threats (cyberattacks) are an inevitable by-product of digital transformation. These may be due to software vulnerabilities. Unresolved digital threats can turn into the following disruptions in the supply chain (Kost, 2022):

- ransomware attacks[8] (Ransomware, 2022);
- security breaches;
- malware infection;
- process disruptions;
- theft of intellectual property;
- Failure to comply with regulatory safety standards (especially detrimental to the medical industry).

Second. Data protection – data integrity in the supply chain is a significant security concern. Security measures should ensure the security of all data states, including at rest and in motion. Data encryption practices are especially important for third-party integrations as hackers know the external destination provider likely has access to sensitive data.

Third. Increasing environmental threats due to the growing challenges facing global supply chains. As a McKinsey report shows (6 Ways Technology Reduces Environmental Impact of Supply Chains, 2022):

- by 2025, nearly two billion people are expected to become global consumers, an increase of 75% compared to 2010;
- the consumer sector is expected to grow by 5% annually over the next 20 years;
- consumer packaged goods (CPG) companies will need to cut greenhouse gas emissions by more than 90% by 2050 to meet their climate change agreements;
- more than 90% of CPG's environmental damage comes from the supply chain, including 80% of greenhouse gas emissions;
- fewer than 20% of supply chain managers say they have visibility into supply chain sustainability practices.

It is important to remember that the environmental impacts of the supply chain are not limited to greenhouse gas emissions. Water scarcity, land use problems, toxic waste, water pollution, deforestation, air quality, and energy consumption are also important factors.

Fourth. Supply chain volatility (fluctuations) caused, among other things, by the following (What Are the Main Supply Chain Challenges?, 2022):

- More and more internationally sourced goods, which causes port congestion. This creates additional difficulties as ships, trucks, and trains must wait for the products to be loaded, unloaded, and transferred. These problems are exacerbated when port authorities and operators charge companies for storing goods at the port;
- Political circumstances and protectionism introduce tariffs across trade routes, resulting in additional fees, delays, and longer customs clearance times. This means slower international shipping and the possibility for competitors from different countries to benefit from lower tariffs;
- A chronic shortage of truck drivers that causes serious capacity problems for trucks, leading to delays in deliveries. The pressure on the truck driver makes it a less attractive profession, and it is harder for logistics service providers to attract and retain the right people;
- Problems with the availability of containers due to the imbalance in trade between China and Europe. As a result of the Covid-19 pandemic, a large number of containers were stuck in Europe. This was further exacerbated by Brexit, which caused many British companies to accumulate significant stocks of goods.

Fifth. The supply chain complexity stems from the following factors:

- e-commerce development;
- last-mile logistics;
- supplier market diversification;
- dropshipping[9] development, which requires fast courier services so that consumers receive the ordered goods as soon as possible;
- geospatial and location technologies (traceability);
- intelligent supply chains that reduce the vulnerability to global pandemics or other unforeseen circumstances;
- digital supply chains that require technology investments in five main pillars (Nelson, 2022):

- insight-driven enterprise,
- digital customer engagement,
- digitally enabled workforce,
- optimization of digital services,
- digital ecosystem.

Sixth. The threat of climate change is increasingly affecting supply chains in various ways. Increasingly, weather anomalies and the frequency of extreme events are already affecting transportation, workers' health and safety, seasonal demand, and other strategic factors.

These threats are an international concern, and the importance of corporate commitment to minimizing and mitigating the damage of climate change is an important part of the global agenda. Consequently, many investors and financial and environmental reporting standards incorporate climate risk and mitigation into their assessments of company performance. A supply chain with mitigation measures and climate resilience both reduces threats and improves reputation (Donovan, 2022).

Seventh. Increased costs throughout the supply chain caused by:

- implementation and operation of information technologies (e.g., IT systems, automatic identification, big data, cloud computing, chatbots, blockchain, 3D solutions);
- rising fuel prices for the transportation of goods by land, sea, or air;
- rising prices of raw materials and semi-finished products;
- growing demand for warehouse space due to the growing needs of consumers and JIC;
- higher labor costs – this applies mainly to digital technology employees;
- growing costs of purchasing, operating, and utilizing logistic resources;
- collapse of supplies due to the changing geopolitical and environmental situation;
- growing customer requirements concerning availability, delivery time, quality, safety, and care for the environment;
- growing environmental charges.

Notes

1. Cloud computing – computing services by an external provider, available on demand at any time, and scaled up as required.
2. Big data – searching, downloading, collecting, and processing available data. It is a method of legally gathering information from a variety of sources and then analyzing it and using it for own purposes.
3. Pooling is based on the multiple use of the same packaging.
4. Corporate social responsibility (CSR).
5. UN Global Compact is the largest sustainable business initiative in the world. Since its establishment in 2000 by the UN Secretary-General Kofi Annan, it has been working for the environment, human rights, anti-corruption, and dignified and legal work. Through cooperation with governments, international organizations, companies, and institutions, it conducts a number of ambitious activities, becoming a catalyst for global change.
6. Cannibalization is not intended to restore the product to a working condition or recover the materials used in production but to use certain elements. In repair, restoration, and remanufacturing – unlike cannibalization – many elements of the original product are used.
7. Mergers and acquisitions (M&A) aim to combine entities with a similar market position to create a completely new legal entity, taking over a company with a weaker position by a stronger company.
8. Ransomware (also known as rogueware or scareware) restricts access to the victim's computer system and requires them to pay a ransom to remove the lock. The most dangerous ransomware attacks were carried out with WannaCry, Petya, Cerber, Cryptolocker, and Locky malware.
9. Dropshipping is a way to run an online store without a warehouse, investing in goods, and packing the parcels. Instead, the store purchases the item from a third party and has it shipped directly to the customer.

Chapter 3

Supply Chains in Reverse Logistics

3.1 Environmental Security

The issue of security is growing in importance in the 21st century. The literature on the subject offers different definitions of security, depending on the scientific discipline. Below are some of them:

- Security is understood as a process that is not so much a specific state of affairs as a continuous social process in which actors try to improve mechanisms that ensure their sense of security (Kulułka, 1982).
- Security includes the guarantee of peace, the stability of the situation in the country, the opportunity for development, and the freedom of an individual to undertake various activities (Majer, 2012).
- Security is a state and a process, that is, it is possible to define hic et nunc (here and now), but it is not invariable over longer periods, as it depends on the shifting balance of power (Stefanowicz, 1984).

The analysis of the above definitions and research on security resulted in a security pyramid presented in Figure 3.1. At its top is military and public security, below political and economic security. On the other hand, the pyramid foundations are a high level of security culture and ecological and health security. The functioning of the above elements is not possible without the others. Gareth Evans, a former Australian MP, has a slightly different

DOI: 10.4324/9781003372615-4

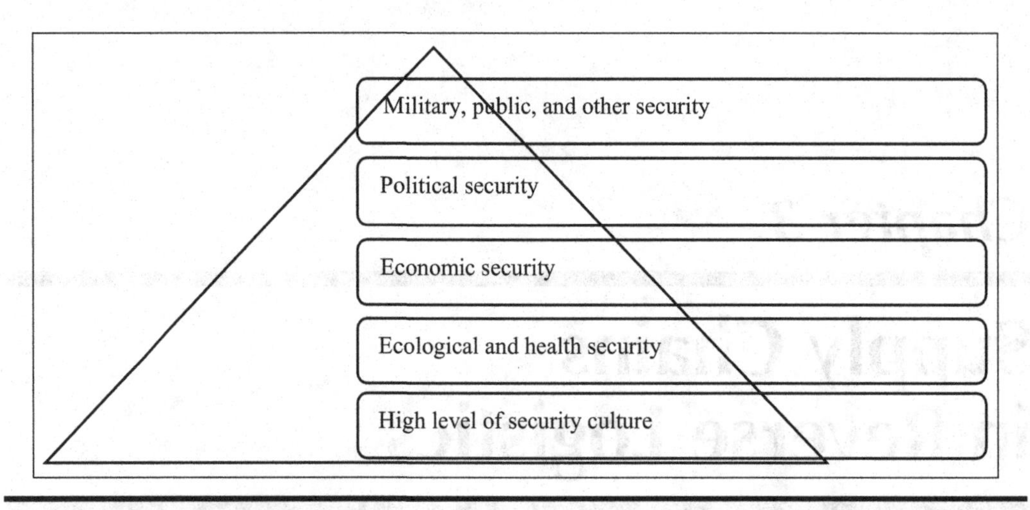

Figure 3.1 Security pyramid.

Source: Based on M. Cieślarczyk, *Teoretyczne i metodologiczne podstawy badania problemów bezpieczeństwa i obronności państwa,* Wydawnictwo Uniwersytetu Przyrodniczo- Humanistycznego w Siedlcach, Siedlce (2009), p. 151.

opinion and describes military, economic, political, social, health, and ecological security (Evans, 1994).

Undoubtedly, it can be stated that ecology[1] is one of the essential components of security, which is more and more often interchangeably referred to as environmental protection. The activities to preserve the natural environment are multifaceted and multidimensional and include the following (Ekologia, 2022):

- rational shaping of the environment and management of natural resources following the principles of sustainability;
- preventing or counteracting phenomena and processes having a detrimental effect on the natural environment;
- preventing or counteracting phenomena contributing to the destruction, damage, pollution, and changes in the physical characteristics or the nature of the components of the natural environment; and
- restoring the environment and natural elements to their proper condition (the state of natural balance).
- Environmental protection covers the air (atmosphere), water, soil, and (renewable and non-renewable) natural resources.

Currently, the main causes of environmental degradation include the following (Zarzycki et al., 2007):

- population growth and concentration, affecting the global amount of products and services needed to meet their needs;
- an increase in the level of consumption as a result of an increase in variety and life requirements, determining the variety of products and the resulting waste;
- technological development influencing the amount of energy consumption, the number of products, their variety and expiry date, and increased threats (unrelated) to human behavior and natural disasters.

On the one hand, civilization mitigates the effects of natural hazards and those caused by existing solutions that increase the comfort of life, but on the other hand, it generates new types of hazards. Therefore, the natural environment determines and impacts the functioning of not only our country, as evidenced by the following:

- Art. 74 of the Constitution of the Republic of Poland of April 2, 1997: Public authorities shall pursue policies ensuring the ecological security of current and future generations[2]; Protection of the environment shall be the duty of public authorities; Everyone shall have the right to be informed of the quality of the environment and its protection; Public authorities shall support the activities of citizens to protect and improve the quality of the environment.
- 2022 National Security Strategy of the Republic of Poland 2022: Bodies responsible for ensuring the external security of the state are obliged to observe and implement tasks and obligations resulting from national legislation on the protection of the natural environment. As actors implementing these tasks throughout the country, they play an important role in this respect, both as direct users of the environment and a real force that can actively shape environmentally friendly activities at the local level. This is also done by raising the environmental protection awareness of the staff.
- White Book of National Security of the Republic of Poland, Warsaw 2013: Protection of the natural environment (ecological security). State policy on ecological security should focus on two areas: improving the quality of the environment and preventive actions.

The analysis of the presented content reveals several important aspects.

First. The environment should be taken care of because it allows us to live on the planet called Earth. We should remember that deforestation means less oxygen, climate change can mean the end of life on our planet, the widening hole in the ozone layer compromises protection from harmful solar radiation, and the polluted environment is a threat of the extinction of flora and fauna species, increases allergies, and causes other diseases. On the other hand, a well-maintained and clean environment attracts tourists and provides us with healthy and comfortable living conditions.

Second. The natural environment is systematically and continuously polluted and destroyed by industry, transportation, agriculture, and municipal utilities management. In an effort to improve the quality of the environment, the following are important (Biała Księga Bezpieczeństwa Narodowego Rzeczypospolitej Polskiej, 2013): advancing reduction of emissions of carbon dioxide, sulfur and nitrogen as well as fine dust in energy production in order to meet the obligations of the Accession Treaty and EU directives; adopting solutions favoring energy savings and the development of renewable sources in the new energy policy of Poland until 2030; taking steps to prepare for the implementation of carbon capture and storage technologies; maintaining or achieving a satisfactory water status by completing the program for the construction and expansion of sewage treatment plants and sewage networks for agglomerations under the EU's Operational Program Infrastructure and Environment; development of a water management plan for each river basin; preparation of the water and environmental program of the country; reducing pollution caused by hazardous substances from industrial sources; increasing energy recovery from municipal waste; increase to over 50% amounts of recovered waste generated in households; creating an effective system of supervision over chemical substances on the market; removal of polychlorinated biphenyl from transformers and other devices as well as removal of asbestos.

Third. Protection of the natural environment is one of the most important tasks undertaken by humankind at the threshold of the 21st century. Responsibility for environmental protection rests with public authorities, which are obliged to ensure ecological security for present and future generations. Environmental protection measures take place at national and international levels.

Fourth. Natural environment security requires the identification of dangers (threats) that may cause disturbances (of existence, development) or loss of value by all of the natural elements, including those transformed as a result of human activity, in particular land surface, minerals, water, air, landscape, climate and other components of biodiversity, and the interactions of these components. After identifying threats, developing an environmental security system (ESS) with specific security potential is possible. This can be achieved by effective prevention (counteraction), protection, and response to the threats (i.e., minimizing their negative effects) (Kołodziński, 2015). Thus, an ESS is a system of actions to secure (protect) the natural environment against the effects of phenomena (processes, events) and their negative consequences (effects, damage).

The concept of a systemic environmental security analysis is presented in Figure 3.2.

Fifth. An ESS includes the following: executive subsystem (forces and resources implementing executive processes, allocated from a fire brigade,

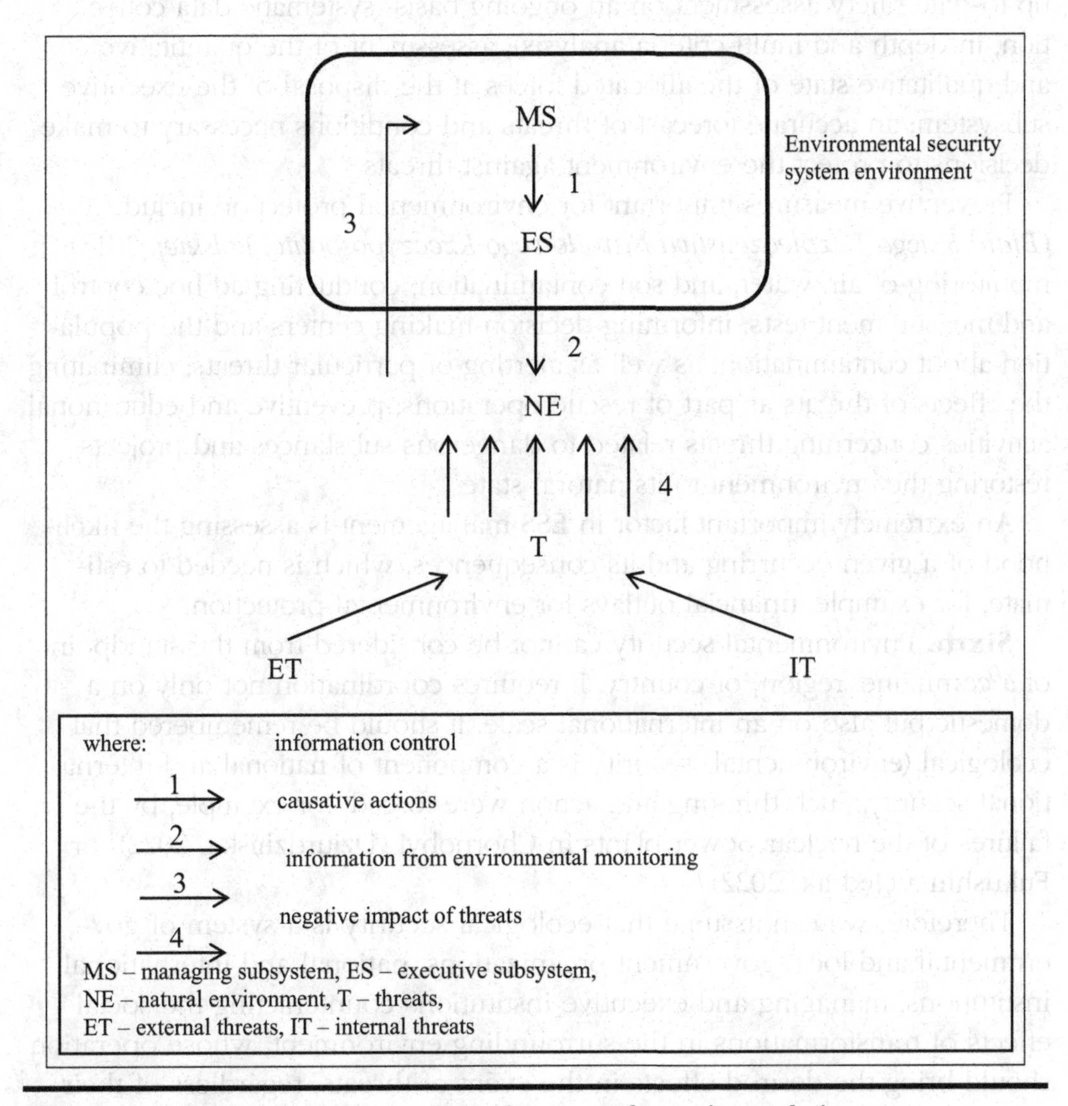

Figure 3.2 The concept of systemic environmental security analysis.

Source: Own study.

emergency medical services, police, army), managing subsystem (performing all management functions, i.e., planning, organizing, motivating, controlling, decision-making, and coordination determining the way of ensuring natural environment security by the executive subsystem), the natural environment, which is the object of impact, threats (any phenomenon undesirable from the point of view of the uninterrupted operation of the ESS).

The information subsystem plays an important role in the ESS managing subsystem, which is responsible for obtaining data necessary for the up-to-date safety assessment on an ongoing basis (systematic data collection, in-depth and multi-criteria analysis); assessment of the quantitative and qualitative state of the allocated forces at the disposal of the executive subsystem; an accurate forecast of threats and conditions necessary to make decisions to protect the environment against threats.

Preventive measures important for environmental protection include (*Biała Księga Bezpieczeństwa Narodowego Rzeczypospolitej Polskiej*, 2013): monitoring of air, water, and soil contamination, conducting ad hoc control and measurement tests; informing decision-making centers and the population about contamination, as well as alerting of particular threats; eliminating the effects of threats as part of rescue operations; preventive and educational activities concerning threats related to dangerous substances and projects restoring the environment to its natural state.

An extremely important factor in ESS management is assessing the likelihood of a given occurring and its consequences, which is needed to estimate, for example, financial outlays for environmental protection.

Sixth. Environmental security cannot be considered from the standpoint of a commune, region, or country. It requires coordination not only on a domestic but also on an international scale. It should be remembered that ecological (environmental) security is a component of national and international security. Such thinking and action were forced, for example, by the failures of the nuclear power plants in Chornobyl (Dziurdzińska, 2022)[3] or Fukushima (Jędrak, 2022).[4]

Therefore, we can assume that ecological security is a system of governmental and local government organizations, national and international institutions, managing and executive institutions counteracting the social effects of transformations in the surrounding environment, whose operation should bring the desired effects in the event of threats, regardless of their type and origin.

3.1.1 Ecological Threats

Large-scale environmental degradation began with the Industrial Revolution in England and Scotland in the 18th century when there was a shift from manual to machine labor. This period saw the creation of new technological solutions (steam engine, telegraph, steam locomotive, internal combustion engine, telephone, light bulb), which caused the development of industry, increased extraction of raw materials, the creation and development of railroads, the use of steam engines in factories, ships, railroads, road transportation, urban development related to the mass migration from the countryside to cities, and population concentration in large cities.

Social, cultural, and economic transformations brought by the Industrial Revolution started the large-scale degradation and pollution of the lithosphere, hydrosphere, and atmosphere. In retrospect, it can be concluded that the negative environmental changes are intensifying, and the proof of this is the disappearance of entire ecosystems, air, water, soil pollution, climate change, rapid extinction of fauna and flora species, and ecological disasters. The threat to the environment by widespread technology, mainly the automotive industry, is one of the most noticeable burdens of the development of civilization today.

Restoring an endangered environment is very difficult. For example, it takes about 100 years to restore a felled forest, many decades to restore water bodies, and thousands of years to restore soils contaminated with heavy metals (Wiąckowski, 2008).

3.1.2 Threat Sources

In the literature, the threat sources are presented in the objective and subjective context (Śladkowski, 2004). Objective – the threat sources are events caused by natural forces and economic activity considered (Szymonik, 2016): natural – the effects of natural disasters and civilizational – various types of material pollution introduced to the environment in the course of human activity. This approach distinguishes the following generic groups (Szymonik, 2016):

- biological: failures or acts of sabotage in laboratories and scientific research institutions involved in the study of bacteria and viruses, and therefore storing biologically hazardous substances (disease viruses, etc.);

- chemical: accidents in industrial plants, laboratories, warehouses, chemical depots, including rail, road, sea, air, and pipeline transportation accidents;
- radiation: accidents and failures of natural radiation sources, in nuclear power plants, or plants using radioactive substances;
- fire: residential buildings, large-scale forests, industrial plants or facilities, public buildings, warehouses, etc.;
- hydrological and meteorological: floods, strong winds, hurricanes, prolonged extreme temperatures, lightning, droughts, heavy precipitation (snow or rain), ice on rivers, lakes, and water reservoirs, etc.;
- damage, failures, and disasters involving technical infrastructure – structural failures, mining disasters, failures and damage to technical, gas, water, and sewage infrastructure, urban cleaning, electricity, fuel, telecommunications, and information networks;
- road, rail, air, or water transportation disasters.

Subjective – results from activities that can lead to population annihilation by changing the natural relationship of humans to biocenoses and biotopes.[5] Their main sources include the breakdown of the natural balance due to the excessive exploitation of environmental resources; pollution of the Earth's spheres and the environment by industrial, transportation, and municipal waste; progressive degradation of ecosystems due to pollution with toxic waste and ecological disasters.

3.1.3 The Most Common Natural Hazards in Poland

There are various natural hazards in Poland. Their frequency, intensity, duration, and likelihood depend on the season. There are times when many hazards may occur simultaneously. However, floods cause the greatest losses. Next, there are windstorms, tornadoes, and severe frost.

Floods – involve a temporary overflow of water that submerges land that is not usually submerged, in particular, caused by water level rising in natural watercourses, water reservoirs, canals, and the sea, excluding water overflow caused by water rising in sewage systems (Ustawa z dnia 18 lipca 2001 r, 2001). There are the following types of floods (Powódź w obliczu zagrożenia, 2013):

- Rainfall floods – due to heavy torrential rainfall, that is, heavy or widespread rainfall occurring over a large area. One of the more dangerous types of pluvial floods that are more and more common in Poland

is the so-called flash flood. It causes rapid flooding of an area due to heavy, short-term rainfall, most often with a thunderstorm. These are the most common floods in Poland;
- Melt floods – caused by rapid snow melting;
- Storm surges – strong (most often northwest) winds cause storm surges of sea waters, which pour into inland waters and hinder the outflow of water from rivers;
- Jam floods – caused by ice jams resulting in a partial or complete reduction of the capacity of the river bed;
- Rainfall and melt floods – caused by snow melting and rainfall.
- Floods due to failures of hydrotechnical structures or improper water management in water reservoirs.

The most common floods are rainfall floods. The areas most at risk of its occurrence are the five southern voivodships: Małopolskie, Podkarpackie, Śląskie, Opolskie, and Dolnośląskie. Flooding involves numerous threats to people, their property, and animals. The transportation infrastructure is destroyed (roads, bridges, viaducts, railroads). Telecommunications, water, gas, and power lines are damaged.

As a result of these losses (which are difficult to list in full due to their quantity and multifaceted nature), secondary effects arise, which include: possible degradation of the natural environment, potential local contamination of the environment as a result of damage to installations and technical facilities and the release of harmful substances, possible shortage of drinking water, possible increase in criminal activity and an increased number of crimes and offenses (burglary, robbery, destruction of property); school closures, epidemics, closure of hospitals and public administration offices. There are also significant financial losses resulting from the losses incurred during the flood.

Windstorms and tornadoes – are the second cause of greatest losses after floods. The wind classification and danger levels are determined by its speed at the height of 10 m (Appendices 3.1 and 3.2).

Windstorms – are winds reaching a speed over 75 km/h. Most often, they occur from November to March. They can damage buildings and break and uproot trees.

Tornado – is a violently rotating column of air created in a thundercloud that develops into a giant sleeve or tail. The base near the ground can be up to 30 m. The tornado reaches a height of 800–1,500 m and can travel a distance of about 50–60 km at a speed of 30–40 km/h. The tornado power is so great that it can snatch people, animals, building elements, and cars (Zagrożenia okresowe występujące w Polsce, 2013). Effects of high winds may cover areas of various sizes depending on wind classification and speed. They can cause human casualties or injuries. Hurricanes damage buildings, telecommunications, and energy infrastructure, disrupt transportation, damage the natural environment, cause failures at industrial plants, combined with the release of hazardous substances and closure of schools, hospitals, and public administration offices.

Severe frost, snowstorms, heavy snowfall, and freezing rain – constitute the third greatest threat to people, the natural environment, infrastructure (energy and transportation), and the economy in Poland. The magnitude of the threat depends on its intensity and severity (Appendices 3.3., 3.4., 3.5., 3.6.). The effects of winter phenomena include an increased risk of hypothermia, frostbite, freezing deaths, freezing of hydrotechnical installations and facilities, transportation difficulties, roadblocks, damage to trees, damage to roofs, danger to life, failures of heating mains, water pipes, sewage networks and high-voltage transmission lines, which can hinder the normal functioning of individuals and the economy in the areas at risk. Mountain areas have the lowest average temperatures in Poland. The north-eastern lowland part of the country is the coldest. In this region, winters are sharper and longer, and summers are relatively short and not very warm.

Apart from the natural hazards mentioned above, there are others, such as landslides, heat waves, forest fires, avalanches, and droughts. Each occurs with a different frequency, and the losses depend on their intensity and severity.

3.1.4 The Most Common Civilizational Threats in Poland

At present, civilizational threats that introduce various types of material pollution to the environment in the course of human activity are the most dangerous. The threats that accompany the civilization development in Poland include (road, rail, sea, mine) disasters; breakdowns and failures (in production, service and commercial enterprises, power lines, dams and water reservoir equipment, municipal utilities management networks), industrial pollution (chemical and radiation contamination of organisms and food, atmosphere, soil, fauna, and flora), transportation, ozone hole (greenhouse effect, ozone layer depletion), other (noise, shocks – vibrations, acid rain, fumes, dust, crude oil, and its derivatives).

Ecological disaster is a new term understood as permanent, irreversible damage to or destruction of the environment with a negative impact on human life and health. Ecological disasters change the structure and functions of entire ecosystems. Due to their origin, they can be divided into two groups (Polcikiewicz, 2012): natural disasters and anthropogenic disasters. Natural disasters are caused by natural forces, for example, floods or landslides, extreme temperatures, droughts, and large forest fires.

Anthropogenic disasters, that is, ones related to intentional or unintentional human activity, are the second group. They most often occur due to failures of various construction objects or machinery and result in the emission of poisonous gases or liquids into the environment. Such disasters can affect water, air, and land. Since the 1990s, experts have identified four main types of global environmental threats (Polcikiewicz, 2012): the spread of non-biodegradable toxic chemical or radioactive substances (nuclear explosions, industrial accidents); the devastation of flora and fauna; pollution of the upper layers of the atmosphere, which causes damage to the ozone layer (ozone hole) and as a result increases the penetration of harmful ultraviolet (UV) radiation; the greenhouse effect.

The spread of toxic substances can take place in water, air, and soil. Their source is mainly: energy (fuel combustion), industrial (technological processes in chemical plants, refineries, steel mills, mines, and cement plants), transportation (mainly by road but also by rail, water, and air), municipal waste (from households and the collection and disposal of waste and sewage, for example, landfills, sewage treatment plants). Road transportation is one of the main sources of anthropogenic air pollution, environmental degradation, and negative impact on humans. As a result of fuel combustion in vehicle engines, toxic substances are emitted into the air, such as carbon monoxide (CO), hydrocarbons (HC), nitrogen oxides (NO_x), aldehydes (RCHO), sulfur dioxide (SO_2), lead compounds, particulate matter.

The most dangerous for humans are **gases and aerosols** in the atmosphere with particles smaller than a micrometer, which easily penetrate the lungs. The main air pollutants include the following (Wolański, 2008): sulfur oxides from coal and fuel oils used in industry; industrial dust and soot, which become the basis for smog in cities; poisonous compounds from motor vehicles causing headaches, indisposition, and in high concentrations, even death; oxidants, resulting from the sunlight impact on unburned hydrocarbons and nitrogen oxides, causing smog that irritates the eyes and reduces visibility; nitrogen oxides from car exhaust and industrial production; lead, added to gasoline and emitted from cars along with exhaust fumes, accumulates in the body with a toxic effect.

The devastation of flora and fauna is on the increase. One of its causes is the so-called acid rain. Industrial areas and large cities are particularly vulnerable to this type of pollution. The source of acid rain that threatens forests and monuments is air pollution. Acid rain results from reactions involving volatile hydrocarbons, sulfur dioxide, and nitrogen oxides from industry, thermal power plants, transportation, and agriculture. The water in the clouds above the factories is saturated with chemicals emitted into the atmosphere. Under these circumstances, reactions take place where sulfuric acid (H_2SO_4) is formed from sulfur dioxide (SO_2), and nitric acid (HNO_3) is formed from nitrogen oxides. Harmful substances travel with the wind and fall to the ground with water molecules, damaging many ecosystems. The prospects for improvement in this area are poor. The positive effect of reducing sulfur dioxide emissions is offset by the fact that pollution with nitrogen oxides continues to increase due to increasing car traffic.

Acid rain has a destructive effect on vegetation. It causes the death of trees and the destruction of the undergrowth. The leaves of trees are damaged, which causes excessive water evaporation and disrupts the photosynthesis process, resulting in low resistance of these plants to climatic conditions. In addition, acid rain acidifies the soil, which contributes to the activation of aluminum and cadmium and the accumulation of nitrates and sulfates. Plant roots have a reduced ability to absorb calcium, magnesium, and potassium because they are washed away by acid rain. This results in a deficiency of essential nutrients. The roots wither, and the plant dies. Acid rain and other precipitation also get into lakes, rivers, etc., acidifying and making them unusable. Harmful substances can get into the water in two ways. They get there together with the water runoff from the surrounding fields, meadows, and other areas or directly with precipitation (Żółtowski & Kwiatkowski, 2012).

The ozone hole is another environmental problem of the 21st century. It is accompanied by a decrease in ozone concentration in the ozonosphere, which extends at an altitude of 10–50 km. It is believed that the ozone hole formation is due to the substances that enter the atmosphere as a result of human economic activity, especially freons and halons, as well as nitrogen oxides (a product of fuel combustion in aircraft and rocket engines). The ozone hole appeared when freon and other fluorocarbons, methane and ethane, began to be used to produce aerosols. The ozonosphere absorbs UV radiation, which is very harmful to all living organisms. The destruction of the ozone layer leads to a decrease in the effectiveness of UV absorption. As a result, organisms are exposed to increased UV radiation. The excess of UV rays can disrupt the balance of entire ecosystems. UV radiation penetrates the water up to several meters deep (in the case of clear waters, over a dozen meters). This causes the death of the particularly sensitive plant and animal species that make up the plankton. The incidence of plankton-eating fish and predatory fish will therefore decrease. UV radiation also adversely affects plants. Among plants that react to UV rays, more than two-thirds of species are sensitive to them. It should be noted that these are mainly cultivated and industrial plant species. The increase in the intensity of UV radiation will certainly affect the human economy. The decline in fish populations due to plankton decline will lead to much smaller catches in the area concerned. So fishing and fisheries will suffer.

However, UV radiation can negatively affect people directly. Due to the production of pigments in the skin, humans have only marginal protection against it. Furthermore, excessive UV radiation can weaken the human immune system and thus reduce resistance to infection and disease. The most dangerous include cancer, especially skin cancers (e.g., melanomas). In addition, UV radiation irritates the conjunctiva, leading to numerous eye diseases, mainly cataracts. UV rays also accelerate skin aging (Żółtowski & Kwiatkowski, 2012).

The greenhouse effect involves the warming of the atmosphere (climate) caused by increased pollution with chemical compounds, mainly carbon dioxide. Solar radiation reaching the Earth reflects off the atmosphere, clouds, and the planet's surface. The rest passes through the atmosphere and reaches the Earth's surface, where it is absorbed. On the other hand, the Earth sends energy in the form of thermal radiation (infrared radiation with a wavelength longer than light radiation), which is absorbed by the atmosphere, more precisely by greenhouse gases. Some radiation is emitted into space, while the rest is reflected and returns to the Earth. This heat warms the atmosphere, the surface of the land, and oceans, providing suitable temperatures for the development of life.

During the Sun-Earth-space exchange, some gases react like glass, allowing sunlight to pass through but stopping infrared. In a greenhouse, the sunlight, coming through the glass, heats the plants, and they radiate heat that remains largely inside the greenhouse. Without this process, the Earth's surface temperature would have been –18 °C. Therefore, the phenomenon itself is not the issue but its intensification caused by human activity. Sunlight (visible light) passes freely through the atmosphere.

Some of it is immediately reflected by clouds, particles in the atmosphere, and bright surfaces. The rest is absorbed by the soil and heats the Earth. Greenhouse gases in the atmosphere slow down the emission of heat into space. Solar radiation reaching the Earth's surface is absorbed by vegetation, soil, and water and reflected and directed to the upper atmosphere. Gases such as carbon dioxide, nitrogen oxides, methane, and fluorinated compounds trap the reflected rays and cause them to be re-emitted to the Earth. The remaining ones leave the atmosphere. The secondary emission maintains the Earth's energy balance and provides an average temperature of 15 °C. The increasing concentration of gases in the atmosphere responsible for the greenhouse effect, especially CO_2, contributes to the intensification of secondary emissions and an increase in the average temperature on Earth.

The sources of gases causing the greenhouse effect are burned fossil fuels (coal, crude oil). The greenhouse effect is amplified by tropical forest depletion and savannah fires. It is estimated that about six billion tons of CO_2 are annually released into the atmosphere. Forest ecosystems absorb part of it; for example, European forests capture between 70 and 105 million tons per year. Thus, afforestation of the world's land resources can significantly reduce the greenhouse effect. Poland also contributes to CO_2 emissions, as shown in Table 3.1.

Below are ten practical micro-scale tips ("for everyone") on how to reduce the greenhouse effect (Sikorska & Józefiak, 2022)

1. Use energy-efficient light bulbs – they use 75–80% less energy than conventional ones, and their lifetime is ten times longer than conventional ones. Replacing five ordinary light bulbs in the house for about five hours a day with energy-efficient ones reduces CO_2 emissions by about 250 kg per year;
2. Save water – you can reduce CO_2 emissions by about 230 kg per person per year;

Table 3.1 Total carbon dioxide emissions in Poland (million tons)

	2010	*2015*	*2017*	*2018*
Carbon dioxide	334.60	313.10	337.30	316.70

Source: Based on Ochrona środowiska 2020 Environment (2020), Zakład Wydawnictw Statystycznych, Warszawa.

3. Boil as much water as you need, and you will not waste unnecessary energy and reduce carbon dioxide emissions – even by about 25 kg per year, according to researchers;
4. Remember to turn off the "standby" mode in your devices – if half of the devices in our homes were unplugged and not left on standby, we could reduce CO_2 emissions by one million tons nationwide;
5. Check the parameters of household appliances. The most energy-efficient devices are marked with the letter A. The further the letter of the alphabet is, the less energy-efficient the appliance is; it consumes more electricity and generates higher bills. In shops, we can also find appliances marked with the symbols A +, A ++ A-10%, etc. They are even more energy-efficient than their counterparts marked A;
6. Segregate waste – if we all remembered to segregate and recycle garbage, processing one ton of waste paper would save 17. A healthy ten-meter tree produces an average of about 118 kg of oxygen per year; a human needs 176 of oxygen, so two medium-sized trees meet the oxygen needs of one person. This alone should be enough to process, for example, waste paper;
7. Lower the temperature at home by 1 °C – lowering the temperature at home by 1 °C reduces CO_2 emissions by up to 300 kg per year. By protecting the climate, you also reduce your energy and central heating bills;
8. Program your home thermostat – program lower temperature at night or when you are away. Most new-generation radiators also allow you to set the thermostat. When you are not home, the lower temperatures will benefit your plants;
9. If you have a car, remember: check tire pressure once a month; remove unnecessary items from the trunk and back seats (the heavier the car, the greater the load on the engine and the greater the fuel consumption); close the windows, especially at high speeds, and remove the empty roof box; use air conditioning only when necessary; start driving as soon as the engine starts and turn off the engine if you are stopping for more than a minute; drive your vehicle at a reasonable speed and, above all, drive smoothly (when you accelerate or brake sharply, the engine uses more fuel and emits more CO_2);
10. Switch from car to bike – cycling to cover short distances is the best way to reduce your carbon footprint. Ten kilometers traveled by a passenger car emits 2 kg of CO_2 into the atmosphere. Additionally, in an hour, one car turns as much oxygen into the exhaust as 800 people use to breathe at the same time.

Noise – a subjective term that defines the unfavorable influence of complex sounds of various frequencies. According to Polish standards, noise is an undesirable sound of any acoustic character in given conditions and by a given person (Rączkowski, 2010). It is caused mainly by the means of transportation: road traffic, rail traffic, air traffic, and industrial activity. Protection against noise involves ensuring the best possible acoustic climate of the environment, that is, the group of acoustic phenomena in a given area, in particular, by keeping the noise level below the permissible value or at this level and reducing the noise level to at least the permissible one.

Environmental noise trends in Poland indicate, on the one hand, an increase in the risk of traffic noise and, on the other hand, a reduction in the growth and the occurrence of downward trends in industrial noise. Monitoring measurements of industrial noise carried out in 2019 (originating, among others, from production plants, wholesalers, hotels, windmills, car washes, or shooting ranges) included the control of 3,646 noise-emitting facilities (plants) in the central records of the acoustic climate control system. Only 837 plants (23%) exceeded the permissible noise levels, which is comparable to previous years. Monitoring of industrial noise showed the highest percentage share of plants exceeding the permissible levels among the inspected plants in the following voivodeships: Lubelskie and Lubuskie (32% each), Małopolskie (31%), and Dolnośląskie (29%), with the lowest in the following voivodeships: Łódzkie (16%) and Podlaskie (17%).

The upward trends in traffic noise relate primarily to road noise and aircraft noise. The increase in road noise pollution in recent years is mainly related to the construction of new roads, bridges, bypasses, and highways, as well as the rapid growth in the number of vehicles in Poland. Measurements of noise monitoring based on acoustic maps showed that in 2019, road noise was a threat mainly in urban areas and was felt by an increasing number of residents. Out of almost 340 km of roads inspected in 2019, less than 8% had road noise emissions up to 60 dB (decibels), i.e., emissions that did not exceed the permissible sound levels during the day in residential areas adjacent to roads. This means that the noise level was exceeded in 92% of inspected roads. For many years, the level of road noise in cities has remained at a high level, about 70–80 dB. The highest percentage of roads where noise emissions exceeded the maximum permissible level of 60 dB to the length of the roads inspected was recorded in 2019 in the cities of Lubuskie and Zachodniopomorskie (100%) as well as Lubelskie (99%) and Śląskie (98%), and the lowest in Warmińsko-Mazurskie (57%).

In the case of **aircraft noise**, the noise level trends are on the uptake due to the development of air traffic. This noise impacts large areas and causes high emissions, with no effective environmental protection measures (Ochrona środowiska, 2020).

3.1.5 Management of Ecological Threats

A threat that affects the life or health of a large number of people, property of significant size, or the environment over large areas should be identified and described on the risk map[6] and the threat map.[7] Any such analysis should identify a risk or threat and determine where it can occur. In order to prepare a partial report for a specific threat that may have a negative impact, among other things, on the environment, an algorithm was developed (Figure 3.3.), which requires standardized information on threats, prevention, preparation, response, historical data, lists, and conclusions.

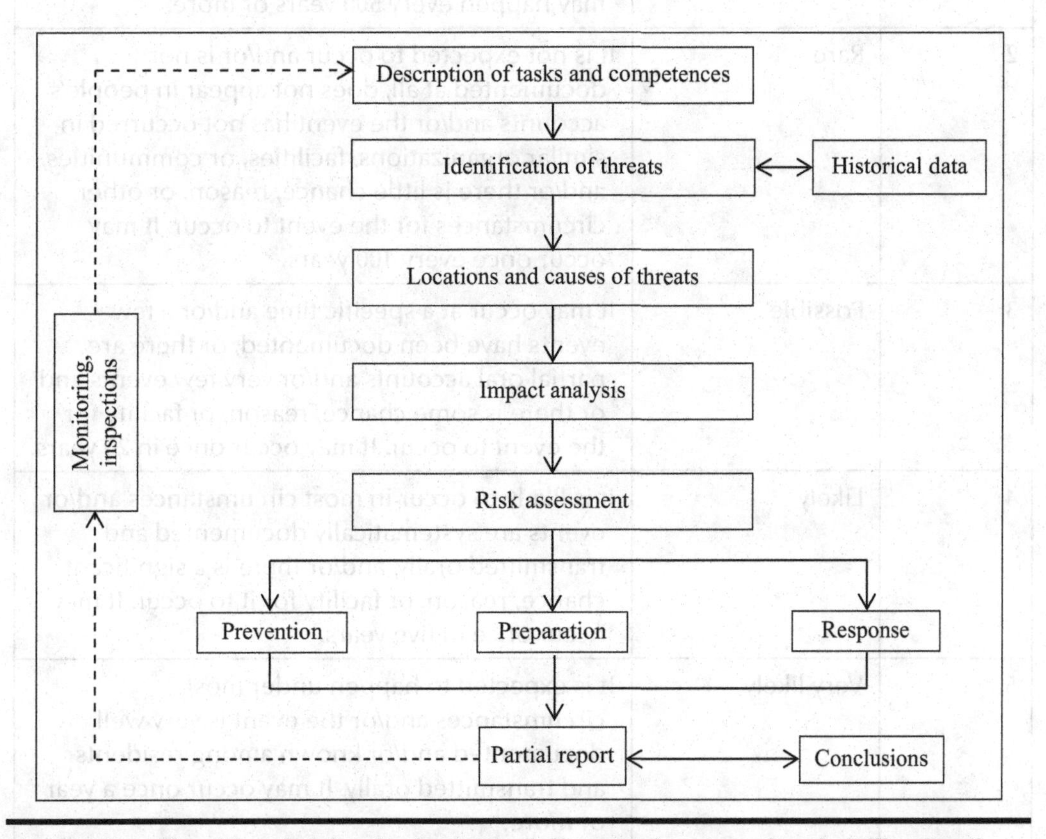

Figure 3.3 Algorithm for developing a partial report for natural and civilizational threats to the natural environment.

Source: **Based on Procedura opracowania raportu cząstkowego do Raportu o zagrożeniach bezpieczeństwa narodowego, RCB Rządowe Centrum Bezpieczeństwa, Warszawa (2010), p. 6.**

3.1.6 Threats – Risk Assessment

All types of threats that may harm the environment are subject to identification. Threats can also be identified through analyzing historical and/or statistical data using expert estimates, field studies, mathematical models, case study analysis, results of data from monitoring systems, and assessment of the international situation. An important identification element is establishing risk assessment criteria, particularly the likelihood of occurrence and effects (consequences). The likelihood is described with a qualitative (descriptive) scale from 1 – very unlikely to 5 – very likely (Table 3.2.).

Table 3.2 The likelihood of risk occurrence on a qualitative scale

Scale	*Likelihood*	*Description*
1	Very rare	It can only occur in exceptional circumstances. It may happen every 500 years or more.
2	Rare	It is not expected to occur and/or is not documented at all, does not appear in people's accounts and/or the event has not occurred in similar organizations, facilities, or communities, and/or there is little chance, reason, or other circumstances for the event to occur. It may occur once every 100 years.
3	Possible	It may occur at a specific time and/or a few events have been documented, or there are partial oral accounts and/or very few events and/or there is some chance, reason, or facility for the event to occur. It may occur once in 20 years.
4	Likely	It is likely to occur in most circumstances and/or events are systematically documented and transmitted orally, and/or there is a significant chance, reason, or facility for it to occur. It may occur once in five years.
5	Very likely	It is expected to happen under most circumstances and/or the event is very well documented and/or known among residents and transmitted orally. It may occur once a year or more.

Source: Based on Ocena ryzyka na potrzeby zarządzania kryzysowego, Raport o zagrożeniach bezpieczeństwa narodowego, Warszawa (2013), RCB, p. 13.

For impacts, a similar solution is proposed with the exception, however, that the parameter closest to reality in categories (Z – life, M – property, S – environment) should be adjusted for the six scales (from A – negligible to E – catastrophic). On the other hand, a scale from A to E, effects from negligible to catastrophic, and categories Z, M, and S are adopted for determining effects, as shown in Table 3.3.

Risk matrices are developed based on two sets of the probability of a risk occurrence and its effects. For each environmental hazard, the risk matrix defines the risk as follows[8]: minimal (blue), low (green), moderate (yellow), high (red), and extreme (brown) – Table 3.4.

Table 3.3 Identification of the effects

Scale	*Effect*	*Category*	*Description (Z – life, M – property, S – environment)*
A	Negligible	Z	No fatalities or injuries. No or a small number of people displaced for a short time (up to 2 hours). No or a small number of people requiring assistance (not financial or material).
		M	Virtually no damage. No or very little impact on the local community. No or little financial loss.
		S	An unmeasurable effect on the natural environment.
B	Minor	Z	A low number of injured, but no fatalities. First aid was required. Necessary displacement of people (less than 24 hours). Some people need help.
		M	Some damage occurs. There are some difficulties (no more than 24 hours). Little financial loss. No additional measures required.
		S	Low environmental impact with short-term effect.

(Continued)

Table 3.3 (Continued)

Scale	*Effect*	*Category*	*Description (Z – life, M – property, S – environment)*
C	Moderate	Z	Medical assistance needed, but no fatalities. Some require hospitalization. Additional hospital beds and additional medical personnel needed. Evacuated people stay in designated areas with the possibility of returning within 24 hours.
		M	Identification of damaged sites that require routine repair. Normal functioning of the community with little discomfort. Significant financial losses.
		S	Some short-term environmental effects or minor long-term effects.
D	Major	Z	Heavily injured, many hospitalized people, a large number of displaced persons (for more than 24 hours). Fatalities. Special resources needed to help people and repair the damage.
		M	Partially non-functioning community, some services unavailable. Significant financial losses. External assistance needed.
		S	Long-term effects in the natural environment.
E	Catastrophic	Z	A large number of seriously injured. A large number of hospitalizations. General and long-term displacement of the population. A large number of fatalities. A lot of help is required for a large number of people.
		M	Extensive destruction. Inability of the community to function without significant external assistance.
		S	High environmental impact and/or permanent damage.

Source: Based on Ocena ryzyka na potrzeby zarz*ą*dzania kryzysowego, Raport o zagro*ż*eniach bezpiecze*ń*stwa narodowego, Warszawa (2013), RCB, p. 14.

Table 3.4 Risk assessment

EFFECTS					
5					
4					
3					
2					
1					
	A	B	C	D	E
LIKELIHOOD					

Description: minimal (dotted), low (Striped), moderate (light grey), high (dark grey), extreme (black).

Source: Based on Ocena ryzyka na potrzeby zarządzania kryzysowego, Raport o zagrożeniach bezpieczeństwa narodowego, Warszawa (2013), RCB, p. 15.

This introduces four risk acceptance categories:

- acceptable (A) – no additional measures are required; applicable solutions and assigned capabilities and resources are sufficient; no action is needed in addition to monitoring activities;
- tolerable (T) – alternatives should be evaluated to see if minor organizational, legal, or functional changes would improve security or the perception of security;
- conditionally tolerable (WT) – additional security measures need to be introduced within six months; solutions need to be improved;
- unacceptable (N) – immediate action should be taken to improve security and introduce additional/new solutions.

However, the methods of risk prevention include:

Prevention – actions to eliminate or reduce the probability of a threat and its impact on the environment. This stage includes, among others, the following measures: legal (acts, regulations, guidelines), organizational (separating human, financial, and equipment resources, conducting research and technology transfer, creating a general social climate that counteracts threats), procedural (removing the threat from what is to be protected, preventing the threat that already exists, cooperation in a broad sense).

Preparation – planning actions regarding the methods of responding to various types of environmental threats, enabling the impact on their course to reduce the negative effects of these events. This stage also includes activities to increase the staffing and resources necessary for effective response, management, organization, and conduct of training and exercises in responding to potential environmental threats (Ustawa z dnia 26 kwietnia 2007, 2007). The preparation includes developing plans, algorithms (scenarios), and operating procedures, organizing communication and communication systems, monitoring systems, organizing and maintaining warning and alarm systems, specialist training and skills improvement, and informing the population.

Response – actions following the occurrence of natural and civilizational threats to the environment. This stage requires the prior definition of response principles and prioritizing actions in the event of a threat. The goal is to provide assistance and reduce secondary damage. Responding requires proper and professional knowledge of the problem, as well as modern, reliable means of communication and accurate data from monitoring of risk areas.

3.2 The Essence of Reverse Logistics in the Supply Chain

Reverse logistics is nothing more than traditional logistics, but the flow is in the opposite direction, and the movement concerns waste and returns. In the case of traditional logistics, the material flow consists of raw materials and components necessary for production, while in reverse logistics, we deal with everything that comes from the consumer and is waste or return (Figure 3.4).

This new application of logistics in managing waste flows is universally called reverse logistics. In the literature on the subject, it is also referred to as retrologistics, reverse supply chain, reverse logistics flow, reverse flow, backward supply chain, returns management, aftermarket logistics, and aftermarket supply chain. Sometimes reverse logistics is identified with green logistics, which is a mistake, as the latter is closely related to environmentally friendly resources, including their transformation favorable to people and not harmful to the existing environment.

By analyzing the literature on the subject, reverse logistics can be defined as taking waste and returns along the supply chain and reworking them (or parts of them) to create a new product that can be sold (Figure 3.5.).

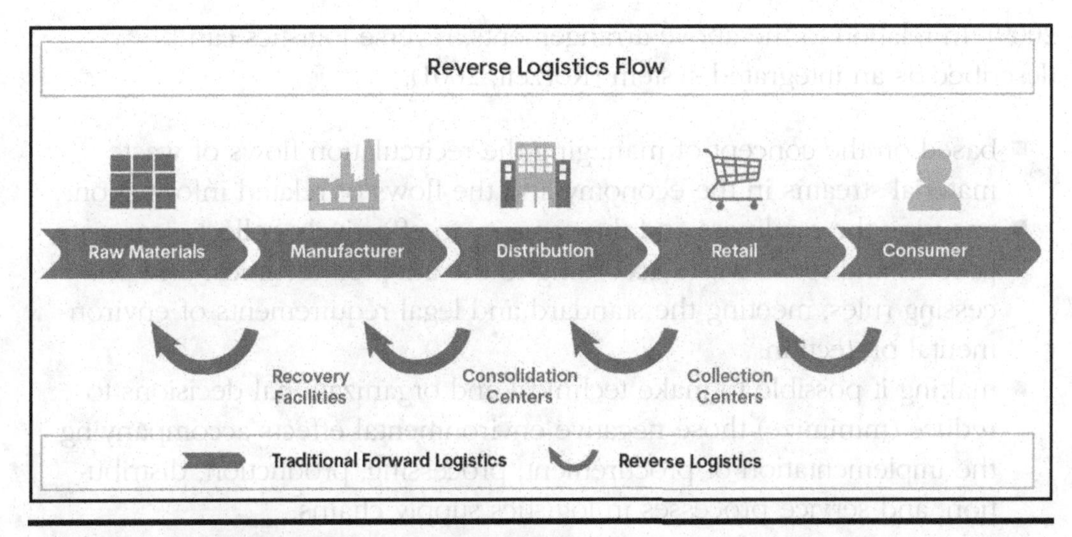

Figure 3.4 Traditional and reverse logistics.

Source: **Based on *What is Reverse Logistics and How Is It Different than Traditional Logistics,* https://www.globaltranz.com/what-is-reverse-logistics/, 4/20/2022.**

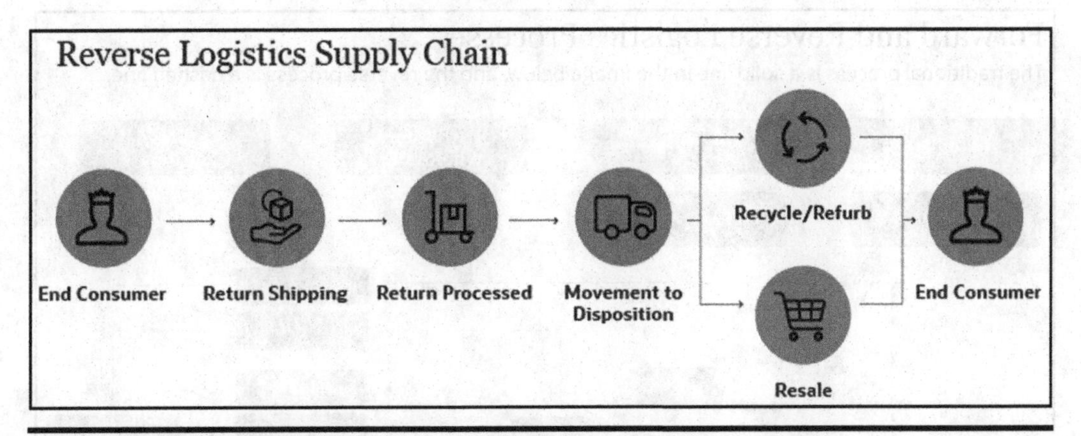

Figure 3.5 Reverse logistics in the supply chain.

Source: **Based on A. Jenkins, *A Guide to Reverse Logistics: How It Works, Types andStrategies,*https://www-netsuite-com.translate.goog/portal/resource/articles/inventory-management/reverse-logistics.shtml?, 4/2/2022.**

Reverse logistics is the management of waste (return) flows (including undamaged and damaged products but considered waste by their holders), as well as information (related to these flows) from their places of origin (in the logistics system) to their destination for reuse, recovery of value (through repair, recycling or processing) or proper disposal and long-term storage in such a way that these flows are economically efficient and minimize negative impacts on the human environment (Kiperska-Moroń & Krzyżaniak,

2009). In relation to the above arrangements, reverse logistics can be described as an integrated system (Korzeń, 2001):

- based on the concept of managing the recirculation flows of waste material streams in the economy and the flows of related information;
- ensuring the readiness and the capacity to effectively collect, segregate, process and reuse waste according to the adopted technical and processing rules, meeting the standard and legal requirements of environmental protection;
- making it possible to make technical and organizational decisions to reduce (minimize) those negative environmental effects accompanying the implementation of procurement, processing, production, distribution, and service processes in logistics supply chains.

Important processes in waste (returns) management that support reverse logistics include (Figure 3.6) (Ustawa z dnia 14 grudnia 2012 r, 2012):

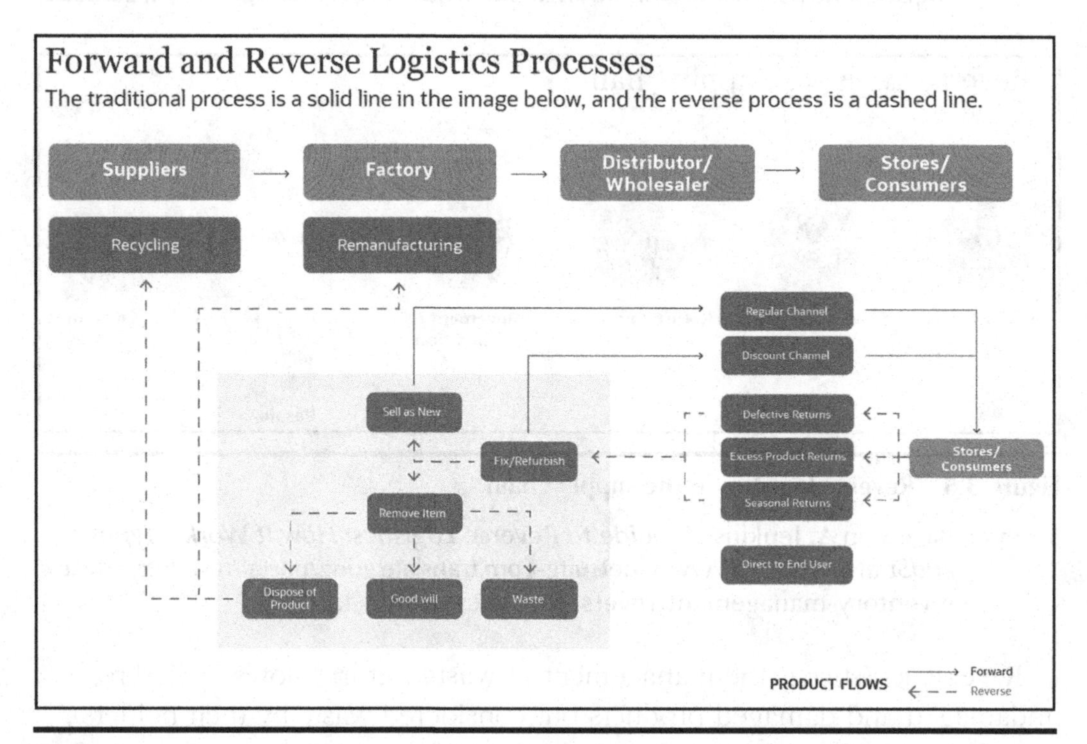

Figure 3.6 Reverse logistics processes – dashed line and traditional logistics – continuous line.

Source: **Based on A. Jenkins, *A Guide to Reverse Logistics: How It Works, Types andStrategies,*https://www-netsuite-com.translate.goog/portal/resource/articles/inventory-management/reverse-logistics.shtml?, 4/2/2022.**

- separate collection, where a given waste stream includes only waste with the same properties and characteristics to facilitate specific treatment;
- storage (preliminary by their generator, temporary by the collector, principal storage by the waste treatment operator);
- recovery (renovation, remanufacturing, reuse of working parts), the main result is that the waste is useful by replacing other materials that would otherwise be used for a given function or as a result of which the waste is prepared to fulfill that function in a given plant or the economy in general;
- energy recovery, incineration of waste to recover energy;
- recycling, recovery involving the reprocessing of substances or materials contained in waste in the production process in order to obtain a substance or material for the primary or another purpose, including organic recycling, except for energy recovery;
- treatment, that is, recovery or disposal, including preparation prior to recovery or disposal;
- waste incineration by oxidation in specially built incineration plants;
- waste disposal – a process that is not recovery, even if the secondary effect of such a process is the recovery of substances or energy.

A significant area that is dealt with by reverse logistics is the return of the product to the manufacturer or distributor or handing it over for service, regeneration, or recycling. There are many aftermarket processes that a product may undergo in reverse logistics, including (Essex, 2022):

- remanufacturing – rebuilding a product with reused, repaired, or new parts;
- refurbishment – resale of a returned product that has been repaired or confirmed to be in good condition;
- service – a broad category covering customer service, off-site service, and product returns, e.g., issuing authorizations to return goods;
- returns management;
- recycling and waste management;
- warranty management;
- warehouse management.

It should be noted that reverse logistics first supports preventing waste generation and second prepares for reuse, recycling, other recovery processes, and disposal. Therefore, it can be said that reverse logistics is a primarily selective collection, transportation, storage, recycling, disposal, sale, and incineration of waste.

3.3 Circular Economy

The circular economy is gaining more and more importance and practical application in economic systems. In Europe, its popularization is related, among other things, to the requirements of the European Union. The following definitions of circular economy can be found (Circular Economy, 2022):

- According to the World Economic Forum – it is an industrial system that is regenerative by intention and design. It substitutes the concept of end-of-life for refurbishment, turns to renewable energy, eliminates the use of toxic chemicals that impede reuse and return to the biosphere, and aims to eliminate waste through better material design, products, systems, and business models.
- According to the Ellen MacArthur Foundation – it involves the gradual decoupling of economic activity from using scarce resources and eliminating waste from the system. The circular model builds economic, natural, and social capital based on the transition to renewable energy sources. It is based on three principles: designing waste and pollution, keeping products and materials in use, and regenerating natural systems.

The following four conclusions can be drawn from the above definitions:

First. In a circular economy, the consumption of resources and materials is not linear (Figure 3.7) but circular (Figure 3.8).

Second. In a circular economy, waste is designed and optimized for the disassembly and reuse cycle. These strict component and product cycles define the circular economy and differentiate it from disposal and even recycling, which lose significant amounts of energy and labor.

Third. In a circular economy, a strict distinction is made between the consumable and durable components of the product. Unlike today, consumables in a circular economy are largely made of organic components that are not only non-toxic but can even be safely returned to the biosphere – directly or in a cascade of subsequent uses. On the other hand, durable

Figure 3.7 A linear economy model.

Source: Based on M.D. Jones, *A new economic model for people and planet,* https://www-metabolic-nl.translate.goog/what-we-do/circular-economy/?,4/30/2022.

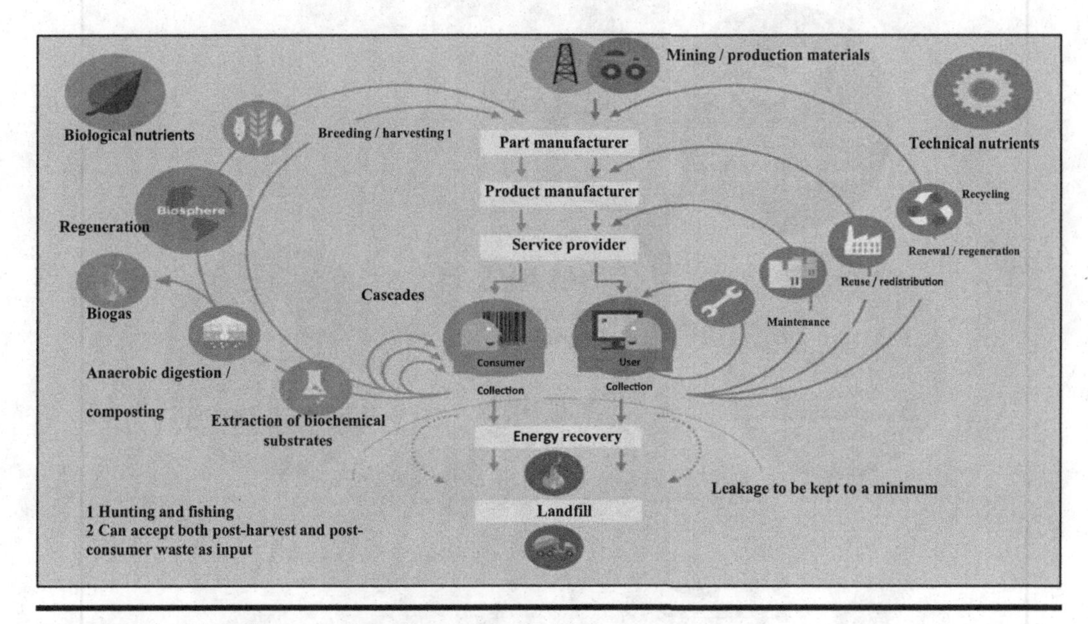

Figure 3.8 Circular economy models – variants.

Source: Based on *Ellen MacArthur Foundation,* https://ellenmacarthurfoundation.org/circular-economy-diagram

components such as engines or computers are made from raw materials unsuitable for the biosphere, such as metals and most plastics, but are designed for reuse from the start.

Fourth. A circular economy tends to use renewable energy.

A circular economy is a form of production and consumption that goes beyond the traditional 3Rs (reduce, reuse, and recycle). This model adds sharing, renting, repairing, and renewing products and their materials as often as necessary to confront the linear economy that has devastated ecosystems and the environment over the years (Gil, 2022).

By analyzing the available literature, it is possible to present seven pillars of the circular economy (Figure 3.9) (Gladek, 2022).

First. Materials are periodically assessed in terms of usefulness and value. Rare materials are preferentially assessed at shorter intervals so they

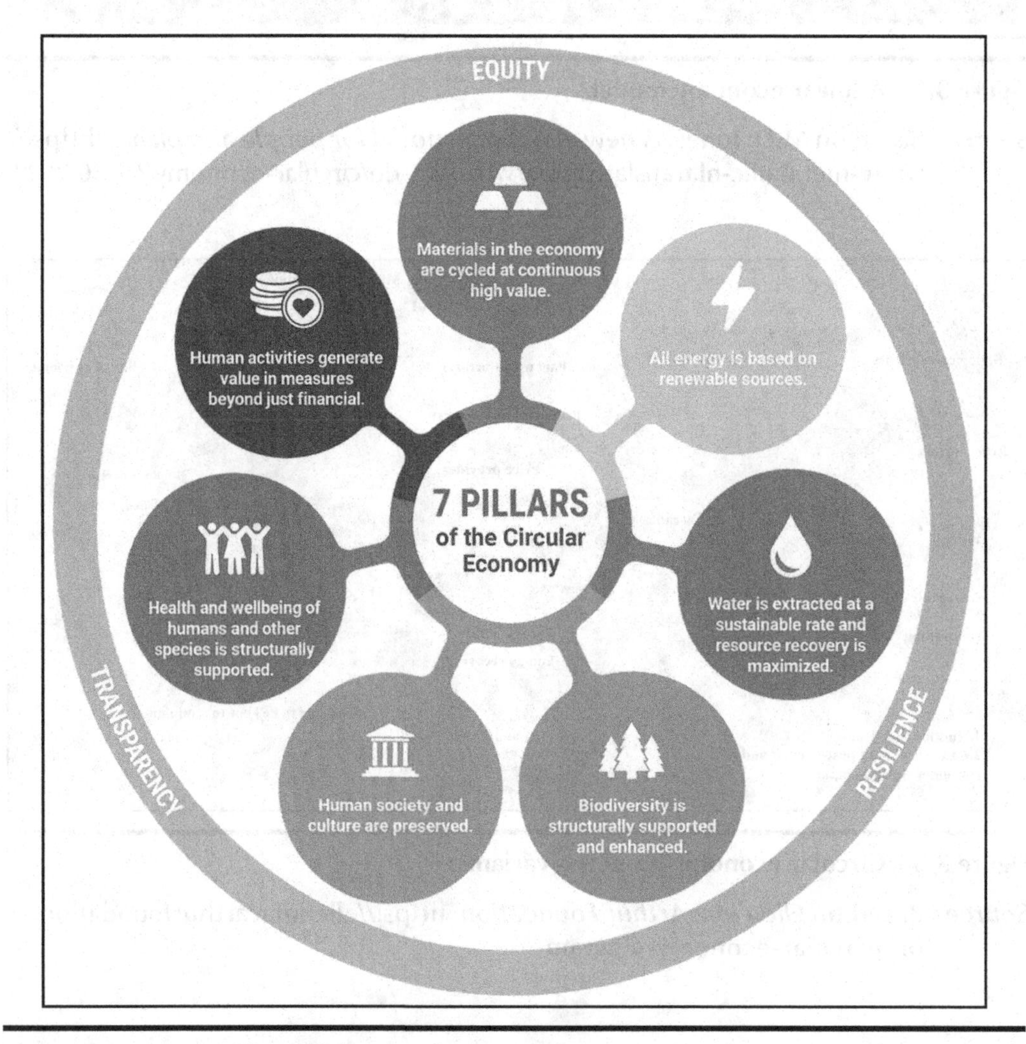

Figure 3.9 The 7 pillars of the circular economy.

Source: Based on E. Gladek, *The Seven Pillars of the Circular Economy,* https://www-metabolic-nl.translate.goog/news/the-seven-pillars-of-the-circular-economy, 4/20/2022.

can be recovered earlier for reuse. Materials are transported over the shortest possible distances. They are not mixed in a way that precludes separation and recovery unless they can continue to be used indefinitely at a high value in their original form. Materials are only used when necessary: there is an inherent preference for the dematerialization of products and services.

Second. All energy is based on renewable sources. Energy is stored intelligently, and consumption is matched to local needs to avoid structural energy losses during transmission.

Third. Biodiversity is supported and enhanced by human activities (Biodiversity, 2022).[9] As complexity is one of the basic principles of operating in a circular economy, preserving biodiversity is a top priority. Habitats, especially rare ones, are not disturbed or structurally damaged by human activity. Preserving ecological diversity is one of the primary sources of biosphere resistance. Material and energy losses are tolerated to preserve biodiversity.

Fourth. Human society and culture are preserved. As another manifestation of complexity and diversity (and therefore resilience), human culture and social cohesion are extremely important to maintain. In a circular economy, processes and organizations use appropriate governance and management models and ensure that they reflect the needs of stakeholders. Activities that structurally undermine the well-being or the existence of unique human cultures are avoided, even at a high cost (Dobrostan, 2022).[10]

Fifth. The health and well-being of humans and other species are supported structurally. Toxic and hazardous substances are minimized and kept in strictly controlled cycles and should eventually be completely eliminated. Economic activities never endanger human health or well-being in a circular economy.

Sixth. Human activity maximizes the generation of social value. Materials and energy are currently unavailable in infinite amounts, so their use should significantly contribute to creating social value. Beyond financial, value can be aesthetic, emotional, ecological, etc. Such values cannot be reduced to a simple measure without making rough approximations or imposing subjective value judgments; they are therefore considered separate value categories. Resource use choices maximize value generation in as many categories as possible rather than simply maximizing financial returns.

Seventh. Water resources are extracted and exploited sustainably. Water is one of our most important shared resources. Sufficient quantity and quality of water are essential to our economy and survival. In a circular economy, the value of water is maintained, allowing it to be reused indefinitely while recovering valuable resources from it whenever possible. Water systems and technologies minimize freshwater consumption and maximize the recovery of energy and nutrients from wastewater.

3.4 Cleaner Production and Waste Minimization

Cleaner production (known by several names with very similar meanings, such as waste minimization, source reduction, pollution prevention, green productivity, clean technologies, and eco-efficiency) is a strategy for environmental protection concerning processes, products, and services to reduce the risk to people and the environment, increase the company's competitiveness, and guarantee its economic viability (Cleaner Production, 2022).

The "cleaner production" program is carried out through technical and organizational measures eliminating or reducing short- and long-term harmful effects of the production process and the product on people and the natural environment. "Cleaner production" refers to both the manufacturing processes and the ecological characteristics of a product throughout its life cycle. In relation to the production processes, this means eliminating harmful raw materials and emissions and rationalizing labor, material, and energy consumption (Adamczyk, 2004).

Cleaner production is defined (understood) in various ways, but all terms have common measures (features), which boil down to the following (Cleaner Production, 2022; Szymonik, 2018):

- minimizing the amount of waste (pollutants) discharged into the environment;
- limiting the use and wastage of raw materials, energy, and human labor in the production system;
- reducing the quantity and toxicity of solid, liquid, and gaseous waste generated in industrial processes, services, and trade while achieving economic benefits;
- limiting the negative impact of the product (service) on the environment – from its manufacture to disposal;
- introducing raw materials and renewable energy that can be reused;
- replacing the non-renewable resources with renewable ones and harmful technologies with ones safer for the environment;
- manufacture of products in the "cleaner production" system, which are:

  - non-toxic,
  - energy-efficient,
  - made using renewable materials that are constantly replenished in a way that preserves the vitality of the ecosystem and the community they come from,
  - made of non-renewable materials, but recycled and recyclable in a non-toxic and energy-efficient manner,
  - durable and reusable,
  - easy to disassemble, repair, or reuse after refurbishment,
  - packed in a minimum and product-specific way, using recycled or recyclable, or reusable materials;
- promoting and informing about the purpose of "cleaner production" using, among other things, magazines (e.g., Czystsza Produkcja EKO Zarządzanie) and organizations (e.g., Polish Cleaner Production Movement Society).

Cleaner production is also considered in the context of life cycle analysis (LCA) and aims to comprehensively study the impact of a product on the environment and natural resources. It begins with preparation for production – specifically, the extraction of raw materials and supply of energy – then covers the production and consumption process and ends with waste management (Analiza cyklu życia, 2022). Systemic LCA of a product must consider the near and far environment, considering internal and external factors. Answering the question of the fate of products that have become waste, that is, substances or objects that the owner discards, is helpful in such an analysis. The following questions can be used:

- What kind of waste are we dealing with: municipal, medical, inert, hazardous, biodegradable, veterinary, green, post-accident, or waste oils?
- How is waste management carried out in terms of collection, transportation, treatment, disposal, and sale?
- How is the waste storage carried out, considering its collection, temporary storage, and accumulation by the entity treating waste?
- What methods are used to prepare waste for reuse without additional technological operations?
- What recovery techniques are used for the further rational use of waste in different production processes – recycling, energy recovery, incineration?
- What ways of preventing waste generation are used?

Cleaner production offers two distinct courses of action:

- the first involves improving techniques and technologies for the manufacture of products that do not harm the environment (neutral or minimal negative impact);
- the second involves managing what is left:
  - at the manufacturer after production (production waste, unnecessary machines, equipment, consumables, etc.),
  - at the customer (e.g., end user, final customer, company) who first purchased (acquired) the product for the purpose of manufacture and then disposed of it because it was unnecessary (lost its use value).

These two courses are shown in Figure 3.10, where the important elements are internal recycling, external recycling, product redesign, process redesign, raw materials change, and energy valuation.

When analyzing the above division, it can be concluded that the first course of action is related to production engineering in a broad (disciplinary)

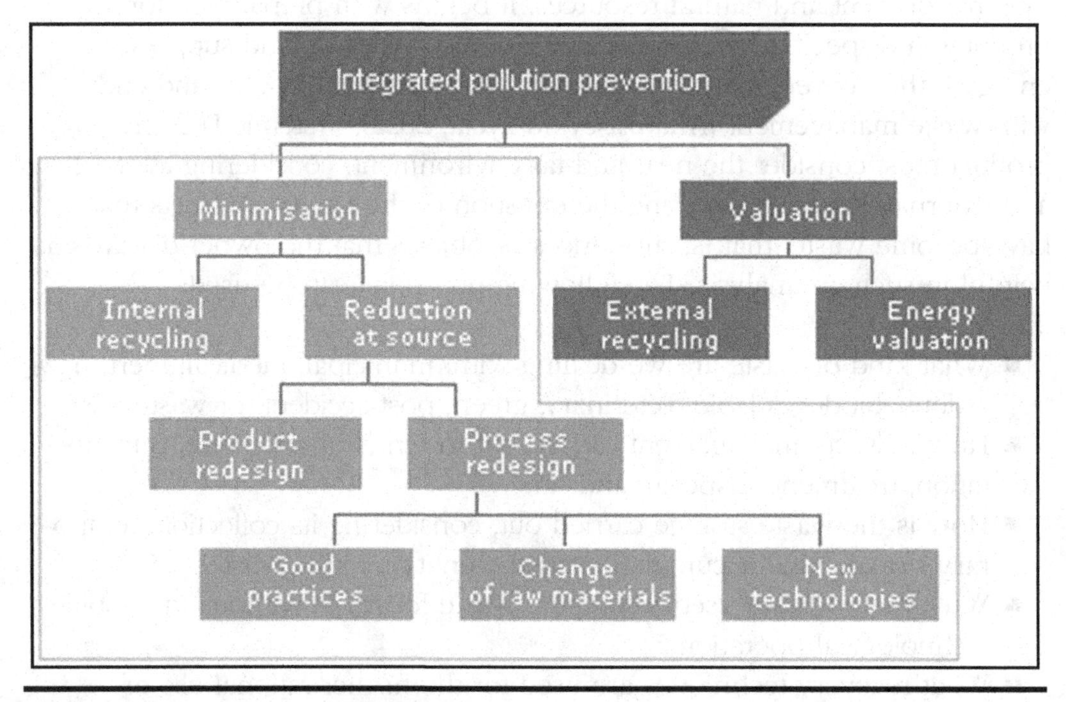

Figure 3.10 Integrated pollution prevention.

Source: **Based on *What is it ?,* https://www-cprac-org.translate.goog/en/sustainable/production/cleaner?, 28.04.2020.**

concept, and the second to waste, and strictly to waste management, in which logistics – or more aptly termed – reverse logistics plays a fundamental role.

3.5 Waste Minimization

The scope of ecological activities in logistics is relatively wide and includes, among others:

- waste minimization (waste prevention) along the entire supply chain ("cradle-to- grave");
- educating society about sustainability.

Waste prevention is the action applied to an object, material, or substance before it becomes waste. These include processes that reduce the following (Ustawa z dnia 14 grudnia 2012 r, 2012):

- the amount of waste, including by reusing or extending the life of the product;
- negative impact of generated waste on the environment and human health;
- the amount of heat, energy, water, and gas consumed;
- the content of harmful substances in the product and material.

Waste minimization is a continuous process that requires regularity and self-discipline. It encompasses processes that start in the upstream supply chain (e.g., raw material mines) and end in the downstream supply chain (e.g., waste generators, waste sellers), including links, which include manufacturing, transportation, and service companies, among others.

Waste prevention should be inextricably linked to all product life cycle stages, which include: idea, specification, technical requirements, product concept, preliminary design, project development, detail development, testing, simulations, analyses, designing tools needed to start production, implementation, production planning, production, final assembly, quality control, organization of customer service/service, sales and delivery, useful life, after-sales service, support, end-of-life, waste treatment.

System analysis carried out to minimize waste in various stages of the product life cycle may reduce the amount and harmfulness of waste and thus positively impact the environment, despite the growing number of products manufactured using new technologies.

Practice shows that reducing waste in the supply chain, along the chain and at the level of individual links, is possible when we reduce unplanned events that may occur at the stage of production, transportation, storage, and sales (Figure 3.11).

These events include the following (Lewandowska & Januszewski, 2013):

- Lack of commitment from top management to:
  - product development,
  - identification of market opportunities,

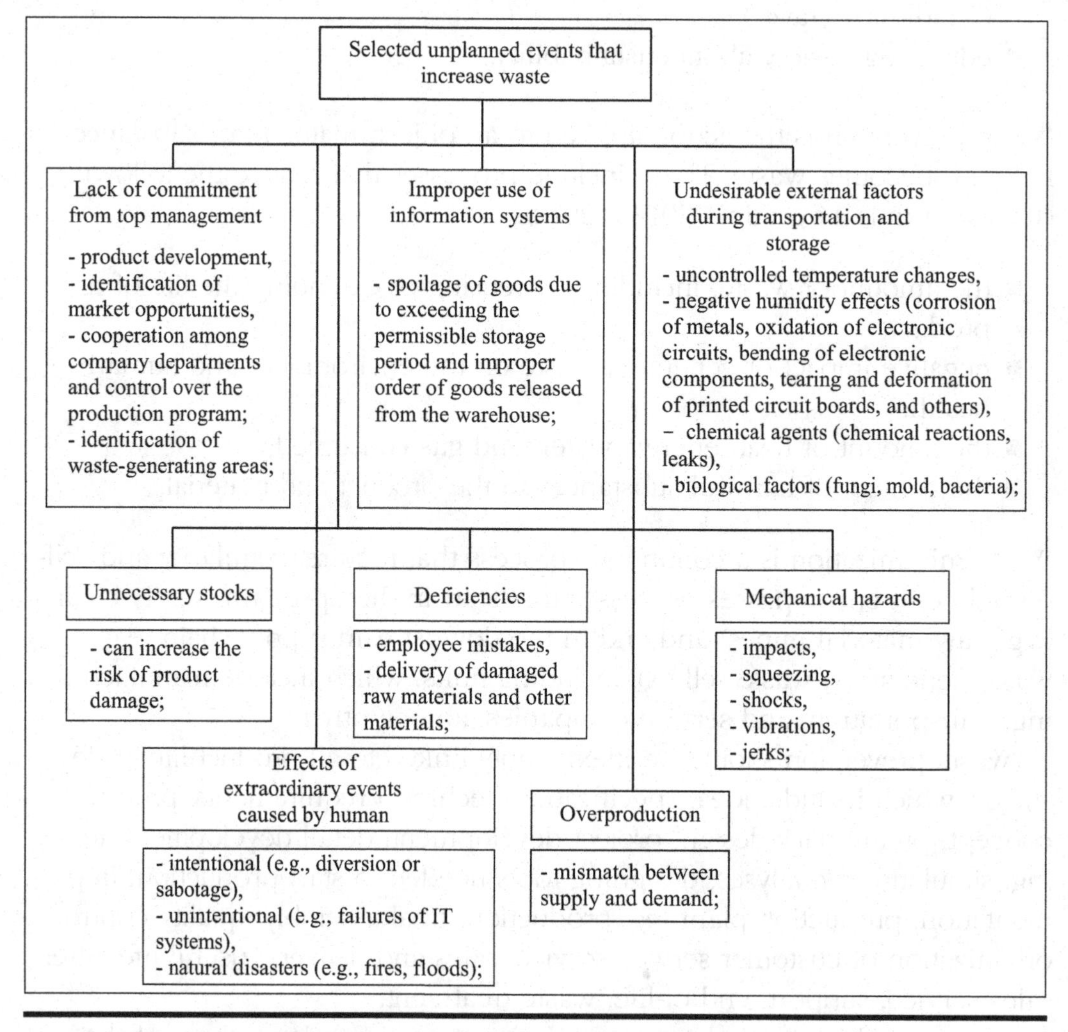

Figure 3.11 Selected unplanned events that increase waste.

***Source:* Own elaboration.**

  - cooperation among company departments and control over the production program;
  - identification of waste-generating areas;
- Overproduction – mismatch between supply and demand;
- Deficiencies resulting from employee mistakes and deliveries of damaged raw materials and other materials, which affect the quality of manufactured goods (cause returns);
- Unnecessary stocks that may increase the risk of product damage;
- Undesirable external factors during transportation and storage:
  - uncontrolled changes in temperature (e.g., some solids lose their shape, properties, and consistency; creams and ointments delaminate, resulting in product disintegration; freezing and sublimation of solutions cause an increase in volume, breaking the containers),
  - negative humidity effects (e.g., metal corrosion, oxidation of electronic circuits, bending of electronic components),
  - chemical agents (e.g., uncontrolled chemical reactions, leaks),
  - biological factors (e.g., fungi, mold, and bacteria);
- Mechanical hazards (impacts, squeezing, shocks, vibrations, jerks) damaging the goods;
- Improper use of information systems (e.g., goods spoilage due to exceeding the permissible storage period and inappropriate order of goods released from the warehouse);
- Effects of extraordinary events caused by human activity: intentional (e.g., diversions or sabotage) or unintentional (e.g., failures of IT systems), and natural disasters (e.g., fires, floods).

In practice, there are many ways to effectively reduce waste in manufacturing. These include the following (How to Effectively Reduce Waste in Manufacturing, 2022):

- Systematic evaluation of existing resources (e.g., work organization, processes, equipment, technology);
- Identification of key waste areas;
- Rational inventory management based on forecasting and planning as well as inventory monitoring (reducing the risk of loss, spoilage, and damage);
- Reduction of packaging materials used (e.g., reusable and recyclable materials);

- Implementation of measures to maintain machines and avoid failures and unnecessary interruptions (zero breakdowns, zero defects, zero accidents during work);
- Protection of order on the premises;
- Implementation of automation of the flow of material stream along the supply chain (thanks to the automated management of the supply chain, reducing the implementation time, labor demand, human error, and operating costs);
- Regular employee training (e.g., safety, new techniques, technologies, manufacturing processes).

Metrics and indicators are helpful tools in ecological management in logistics in waste prevention. They help assess economic processes related to waste generation, considering the near (waste source) and far (consumers) environment and providing the necessary information to describe this process. Indicators in ecologistics boil down to activities that reflect the events and facts of waste minimization in the economic system (Rokicka-Broniatowska, 2006)[11] and its environment, expressed in appropriate measurement units (allowing comparison with other phenomena). These parameters include the inputs and outputs of any economic system. The inputs include:

- raw materials, materials, and components used in product manufacture [e.g., kg, t];
- consumables (e.g., lubricants, oils, inks, toners, spare parts for machinery and equipment used during repairs and maintenance, as well as packaging not directly related to finished products) [e.g., t, pcs];
- energy, water, gas [e.g., m^3];
- auxiliary materials (e.g., tools, cleaning agents, agents giving the manufactured products a specific characteristic or appearance) [e.g., PLN];
- fuel used for technological, transportation, and heating purposes (e.g., coal, coke, briquettes, diesel oil, gasoline, gas) [e.g., t, PLN];

While outputs include:

- quantity of solid and liquid waste [e.g., kg, t, m^3];
- number of complaints [e.g., pcs];
- emission of air pollutants [e.g., CO_2 kg/GJ];
- wastewater [e.g., m^3].

Ecological indicators in logistics are technical and economic measures that assess the dynamics of waste generation and compare it in similar companies in different branches, for example, chemical, metal, and clothing industries (Ustawia z dnia 11 września 2015 r. o zużytym sprzęcie..., 2015).[12] Examples of indicators include:

- share of complaints regarding deliveries of raw materials = (number of complaints regarding deliveries of raw materials/total number of raw materials deliveries) × 100 [%];
- share of raw material delivery returns = (number of raw materials returned/total number of raw material deliveries) × 100 [%];
- share of proper production = (number of defective products/total number of products) × 100 [%]
- share of downtime in production = (production downtime/total working time) × 100 [%];[13]
- share of product delivery returns = (number of returned product deliveries/total number of product deliveries) × 100 [%];
- accuracy of deliveries = (number of damaged parcels/total number of parcels) × 100 [%];
- share of damage during transportation = (number of damaged transport units/total number of moved transport units × 100) [%].

Ecology in logistics also involves the implementation of technical and managerial solutions that minimize the negative environmental impacts. These include the following (Radomska-Deutsch, 2010):

- solutions that generate energy and heat from renewable sources (e.g., wind farms, hydropower plants – hydropower, geothermal energy, biomass power plants);
- energy-efficient lighting systems with integrated twilight and motion sensors;
- reducing energy consumption by using LED (Kalicka, 2022)[14] lighting and lowering the height of light points, adjusting the intensity to the operating areas, placing motion detectors on the tops of the racks of each lighting section;
- photovoltaic systems and renewable energy sources that do not generate air pollution (zero greenhouse gas emissions) – the panels are recyclable after their useful life;
- maximum use of natural light in the warehouse and office space;

- water heated by solar panels;
- water saving – water supply in washrooms when needed (automatic shut-off after releasing the faucet mechanism);
- modern elevators of various sizes, which move vertically and horizontally, make the most of natural lighting, recover electricity to their full potential, and move at a speed of 5–8 m/s (three times faster than traditional ones);
- rainwater tanks, which can be used in toilets, to clean the floor, water plants near the warehouse, and wash concrete mixers and cars;
- kinetic plates on access roads – their pressure produces electricity, which is then accumulated.

3.6 Environmental Management System

Cleaner production is not a one-off action; it is an environmental protection strategy based on continuous, integrated, preventive action concerning processes, products, and services, aimed at increasing the efficiency of production and services and reducing the risk for people and the natural environment (Programu Ochrony Środowiska Narodów Zjednoczonych, 2022). Cleaner production is the foundation of an environmental management system in line with the requirements of:

- ISO 14001 and EMAS (EMAS, 2022);[15]
- corporate social responsibility (CRS).

The 14,000 series of standards has been developed by the ISO/TC 207 and is designed to assist organizations in improving their environmental performance. ISO 14001 (the latest version 14001: 2015, which has been in force since 2018) is the basis for the environmental management system certification. The basic assumptions for environmental management systems are to balance the environment, society, and economy. ISO 14001: 2015 "specifies the requirements for an environmental management system that an organization can use to enhance its environmental performance," considering internal and external factors.

The most important benefits of the environmental management system include the following (ISO 14001: 2015, 2022; ISO 14001: 2015 certification process, 2022):

- increasing the company's competitiveness (compared to organizations without an implemented and certified environmental management system);
- reducing generated pollutants and waste along with the reduction of disposal costs as a result of constant and systemic supervision over the environmental aspects of the organization;
- improving organization performance;
- increasing the profitability of production resulting from the optimization of the consumption of energy, raw materials, and materials;
- improving the environment near the company, for example, as a result of reduced emissions and pollutants;
- improving the relationship between the organization and local residents;
- increased trust of customers and contractors;
- increasing the legal security of the company.

The environmental management system considers the following:

- legal requirements;
- customer requirements regarding the environmental impact of products;
- requirements for suppliers;
- requirements resulting from the organization's environment;
- inspections by environmental protection authorities.

A company implementing ISO 14001 requirements should consider its environmental impact in all its business processes, as shown in the simplified form in Figure 3.12.

During the implementation of internal and external processes, measures and indicators (quantitative and qualitative) are used to assess their environmental impact. Examples of internal company activities subject to assessment include (Szymonik, 2018):

- the amount of water used for domestic purposes in the plant;
- the amount of water used in the production process;
- amount of water used in auxiliary processes (washing floors, washing elements, flushing installations, etc.);
- chemicals used in the production process (generation of industrial wastewater and air emissions);
- chemicals used in auxiliary processes (washing floors, washing elements, flushing installations, air conditioning emissions, etc.);

Environment area	Preparation of production	Production	Packing and distribution	Usage	Removal
Waste					
Soil contamination and degradation					
Air emissions					
Wastewater					
Energy consumption					
Natural resource consumption					
Ecosystem impact					
Other					

Figure 3.12 Business processes and their impact on the environment.

Source: Based on A. Szymonik, *Ekologistyka Teoria i Praktyka,* Difin, Warszawa (2018), p. 120.

- energy consumption in the production process;
- energy consumption in production-related processes (offices, air conditioning, hand dryers in toilets, etc.).

However, in the case of outsourced processes, it is important that the ordering party monitors the activities. Thus, when outsourcing the service of painting elements, the following should be checked (Szymonik, 2018):

- the type of packaging in which the varnishes are stored (related to packaging waste and waste in the form of out-of-date paints and varnishes);
- fire safety and environmental protection of paint and varnish storage – protection against uncontrolled pollution of air, soil, and groundwater;
- how to reduce gas and dust emissions to air from coating processes – whether filters are used and whether their type is appropriate to the emission,
- fire safety and environmental protection of waste storage – protection against uncontrolled pollution of air, soil, and groundwater;
- how to handle waste in the form of packaging, out-of-date paints, paint sludge, defective elements, etc.

Corporate social responsibility (CSR) is the responsibility of companies for their impact on society. CSR in sustainability involves maintaining a balance between activities aimed at achieving goals in the context of (Kazojć, 2014):

- environment;
- society;
- economy.

According to corporate social responsibility, companies should similarly assess the social, ecological (environmental), and financial spheres. In conclusion, the company should undertake such activities that are economically viable and, at the same time, socially responsible and environmentally friendly.

In the environmental sphere, CSR activities include, among others (Ustawa z 14 grudnia 2012 r. o odpadach, art. 3., 2012; Kondraciuk, 2022):

- eco-labeling and social labeling consist of placing additional information on environmental or social responsibility on the packaging or labels of products;
- reducing emissions of waste, pollutants, and greenhouse gases by optimizing production, transportation, and logistics processes;
- preparatory work aimed at creating suitable facilities (racks, boxes, etc.), ensuring appropriate conditions for the collection of waste and products resulting from returns;
- rationally structured product return processes, which provide different usage scenarios for the returned goods (Domagała & Wolniak, 2014):
  - products are reprocessed and re-sold on the secondary market, especially to those who are not interested or unable to buy a new product,
  - returns can be used as spare parts for warranty claims to reduce the cost of providing the services to the customer,
  - products that are not reused are sold as waste or recycled,
  - returned products may be new and unused – they return to the distribution channel after evaluation;
- separate collection, where a given waste stream includes only waste with the same properties and characteristics to facilitate specific treatment;
- accumulation of collected waste, for example, by using:
  - balers and presses for compressing paper, waste paper, plastic (PET bottles), cans, foil, textiles,
  - crushers, shredders, and kneaders for recyclable materials and garbage,
  - modern glass crushing equipment, the so-called imploders,[16]

- presses, briquetting machines for styrofoam,
- packers for aluminum cans and scrap presses.

- modern means of transportation that use activities such as grabbing, loading, pushing and scooping, gravitational discharge and runoff on chutes (ramps), mechanical surveillance;
- waste storage for further management;
- waste incineration by oxidation in specially built incineration plants (if any).

Life cycle engineering should not be underestimated in reverse logistics, as it offers the possibility of decomposing and recovering products and components so that they can be reintroduced into the manufacturing process.

3.7 Passive Building Infrastructure

Logistics infrastructure also includes buildings (warehouses) where appropriate conditions such as temperature and humidity should be maintained. Meeting such requirements generates costs that can be minimized through modern technologies, such as passive buildings.

The creator of this concept is Dr. Wolfgang Feist, founder of the Passive House Institute in Darmstadt. In 1988, he formulated the following definition of a passive house: A passive house is a building with extremely low energy demand for interior heating (15 kWh/(m^2 year)), in which thermal comfort is provided by passive heat sources (residents, electrical appliances, "solar" heat, heat recovered from ventilation) and additional heating of the air ventilating the building. Therefore, it does not need an active autonomous heating system (*Budynki pasywne*, 2022).

Other similar definitions can be found in the literature on the subject. Below are two examples:

First. A passive house is a type of building that uses solutions to significantly reduce the energy consumption needed to heat it. Great importance is attached to the use of sunlight as the main source of heat, and systems such as recuperation are used to recover it. As a result, the annual energy demand of a passive house is only 15 kWh per square meter. For comparison, a traditional house may require up to 120 kWh per square meter (Skorżepo, 2022).

Second. A passive house is a building with annual energy demand not exceeding 15 kWh per square meter (Co to jest budownictwo pasywne, 2022).

Passive house designs are based on six principles that ensure optimal temperature, comfortable air, minimum energy consumption, and noise reduction (Figure 3.13) (Olczak, 2022).

These principles are the following:

1. Achieving indoor comfort with the lowest possible energy consumption.
2. No thermal bridges – walls, floors, and roofs are well insulated and have no gaps. The need to heat or cool the rooms is minimized as a comfortable temperature is maintained.
3. Good insulation – high-quality insulation is a key element of passive houses. Insulation prevents the exchange of energy with the external environment.
4. Excellent windows – top-quality windows prevent unnecessary heat loss; therefore, the chosen solution should have low thermal conductivity. Additionally, passive houses often have large glazing facing south.
5. Hermetic design – a good home design will reduce uncontrolled air flow and heat loss.
6. Mechanical ventilation with heat recovery – high-quality ventilation will recover heat from used air and direct it to fresh air. This ensures the minimization of energy losses and good air quality.

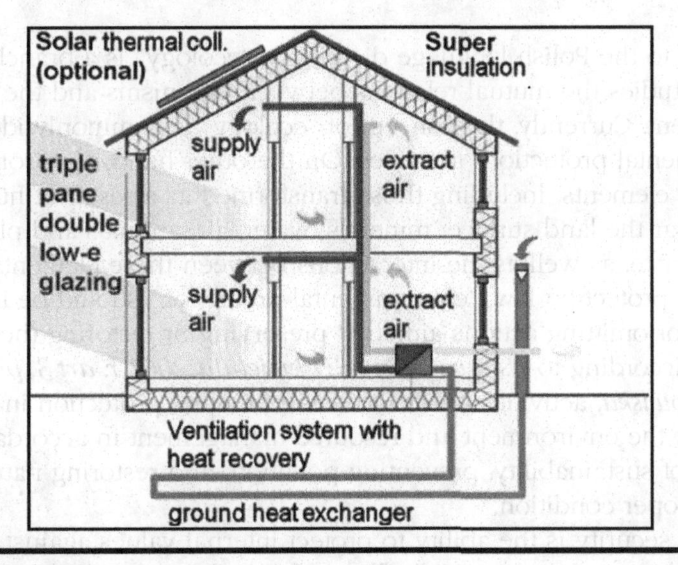

Figure 3.13 Passive system model.

Source: **Based on What is a Passive House?, https://passipedia-org.translate.goog/basics/what_is_a_passive_house, 4/28/2022.**

In a passive house, there is practically no heating system. In principle, the passive house design reduces the demand for heat to such an extent that the necessary amount of heat can be provided by appropriate heating of the ventilation air. Thus, in passive houses, the ventilation system also plays the role of a heating system. Then, a small amount of heat is supplied by heating the air supplied to the rooms. The heating power is only 10 W/m^2. An air heater is often placed in the main supply air duct. This heater can be powered by a heat pump. It is also used to heat water (Lont, 2022). The advantages of passive buildings include (Rinkesh, 2022):

- Energy efficiency and savings – passive houses save their owners an average of 90% on utility bills. Some passive houses feed electricity back into the grid.
- Individualism – a passive house can be tailored to the investor's needs.
- Environmental friendliness – using renewable energy does not hurt the environment.

However, the disadvantages include the cost of construction and the fact that it can practically only apply to newly built houses.

Notes

1 According to the Polish language dictionary, "ecology" is a branch of biology that studies the mutual relations between organisms and the surrounding environment. Currently, the concept of "ecology" is commonly identified with "environmental protection" activities. On the other hand, "environment" means all natural elements, including those transformed as a result of human activity, in particular the land surface, minerals, water, air, animals and plants, landscape, climate, as well as the interactions between these elements. In the environmental protection law, "environmental protection" should be understood as taking or omitting actions aimed at preserving or restoring the natural balance. According to *Ustawa z dnia 27 kwietnia 2001 r. art.3. prawo ochrony środowiska,* activities related to environmental protection include rational shaping of the environment and resource management in accordance with the principle of sustainability, preventing pollution, and restoring natural elements to their proper condition.

2 Ecological security is the ability to protect internal values against threats or the state of counteracting the social effects of transformations in the surrounding environment.

3 The explosion of the fourth reactor of the power plant, which took place on the night of April 25–26, 1986, contaminated parts of the territories of Ukraine and Belarus. Radioactive substances also reached Scandinavia, Central Europe, including Poland, and the south of the continent – Greece and Italy. Currently, the reactor of the fourth block is covered with a protective "Sarcophagus" and "Ark." 31 people died directly as a result of the Chornobyl disaster and during the rescue operation. According to some studies, about 600,000 people worldwide were exposed to increased radiation, equivalent to two X-rays. The number of cancer deaths that developed in people exposed to heavy radiation was estimated at around 4,000.
4 The tsunami on March 11, 2011, caused by a Richter 9 earthquake, hit the northeast coast of Japan, killing almost 20,000 people and flooding Fukushima Daiichi Nuclear Power Plant. Due to the destruction and radioactive contamination, over 160,000 people were evacuated.
5 Biocenosis – a group of living creatures inhabiting a homogeneous section of the biosphere, in which the number of species and individuals corresponds to the average capacity for life. Each biocenosis has plant and animal species. Biotype – a group of individuals with the same hereditary characteristics, that is, the same genotype. An example may be bacterial flora inhabiting humans. Every person has many specific bacterial biotypes developed over their lifetime.
6 Risk map is to be understood as a map or description showing the potentially negative effects of a threat's impact on people, the environment, property, and infrastructure, according to Ustawa z dnia 26 kwietnia 2007 r. o zarządzaniu kryzysowym, Art. 3.
7 Threat map is to be understood as a map showing the geographical area affected by a threat that includes various event scenarios, according to Ustawa z dnia 26 kwietnia 2007 r. o zarządzaniu kryzysowym, Art. 3.
8 The procedure of developing a partial report (an integral part with the spreadsheet) to *Raportu o zagrożeniach bezpieczeństwa narodowego* Rozporządzenie Rady Ministrów z dnia 30 kwietnia 2010 r. w sprawie Raportu o zagrożeniach bezpieczeństwa narodowego (Dz.U. Z 2010, Nr 83, poz. 540).
9 Biodiversity is the name given to the variety of ecosystems (natural capital), species, and genes in the world or in a particular habitat. It is essential to human well-being, as it delivers services that sustain our economies and societies. Biodiversity is also crucial to ecosystem services – the services that nature supplies – such as pollination, climate regulation, flood protection, soil fertility, and the production of food, fuel, fiber, and medicines. Biodiversity, https://www.eea.europa.eu/pl/themes/biodiversity/intro, 4/292022.
10 Well-being – a person's subjectively perceived sense of happiness, prosperity, satisfaction with the state of life, Dobrostan, https://encyklopedia.pwn.pl/haslo/dobrostan;3893293.html, 4/29/2022.
11 An economic system is an open, dynamic social and technical system that pursues specific economic goals, according to A. Rokicka-Broniatowska, *Wstęp do informatyki gospodarczej*, SGH, Warszawa 2006, p. 111.

12 Ecological indicators, do not concern, for example, the obligatory amounts of recovery, reuse and recycling of electronic equipment included in *Ustawia z dnia 11 września 2015 r. o zużytym sprzęcie elektrycznym i elektronicznym.*
13 The number of waste increases during an interrupted technological process (e.g., during food production) or damage to machinery (e.g., recalibration of the size of ceramic tiles).
14 LED lighting advantages include efficiency – LEDs are the most energy-efficient lighting type on the market; luminous efficacy, that is, the energy converted into visible light, is 80%–95% (efficacy of an ordinary light bulb is 5–10%); durability – they last about 50,000 hours on average, ten times longer than a halogen bulb and 25 times longer than an ordinary bulb (the average lifetime of a LED module is 5–7 years).
15 Eco-Management and Audit Scheme (EMAS), an instrument of the European Union for businesses and other organizations that voluntarily undertake to assess their environmental impact and improve their environmental performance. EMAS is currently the most reliable environmental management system. The legal basis of EMAS is Regulation (EC) No. 1221/2009 of the European Parliament and of the Council of 25 November 2009 on the voluntary participation by organizations in a Community eco-management and audit scheme (EMAS). In Poland, it is additionally regulated by the Act of 15 July 2011 on the national eco-management and audit scheme (Journal of Laws No. 178, item 1060, EMAS, https://www.mos.gov.pl, 4/22/2022.
16 Imploders are an alternative to glass crushers. They replace traditional glass crushing methods with a technology that uses targeted sound vibrations to create non-sharp glass cullet.

Chapter 4

Processes and Logistics

4.1 Logistics Process

In the literature on the subject, it is difficult to find an unambiguous definition of a *process*, especially a *logistics process*. The process can be defined as:

- the course of consecutive and related cause-specific changes (Słownik języka Polskiego, 2022);
- an orderly sequence of changes and states occurring one after another (the carrier of each process is always, in effect, a physical system, and each subsequent state/change of the system is caused by the previous state/change or by an external influence on the system) (Encyklopedia naukowa, 2022);
- a set of procedures or activities that allow us to jointly achieve a business goal, considering the care of employees and the natural environment, with the involvement of possible resources and legal regulations (Rodriguez, 2022);
- a set of logically related tasks or activities performed in order to achieve a specific business result (Bozarth & Handfield, 2007);
- an orderly and regulated chain of operations closely related to the flow of materials (Vademecum logistyki, 2020);
- a whole range of different activities covering the movement of goods from their production at the producer until their receipt by the recipient (Procesy logistyczne w przedsiębiorstwie – etapy przygotowania, wykorzystanie nowoczesnych technologii, 2022);

DOI: 10.4324/9781003372615-5

- transformation of input data (quantities) into output data (quantities) and information accompanying activities, as well as disruptions that may appear during the creation of added value (Figure 4.1) (Smid, 2012).[1]

The processes are primarily carried out by economic entities (systems) whose main task is to create added value for a product or service. On the other hand, *the logistic process is understood as the successive facts (past and future phenomena) in the physical flow of products, services, and information, as well as the risks that accompany each action at a specific time and place.*

These facts may concern:

- performance of the management function in logistics activities;
- material events (e.g., supply, production, distribution, transportation, waste management in reverse logistics, etc.);
- intangible events (e.g., logistic costs, threats, etc.);
- information related to the physical movement of goods and services from origin to destination (e.g., confidentiality, security, timeliness);
- risk (disruptions) related to logistic, ecological, and energy activities.

Logistics processes can be divided into various types. For example, due to the creation of added value, P. Blaik (2001) proposed the following division:

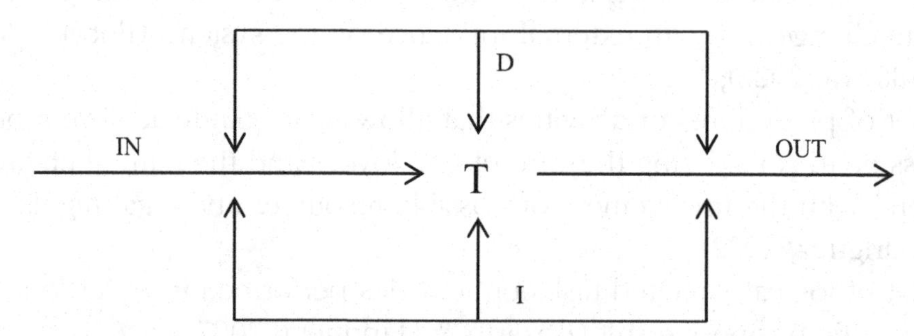

Where: IN – input (e.g., collection and storage in the case of a warehouse); OUT – output (e.g., these are activities related to forming a logistic load and sending it to the customer in the case of a warehouse); T – transformation (e.g., related to cross-docking or picking in the case of a warehouse); I – information, D – disruptions in the process

Figure 4.1 Process model.

Source: **Own elaboration.**

- directly creating added value, characterized by a direct and close relationship with customers and the environment – the so-called primary processes (e.g., delivery of goods in accordance with customer requirements and invoice, delivery of waste to a landfill);
- indirectly creating added value, characterized by an indirect relationship with customers and the environment – the so-called secondary processes, from the point of view of contributing to the creation of added value (supporting processes, e.g., packaging of goods, waste segregation);
- relatively creating added value, showing a relative (conditional) relationship with customers and the environment – the so-called tertiary processes, from the point of view of contributing to value creation (e.g., placing non-obligatory information on packaging, waste minimization);
- not creating added value, no relationship with customers and the environment – the so-called potential signs of waste (e.g., delivery of goods not in accordance with the invoice, non-ecological handling of packaging, waste).

For a different breakdown of logistics processes, see *Introduction to Operations and Supply Chain Management*. The authors distinguished three types of processes (Bozarth & Handfield, 2007):

- primary processes, which cover the most important activities carried out by the organization with high added value (these include such activities as the provision of transportation, storage, picking, packaging management services, etc.), for a result that the customer is willing to pay;
- support processes include activities that are needed but offer no added value (e.g., packaging, labeling, waste sorting);
- development processes increase the efficiency of primary and support processes (these include employee training, market research, designing new products, use of IT systems in reverse logistics, etc.).

The basic components of logistics processes include (Słownik biznesu i ekonomii, 2022): tangible goods flow processes, information and decision-making processes, inventories and warehouse infrastructure, logistic flow infrastructure, customer service, waste management, costs of logistics processes. They are implemented, among other things, by forecasting supply and distribution, placing orders, procurement, storage and stock management, supplying workstations with materials, raw materials, components, packing and confectioning, transportation, packaging management, waste management in reverse logistics, information flow, service, collecting, processing, and transferring information related to the above activities.

By analyzing the definitions of logistics processes and their types and components, it can be concluded that they consist of the physical movement of goods and related information. In the course of these processes, further transformations (appreciation – the creation of added value) of semi-finished products take place, which can ultimately be finished products or waste that can be reused.

4.2 The Flow of the Material Stream

According to the definition given in the *Glossary of Logistics Terminology*, logistics is the *management of the processes of movement of goods* (Słownik języka polskiego, 2022) *and/or people and activities supporting these processes in the systems in which they occur* (Słownik terminologii logistycznej, 2006). Thus, logistics is the physical flow of primarily material goods (their value can be estimated in money) from the sources of their acquisition through manufacturing to the customer (final consumer).

To conclude, there are different views on logistics. For example, the Byzantine Emperor Leo VI (886–911), in the definition of logistics, considered the object of logistics to be pay (today's cash for wages), armaments, cannon and war equipment, and the movement of troops (including transportation) (Kortschuk, 1992). J.P. Guillaume (1993), on the other hand, believed that the object of logistics is "the total flow of goods and the flow of information" (Blaik, 2001). The scope of logistics is constantly expanding. In 1999, M. Wasylko took the following position on this matter (Wasylko, 1999):

> From the theoretical point of view, several variants of the logistic chain (channel) capacity can be considered. **The first** includes the supply streams of the logistics chain, i.e., materials, parts, assemblies, and subassemblies necessary to manufacture a specific product.[2] **The second** covers the scope listed as the first, as well as electricity, gas, cash, personnel, water. **The third** covers the

scope listed as the second, as well as infrastructure and operation.
The fourth covers the scope listed as the third, as well as the supply of machinery and equipment for production.

From the point of view of the essence of logistics and its object, it can be stated that the identification of participants improves economic activities by:

- improving the management of product flow processes for all participants in the logistics chain;
- subordinating all activities to create added value and meet customer expectations;
- minimizing logistic costs (in some situations, this problem is of secondary importance, e.g., helping people affected by a natural disaster).

The implemented processes related to the physical flow of goods are to efficiently (wisely, without wastage) and effectively ("doing only the right things") provide customer service following the "7 R's" (*Czym właściwie jest logistyka? Poznaj zasadę 7W, 2022*): right product, right customer, right quantity, right condition, right place, right time, right cost.

The efficiency and effectiveness of the flow of physical material goods are achieved by performing all management functions, that is (Wstęp do informatyki gospodarczej, 2006):

- Planning, that is, setting goals that the logistics system intends to achieve in a given time and assigning tasks in the area of product movement, the implementation of which ensures the achievement of these goals.
- Organizing, that is, acquiring and allocating resources (funds necessary to carry out the flow of material goods). They include human, material, financial, and information resources. The first three types are market-based, while information resources are the only own resources of the functioning logistics system. Therefore, these resources must be both acquired and properly allocated (assigned) within the logistics system.
- Motivating, that is, creating conditions for efficient and effective work of people employed in the logistics chain, considering the goals and tasks to be implemented and the resources at hand. This purpose is mainly used by the HR and payroll policy implemented for the benefit of, among others, those who work in a given logistic system.

- Control, that is, comparing the achieved effects with the assumed goals and tasks, plans, standards, etc., in order to gain insight into the flow of the material stream (based on feedback reports and analyses).
- Coordinating, that is, ensuring harmonized cooperation of the discussed functions. In many practical situations, it is necessary to simultaneously engage in many activities representing many functions.
- Deciding, that is, making a non-random selection of an action from a set of acceptable and rational actions. It is a "cross-sectional" function, that is, a common feature of the previously mentioned ones.

All types of functions that participate in the movement of material goods in time include the following process spheres:

- real (actual activities related to the material stream, e.g., packing, picking, shipment, storage, waste from segregation sites to the customer);
- regulation (actions taken to properly direct the material flow by performing management functions such as planning, organizing, motivating, controlling).

The physical flows of material goods can be considered in many ways. Considering the classification of logistics systems, they can be divided into two ways. According to the institutional criterion, physical flows can be realized in the following systems:

- micrologistics (e.g., within individual economic organizations such as a company in the chemical, metal, clothing, and mineral industries or a waste incineration plant);
- macrologistics (integration of flows in the entire economy, e.g., rail transportation, car transportation, electricity);
- external (between suppliers and customers in the international dimension, an example may be logistics, transportation, and forwarding companies).

In the case of the functional criterion, the flows may take place, among others, in the sphere of supplies, production, sales, return of goods, packaging, and waste (as well as in the area of logistics), material, marketing, suppliers, and customers. K. Ficoń proposed a slightly different division, considering (Figure 4.2) (Ficoń, 2001): generic, technological, assortment, destination, and spatial criteria

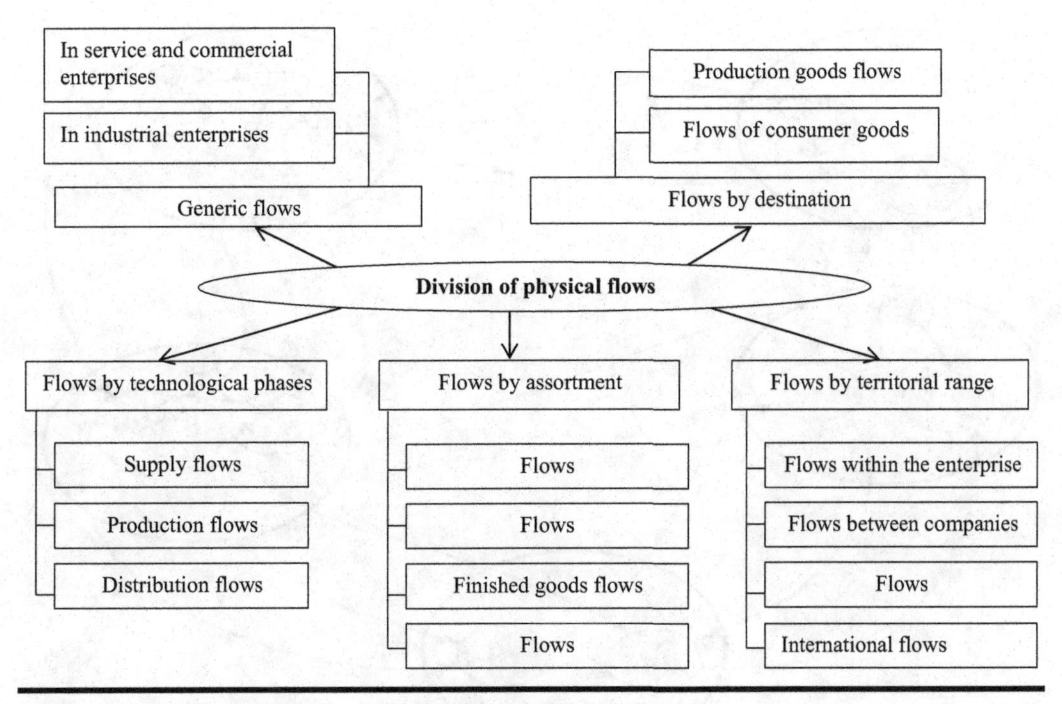

Figure 4.2 Classification system of physical flows.

Source: **Based on K. Ficoń, *Procesy logistyczne w przedsiębiorstwie,* Impuls Plus Consulting, Gdynia 2001, p. 71.**

The total flow of goods in the economy includes several basic phases (Figure 4.3) (Skowronek & Sarjusz-Wolski, 2007):

- obtaining raw materials from nature and production management (e.g., mines, storage, transportation);
  - processing of raw materials into materials and semi-finished products with various degrees of processing and refinement (e.g., steel mills, rolling mills);
  - processing of materials, production of final products (e.g., companies producing home appliances, electronic, automotive equipment);
  - trade in means of production and consumption (real and virtual wholesalers, e-commerce, retail);
  - after-sales service (delivery, assembly, start-up, operation, withdrawal of unnecessary product);
  - waste management (sorting, recycling, utilization, cleaner production) (Encyclopedia PWN, 2022).[3]

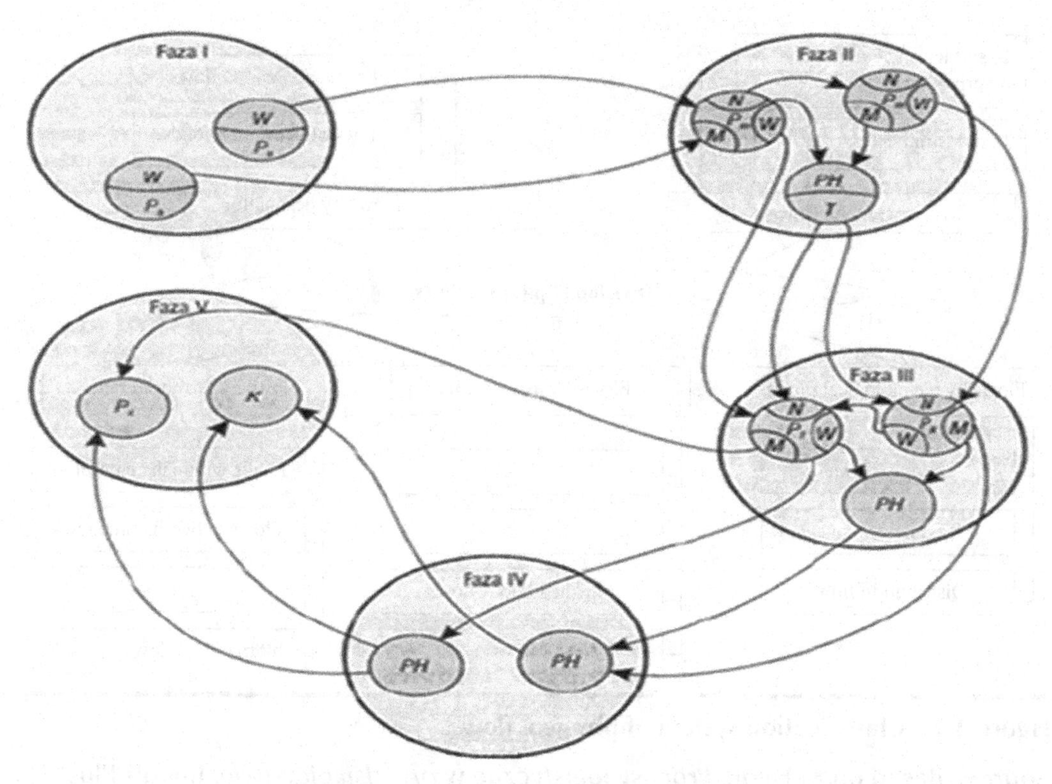

Labels: Phase I – obtaining raw materials; Phase II – raw materials processing, material production; Phase III – materials processing, production of final products; Phase IV – trade in means of production and consumption; Phase V – exploitation (consumption); Ps – producers of raw materials; Pm – producers of materials; Pt – producers of final products; Pk – producers of parts and elements; PH – commercial enterprises; Pe – enterprises operating machines and devices; K – consumers, M – material stocks, N – work-in-progress inventories, T – inventory of goods, W – inventory of finished products

Figure 4.3 Basic phases of the flow of material goods.

Source: **Based on A. Szymonik, *Logistyka i zarządzanie łańcuchem dostaw,* part 1, Difin, Warszawa 2010, p. 36.**

4.3 Information and Decision-Making Processes

Information flow and resources are important components of logistics processes along logistics chains, including reverse logistics. They reflect the flow and state of material resources and, at the same time, are used to control the flow processes. The information must be obtained, properly classified, encoded, collected, and used (shared, transmitted) in decision-making processes.

This information facilitates the implementation of processes in the logistics supply chain. For example, implementing procurement, distribution, stock management, warehouse layout and design, material handling and packaging, transportation, order processing, waste management, and logistics costs would not be possible without effective information systems.

The basic components of logistics information processes include (Szymonik, 2010):

- systems for coding and identifying products as well as raw materials, materials, finished products, goods (e.g., barcodes, EPC, RFID);
- documentation of the flow: records of receipt and issue, invoices, orders, waybills, specifications, etc. (preferably EDI – transfer of business transaction information from computer to computer using standard, accepted message formats);
- coding systems for documents, contractors, internal organizational units, workstations, etc. (e.g., application identifiers in accordance with GS1);
- information processing as well as grouping and aggregation in various time sections, according to the needs of various decision-making functions (e.g., creating databases, data warehouses, big data (Poradnik przedsiębiorcy, 2022)[4];
- technical means and computer programs for emission, collection, processing, and transmission of information (e.g., transaction information systems, information systems supporting decision-making processes, enterprise resource planning systems, effective customer service systems, customer contact management systems, warehouse management systems, transportation management system, supply chain management systems, customer relationship management systems, chatbots (Włodarczyk, 2022).[5]

The flows in question can be dealt with information that controls and regulates material flows, as well as reporting and control. The first of them runs in the opposite direction to the material flows. They originate in the market and take the form of demand forecasts or customer orders. This information is transformed appropriately. This transformation results in production plans, programs, and schedules, including those related to waste management. Information about production (processing) objectives then moves to the supply phase, enabling the development of material needs plans (waste collection). These plans are the basis for preparing purchase (recovery) plans, resulting in orders, contracts, etc., directed to the market. On the other hand, reporting and controlling information additionally flows in accordance with the course of material processes. It reflects the implementation of previous planning decisions. In logistics management, the addressee of the decision is a person or a group of people.

Logistics decision-making is a process that starts when there is a problem to be solved in the movement of goods and services (and accompanying information). This problem involves inherent features and actions:

- there must be at least two variants; otherwise, there is no choice;
- these solutions are important for some reason;
- solutions differ in the amount of added value.

The decision can be defined as *a non-random selection of one of the variants provided for by the set of admissible variants,* and it can be formally presented as a transformation [T2] of the set into decision D (Rokicka-Broniatowska, 2006):

$$D = T2\ [W] = T2\ \{T1\ [B]\}$$

Where: W – a set of variants of acceptable solutions to a given problem (e.g., selection of a warehouse location, inventory management method, warehouse management method); B – a set that can be transformed by T1 into at least two-element set W. Converting T2 requires knowledge of both the selection criteria used and the selection procedures.

The decision-making process consists of the following steps (*Encyklopedia zarządzania*, 2022):

- identification of the decision situation (e.g., choice of the means of transportation);
- identification and design of decision variants (at least two ways, e.g., rail or car);
- evaluation of the designed variants and selection of the rational one (using, e.g., IT systems supporting decision-making processes);
- creating conditions for the implementation of decisions;
- control of the effects of the decision made.

Each step is important, but the priority is determining each option's consequences. The logits must analyze the impact that a change in conditions could have on the results of various activities and answer whether it is possible to obtain more comprehensive information to predict the results. Properly designing and forecasting the consequences is not always an easy task. Sometimes, simple calculations are sufficient. Often, however, a complex analysis will be needed to determine the results and the probability of their occurrence.

It can use a model, that is, a simplified description of a process, relationship, or phenomenon. In the case of forecasting, we can use deterministic and probabilistic models. Each of these models requires satisfying specific information needs, and the continuous flow of relevant information is possible only with an efficiently operating information system. Decision-making issues always involve two primary levels (Słowiński, 2008):

- decision makers' beliefs about cause–effect relationships in a given problem ("if this, then that");
- their preferences with regard to possible outcomes.

These are the basic decision variables. Different decision-making strategies are appropriate when considering these two variables. The formulation of a decision problem is the first step to building a decision model, that is, a theoretical representation of a fragment of reality that synthetically binds decision variables. Such a model should enable the determination of a set of optimal decisions. Building such a model that represents the real situation well is a task that requires a lot of knowledge, work, and considerable skills. Although not all decision models are complex, they all require using operations research supported by modern IT systems.

An important issue when making decisions is having "the right amount of information" that can be obtained from: search engines – we use them in various environments and for various purposes; agent-based technology – computer programs, similar to searchers, that identify a specific material in terms of content, structure, and properties (email filtering, transaction handling, text analysis, news management); personalization technology (uses agent-based technology) to meet 100% of the user's needs (companies use it to gain knowledge about the customer, e.g., through the so-called "cookies" – a small file placed on the user's computer); OLAP (online analytical processing) – multidimensional data processing, for example, of a company important to the user; exploration of databases – generating knowledge from a set of structured data (providing ready-made solutions in areas such as distribution, fraud detection, and production control); the Internet; an intranet; an extranet – a closed network designed to exchange information with business partners; Web 2.0 platforms; social networks (e.g., MySpace, Facebook, LinkedIn); blogs – online journals (posts, podcasts, photoblogs, microblogging – Twitter), virtual world (Second Life) – three-dimensional virtual world, wiki sites; videoconferencing; expert telephone directories – skill catalogs; e-learning; data warehouses (thematic orientation, homogeneity, variability over time, stability).

Due to the information, decision problems can be divided into three groups, that is, undertaken under the following conditions:

- certainty – each decision has specific, known consequences (the largest share of these decisions occurs at the operational management level; an example may be the choice of one of two proven, reliable suppliers);
- risk – each decision entails more than one consequence, but we know them and the probability of their occurrence (such decisions are made mainly at the tactical management level, and an example may be the choice of a tailor-made IT system for the needs of warehouse management, selection of partners for cooperation within the supply chain);
- uncertainty – we do not know the probabilities of the consequences of a given decision (such decisions are made mainly at the strategic management level, and the translation may be the number of forecasted inventories in the enterprise for the next calendar year, forecasts of logistic costs).

Decisions should result from a rational solution to the problem, assessment of the situation being a derivative of the collected information (using modern IT solutions), human knowledge and experience, imagination, and intuition. Therefore, the area of decision-making, which is a non-random selection of one variant (from the set of acceptable options), is multi-faceted and multi-criteria and concerns material and information processes. Decisions may concern many logistics problems, which include:

- inventory control method – depends, among other things, on the type of production organization (individual, small, medium, multi-series, mass), the form of production organization (rhythmic, non-rhythmic, traditional, modern based on digital technologies, e.g., flexible production systems or computer-integrated manufacturing systems), product features (design, structure, complexity, processing degree, manufacturing technology), location and distribution of individual devices involved in the manufacturing process (technological and object distribution);

- "make or buy" – deciding to make or buy means to produce at home or obtain from outside (in an industrial enterprise, make or buy may apply to products, their parts or production processes, and logistics processes such as transportation, storage, packaging, etc.);
- doing something or outsourcing – the decision problem may concern all spheres of material flow activities related to the subsystem of logistics, supply, production (make or buy), distribution, transportation, storage, raw materials and waste management, logistics costs, IT systems, human resources management in logistics, security;
- selection of the logistics information system – before we proceed to the purchase and implementation, we must consider: which computerization variant to choose; to what extent we will implement the IT system; whether we are able to prepare the company for computerization on time; are we able to overcome all barriers of computerization;
- choice of a transportation company – the problem concerns not only the carrier but also the transportation sector in which road transportation is at the forefront (advantages: the best adaptation of the road network to the distribution of sales and supply markets, availability in time and space, high operational speed) and rail (advantages: favorable availability of the railway network, the size of the rolling stock, speed, long-distance cost advantage, transportation safety, low environmental impact);
- selection of waste management in the context of waste segregation, waste storage, recovery, disposal, recycling, waste prevention, etc.;
- use renewable or non-renewable electricity or both.

4.4 Intralogistics in Warehouse Management

Intralogistics is a logistics subsystem in which the flow of the material stream inside the company starts with the receipt of goods (parts, components, waste) to the warehouse and ends with sending the finished products to the final customer. The areas of intralogistics include (Czym jest intralogistyka?, 2022):

- Internal transportation of materials – including both within the warehouse and between individual production (processing) plants and warehouses belonging to one production or service company. Contemporary, extensive, global supply chains contribute to the organization of the flow of the material stream and accompanying information within the so-called Logistics 4.0, which is based on new digital technologies ensuring exchange between people, devices, machines, products, and internal transportation (Scherf, 2022):
  - automation – examples include automated systems such as stacker cranes, pallet conveyors;
  - robotization supporting picking and packaging – a good example of such an approach is the so-called cobot, that is, a collaborative robot, for example, robotic mechanical arms or packaging machines, that relieve staff during order picking and packaging, thus reducing the feeling of fatigue.
- Inventory and information flow management – the company must keep track of the physical movements of goods using an IT system that allows controlling fluctuations in inventory, locating available inventory, and managing its replenishment. Various highly specialized programs such as WMS are usually used for comprehensive tracking of the flow of goods, handling of the purchasing process, and invoicing. In addition, a system of interconnected devices in the warehouse (IoT technology – Internet of Things) is used to collect and transfer information from the real to the digital environment. It employs, among others, headphones (voice picking – pick by voice), radio terminals, or traffic lights (pick-to-light systems).

Inventories play an important role in running a business in every economic system, ensuring the continuity of economic processes (Marciniak, 2006)[6] and the continuity of production and sales. A company can accumulate different inventories, each with a completely different role. Manufacturing companies mainly stock up on materials and finished products. Stocks dominate in trading companies. Service companies have stocks of materials, including waste, that can be used to perform the service (including waste management).

The main factor influencing the demand for materials (including waste) or goods is the volume of planned sales of products or goods. If companies fully implemented the just-in-time strategy, stocks would not be needed, but it is impossible in practice. The main reason for creating inventories is that the inflow and outflow streams cannot be fully synchronized. The second reason is the impact of a random factor on the logistic processes. It makes it impossible to build error-free forecasts, forcing companies to apply safeguards against the effects of random disruptions. Other reasons for inventory build-up are related to (Buczacki, 2022): uncertainty of deliveries and their delays, greater market needs than anticipated, obtaining a lower purchase price, seasonality of deliveries, the need to ensure the rhythm of production, economies of scale of production, economies of scale of supplies, seasonality of demand, providing full customer service (otherwise you may lose your reputation), ensuring that the transportation of products is profitable (stocking is associated with sending a minimum batch size ensuring profitability), customer requirements (creating an inventory is related to the need to deliver the ordered quantity of the product to the customer at a specific place and time).

APICS defines inventory as *those stocks or items used to support production (raw materials and work-in-process items), supporting activities (maintenance, repair, and operating supplies), and customer service (finished goods and spare parts)* (Bozarth & Handfield, 2007).

Modern logistics defines inventory as the phase of the flow of goods through the logistics channel. This approach to inventories makes it easier to illustrate the principles used so that the inventories fulfill their primary tasks in the logistics system (Szymonik, 2010):

- stocks should be stored in this area of the logistics chain where it is associated with the optimization of total costs (with a certain level of customer service);
- the place of storage, quantity, and type of stocks should enable full synchronization of supply and demand;
- the current and projected level, costs, and rate of inventory flow should be known to all entities in the logistics system.

In addition to applying the above principles, in order to properly manage stocks, it is necessary to have detailed knowledge of the phenomena occurring in the logistics chain itself and in its environment, which may greatly affect all parameters of the inventory used in the enterprise, including waste. These phenomena primarily include:

- adopted policy of servicing internal and external customers;
- the staff available;
- reliability of suppliers and customers;
- capabilities of information and IT systems;
- macroeconomic situation and forecasts;
- actions of competition, both within one supply chain and between different chains;
- the company's financial condition and negotiation skills.
- Generally, stocks can be divided into the following (Szymonik, 2010):
- current – consumed on an ongoing basis for production;
- cyclical – those for which there is a seasonal demand;
- safety – collected due to the possibility of unforeseen circumstances to maintain the pace of production;
- speculative – (surplus stocks) created in advance for financial or supply reasons.

The fundamental determinant of the logistics approach is also the extremely diverse sphere of inventories and the associated warehouse management, which is the opposite of mobile transportation systems.

Warehouse management symbolizes statics and the stoppage of economic processes, while transportation is the epitome of dynamics and intensity of physical flows. The minimax decision problem (minimum inventory and maximum transportation as well as minimum transportation and maximum inventory) has been theoretically and practically solved in an optimal way using the just-in-time principle (*Modelowanie ryzyka gospodarczego przedsiębiorstwa produkcyjnego*, 2022). It reduces inventory as a sign of waste in favor of punctual and reliable deliveries, most often when meeting the 7 R's – the right product, the right consumer, the right quantity, the right condition, the right place, the right time, and the right cost. For economic, technical, and organizational reasons, every enterprise must have a certain minimum stock called safety stock, which should be optimized with appropriate models and modern computer applications.

The category of traditional inventories refers primarily to the inventories of supply materials and finished products. In the case of large production enterprises, an important category is various work-in-process inventories resulting from the adopted technological processes. A unique category of inventories is waste, including both unused raw materials, used materials, as well as full-value finished products that have not found a buyer. The symbolic topology of the collection of inventories and their accompanying waste can be described as follows (*Modelowanie ryzyka gospodarczego przedsiębiorstwa produkcyjnego*, 2022):

$$\underset{O}{M} = \underset{OZ}{MZ} \approx \underset{OP}{MP} \approx \underset{OD}{MD} \varnothing \text{ min}$$

Where:

M – warehouse stock in the enterprise;
MZ – supply stocks (raw materials, materials, semi-finished products);
MP – production inventories (work in process);
MD – distribution inventories (finished goods);
O – waste in the enterprise;
OZ – supply waste;
OP – production waste;
OD – distribution waste.

Currently, inventory management focuses on maximum inventory reduction, including waste and optimization of material streams. Inventory management aims to ensure the size necessary to run the business at the lowest possible cost. The primary objectives of inventory management are:

- minimizing the maintenance of operating, maintenance, and risk costs;
- ensuring continuity of production and customer service rhythmicity at the lowest inventory costs;
- preventing the formation of excessive and unnecessary stocks and their optimal management in the event of their occurrence;
- counteracting quantitative and qualitative losses as well as normal consumption of stocks.

Examples of classic methods of inventory management, supported by automatic identification and IT systems, include:

- the 80/20 rule states that in a heterogeneous group, 20% of elements represent 80% of the cumulative value of the feature, which serves as a classification criterion (in logistic practice, the 80/20 rule became the basis for inventory analysis and the methodology of the widely used ABC analysis was created on its basis, which breaks down inventories by value);

- ABC analysis divides the supply goods into three groups according to their proper share in the value of material consumption;
- XYZ analysis examines the regularity of the demand for individual materials.

It cannot be managed well, which cannot be expressed in numbers, and therefore inventory management uses various indicators, such as (Encyklopedia zarządzania, 2022):

- quantitative inventory structure = quantity of a given type of stocks/stocks in the analyzed period;
- inventory structure = value of a given type of stocks/stock level in the analyzed period;
- inventory dynamics = stocks at the end of the analyzed period/stocks at the beginning of the analyzed period;
- turnover of material stocks = value of materials used during the year/average stock in the analyzed period;
- material inventory turnover (base) = value of materials used in the base period/average inventory in the base period;
- reserve intensity = average stocks over the analyzed period/net sales;
- increase in material stocks = increase in stocks/increase in production;
- cost of holding stocks = cost of holding stocks/average stocks over the analyzed period.

It should be remembered that the assessment with the use of measures will be objective when the surveys are:

- implemented with the use of the same: key values (measures), time divisions, types of stocks, markets, warehouse infrastructure;
- carried out systematically on the same (similar) representative group of customers, warehouse employees, and infrastructure components;
- implemented using an up-to-date historical database (data warehouses).

4.5 Infrastructure of Logistics Flows

Logistics processes require infrastructure that facilitates efficient and effective physical movement of products and services from the place of shipment to the destination (including temporary collection, issuance, rotation, completion, protection) and the accompanying information.

Although it has been used in Polish for many years, infrastructure has not yet had a generally accepted definition and thus is not clearly understood. The very term taken from the English language means "foundation of the base, i.e., the necessary foundation of the economy." Infrastructure can also be defined as physical objects, institutions, organizations, and structures that provide social and economic support for the functioning of society (economic systems in the micro and macro dimensions) (Vilko et al., 2011.

The place of infrastructure in the logistics system is presented in Figure 4.4. It consists of the following (Banomyong, 2008):

- human resources and their capabilities;
- logistics and transportation service providers from the public and private sectors;
- administration – government and local government institutions, their policy;
- infrastructure, including transportation and communication.

In the literature on the subject, there are many attempts to define the logistics infrastructure, but the most interesting one can be found in *the Glossary of Logistics Terminology*, which illustrates the essence of the matter. Here it is: *Logistics infrastructure is a system of land, waterways, airports, seaports and/or telecommunications networks located in a specific area (Słownik terminologii logistycznej, 2006).*

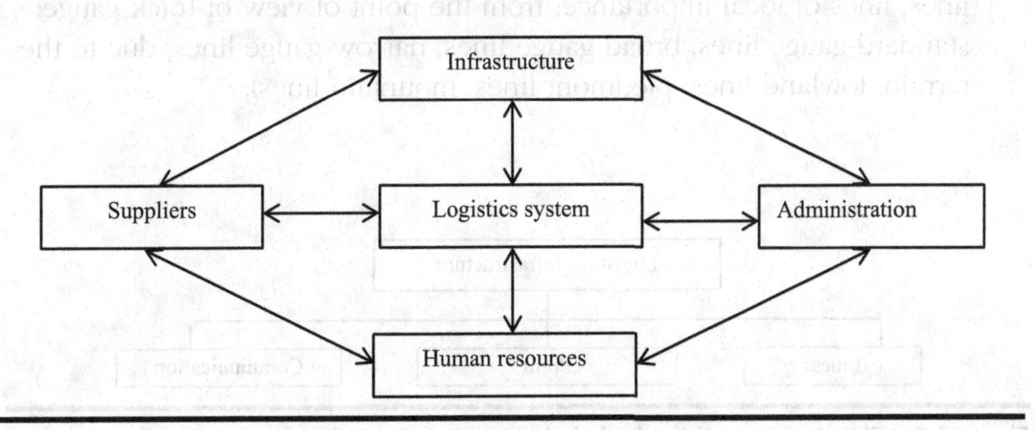

Figure 4.4 The place of infrastructure in the logistics system.

Source: Own study.

In the systemic approach to logistics, three components of the logistics infrastructure are distinguished:

- linear network, which is constituted by the network existing in the country, understood as each separated strip of land intended for the traffic or parking of means of transportation along with the engineering facilities within it;
- point, consisting of separate facilities for stationary cargo handling (generally accessible unloading stations, yards and reloading points, logistic centers) and means of transportation;
- communication infrastructure, which includes media, data exchange standards, and measures ensuring their flow. This is illustrated in Figure 4.5.

Linear and point infrastructure is a system, and therefore a classification can be proposed that considers both components (*Encyklopedia zarządzania*, 2022):

- car – point (it includes facilities for stationary passenger service, e.g., bus stations, parking lots, cargo, e.g., warehouses, logistics centers, and means of transportation in road transport), linear (it is the road network existing in the country, including national roads, voivodeship roads, poviat roads, local city roads, municipal roads, company roads);
- railroad – point (sidings, stations, reloading points), linear (all railroad lines that can be divided according to several criteria – from the socio-economic point of view: main lines, primary lines, secondary lines, lines of local importance; from the point of view of track gauge: standard-gauge lines, broad-gauge lines, narrow-gauge lines; due to the terrain: lowland lines, piedmont lines, mountain lines);

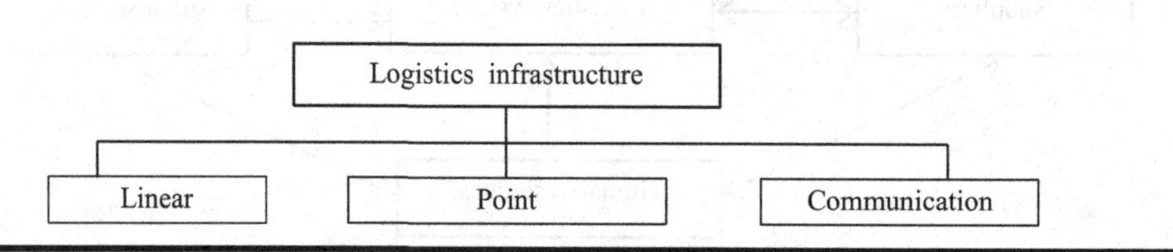

Figure 4.5 The structure of the logistic infrastructure.

Source: Own study.

- sea/inland waterway – point (port waters, port territory, port network of railroad and roads, port stations, networks, and nodes making up the so-called port installation networks), linear (water routes leading to and from the port, mainly water in the areas of port waters, in addition, river beds and water channels);
- air – point (airports, international airports, landing fields), lane (air lane).

The term telecommunications infrastructure should be understood as a set of all technical means to provide various services, such as intelligent networks,[7] mobile telephony, data transmission, access to the Internet, transmission of television signals, creation of virtual corporate networks, radio and wired access, voice calls, etc. (Vademecum teleinformatyka, 2002). The telecommunications infrastructure consists of cables and wires (copper and optical fibers), telecommunications cable lines (overhead and underground), cable ducts (underground and municipal sewage systems), radio lines (tropospheric, satellite), poles, towers, active and passive devices processing and transmitting (analog and digital) telecommunications signals.

In addition to the above-mentioned elements of the telecommunications infrastructure, there is a very wide range of other systems and devices used to ensure the continuity of telecommunications services at an appropriate quality level guaranteed by telecommunications companies. The so-called accompanying infrastructure can include, among others, uninterruptible power supply systems, precision air conditioning, ventilation, fire protection systems, access control systems, remote supervision systems, management and maintenance of telecommunications networks and devices (Rozporządzenie Ministra Infrastruktury z dnia 26 października 2005 r., 2005).

4.6 Waste Management

4.6.1 Waste in Numbers

The production of waste accompanies every human activity. Initially, people naturally sensed and made decisions about how to handle the waste. However, as time passed and the waste increased, this problem only grew. Examples include packaging and waste. In 2019, almost 225 million tons of municipal waste were generated in the EU. This represents 502 kg per person, a slight increase compared to 2018 (495 kg), although there has been a decrease compared to the 2008 peak (518 kg), according to Eurostat. Poland was at the bottom of the list, generating relatively the least amount of waste.

The highest volume of municipal waste per person among the EU Member States was generated in 2019 by Denmark – 844 kg. Other countries that produced more than 600 kg of municipal waste per capita are Luxembourg (791 kg), Malta (694 kg), Cyprus (642 kg), and Germany (609 kg). In contrast, Romania produced 280 kg of municipal waste per person in 2019. Three more EU Member States also generated less than 400 kg per person: Poland (336 kg), Estonia (369 kg), and Hungary (387 kg) (Pół tony odpadów komunalnych ..., 2022).

According to the data provided by Statistics Poland, waste is generally divided into municipal waste and waste other than municipal waste. In 2020, almost 123 million tons of waste was generated, of which 10.7% was municipal waste (13.1 million tons). The amount of generated waste (excluding municipal waste) since 2000 was between 110 and 130 million tons. In 2020, it decreased compared to the previous year (4%) and amounted to 109.5 million tons. The amount of waste generated each year remains at a similar level. In 2020, in the economic slowdown caused by the pandemic, the observed decline in GDP was accompanied by a decrease in the amount of waste generated in the country (Ochrona środowiska 2021 Environment).

Municipal waste is generated in households and in retail, business, office buildings and educational institutions, medical facilities, and public administration, similar in nature and composition to household waste. The amount of generated municipal waste depends, among other things, on:

- population and density per km;
- degree of industrialization;
- production sites (in the western voivodships, much more municipal waste was generated per capita than in the eastern voivodships);
- consumption patterns and the level of education of the society.

It is also worth noting that the amount of waste generated is not synonymous with the impact of a given society on the environment. An important issue is also how waste is processed and whether it is recycled. This is important because it may turn out that a society where 400 kg of waste is produced per person has a much more negative impact on the environment than citizens of a country with 800 kg of waste per person.

According to Eurostat data, the amount of waste recycled in 2019 reached a new record. Recycled and composted waste has almost tripled in recent years, from 37 million tons (87 kg per person) in 1995 to 107 million tons (239 kg per person) in 2019. Since 1995, the amount of municipal waste incinerated in the EU has doubled from 30 million tons (70 kg per person) to 60 million tons (134 kg per person) in 2019. Although slightly more waste is generated, the total amount of municipal waste disposed of in landfills in the EU has more than halved since 1995: from 121 million tons (286 kg per person) in 1995 to 54 million tons (120 kg per person) in 2019 (Ochrona środowiska 2021 Environment, 2021). When it comes to generating and managing waste, the following should be kept in mind (Szymonik & Stanisławski, 2021):

- processing a pile of waste paper, for example, a 1.25 m pile of newspapers, allows you to save a 6-meter pine tree;
- 1 ton of recycled paper saves 1,200 liters of water in the paper industry;
- 400 million aluminum cans are used annually in Poland, which can be recycled and reused an infinite number of times;
- 95% less energy is needed to produce a can from recycled aluminum than from aluminum extracted from bauxite ore;
- by processing PET bottles, we obtain granules for the production of fleece, backpacks, or toys;
- an aluminum can that we throw away takes up to 100 years to decompose, a plastic bag takes up to 450 years, and a plastic bottle takes up to 1,000 years.

The amount and type of waste are not the same everywhere in the world. It depends, among other things, on society's standard of living, education, renewable and non-renewable resources, technology of production, and consumption. According to a report by IQAir and Greenpeace, three countries from South Asia made the top five of the world's countries with the worst air. Bangladesh came first with a PM2.5 of 83.3, and Pakistan second (65.8). India is fifth (58.1). Poland, with a score of 18.7, was 53rd among 98 countries (Sprawdzili najbardziej zanieczyszczone państwa świata, 2022).

According to a 2019 ranking by the World Health Organization in cooperation with the International Energy Agency, New Zealand, Sweden, Brunei, Australia, Canada, Finland, the United States, Iceland, Estonia, and Spain are among the 135 countries with the least polluted air. Sweden has the best air in Europe. The United States ranks 7th and has one of the lowest death rates due to air pollutants. Poland was not in the top ten of any of the rankings, but we are one of the smog leaders among European countries. Poland's only place where the air is clean and completely free from pollution is located underground, more precisely in the "Wieliczka" Salt Mine (Gdzie najczystsze powietrze na świecie, 2021).

4.6.2 Characteristics of Selected Waste

Waste management problems are more and more often included in the competences of people employed in logistics companies. It should be noted that waste is not only something of inferior quality, which is a waste of human activity or economic systems, or of little or no further use. It must not be forgotten that something considered waste by some people can be a useful resource for others.

Waste retains specific features and is a commodity, as evidenced by, among other things, national waste exchanges. According to experts, the waste trading market may double in the coming years. Obtaining energy from the incineration of waste is becoming more and more common practice, for example, in Sweden and Denmark. In the Netherlands, the largest importer of waste in the European Union, waste has become an important source of energy and savings.

In developed EU countries, as well as in Switzerland and Norway, there are currently over 400 installations that recover energy from municipal waste. They currently burn 70 million tons/per year of municipal waste in the EU, provide electricity to around 13 million people, and provide heat for 12 million city dwellers (Blumenthal, 2011).

By the end of 2021, eight incineration plants operated in Poland, processing a total of approx. 1.1 million tons of municipal waste per year, producing electricity and heat. Thanks to the expansion and construction of new facilities, their processing capacity will reach approx. 2 million tons in the coming years. The number of waste incineration plants and combined heat and power plants are presented in Figures 4.6 and 4.7.

Waste management is *closely related to sustainability, which meets the basic needs of all people and preserves, protects, and restores the health and integrity of the Earth's ecosystem without endangering the ability to meet the needs of future generations and without exceeding the long-term limits of the Earth's ecosystem capacity* (Stappen, 2006). The primary factors for the functioning of the waste management system include the following (Stappen, 2006):

- quantity, nature, and spatial distribution of waste;
- degree of regularity and dynamics of waste generation;
- adopted rules for the implementation of environmental protection;
- spatial and urban factors: structure and shaping of the settlement network of the region, possibilities of locating system objects, communication routes, the spatial structure of economic activity, etc.;

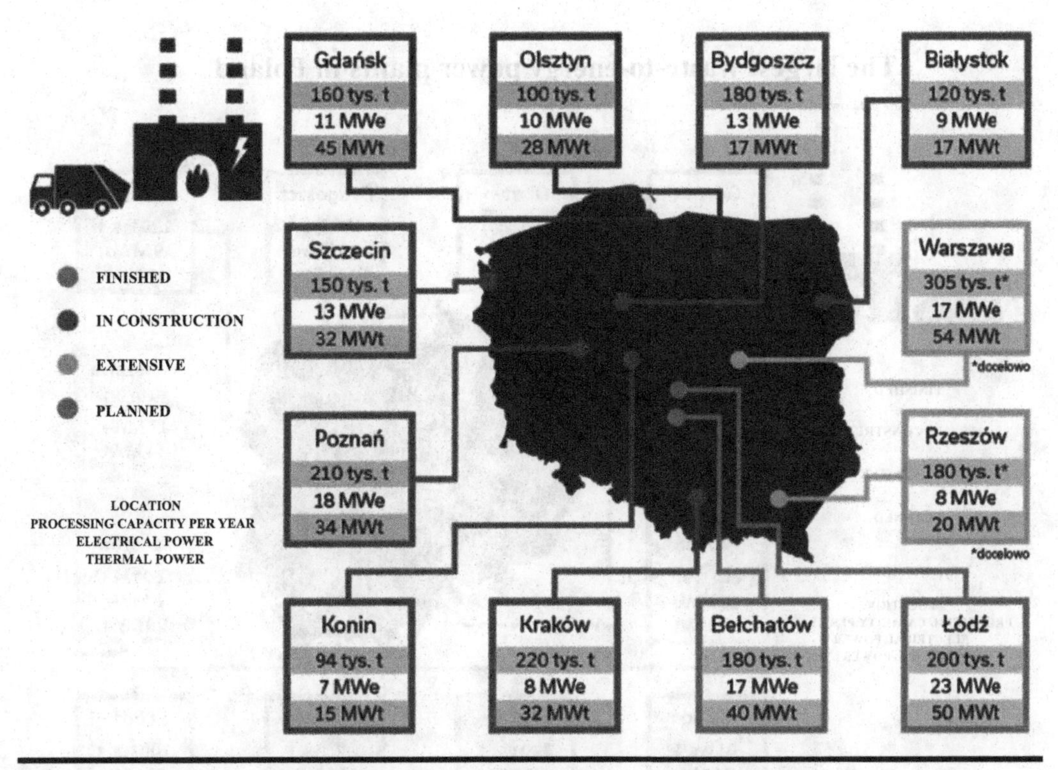

Figure 4.6 Incineration plants in Poland at the end of 2021.

Source: **Based on M. Skłodowska, T. Elżbieciak, *Śmieci zamiast węgla i gazu. Przybywa spalarni,* https://wysokienapiecie.pl, 2/18/2022.**

- general standards and local (regional) requirements for permissible loads on environmental elements.

On the other hand, the basic principles of waste management result from the assumptions of waste management defined in European law (Ustawa z dnia 14 grudnia 2012 r. o odpadach, 2012) (Kisperska-Moroń & Krzyżaniak, 2009):

- preventing the generation of waste or reducing its negative impact on the environment during production and after product use;
- providing recovery in accordance with the principles of environmental protection if waste generation cannot be prevented;
- ensuring that waste disposal complies with environmental protection principles if waste generation cannot be prevented or waste cannot be recovered.

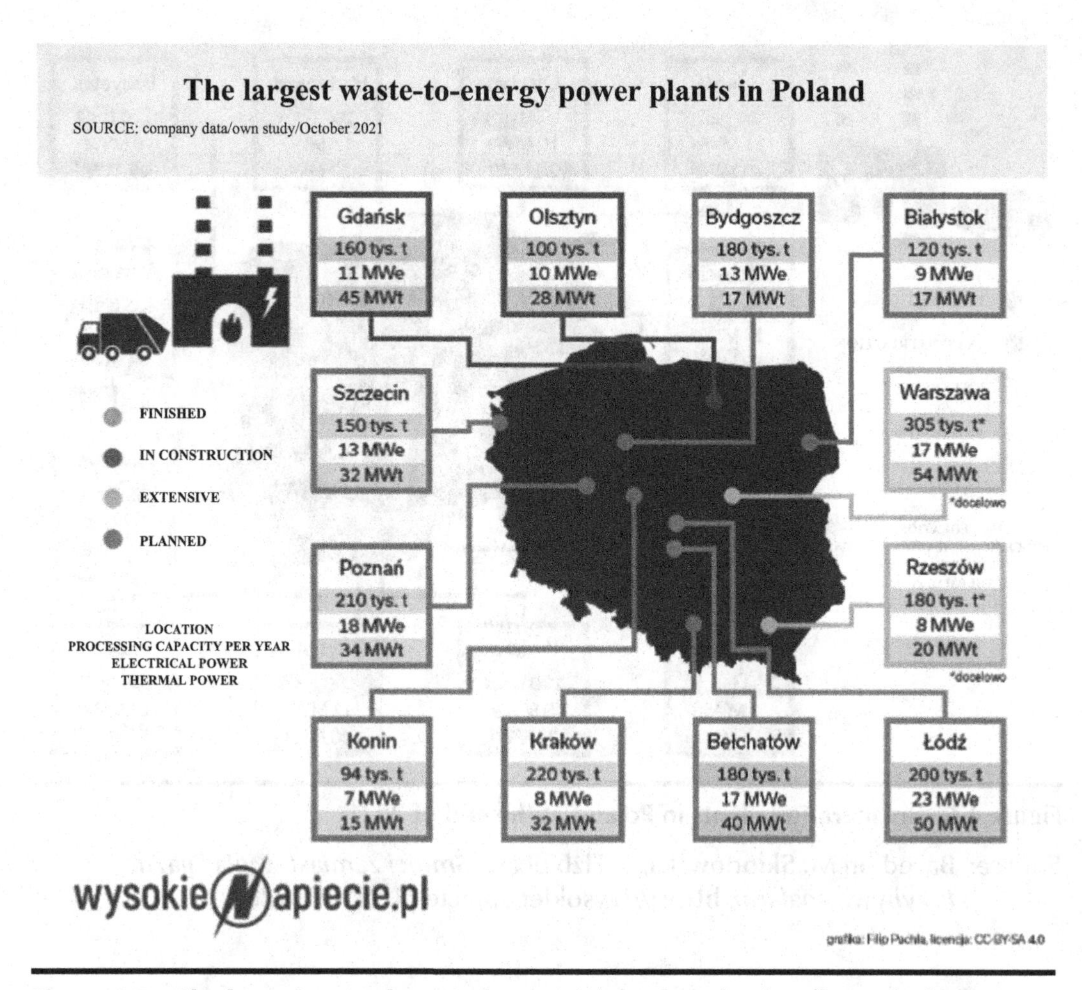

Figure 4.7 The largest waste heat and power plants in Poland at the end of 2021.

Source: **Based on M. Skłodowska, T. Elżbieciak, *Śmieci zamiast węgla i gazu. Przybywa spalarni,* https://wysokienapiecie.pl,18.02.2022.**

According to Polish law, waste can be divided into two groups. **The first is non-hazardous waste**, which includes municipal, medical, inert, biodegradable, veterinary, and green waste and waste from accidents and processes of recovery and disposal. **The second is hazardous waste**, including (Ustawa z dnia 14 grudnia 2012 r. o odpadach, 2012): the source of its formation, properties that make waste hazardous, as specified in Annex 4 to the Act of December 14, 2012, components of waste exceeding the limits of hazardous substances that may cause the waste to become hazardous.

A slightly different division of waste is presented in the National Waste Management Plan 2022, which distinguishes (Uchwała nr 88 Rady Ministrów z dnia 1 lipca 2016 r., 2016): municipal waste, including food waste and other biodegradable waste, waste arising from products such as waste oils, waste batteries and spent accumulators, WEEE (waste electrical and electronic equipment), end-of-life vehicles, worn tires, packaging, and packaging waste. Another group includes hazardous waste (medical and veterinary waste, waste containing PCBs (polychlorinated biphenyls), asbestos-containing waste, waste repositories). The last group is "other waste," which consists of waste from construction, renovation, and dismantling of buildings and infrastructure, road waste, MSS (municipal sewage sludge), biodegradable waste other than municipal waste, waste from selected economy sectors, the management of which causes problems, according to the "Waste Catalog" (Rozporządzenie ministra środowiska z dnia 27 września 2001 r., 2001) (01 – wastes resulting exploration, mining, dressing and further treatment of minerals and quarry; 06 – wastes from inorganic chemical processes; 10 – inorganic wastes from thermal processes) and waste in the marine environment.

Municipal waste is waste generated in households and in retail, business, office buildings and educational institutions, medical facilities, and public administration, similar in nature and composition to household waste.

The amount and morphological composition of municipal waste largely depend on the place where it is generated, including, first of all, the wealth of the society and the related level of consumption of products, as well as the season of the year. It should be mentioned that the amount of municipal waste collected yearly per capita is strongly correlated with the economic condition of individual regions of the country. The type and quantity of generated waste are also influenced by the type of area (city, village) where it is generated, population density, development type (single-family, multi-family buildings), number of tourists, public utility facilities, and the type, size, and number of commercial establishments and small industry or services (Uchwała nr 88 Rady Ministrów z dnia 1 lipca 2016 r., 2016), (Uchwała nr 67 Rady Ministrów z dnia 6 maja 2021 r., 2021). The amount of municipal waste in Poland, based on Statistics Poland data, is presented in Table 4.1.

Product waste is another group resulting from manufacturing and service activities. The group includes the following (Uchwała nr 67 Rady Ministrów z dnia 6 maja 2021 r., 2021):

- waste oils – all lubricating or industrial oils that are no longer suitable for the application for which they were originally intended, in particular, used oils from combustion engines and gear oils, as well as lubricating oils, turbine oils, and hydraulic oils (Ustawa o odpadach z dnia 27 kwietnia 2001 r.);

Table 4.1 Information on municipal waste in 2013–2020

Year/Quantity	*2013*	*2014*	*2017*	*2018*	*2020*
Waste converted to 1 inhabitant per year [kg]	246	268	311	325	342
Manufactured waste [million Mg]	11.30	10.30	12.0	12.5	13.1

Source: Based on *Ochrona środowiska 2014–2021 Environment 2014–2021*, Zakład Wydawnictw Statystycznych, Warszawa 2018–2021.

- worn tires – result from the use of vehicles and during the dismantling of end-of-life vehicles; they are:
  - subjected to a regeneration process by the so-called retreading,
  - used to produce rubber granules for manufacturing asphalt intended for the construction of safer roads,
  - used as an alternative fuel in the co-combustion process, for example, in cement plants, heat and power plants;
- waste batteries and accumulators and their management to:
  - limit the negative impact on the environment by reducing the number of hazardous substances,
  - collect and recycle waste generated from them (including by supporting a high level of collection of waste portable batteries and accumulators) – the number of introduced and collected waste batteries and accumulators in Poland as well as the required and achieved collection level (in a 2019 ranking of collected waste batteries and accumulators waste from batteries and accumulators was ranked 5th in the EU) (Ustawa z dnia 24 kwietnia 2009 r. o bateriach i akumulatorach) – Table 4.2;
- waste electrical and electronic equipment (Ochrona środowiska 2019 Environment 2019, 2019) – the weight of equipment placed on the market and weight of waste equipment collected in 2014–2018 are presented below (per capita, 8.6 kg of used equipment was collected, and this indicator is constantly growing, compared to the previous year it was more by 2.2 kg per capita, and in the last five years it has almost doubled – it amounted to 4.5 kg per capita in 2013 (Ochrona środowiska 2020 Environment 2020, 2020) – Table 4.3;

Table 4.2 The number of introduced and collected waste batteries, accumulators, and the required and achieved collection level

Year/Quantity of equipment	*2016*	*2017*	*2018*
Introduced batteries and accumulators (in thousand tons)	12.6	13.3	13.2
Collected waste batteries and accumulators (in thousand tons)	4.8	8.4	10.6
Required level of collection of waste batteries and accumulators (in %)	43	43	45
The achieved level of collection of waste batteries and accumulators (in %)	39	66	80

Source: Based on *Ochrona środowiska 2019–2021, Environment 2019–2021,* Zakład wydawnictw statystycznych, Warszawa 2019–2021.

Table 4.3 Information on the weight of equipment placed on the market and the weight of the collected waste equipment in 2014–2018 in Mg

Year/Quantity of equipment	*2014*	*2017*	*2018*
Equipment placed on the market	518,868	607,000	660,000
Total waste equipment collected	168,938	246,000	330,000
Waste equipment collected from households	159,756	227,000	302,000

Source: Based on Uchwała nr 88 Rady Ministrów z dnia 1 lipca 2016 r. w sprawie Krajowego planu gospodarki odpadami 2022, Warszawa, dnia 11 sierpnia 2016 r., *Ochrona środowiska 2019 Environment 2019,* Zakład Wydawnictw Statystycznych, Warszawa (2019), p. 155.

- packaging and packaging waste (Ustawa z dnia 13 czerwca 2013 r., 2013)
  - during production and management, in order to reduce the amount and harmfulness of materials and substances contained in packaging and packaging waste impacting the environment, it is necessary to:
  - define the requirements to be met by packaging on the market,
  - develop the rules of operation of the packaging recovery organization,

  - develop rules for dealing with packaging and packaging waste,
  - establish the rules for setting and collecting the product fee;
- end-of-life vehicles[8] – the activities are primarily aimed at their collection and disassembly, which include the following (Ustawa z dnia 20 stycznia 2005 r.):
  - removal of hazardous elements and substances, including liquids, from end-of-life vehicles,
  - dismantling of equipment and parts suitable for reuse from end-of-life vehicles,
  - dismantling of recoverable or recyclable components from end-of-life vehicles.

The number of deregistered and dismantled vehicles is shown in Table 4.4.

It should be noted that, in practice, there is a relatively high recovery and recycling of end-of-life vehicles; for example, in 2018, the recovery and recycling of end-of-life vehicles reached 95.3% and 93.4%, respectively (with the recovery and recycling rates required by the European Commission of 95% and 85%, respectively). These rates are slightly lower than in 2017, when they were 98.6% and 95.6%, respectively.

Hazardous waste is another group that shows at least one hazardous property and may arise at the stage of production and use of chemicals and other products containing hazardous substances, as well as a result of work carried out by medical facilities and veterinary clinics (infectious medical waste and infectious veterinary waste), carrying out repairs (asbestos-containing waste), or as a result of withdrawal from use devices containing polychlorinated biphenyls (Ustawa z dnia 14 grudnia 2012 r. o odpadach). Hazardous waste includes the following:

Table 4.4 The number of deregistered and dismantled vehicles

Year/Number of vehicles	*2014*	*2016*	*2017*	*2018*
Deregistered	490,000	444,000	475,000	595,600
Due to dismantling	450,000	339,000	425,000	538,500
Due to exportation	10,000	31,000	44,000	18,000

Source: Based on Uchwała nr 88 Rady Ministrów z dnia 1 lipca 2016 r. w sprawie Krajowego planu gospodarki odpadami 2022, Warszawa, dnia 11 sierpnia 2016 r., *Ochrona środowiska 2019–2020, Environment 2019–2020,* Zakład Wydawnictw Statystycznych, Warszawa 2019–2020.

- medical and veterinary waste (Ustawa o odpadach medycznych z dnia 27 kwietnia 2001 roku, 2001)[9] – solid, liquid, and gaseous substances generated during treatment, diagnosis, and prevention in medical activities carried out in inpatient and outpatient treatment facilities as well as in research and experimental facilities;
- waste containing polychlorinated biphenyls – the ban on marketing these substances means that in the future, waste containing these substances will not be produced (these were additives to oils in transformers, capacitors, and switches, as well as ingredients for paints, varnishes, and plasticizers, as well as preservatives and impregnating agents);
- asbestos-containing waste – the "Program for Asbestos Abatement in Poland 2009–2032" assumed the elimination of asbestos-containing products from use by 2032 (a consequence of this is the expected increase in the amount of waste generated, which will be neutralized in special landfills or stored in properly prepared landfills) (Uchwała Nr 39/2010 Rady Ministrów z dnia 15 marca 2010 r., 2010);
- 3 out of 242 waste repositories,[10] according to the current state (July 2018), remain to be liquidated (Szekalska, 2022).

Other waste – the last group, which includes the following:

- waste from the construction, renovation, and disassembly of buildings and road infrastructure, produced in residential and industrial development as well as in railroad and road development, both at the stage of construction, extension, modernization, and demolition works (this waste is subject to, among others, recovery beyond installation, and used in the construction of new road and rail infrastructure) (Rozporządzeniem Ministra Środowiska z dnia 11 maja 2015 r., 2015);
- municipal sewage sludge is subject to a specific further procedure, which includes the following (Rozporządzenie Ministra Środowiska z dnia 6 lutego 2015 r., 2015):
  - preventing the formation, for example, by subjecting the sludge to such treatment processes as disintegration, deep stabilization, hygienization, and dehydration, or end-of-waste activities transforming waste, for example, into organic fertilizers,
  - recycling (e.g., obtaining material after the composting process used for fertilization):

- use of a recovery method, including energy recovery – for example, for sludge as biomass, this means incineration or recovery outside installations,
- neutralization, where the sludge in this process can be thermally transformed in incineration plants or waste co-incineration plants without energy recovery or stored after processing if it meets the legal requirements;

- non-municipal biodegradable waste includes the following groups (Rozporządzenie Ministra Środowiska z dnia 9 grudnia 2014 r., 2014):
  - 02, that is, wastes from agricultural, horticultural, hunting, fishing, and aquacultural primary production, food preparation and processing,
  - 03, that is, wastes from wood processing and the production of paper, cardboard, pulp, panels, and furniture,
  - 19, that is, wastes from waste treatment facilities, off-site wastewater treatment plants, and the water industry;
  - wastes from selected branches of the economy, the management of which causes problems, are mainly those that we include in the following groups:
  - 01, that is, wastes resulting from exploration, mining, dressing, and further treatment of minerals and quarry,
  - 06, that is, wastes from inorganic chemical processes,
  - 10, that is, inorganic wastes from thermal processes;
- the marine environment wastes have the following sources:
  - pollution carried along with the current of rivers reaching the sea,
  - wastes from ships (fishing boats, wrecks) in the Baltic Sea.

When analyzing legal acts and literature on waste management, it can be concluded that this problem is of interest to government and local government institutions and every human being. Its goals include the following:

- effective waste management aimed at prevention, preparation for re-use, recycling, as well as other methods of recovery and disposal;
- striving to improve energy recovery from non-recyclable materials;
- increasing efforts to combat pollution, including sea and air pollution;
- systematic phasing out of landfilling of recyclable or recoverable waste;
- introduction of new environmentally friendly technologies of waste management;
- educating society on the "culture of ecology."

4.6.3 Logistics Processes in Waste Management and Their Optimization

In the literature on the subject, it is difficult to find an unambiguous definition of a *process*, let alone the logistics process – waste. The logistic process in waste management should be understood as the successive facts (past and future phenomena) in the physical flow of waste and information, as well as the risks that accompany each activity at a given time and place. These facts may concern:

- performance of the management function in waste-related logistics activities;
- material incidents (e.g., collection of waste, transportation, storage, processing, etc.);
- intangible events (analysis of logistics costs, etc.);
- information related to the physical shipment of waste from origin to destination;
- the risk (disruptions) associated with logistica processes related to waste management.

In waste logistics, three types of processes can be distinguished (Bozarth & Handfield, 2007):

- primary processes, which cover the most important activities carried out by the organization with high added value (these include activities such as the provision of transportation and storage services, processing, etc.), for a result that the customer is willing to pay;
- support processes include activities that are needed but offer no added value (e.g., packaging, labeling);
- development processes increase the efficiency of primary and support processes (these include employee training, waste market research, designing new disposal, recycling, etc.).

The basic components of logistic processes in waste management include collecting, transportation, storing (warehousing), processing (recovery, neutralization, incineration), and costs of logistics processes.

Waste collection – or selective collection – is to be a planned, organized, and controlled process as part of environmental protection. Selective collection means collection in which a given waste stream covers only waste with the same properties and of the same type to facilitate a specific treatment method. In the case of selectively collected municipal waste, it is forbidden to mix it with mixed municipal waste collected from property owners. The type and quantity of waste are presented in Table 4.5.

In 2020, 144 kg of waste per capita was collected selectively in cities and 108 kg per capita in rural areas. The amount of selectively collected waste varies greatly in individual poviats and communes and depends to a large extent on how the local authorities have organized the waste collecting system. In 2020, eleven municipalities obtained over 90% of the level of selective collection for all collected waste, while in two municipalities, less than 3% of waste was collected selectively (Ochrona środowiska 2021 Environment 2021). Selective collection applies to the following (Dziennik Ustaw Rzeczypospolitej Polskiej Warszawa, z dnia 7 października 2019 r., 2019):

- paper that accumulates in blue containers marked with the word "Paper," this applies to cardboard, packaging waste made of paper and cardboard, paper;
- glass collected in color containers:
  - green, marked with the word "Glass," this applies to glass mixed in terms of color,
  - white, marked with the words "Clear glass," this applies to clear glass,
  - green, marked with the word "Colored glass," this applies to colored glass;

Table 4.5 Amount of waste collected or collected selectively in Poland in 2017 and 2018 per capita in kg

Year/Amount	*2017*	*2018*	*2020*
Biodegradable waste	23	26	31
Mixed packaging waste	14	15	14
Bulky waste	11	14	19
Glass	12	13	19
Plastics	8	9	13
Paper and cardboard	6	7	13

Source: Based on *Ochrona środowiska 2019 Environment 2019*, Zakład Wydawnictw Statystycznych, Warszawa (2019), p. 158, *Ochrona środowiska 2021 Environment 20201* Zakład Wydawnictw Statystycznych, Warszawa (2021), p. 160.

- metals and plastics include metal waste, including metal packaging waste, plastic waste, including plastic packaging waste, and multi-material packaging waste, collected in yellow containers marked with the words "Metals and plastics;"
- biodegradable waste, with particular emphasis on bio-waste, is collected in brown containers marked with the word "Bio."

An obligatory element in creating a waste collection system is the creation of points facilitating access, with particular emphasis on waste electrical and electronic equipment from households.

Selective collection is a process that requires segregation and self-discipline. As practice shows, not everyone does it because it involves some effort. The following steps need to be taken before putting waste into the correct container:

- glass bottles and jars require emptying and removing the caps;
- plastic bottles for cosmetics and household chemicals and PET bottles require emptying and crushing;
- juice and milk cartons require crushing (it is not necessary to remove caps or lids);
- cardboard boxes should be flattened and folded (large ones are best tied with a string);
- aluminum cans should be emptied and crushed (no need to tear off paper labels);
- hazardous waste (paints, varnishes, used oils, tires, batteries, fluorescent lamps, electronics, and household appliances) should be taken to a PSZOK (point of selective collection of municipal waste);
- packaging with hard covers coated with plastic or leather-like material requires the removal of the outer coating;
- medicines and medicine packaging should be returned to pharmacies or medical clinics.

Waste transportation is one of the elements of waste management. It is carried out in accordance with the requirements of environmental protection and human safety, in particular considering the chemical and physical waste properties, including its physical state and potential hazard. The waste is transported together with a document confirming the waste type and transportation order. In the case of collecting municipal waste from property owners, the name of the commune of waste collection and a document confirming the waste type are required. The required documents include (Rozporządzenie Ministra Środowiska z dnia 7 października 2016 r., 2016): waste transfer card, waste sales invoice, basic waste characteristics, a document on the transboundary waste shipment, other documents confirming the type of transported waste and data of the party ordering waste transportation if the transported waste does not have the above-mentioned documents available.

Means of waste transportation are marked with the following plate:

- a white plate, 400 mm wide and 300 mm high;
- the word "WASTE" in black capital letters, at least 100 mm high with a line width of at least 15 mm on the plate.

If there is no space to place a plate with the recommended dimensions due to the size or design of the means of transportation, the plate size can be reduced as follows:

- dimensions to at least 300 mm in width and 120 mm in height;
- the height of the inscription "WASTE" to at least 80 mm and the line width to at least 12 mm.

In the case of means of transportation intended for the transboundary transportation of waste, instead of the indicated marking, the following plate can be used (Rozporządzenie Ministra Środowiska z dnia 7 października 2016 r., 2016):

- a white plate, 400 mm wide and 300 mm high;
- a black capital letter "A" at least 200 mm high and a line width of at least 20 mm on the plate.

The marking should be placed in a visible spot on the front of the means of transportation on its external surface, bearing in mind that the lettering is legible, durable, and resistant to weather conditions. The transportation of hazardous waste also complies with relevant regulations (Ustawa z dnia 14 grudnia 2012 r. o odpadach, 2012).

The following are used for transporting waste (Korzeń, 2001): grabbing, loading, dozing and raking, gravitational discharge and runoff on chutes (ramps), and mechanical dosing. The means of transportation used in waste management depend primarily on the type of containers used in the waste collection system and waste treatment, for example, initial segregation at the same time and on the same vehicle, crushing, or carriage. It is also important whether there are various intermediate points in the waste transportation system – for example, transfer stations. The transportation of waste uses, among others:

- garbage trucks, the characteristic element of which are loading devices that enable putting waste into the loading box (16 m3 two-axle, 21 m3 three-axle, and 10 m3 mini-garbage trucks) directly from adapted containers;
- hook lift trucks, the so-called hook lifts – special vehicles equipped with hydraulically controlled superstructures, enabling the stacking and transportation of containers, platforms, tanks, etc. (the vehicles used are additionally equipped with hydraulic lifting devices used to operate the systems of publicly available selective collection of waste);
- tractor units with semi-trailers are a road set adapted to transport large loads over long distances (these vehicles transport containers, segregated waste, and alternative fuels);
- vans are mainly used to transport containers to and from customers and to collect segregated waste from educational institutions for cleanup at generally accessible containers when the residents clutter up these places.

Devices facilitating transportation include:

- containers are the most important element of the waste transportation chain, which allows the use of the same vehicles to transport various types of cargo (containers are mainly used to transport segregated waste from generally accessible containers, for the transport of mixed municipal waste, sewage sludge, construction waste, vehicle maintenance and waste industrial and hazardous materials such as asbestos roof tiles);
- side-loading containers are used for self-loading without the need to use truck-mounted cranes (e.g., for the selective collection of packaging glass or debris);
- press containers are containers with a specific structure and purpose, which use a type of hydraulic press that ensures the crushing of the waste collected, for example, paper or cardboard boxes.

Landfilling is the most common method of neutralizing municipal, industrial, and hazardous waste. It is a method of final disposal but should not be used for the disposal of untreated waste. The method of storage and the technologies used should also minimize the impact of the stored waste on all elements of the natural environment and meet all safety requirements. Waste is neutralized in: landfills (construction facilities intended for the storage of waste), bunkers (specialized tank structures) (Ustawa z dnia 9 czerwca 2011 r., 2011),[11] underground landfills and mining waste treatment *facilities* (*Ustawa z dnia 10 lipca 2008 r., 2008*).[12] The following types of landfills can be distinguished: hazardous, neutral, and other than hazardous and neutral landfills.

In terms of spatial form, the following landfills are distinguished (Korzeń, 2001):

- in a basin or in a ravine, using the existing depressions of the terrain;
- in a canopy created during earthworks;
- on surface areas, where waste is collected on the ground;
- slope landfills, one of the walls/slopes of the landfill forms a natural slope.

When storing waste, the following rules should be followed (Ustawa z dnia 14 grudnia 2012 r. o odpadach, 2012):

- it is forbidden to store waste in a landfill;
- before being placed in a landfill, waste shall be subject to a physical, chemical, thermal, or biological treatment process, including segregation, to reduce the risk to human life and health or the environment, and to reduce its quantity, volume, and facilitate its handling or recovery;
- only passive waste (municipal, non-hazardous waste) may be collected on an inert landfill;
- at a hazardous waste landfill, no other than hazardous waste may be stored;
- the information contained in the prepared characteristics of waste shall include:
  - name and surname or name of the entity and the address of residence or registered office,
  - type of waste,
  - concise description of the waste generation process, considering the basic raw materials used and products manufactured,
  - a statement about the absence of waste covered by the storage ban,

- description of the waste treatment process used, waste sorting method,
- a description of the waste specifying its color, physical form, and smell,
- an indication of the type of landfill on which it can be stored after conducting tests,
- declaration of no possibility of recovery, including recycling of waste,
- specification of the frequency of compliance tests.

To mechanize waste storage, specialized equipment is used, which includes:

- front loader – a machine used for loading and transporting materials over short distances with the use of a loading bucket (in practice, it is used for reloading and work in municipal waste landfills);
- telescopic loader – a piece of equipment that uses a retractable working arm for assembly, making it possible to feed the load at greater heights than traditional bucket loaders (it is mainly used in the production of alternative fuels and in waste sorting plants);
- compactor is used to reduce the volume of waste by compacting it with weight and wheels equipped with a series of metal spikes;
- rotary sieve – a machine for the mechanical separation of mixed materials of different granulation, for example, earth, ash, and small organic waste (the required size of granules of the separated material is obtained using sieves of different sizes);
- sludge mixer (also called a crusher-mixer), used to mix and crush compost components such as sewage sludge, organic municipal waste, branches, green waste, and sawdust (the main element of the mixers are rotating shafts equipped with sets of cutting blades);
- mobile waste shredder, the main task of which is to reduce the granulation and volume of waste such as: tires, furniture, window frames, branches, boards, wooden pallets, etc.
- stationary waste shredder – a machine whose primary task is to reduce the granulation and volume of waste;
- compost turner – used for dynamic shifting of humus heaps to aerate, crush, and mix the mass in the pile;
- sorting line, the main task of which is to reduce the amount of landfilled waste by segregating as many recyclable fractions as possible, such as plastic, glass, waste paper, steel scrap, and non-ferrous metals;

- hydraulic press – its main task is to reduce the volume and form bales of recovered raw materials, such as PET plastic packaging, foil, and waste paper (formed bales of raw materials have a standardized size that allows them to be conveniently transported to processors on euro pallets).

Waste treatment is recovery or disposal processes, including preparation for recovery or disposal (Ustawa z dnia 14 grudnia 2012 r. o odpadach, 2012). Preparing for reuse through recovery, inspection, cleaning, or repair, in which products or parts of products that have previously become waste are prepared for reuse without any other pre-treatment. Recovery is primarily recycling, where waste is reprocessed into products, materials, or substances used for its original purpose or other purposes. Recycling does not include energy recovery and reprocessing into materials that are to be used as fuels or for backfilling. Waste recovery includes, among other things(Ustawa z dnia 14 grudnia 2012 r. o odpadach, 2012):

- use as a fuel or other means of energy generation;
- recovery/regeneration of solvents;
- recycling or recovery of organic substances that are not used as solvents (including composting and other biological transformation processes);
- recycling or recovery of metals and metal compounds;
- recycling or recovery of other inorganic materials;
- regeneration of acids or bases;
- recovery of components used for pollutant reduction;
- recovery of components from catalysts;
- re-refining (purification) or other reuse of oils;
- surface treatment with agricultural or environmental benefits.

In practice, waste processing is supported by specialized machines, which include (Szymonik, 2018):

- Presses (automatic, or manual) that effectively solve the problem of packaging solid waste and materials intended for recovery plants, including paper, corrugated cardboard, nylon, plastic, packaging for liquids, PET bottles, municipal solid waste, and industrial waste. The devices come in various configurations, for example, the PC 100L series press, with a volumetric capacity of 530 m^3/h (weight 20–22 tons/h).
- Rotary screens that make it possible to screen various types of municipal waste and recyclable materials and direct them for further

processing. They come in various sizes (VT 1.800 × 7.000 mm, VT 2.000 × 8.000 mm, VT 2.500 × 9.000 mm, or VT 2.500 × 12.000 mm). It is designed from special types of steel, making the machine durable and reliable. A rotary sieve is presented as an example.

- Shredders are useful machines for reducing the volume of bulky waste (e.g., reams of paper, stationery, bumpers, tires, refrigerators) and mulching. They are also used for crushing materials such as scrap metal, iron, aluminum, copper, plastics, and municipal and industrial waste. The machine is especially useful for recycling raw materials, materials, and energy. The devices come in various sets and configurations, for example, TR 100 100L shredders (grinding chamber size 1110 × 1500 mm, plastic processing capacity 7–10 tons/h, tires 4–7 tons/h, industrial waste 4–8 tons/h).
- Wrappers are special devices that enable the automatic wrapping of baled waste in foil. The use of these devices is intended for packing materials of small size and lightweight for ease of transport and to protect the waste against dispersion and weather conditions. Wrapping the waste makes it easier to store it in open spaces and protects against unpleasant odors and negative effects from birds and rats. These machines pack 20–50 bales per hour, depending on the size of the packed waste.
- Belt conveyors are used for transporting loose and solid materials. The following types of conveyors are used belt conveyors with a rubber belt on rollers, channel conveyors, inclined conveyors, inclined-rising conveyors, chain conveyors, vibrating conveyors, push-pull conveyors, spiral conveyors, and devices for loading containers and silos.
- Waste selection installations are devices that carry out transport, sort secondary raw materials such as paper, industrial waste, segregated municipal waste, etc., as well as recycle selected categories of waste. This type of industrial equipment includes:
  - Tire processing plants that mechanically granulate tires with automatic separation of steel and textiles ensuring full recovery of rubber without harmful environmental impact;
  - Machines for mechanical grinding of refrigerators with the recovery of plastic parts, iron, aluminum, copper, polyurethane, and gas from cooling systems, making it possible to recover about 85% of the materials (for recycling refrigerators);
  - Installations for recycling waste electrical and electronic equipment from groups R2, R3, and R4 (Annex 1 to Ustawa z dnia 14 grudnia 2012 r. o odpadach);

  - Installations for the treatment of non-recyclable waste (energy generation, biofuel) that allow the refining (Słownik wyrazów obcych, 2022)[13] of dry waste that cannot be treated and recycled to obtain a homogeneous metal-free final product.
- Tearing machines – innovative machines that enable the tearing and emptying of bags with waste of various sizes, without disturbing their content. These devices come in various sets and configurations, for example, the ARP 200 series ripper (bursting chamber size of 1650 × 1780 mm, and a processing capacity of 30–37 tons/h for municipal waste bags).

4.6.4 Waste Storage Management

Efficiency in warehouse management is the key to success as it means "doing things the right way" (i.e., minimizing the use of resources to achieve goals) and "doing the right things" (i.e., being able to set the right goals) (*Stoner* et al., 2001). This approach to mapping and measuring the efficiency of processes favors the improvement and productivity, as well as the efficiency of such activities in the warehouse as receiving, storing, issuing, documenting, and informing.

In practice, there are many concepts, tools, and techniques that make it possible to increase the efficiency of warehouse processes. Here is one of them.

5S – the name comes from five Japanese words starting with "s" (i.e., seri, seiton, seiso, seiketsu, shitsuke) and refers to systematic cleaning, maintaining a clean, efficient work environment, as well as compliance with the standards and discipline needed to manage an organization. The 5S system involves five stages leading to transparency and neatness of the places where production and service systems operate, which include, among others, the warehouse.

Stage one – sorting. In the case of warehouse management, it is nothing more than the physical separation of needed items from unnecessary ones during the implementation of business processes. What is necessary in stock is either sold or donated for free (which for some is waste, while for others is valuable and useful), handed over to the supplier, segregated and reused or treated as waste, or recycled.

On the other hand, items that can be useful in practice should be marked with a "red label" and stored in an appropriate place (e.g., on a shelf with a low level of consumption value, and low forecast accuracy) (Encyklopedia zarządzania, 2022). However, it should be remembered that this place should be constantly segregated so that the goods stored in such a way do not become useless and redundant. It should not be forgotten that unnecessary products and packaging generate inventory, which in turn leads to waste and unnecessary costs. Proper selection in the warehouse favors (Jędrzejak et al., 2014):

- eliminating unnecessary supplies, packaging, labels, samples, advertising materials, and waste;
- providing free space that can be managed, for example, in accordance with commercial warehouse indexes or for communication routes;
- eliminating used or damaged tools (packaging) that may have a negative impact on the quality of warehouse processes and work safety;
- increasing space and providing the worker with freedom of movement.

Stage two – setting in order. The classification and naming of devices for storage, transport, and auxiliary works carried out in the warehouse facilitates the identification of everything that improves logistics processes. Qualifying (classifying) places for all necessary infrastructure devices in the warehouse makes it possible to:

- locate storage facilities and equipment;
- put the device back in a suitable, previously prepared place, after its use;
- visualize the necessary storage facilities;
- control the current location and condition of storage devices;
- manage waste rationally.

When grouping devices, one should consider such parameters as distance (ensuring that everything is "at hand"), dimensions (small items should be as close as possible), frequency of use (the more often the devices are used, the closer they should be), maximum and minimum states (nothing should be missing and nothing should be left behind), the reliability and importance of the tools used (basic processes should be run without failure of the technique used).

Stage three – cleaning. Only the permanent elimination of all kinds of contamination, waste, pollution, dust, and rubbish makes the work environment friendly, not only for employees but also for future customers.

Activities using techniques applied in the warehouse occupy a special place in cleaning. They include, among others, cleaning, washing, and anti-corrosion protection. Regular care for the workplace and equipment (tools, cabinets, shelves) also helps to identify defects (damage). Unusual smells and unusual noises are often signs that something wrong is happening with technology, people, or warehouse processes. Proper cleaning in the warehouse is conducive to (Jędrzejak et al., 2014):

- reducing the failure rate of infrastructure;
- positive attitude of the employee;
- the employee's sense of responsibility for warehouse management,
- full preparation of tools for use.

Stage four – standardization (normalization). The main purpose of these activities in the case of warehouse management is (Ustawa z dnia 12 września 2002 r., 2012):

- rationalizing (modernizing) warehouse processes through the use of recognized technical rules (e.g., forklifts, including truck capacity, mast type, maximum lifting height, mast height, and travel speed) or organizational solutions (e.g., containers labeled with their external and internal length, external and internal width, internal and external height, maximum weight in tons, and internal volume in m^3);
- removing technical barriers to trade (e.g., through the use of GS1 auto-identification solutions) and preventing them (e.g., by shifting from national to international solutions);
- ensuring the protection of life, health, the environment, and the interests of consumers as well as work safety (e.g., drawing lines that facilitate the functional and spatial layout of the warehouse, the flow patterns in the warehouse, warehouse processes, technical specification of devices);
- improving the functionality, compatibility, and interchangeability of products, processes, and services and regulating their diversity;
- facilitating communication by providing terms, definitions, markings, and symbols for common use (e.g., warehouse system, IT pick-by-voice).

Standardization of stock:

- facilitates the identification of devices, places, and warehouse processes;
- facilitates the implementation of clear and comprehensible procedures in various situations (e.g., in the event of fire, theft, flood, or electricity failure);

- makes it possible to reduce costs;
- enables mass complementation;
- enables the cooperation of devices from different manufacturers during the implementation of logistic processes;
- enables the replacement of worn-out parts, making it easier to place commercial orders.

Stage five – self-discipline, in other words, self-imposed discipline (Słownik języka Polskiego, 2022). The first steps in the 5S method, even if efficiently implemented, will not bring the intended results when the human factor fails. An employee's approach to work, commitment, applied humanistic methods, and well-designed tasks are the paths to success. Self-discipline in the warehouse includes the search for solutions that eliminate mismanagement and strengthen self-discipline. Typical actions to identify waste that should be eliminated are (*8 typów marnotrawstwa*, 2022):

- waiting (unproductive time) – when employees are waiting for the next set of tasks to be completed or the completion of the order process (e.g., no order, no redundant goods, no means of transport);
- excessive processing – repeating activities/returning to activities that were already performed at previous work stages (e.g., rewriting orders, performing all or part of a particular picking task, improving previously performed work in collecting inventory, waste, packaging);
- excessive transport – inadequate internal transport, which includes: cranes, transport carts, conveyors, loaders, manipulators and industrial robots, palletizers, or depalletizers;
- excessive storage of, for example, additional stocks, packaging, unused racks, and products with non-commercial indexes, and, as a consequence, capital freezing;
- excessive traffic – the process can be observed during (Michalik, R. Budzik, 2011): unloading of means of transport, transfers to the reception area, quantitative and qualitative acceptance, dismantling of loading and transport units, sorting, repacking, formation of loading and storage units prepared for picking, moving to a storage area, storage, picking in the storage area or moving to the picking area, temporary storage in the area of picking and picking loads for release, relocating completed loading units to the release area, quantitative and qualitative acceptance, loading onto an external means of transport;

- errors and defects in the course of physical and information warehouse processes (whether caused through fault or not);
- unused human potential – including low creativity, low competencies, low discipline, lack of ideas, and lack of information boards presenting improvement activities and visualizing the results.

4.7 Logistic Customer Service

Logistic customer service (LCS) is an important element for rational and effective operations for all links along the supply chain. There is no single universally accepted definition of customer in logistics, just as there is no single definition of logistics. In the literature on the subject, LCS is defined, among others, as:

- a system of solutions providing the customer with a satisfactory relationship between the time of placing the order and the time of receiving the ordered product, intended to maintain this relationship and positive cooperation with the customer for the longest possible time (*Logistyczna obsługa klienta – definicja, elementy, strategii*, 2022);
- activities involving all interactions, both in the real world and on the Internet, between the current or potential customer and the company (processes cover the entire consumer experience – from the first contact to selling and maintaining further relationships) (Pruziński, 2022);
- a set of activities carried out from the moment the order is placed until the goods are delivered, the purpose of which is to meet customer requirements in the long term (Słownik logistyczny, 2022);
- support that is offered to customers – both before and after the purchase and use of products or services in order to establish and maintain positive relations and cooperation with the customer for the longest possible time (What is Customer Service?, Definition & Tips, 2022);
- the help and guidance the company provides to people before, during, and after the purchase of a product or service (*What is customer service: Definition, types, benefits, stats*, 2022).

An analysis of the presented definitions and terms leads to the conclusion that LCS:

- covers the acceptance, preparation, execution, and financial handling of customer orders as well as explaining any irregularities that may arise;
- ensures certainty and reliability of delivery of materials to the customer in line with the customer's expectations;
- includes comprehensive activities (order handling, loading, transport, invoicing, product control, and warranty services) involving all logistic processes along the supply chain aimed at the delivery of goods and information in accordance with the 7R principle[14];
- applies to the order – all activities performed in connection with the customer's order, from the moment the inquiry is received until the finished product is shipped
- concerns e-service – it aims to efficiently and effectively integrate the processes, tasks, and functions performed within the company, which begin at the time of placing the order by the customer and last until the delivery of the ordered goods or service.
- concerns e-logistics – it includes the use of IT technologies to improve the implementation of logistics processes along the entire supply chain and concerns, for example, order handling, warehouse management (safety stock management), as well as contacts with customers and customer service.

Customer support has come a long way since a phone call or a visit to the store were the only ways to reach a particular brand. Currently, a wide range of tools for communication with clients, such as C2C, B2B, and B2C, is widely used. These include, among others (What is customer service: Definition, types, benefits, stats, 2022):

- Social Media – responding to questions, requests, and complaints on social media channels such as Twitter, Facebook, and Instagram. Social media allows customers to instantly contact the brand at any time.
- Chatbots – these online tools allow customers to get very quick answers to frequently asked questions or refer them to a customer service representative for help. They use artificial intelligence to automate calls, providing a cost-effective 24/7 service.
- SMS/Mobile –people love to text, especially the younger generations, so SMS service has become commonplace. Brands send text messages with order, shipment and delivery confirmations, and can also answer questions through this channel.

- Telephone calls – the use of IVR (interactive voice response in which artificial intelligence helps to answer frequently asked questions and direct customers to the appropriate representative).
- E-mail Support – responding to customers by e-mail has its downsides (is more time-consuming) but gives customers the ability to clearly explain what they need.
- In-person (traditional, in-store) customer support – this type of service can make it easier for customers to learn about a product or service and make it easier for service representatives to establish customer relationships.

It should be remembered that LCS is a system that includes three elements: a specific activity (customer service as an activity), the level of customer service offered (customer service as a performance level), and a management concept (customer service as a management concept). For proper and effective operation, this system requires the development and implementation of, among others, appropriate metrics that will be used in pre-transactional, transactional, and post-transactional activities. Such an approach allows us to meet the customer's needs in the area of service quality, customer satisfaction, and customer loyalty. Various constructs of indicators assessing LCS can be found in the literature. In practice, the criteria that are most often considered are availability (e.g., delivery time), capabilities (e.g., delivery flexibility), and quality (e.g., delivery reliability, advertising).

In assessing the level of LCS, attention should be paid to the solution developed by Systell, which is a contact center system using a modern platform for servicing all communication channels (an omnichannel platform). It stores all business communication in a single centralized system in which eight indicators for effective customer service have been presented (8 key indicators for effective customer service, 2022).

First. Service Level (SLV) – The most important indicator of operational performance. It expresses the percentage of calls answered within the assumed time. This indicator should be determined independently for each contact channel. In multi-channel service, the behavior and expectations of customers vary depending on the selected medium. The universal formula for calculating SLV is as follows:

SLV = (number of calls received during the specified time frame/ number of calls offered[15]) × 100%

Second. First Contact Resolution (FCR) – this indicator relates directly to the result of the customer's contact with the company. It describes what percentage of cases were resolved at the first contact. FCR reflects the actual efficiency of the organization in the area of handling requests. Its result is primarily influenced by: correct routing design (matching the caller to the agent), consultants' competencies and rights, the number of consultants available, and access to information.

Third. Call abandonment rate, that is, abandoning a call before connecting to the operator. This customer service metric reflects the performance of a helpline. The most common reasons for abandonment include:

- too long waiting times for a consultant to answer;
- complicated IVR[16] (Słownik pojęć, 2022);
- long waiting times in the HOLD mode before a call can be resumed[17] (Podrecznik-uzytkownika-Yealink-SIP-T26P-PL).

The indicator most often is high in the case of increased demand for service, the direct symptom of which is the extended waiting time for a connection. There is a strong correlation between this indicator and the level of satisfaction with contact with the company.

Fourth. Average time on hold. It significantly affects customer satisfaction. The call hold mode is used by consultants who have to contact an expert in complicated and difficult situations. The length of time a call is on hold is a consequence of the service structure, the service model and the competence and authority of the consultant. This indicator will also be sensitive to elements such as the importance of the issue the customer is facing and the way the HOLD mode is handled (messages about waiting, background music).

Fifth. Call scoring, that is, monitoring the interaction between the customer service department and customers. This measure makes it possible to identify the elements that affect the quality of the service provided. Quality assessment should be performed based on a standardized set of parameters. They may concern the application of the contact practices adopted by the organization, the correctness of the information provided, and the form of communication. Most often, such monitoring involves analyzing a random sample of calls recorded in the system. When conducting such an analysis, it is worth focusing on the interactions labeled in the system as exceptions. These include complaints, service cancellations, or giving a low rating in the customer satisfaction survey after contact.

Sixth. Agent turnover rate – contact center structures have one of the highest employee turnover rates of all occupations[18] (Słownik pojęć, 2022). Lack of knowledge about agent turnover rates, and thus the inability to take remedial actions, is the reason for:

- lack of continuity of work and staffing problems;
- low brand reputation caused by deficiencies in the service team and insufficient competencies;
- high costs of training and continuous recruitment.

Seventh. Customer Satisfaction Index (CSI) – an indicator to determine the level of customer satisfaction with products or services offered by the company. Knowledge about CSI is obtained through a short questionnaire, carried out after contact. This survey examines the level of customer satisfaction with the interaction that has just ended. The information collected is analyzed using two different approaches. The first is from a global perspective, determining the level of customer satisfaction with customer service in a particular channel. The second relates to the individual consultant. This is part of the evaluation of his or her work. The survey can be carried out during a telephone call, in the form of an e-mail survey, a web form, or a Voice-SMS or a Text-SMS survey.

Eighth. Net Promoter Score (NPS) is used to measure customer loyalty by asking how likely they are to recommend the company, brand, website, product, or service to their friends or family. The surveyed user provides answers on an 11-point scale ranging from 0 to 10. In the form, zero means no willingness to recommend, and "10" means full loyalty and satisfaction. Based on the collected responses, users are divided into three groups:

- critics – those who answered between 0 and 6;
- passive users – responding in the 7–8 range, that is, people relatively satisfied but less willing to recommend;
- promoters – people who have declared their willingness to express their positive opinion and recommend the company/product/website to their friends.

4.8 Costs of Logistics Processes

From the model perspective, useful in logistics in security, the structural cross-section of logistics costs from the point of view of the basic components of logistics processes is their division into three groups: physical material flow, inventories, and information processes.

Physical material flow costs. The costs of physical material flow are shaped by the following components:

- depreciation costs of fixed assets involved in logistic processes, which are calculated as the product of the initial value of fixed assets in logistic processes and the average depreciation rate of these assets:
- **costs of fixed assets** = initial value of fixed assets • average depreciation rate
- labor costs, which are calculated as the product of the employment size in the logistics process and the average wages and salaries together with the overheads:
- **labor costs** = employment size • average wages and salaries together with the overheads
- costs of materials, fuels, and energy consumption are the sum of the costs of consumption of particular types of these materials;
- transport costs;
- other flow costs, such as costs of real estate tax, tax on means of transport, losses, and damages.
- The costs of physical material flow are internal costs arising in the economic system and costs of external services. Physical material flow costs include:

Physical material flow costs = costs of fixed assets + labor costs + costs of materials, fuels, and energy consumption + other flow costs + transport costs

Transport costs are the largest contributor to the structure of physical flows and can be divided into: global, internal, external, and other costs. Transport costs can be expressed as:

Transport costs = car and building depreciation costs + costs of work of drivers and transport service + costs of consumption of materials, fuels and energy related to car operation + office costs + costs of insurance and means of transport + repair and maintenance of equipment costs + lease costs + transport and repair costs + external transport service costs

Inventory costs. Inventories are goods with a precisely defined location, expressed in terms of quantity or value. These goods can be found, for example, in the distribution channel, warehouse, production, or control process (Słownik terminologii logistycznej, 2006).

Maintaining stocks of raw and other materials is associated with the need to ensure that the economic system achieves the goal in a planned and regular manner, and also reduces the uncertainty related to the deliveries and their timeliness, as well as protection against emergencies. Other reasons for maintaining stocks include ensuring the availability of raw materials, materials, products, and finished products in a specific place and in the required amount while meeting the requirements of minimizing the costs of maintaining these stocks.

Maintaining stocks for security purposes is also assessed through the criteria of rational management, but in the final assessment, what is the decisive factor is the level of goal achievement, that is, meeting the needs of people (society) such as existence, survival, completeness, identity, independence, peace and certainty of development.

The global costs of collecting and maintaining stocks, apart from transport costs, are among the highest, and their total share is estimated at 80–90% of logistics costs. The essence of inventory management results from the need to reduce the enormous costs of its maintenance, which, according to American sources, amount to 20–40% of their value per year (Ficoń, 2021).

Among the costs related to inventory management, three groups of costs can be distinguished (Figure 4.8): creation, maintenance, and exhaustion.

Each of these groups can be additionally divided into two subgroups: fixed costs independent of stock size and variable costs (dependent on stock size).

Inventory creation costs include the costs of physical inventory building and the costs of information processes related to the procurement of materials. The informational costs of creating inventories include (Figure 4.9): supplier selection, conducting negotiations, preparation of orders, opening orders, and execution of orders.

Inventory maintenance costs are a major part of a company's logistics costs. They consist of the following components: capital costs, warehousing costs, inventory servicing costs, and risk costs.

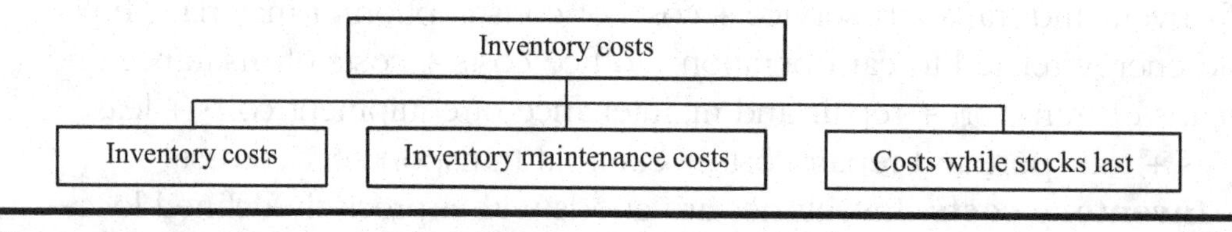

Figure 4.8 Inventory cost breakdown.

Source: Based on Cz. Skowronek, Z. Sarjusz-Wolski, *Logistyka w przedsiębiorstwie*, PWE, Warszawa 1995, p. 249.

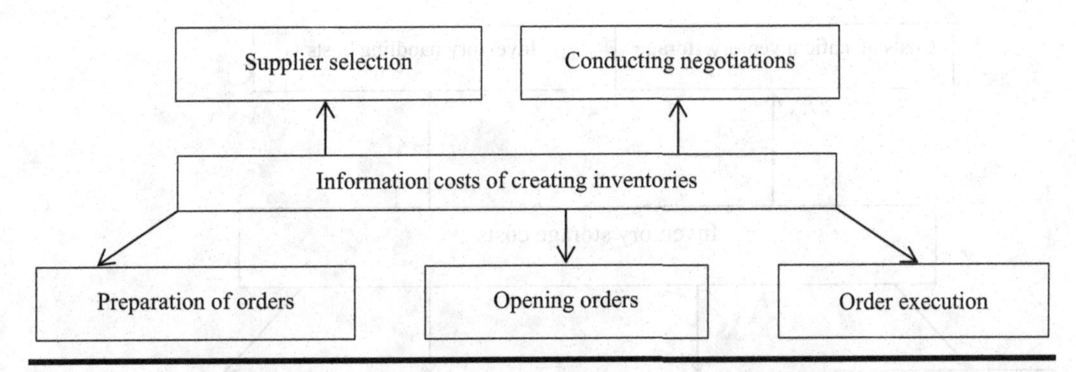

Figure 4.9 Classification of information costs of inventory building.
Source: **Own study.**

Capital costs express the losses incurred by the economic system as a result of the freezing of capital in stocks and are therefore referred to as the costs of unused opportunities. Equity and foreign capital take part in financing the stocks of the economic system. The cost of foreign capital is the rate of interest that the economic system pays to lenders. This cost is reflected in the calculation of the economic system. The cost of equity capital is not reflected in cost accounting. The measure of this cost may be the interest rate on capital deposits or, alternatively, a bank deposit. It is the minimum rate of return on debt capital in financing inventories. The cost of capital employed in inventories is variable. It is expressed as the product of the value of inventories and the average interest rate:

cost of capital involvement = average stock level in a given period • average interest rate

Warehouse costs include the costs related to the movement of inventories, and their maintenance in the warehouse, and thus include the costs of storing the inventory and the costs of the manipulation related to the flow of inventory.

Due to the generic criterion, the costs of storage include the costs of meeting the requirements of storage, protection, and security of stocks, occupancy of warehouse storage space, handling of stocks, and static storage of stocks – Figure 4.10.

Storage costs can be broken down by type. They may include the following costs: depreciation of fixed assets employed in warehouses, consumption of materials, fuels, and energy for storage, work with overheads, external services, and other costs such as property taxes and vehicle taxes.

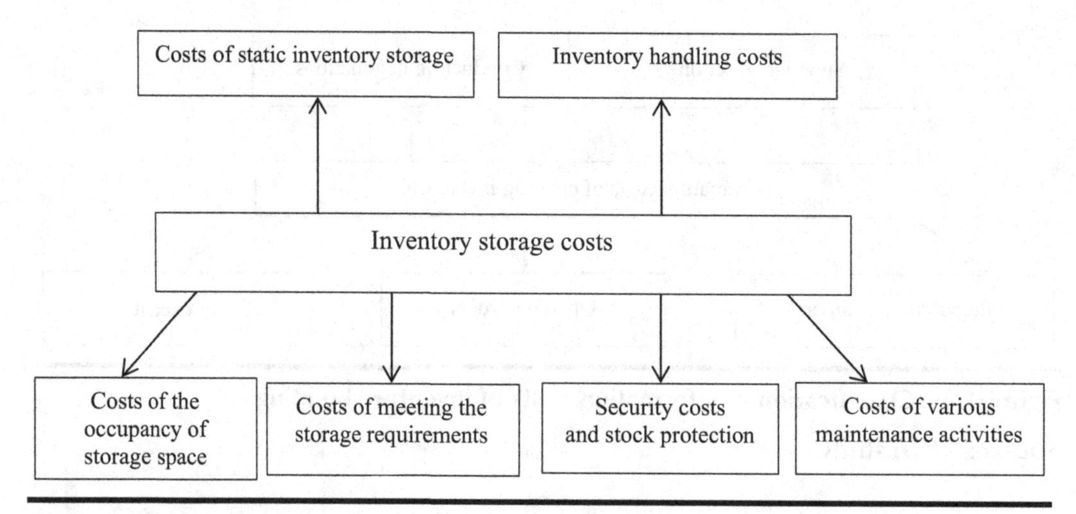

Figure 4.10 Storage costs.

Source: **Based on K. Ficoń, *Procesy logistyczne w przedsiębiorstwie,* Wyd. Impuls Plus Consulting, Gdynia (2001), p. 382.**

All storage costs can be treated as fixed costs. They are calculated from the formula:

All storage costs = average stock • empirically determined index of storage costs in % of inventory value

Inventory servicing costs include expenses related to insurance (against fire, flood, theft, etc.) and taxes on the value of inventories held.

Risk costs result from a decrease in the value of inventories for reasons beyond the control of the economic system (e.g., a sudden change in fashion, or crises), and their level depends on the amount and type of inventories stored.

One of the most important groups of inventory maintenance costs is the costs of aging and spoilage of inventories. The costs of stock aging can be broken down into costs of physical aging of inventories, and costs of economic aging of inventories.

The costs of obsolescence of inventories express the economic effects of reducing the quality of inventories and the loss of their commercial and functional value. The cost of aging stocks is significantly influenced by their non-use due to the absence of specific emergencies (droughts, floods, conflicts, wars, etc.). Low demand increases the cost of obsolescence (it cannot be avoided as it is difficult to predict floods, fires, air accidents, influenza epidemics, terrorist attacks, or other similar crises). Only the right set of actions, including forecasting, can protect the economic system against (or, more strictly, limit) the risk of incurring excessive costs of inventory obsolescence.

Another breakdown of the cost of inventory was proposed by D. M. Lambert, considering such cost items as capital (investments in inventories), inventory handling (insurance, taxes), maintenance of warehouses (own, leased, public), risks ("aging", damage, wastage, location changes) (Figure 4.11).

The ability to efficiently manage and optimize all information processes is a prerequisite for the economic provision of services supporting the achievement of the goals of economic systems.

Proper information management contributes to risk reduction by identifying formal requirements, and then monitoring and documenting activities aimed at meeting such requirements. The lack of an interdisciplinary strategy to manage information processes, such as resources, services, change, and configuration, makes it difficult for organizations to combine cost reduction, investment efficiency, and high SLVs.

Costs of information processes in the knowledge-based economy (KBE) are essentially generated in modern IT systems (*Wstęp do informatyki gospodarczej*, 2006), which include the costs of creating the system and the costs of its use[19] – Figure 4.12.

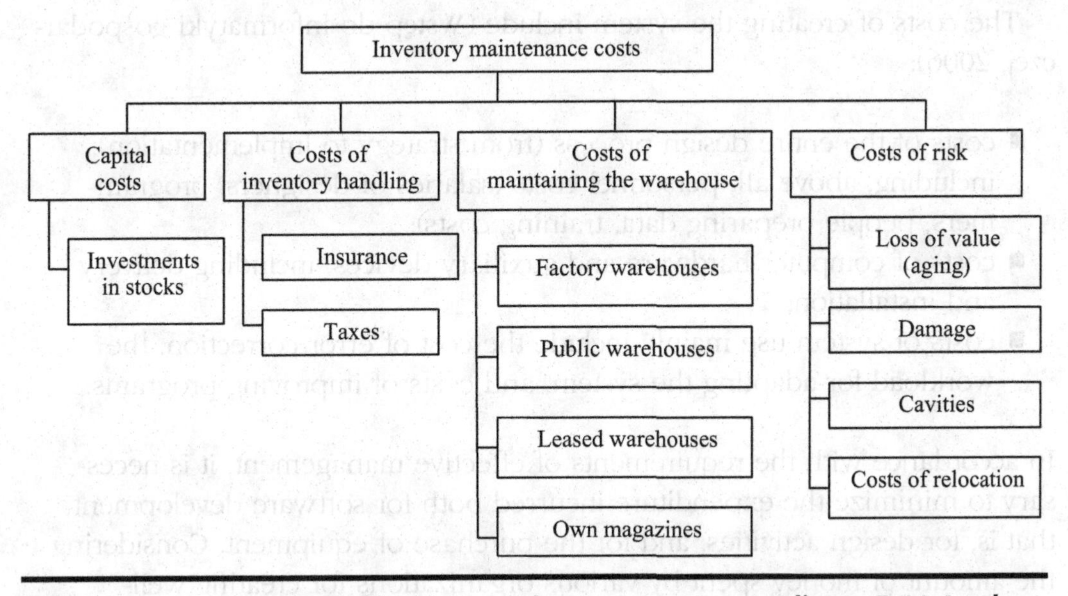

Figure 4.11 The structure of inventory maintenance costs according to D.M. Lambert.

Source: **Based on D.M. Lambert, J.R. Stock, *Strategic Logistic Management*, R.D. Irwin Inc., Boston, 1993, pp. 113–116.**

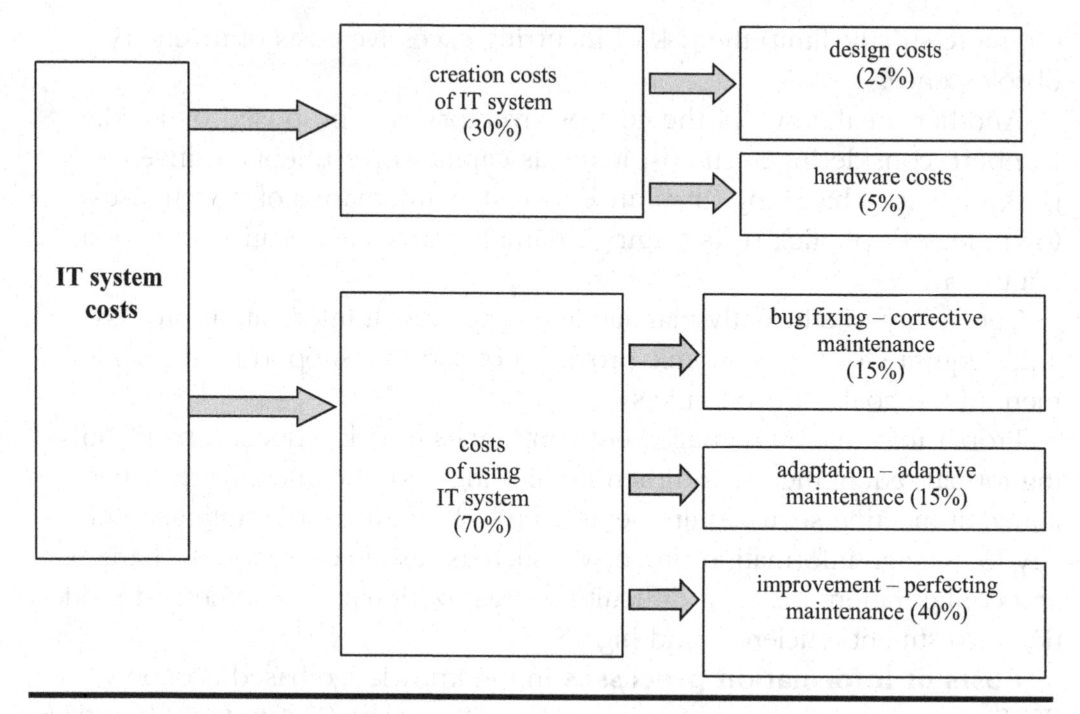

Figure 4.12 Breakdown of IT system costs.

Source: **Based on: Rokicka-Broniatowska A., Wstęp do informatyki gospodarczej, SGH, Warszawa (2006), p. 529.**

The costs of creating the system include (Wstęp do informatyki gospodarczej, 2006):

- costs of the entire design process (from strategy to implementation), including, above all, personnel costs (salaries of designers, programmers, people preparing data, training costs);
- costs of computer hardware and auxiliary devices, including delivery and installation;
- costs of system use mainly include the cost of error correction, the workload for adapting the system, and costs of improving programs.

In accordance with the requirements of effective management, it is necessary to minimize the expenditure incurred both for software development, that is, for design activities, and for the purchase of equipment. Considering the amount of money spent by various organizations for creating well-functioning applications, it is essential to reduce the cost of software development. These costs currently show a growing tendency, in contrast to the costs of computer hardware (Szymonik, Logistyka w bezpieczeństwie, 2010).

Notes

1 Value added is the difference between the market value of a product or service and the cost of production (Smid, 2012).
2 A product is the result of activities, processes and tasks. The term "product" may include a service, a tangible object (mechanical part), processed materials, an intellectual product or a combination thereof, it may be tangible (components for assembly or processed and other materials) or intellectual (e.g., knowledge or ideas), or be a combination of them, it can also be intentional (offered to clients) or unintentional (side or unwanted), according to Annex A to AGAP 2070 (1st edition) – NATO document.
3 Cleaner production – the process of managing and controlling production in such a way as to prevent pollution and its release to the environment, and to reduce the waste of raw materials, energy and human labor; (Encyklopedia PWE, available at: https://encyklopedia.pwn.pl/, 22.02.2022).
4 Big data is defined as the tendency to search, download, collect and process available data. It is a method of legally gathering information from a variety of sources, and then analyzing it and using it for your own purposes. As a result, for example, a consumer profile is created, which is later used to increase sales, acquire a colleague in business transactions in the TFL industry, How to use the potential of big data in the company's development.
5 Chatbot - software for marketing, sales or customer service, using artificial intelligence (AI) and machine learning (ML), which can simulate a conversation (chat) with the user in his natural language – the everyday language of everyday life. It is also often referred to as an Intelligent Assistant, Virtual Advisor, or just a Bot. (D. Włodarczyk, *Chatbot – czym jest, jakie są typy i jakie przynosi korzyści?*, https://inteliwise.com/pl, 04.02.2022).
6 Economic process – a set of activities that require input and give output a result that has a certain value for the client (J. Marciniak, *Standaryzacja procesów zarządzania personelem*, Oficyna Ekonomiczna, Kraków 2006, p. 22).
7 Smart networks are those in which new overlay software are installed in the already existing digital exchanges and are supported by computers for the implementation of services.
8 End-of-life vehicles are waste vehicles within the meaning of the Waste Act. A vehicle means motor vehicles for the transport of passengers, with no more than eight seats in addition to the driver's seat, or vehicles designed and constructed for the carriage of goods and with a maximum total weight not exceeding 3.5 tons, and three-wheeled mopeds.
9 Medical waste is waste generated in connection with the provision of health services and the conduct of research and scientific experiments in the field of medicine. Veterinary waste is waste generated in connection with the examination, treatment of animals or the provision of veterinary services, as well as in connection with the conduct of scientific research and experiments on animals. (Ustawa o odpadach medycznych z dnia 27 kwietnia 2001 roku).

10 Graves are structures in which unsuitable toxic substances are stored (e.g., expired plant protection products) – these are earth pits, tanks made of concrete coils or blocks, bricks.
11 Underground landfill is a part of the rock mass, including an underground mineg workings, used for neutralizing waste by depositing it, (Ustawa z dnia 9 czerwca 2011 r. – Prawo geologiczne i górnicze).
12 Mining waste disposal facility – a facility intended for the storage of mining waste in solid, liquid, solution or suspension form, including bings and tailing ponds, that includes dams or other structures used to contain, retain, confine or reinforce-such a facility; a mining excavation filled with mining waste for reclamation and technological purposes is not considered a mining waste disposal facility, (*Ustawa z dnia 10 lipca 2008 r. o odpadach wydobywczych*. Dz. U. 2008 Nr 138 poz. 865).
13 Refining – purification and treatment of natural products and substances, to obtain a smell or color using chemical and physical means, according to *Słownik wyrazów obcych*, (http://slownik-wyrazowobcych.eu/, 1/7/2022).
14 7R – delivering the right products, in the right quantity, at the right price, with the right quality, to the right place, at the right time, to the right recipient.
15 Offered calls – the number of incoming calls received by the system and these include dropped and received calls, and calls redirected to the queue, where callers hang up or receive a busy message, calls sent to voicemail or chat and those conducted by chatbot, etc.
16 IVR (Interactive Voice Response) – a system of voice announcements. An automatic voice menu technology where the caller dials one of the numbers during a call. The digits have assigned numbers to which the caller is redirected. After listening to the messages, the caller selects one of the digits. Then the system directs ther call to a specific department, e.g. complaints, registration, customer service, call center (Słownik pojęć, https://systell.pl/slownik-pojec/ivr/, 2/20/2022).
17 HOLD Mode – a function that allows the caller to keep the call active. The caller in the HOLD mode may activate a melody or a voice announcement. While a call is on hold, the user can answer or make other calls (Podrecznik-uzytkownika-Yealink-SIP-T26P-PL.pdf - 4IP.pl, s. 27, http://www.4ip.pl›file, 27.02.2022.).
18 Contact center – the central place of communication with the client in a company. It is in the Contact center that all contacts are managed. How? A dedicated system manages incoming and outgoing calls. Modern programs also record other forms of contact with the customer, such as live chat, web forms, SMS, e-mails. The software collects all inquiries/complaints/registrations/orders into one convenient agent panel. An additional option is the manager panel. This extensive function allows greater control and supervision over the efficiency of consultants' work. Thanks to it, the manager can see contact attempts on an ongoing basis and is able to collect data in a report. There are many types of reports, depending on the needs of a call center or customer service office (Słownik pojęć, https://systell.pl/slownik-pojec/ivr/, 2/20/2022).
19 Information system is the information system of the institution in which the data processing process is supported by computer technology (*Wstęp do informatyki gospodarczej, 2006*).

Chapter 5

Modern Logistics and Information Systems

5.1 Selected IT Technologies for Logistics

Logistics involves the acquisition, collection, processing, and transmission of large amounts of information. Satisfying the information needs for the implementation of logistics processes calls for an information system ensuring continuous access to up-to-date, accurate, and true information.

From the perspective of logistics, the main benefits of implementing information systems include (Rutkowski, 2001):

- improving customer service;
- a climate of trust thanks to good communication of the participants in the logistics chain;
- the possibility of using an electronic signature, protection and certification system, standardization in the area of electronic business;
- a lower level of inventories held;
- synchronization of supply, production, and distribution processes;
- replacing make-to-stock production with make-to-order production;
- reducing downtime caused by a shortage of materials for production;
- reducing costs, especially those related to transport and storage;
- improving the timeliness of deliveries as well as reducing errors in orders;
- effective management of internal and external transport;
- reducing the number of documents in circulation.

DOI: 10.4324/9781003372615-6

An information system consists of information streams connecting the executive elements of the logistics system with the management system and a set of information processing procedures.

Appropriate implementation and application of measures and IT techniques supporting the functioning of logistic information systems guarantee the improvement of the efficiency of economic systems that function in supply chains. These activities are reflected in:

- improving the speed and quality of the implemented logistics processes;
- improving the level of customer service;
- reducing costs and thus increasing competitiveness in the market.

The main functions of logistic for the implementation of which information technologies are used include (Christopher, 1996):

- customer service and communication focused on improving the customer–supplier relationship;
- planning and control related to advanced customer requirements and monitoring of physical flows to identify deviations from the plan;
- coordination, responsible for linking logistics activities into one coherent system.

The implementation of all the above-mentioned functions is possible if there is a single shared database.

Each of these functions can be part of a logistics information system that usually does not function autonomously but is integrated with the management system of the company and other companies performing tasks within the supply chain. The logistics information system includes the following subsystems: information collection subsystem, information processing subsystem, and information collection and decision support subsystem. The basic task of the information collection subsystem is to monitor the environment and the company itself to collect information necessary to make logistic decisions.

The essential information obtained for the logistics management system includes information on the company's objectives and its logistics resources, customer orders, results of marketing research, the condition of the executive elements of the logistics system (links in the logistics chain), and the implementation of logistics processes, as well as the conditions and limitations of the logistics system operation.

Reports on the condition of the logistics system and the implementation of logistics processes are significant sources of information on sales trends and forecasts, customer service quality, logistics costs, inventory, supply orders, production schedules, logistical needs, etc. To sum up, the methods and content of the obtained information can be grouped into six areas. The first one is a new market environment generated by access to the global network through the telecommunications infrastructure. The second one is the convergence of market space resulting from eliminating the geographic isolation of companies and economies. The third one is new technologies that enable individuals and organizations to interact in the network as well as create and implement new solutions and products. The fourth one is the convergence of infrastructure combining various data and information transmission technologies (cable networks, GSM, social networks, chatbots, satellite solutions, instant messaging, internet phones, etc.). The fifth one is process convergence involving, for example, the personalization (customization) of products through the integrated virtual connection of customer expectations with online sales (e-logistics), e-payments, and modern distribution processes. The sixth one is the convergence of products that can exist in various physical and electronic forms depending on the level of usability for the consumer, for example, books, knowledge, etc.

In a computerized information system, the technical means of data collection include:

- information and communication technologies (ICT) networks with the technology of electronic data interchange (EDI);
- automatic identification systems;
- navigation systems.

The quality of information depends on the methods of processing and the way data is presented. The task of the data processing subsystem is to evaluate information in terms of relevance, eliminate information noise and excess of less relevant information, sort information and display it appropriately. Information sorted in this way should be collected in an appropriate form in databases. Both physical media and the software managing them are used for this purpose.

Decision support systems are computer programs operating on a database, a database of procedures, and a database of models. They enable logistics management to use mathematical models and computer simulation techniques to analyze the effects of different decision options. The most common applications of decision support systems in logistics are (Gołembska, 2001):

- production planning, including assortment shaping, production hall development planning, material flow shaping, task scheduling on production machines, and minimization of work-in-progress inventories;
- planning of raw material supplies, including supplier selection, supply forecasting, and planning the possibility of substitution of materials and components;
- customer service, including identifying customer needs and requirements;
- forecasting the volume of demand in terms of time and space;
- distribution planning, including the selection of distribution channels;
- planning the distribution of storage facilities, including determining their capacity and number;
- warehouse management, including the planning of warehouse development, planning of receipts and releases, planning of inventory allocation;
- inventory control, including determination of safe inventory levels;
- customer service management (customer relationship management, CRM);
- modeling the distribution network, including the location of logistics centers, warehouse and transport facilities, and transport nodes, shaping transport connections between them;
- cargo shaping, including the organization of goods into loading units;
- transport management, including shaping the ownership structure of the transport fleet, selection of the mode of transport and carrier;
- management of the transport fleet, including assignment of the rolling stock to transport orders and the assignment of crews to the rolling stock, control of rolling stock renewal processes;
- transport planning, including the planning of cargo delivery and completion, and planning of traffic (routing).

In practice, typical IT systems supporting logistic processes can be used for:

- effective consumer service (ECR – efficient consumer response);
- customer relationship management (CRM);
- supply chain management (SCM).
- distribution requirement planning (DRP);
- combining calendar and database functions (CM – contact management);

- warehouse management system (WMS);
- transportation management system (TMS);
- enterprise asset management (EAM).

The systems that support also logistic management include systems and some modules of such solutions as:

- material requirements planning (MRP);
- manufacturing resource planning (MRP II);
- sales force automation (SFA);
- enterprise resource planning (ERP).

The presented list of IT systems used in the supply chain indicates that system developers attach increasing importance to developing scalable applications, that is, those that will "grow" with the increasing length and capacity of the supply chain. Usually, they offer their clients a new application, externally very similar to the one offered so far, but functionally extended, using a modern, efficient database. As a result, supply chain participants who decide to purchase and implement a program corresponding to the current situation can easily replace the software in the future as their needs increase.

The new program is similar in use, so the employees using it do not have to learn it from scratch. Moreover, the time and costs of implementing the system are significantly reduced. An important tendency in enterprise management support systems is their systematically increasing flexibility. Nowadays, software is becoming easier to modify.

Research shows that the necessary conditions for IT integration within multinational and cooperative supply chains are (Szymonik, Technologie informatyczne w logistyce, 2010):

- information technologies existing in enterprises and supply chains;
- uniform standard of identification;
- automatic identification;
- electronic communication, including electronic data exchange;
- integrated IT system;
- securing the flow of information against interference by unauthorized persons and guaranteeing its credibility.

The condition for building a network of external links of companies within the supply chain, also as indicated by the results of own research, is that they have the appropriate class of IT systems. These should be ERP systems that make it possible to expand business operations with e-business, that is, ERP II solutions, which also take into account the external elements of the business environment. Seventy per cent of Western companies and the majority of NATO members (Germany, Turkey, the United States, Canada, Great Britain, Spain, Portugal, France, Italy, the Netherlands, and others) use ERP IT systems, which confirms that Polish companies should also implement IT systems of this class (Szymonik, Technologie informatyczne w logistyce, 2010).

Depending on the type of business, different strategies can be used for comprehensive integration of IT systems. The goal of such integration is to optimize the entire supply chain and then individual participants. To meet this condition, the information system must ensure:

- the possibility of obtaining information at any desired point of flow along the logistics chain;
- availability of information for all cooperating partners;
- accuracy of information;
- satisfactory speed of information flow and its timeliness;
- the ability to process information to support the decision-making process;
- the ability to automate activities related to the production, acquisition, and processing of information and decision-making.

5.1.1 The System of Effective Customer Service

ECR is a customer-oriented supply chain. It is a modern supply chain strategy based on a partnership of its participants, consisting of the synchronized management of supply and demand with the involvement of technologies supporting the flow of products, information, and financial resources, aimed at increasing the competitiveness of the entire supply chain and maximizing the benefits of all participants in the chain while increasing the satisfaction of the final recipient (Baraniecka, 2004). The general areas of interest for ECR are presented in Figure 5.1.

The collective pursuit of maximizing the efficiency of the entire chain, rather than the traditional focus on the efficiency of its individual links, leads to lower total system costs, inventory levels, and capital employed while increasing value for the end customer. These activities focus on the use of modern management methods and technical means aimed to shorten the time a product takes to travel from the production line to the store shelf

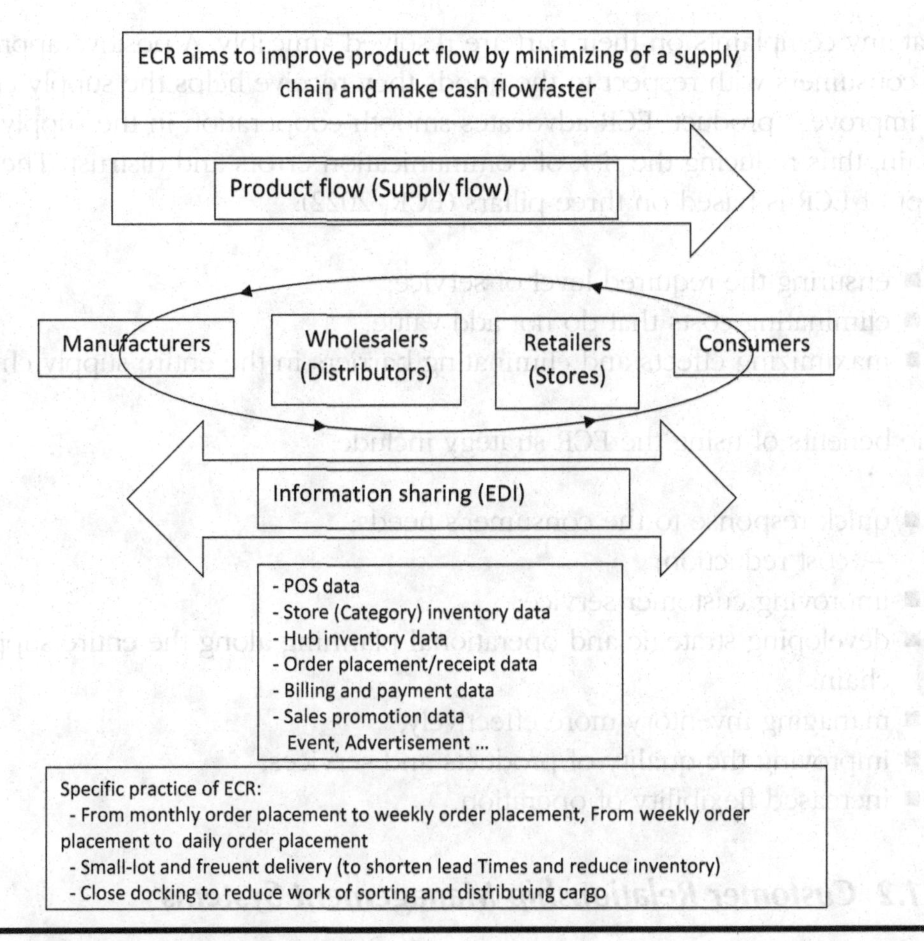

Figure 5.1 ECR areas of interest.

Source: **Based on Efficient Consumer Response (ECR): Adding Customer Value to the Supply Chain using Collaboration, https://www.globaltranz.com/efficient-consumer-response/,3/28/2022.**

and to reduce costs in the entire circulation of goods. As a result of these activities, the customer receives the product at the price he or she is willing to accept and with a satisfactory level of service.

The strategy of ECR is founded on reliable information exchange and constant staff development. ECR reduces supply chain risk and thus reduces the risk of reluctance to purchase products. It also ensures that products that reach the consumer are of high quality and fresh (Kurnia & Johnston, 2001).

The processes of the warehouse strategy involved in the supply chain enable the efficient delivery of better raw materials, resulting in the production of high-quality products to the satisfaction of the consumer. This is of critical importance as it ensures that customers receive products on time and that any complaints on their part are resolved amicably. A positive approach to consumers with respect to the goods they receive helps the supply chain to improve a product. ECR advocates smooth cooperation in the supply chain, thus reducing the risk of communication errors and distrust. The concept of ECR is based on three pillars (ECR, 2022):

- ensuring the required level of service;
- eliminating costs that do not add value;
- maximizing effects and eliminating barriers in the entire supply chain.

The benefits of using the ECR strategy include:

- quick response to the consumer's needs;
  - cost reduction;
- improving customer service;
- developing strategic and operational planning along the entire supply chain;
- managing inventory more effectively;
- improving the quality of products and services;
- increased flexibility of operation.

5.1.2 Customer Relationship Management Systems

One of the types of systems supporting the company's operations is CRM system. According to Harvard Business Review research, a typical American company loses half of its customers in the period of five years. Other studies indicate that acquiring a new customer is seven to ten times more expensive than maintaining an existing one. Undoubtedly, the condition for the existence of many companies on the market is their ability to retain their customers and attract new ones. This is how the concept of customer-oriented systems was born. These are the systems of Efficient Customer Service (ECS) and CRM (Szymonik, 2015).

The literature offers many definitions of CRM. Here are some of them:

- CRM is an infrastructure that allows to define and increase the value of customers and appropriate means by which the best customers are motivated to be loyal, that is, buy again. CRM is much more than simply managing customer knowledge and monitoring customer behavior (Dyché, 2002).

- CRM is a customer-oriented, integrated, multi-access, and open IT system designed to support the management of marketing, sales, service, and technical support, that is, data on the seller-customer relationship and characterizing the customer in terms of obtaining and continuing it over a long period of time (Rokicka-Broniatowska, 2006).
- CRM is a business strategy of relationship building and customer management to optimize long-term benefits. CRM requires the introduction of a customer-centered business philosophy and culture that ensures effective marketing, sales, and service processes (Lotko, 2003).
- CRM is an integrated IT system that makes the interaction with potential customers deeper, streamlines the process, and facilitates the creation of personalized activities with recipients, and the creation of a database for the needs of potential customers (5 Benefits of Using Customer Relationship Management (CRM), 2022).

The functions of CRM systems include (Rokicka-Broniatowska, 2006):

- collection and processing of archival data on the cooperation with the client, contacts, and business talks, orders, and activities of sales representatives and employees who are in direct contact with the client;
- automation of organization and sales management;
- configuration of orders (products) at the client's individual request – CRM systems support sellers at the point of sale and enable the compilation of selected elements of products and services;
- preparation of offers;
- marketing encyclopedias, helpful for sales representatives as they contain comprehensive information about products, and competitors, as well as other marketing information about the sales process;
- search for relevant data;
- preparation of analyses and forecasts regarding sales and the market;
- management of technical support departments and call centers;
- development of a strategy for acquiring a client from a selected industry based on detailed information about clients;
- preparation of an advertising campaign to promote the product by the marketing department;
- preparation of a list of customers to whom offers, information materials, etc. are sent;
- care about the already acquired customer (service and handling of possible complaints, technical support);

- communication with the market – search for contacts with business partners;
- administration – daily organization of tasks (deadlines, contacts, reporting, presentations).

CRM software consists of three elements (Figure 5.2) (Malczan, 2022):

- operational CRM (it is used to consolidate through automation the data about the customer, their needs, behaviors, or history of cooperation, especially in the areas of services, sales, and marketing);
- collaborative[1] CRM (covers only customer contact solutions) based on telephone, e-mail, social media, interaction management, and the like;
- analytical CRM (helps to understand the customer's actions taken during contact with the organization, carries out all customer contact processes and all other processes taking place in the organization that are of any importance from the customer's point of view), works based on OLAP (Encyklopedia zarządzania, 2022),[2] data mining (Techniki zgłębiania danych, 2022),[3] and data warehousing.

The structure of the CRM system is presented in Figure 5.3

Where: PDA – Personal Digital Assistant

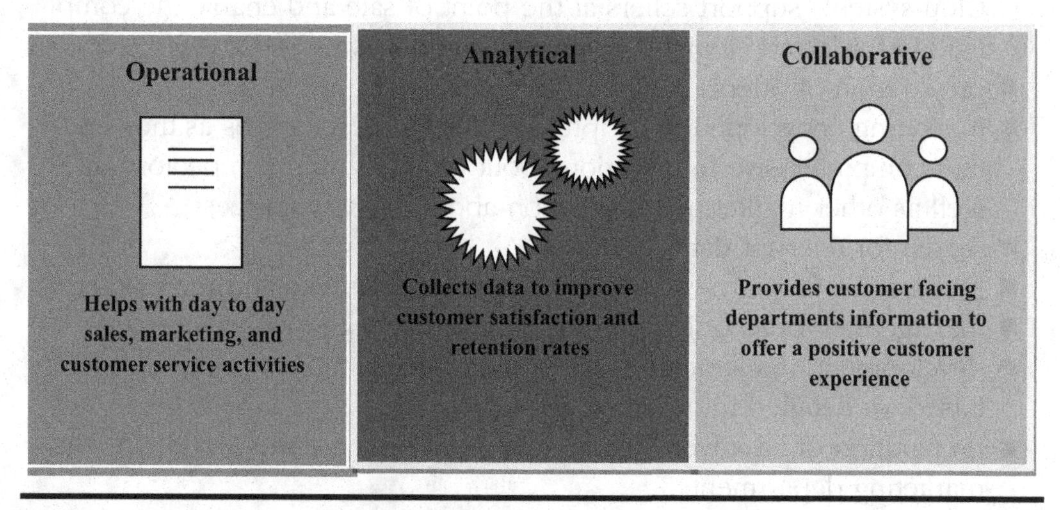

Figure 5.2 CRM software components.

Source: Based on N. Malczan, CRM Database: Overview, Structure, Strategies & Maintenance Tips, https://www-engagebay-com.translate.goog/blog/what-is-a-crm-database/?, 20.07.2022

The benefits of using CRM systems include (Rokicka-Broniatowska, 2006, What is the CRM process? 5 key steps, 2022):

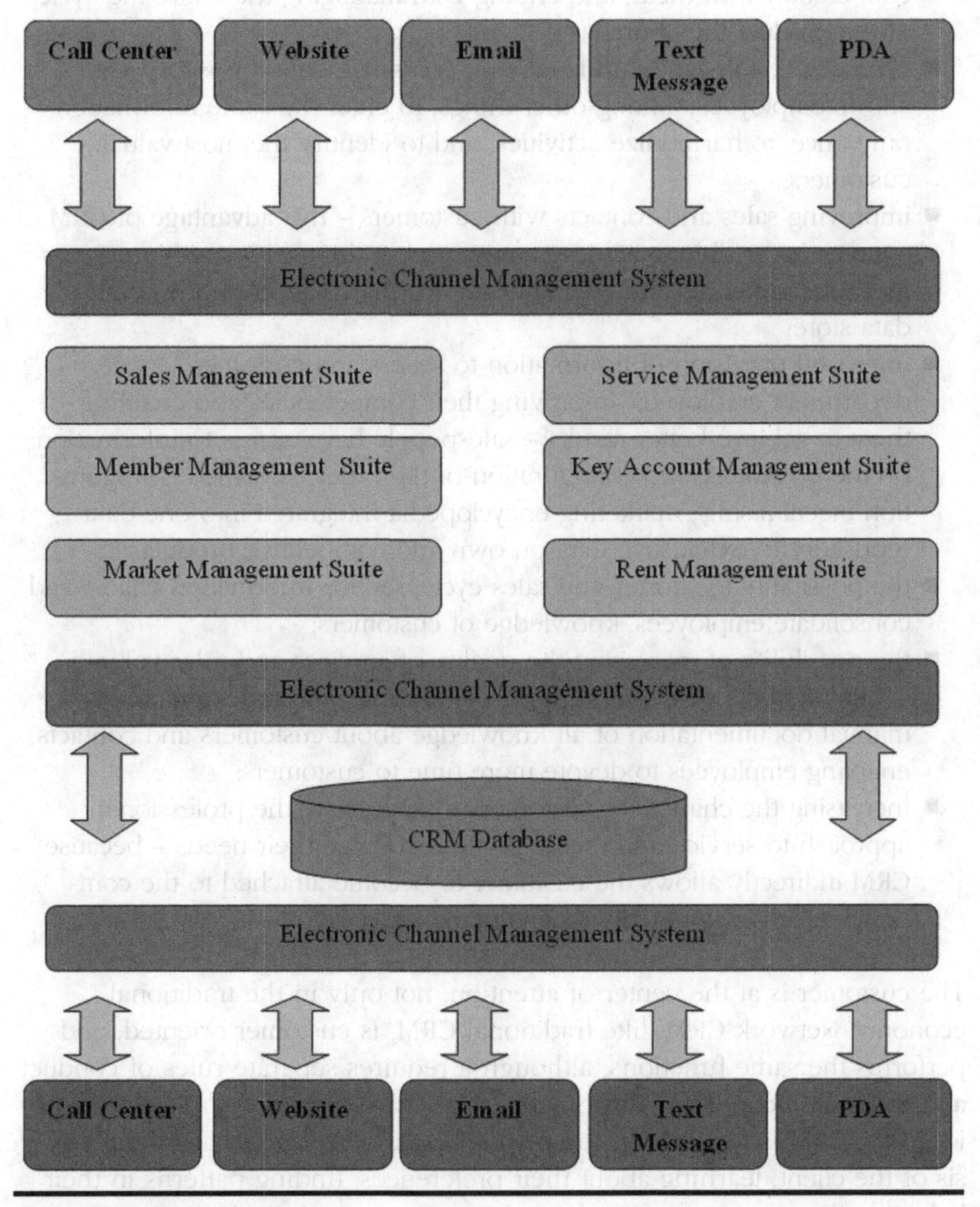

Figure 5.3 CRM structure.

Source: **Based on N. Israni, CRM Database: Overview, Structure, Strategies & Maintenance Tips, https://www-engagebay-com.translate.goog/blog/what-is-a-crm-database/?, 25.07.2022.**

- establishing and maintaining contacts with customers – starting from identifying a potential customer, through establishing possible real cooperation with them, and ending with managing the entire life cycle of the product they purchase;
- centralized, constantly updated, and accessible data repository – it allows employees, among other things, to enter the same information only once, to harmonize activities, and to identify the most valuable customers;
- improving sales and contacts with customers – this advantage of CRM systems is possible to achieve, among other things, by combining commercial, marketing, and customer service information in one central data store;
- improved provision of information to sellers and customer service department employees, improving their competencies and enabling them to achieve better results – salespeople have access to information on the possibility and configuration of the order (so-called configuration mechanisms), marketing encyclopedia integrated into one data repository to exhaustive data on own and competitive products;
- the possibility to shorten the sales cycle, reduce information chaos, and consolidate employees' knowledge of customers;
- the possibility of increasing the quality of services and sales volume – CRM systems allow minimizing the onerous and time-consuming manual documentation of all knowledge about customers and contacts, enabling employees to devote more time to customers;
- increasing the chance for customers to appreciate the professional approach to service and the ability to recognize their needs – because CRM indirectly allows the customer to become attached to the company, which undoubtedly means market success.

The customer is at the center of attention, not only in the traditional economy. Network CRM, like traditional CRM, is customer-oriented, and performs the same functions, although it requires separate rules of conduct and different technology. Customer service has changed completely. The idea of e-CRM is focused on the personalization process, that is, analysis of the client, learning about their preferences, finding patterns in their behavior, etc.

The personalization process is used on an increasing scale on the internet, which is perceived as another market because it offers specific benefits, including:

- the possibility of placing orders for non-standard (individual) products;
- use of promotions and efficient and friendly service;
- quick access to the resources sought.

The development of information and communication technologies, the increasing length of the logistics supply chain, and the growing competition force us to look for more advanced solutions for management support systems.

Two classes of ERP and CRM systems can use new communication possibilities to make management functions, that is, planning, execution, motivation, and control, more effective. These two systems cooperate and comprehensively cover the logistics supply chain.

The cheapest way to maintain your market position is to build a solid customer base. Retaining customers, however, requires increasingly more effort, and above all, perfect knowledge of their needs. This is where computer technology comes in handy, and in particular, two of its aspects:

- the ability to store customer data in an integrated manner so that all authorized persons in the company can view customer information at the same time;
- the ability to automate the analysis of customer data and contacts with customers (data mining), aimed at turning information into knowledge.

Advanced CRM solutions make it possible to view each recipient, their behavior toward service support, reactions to marketing campaigns, sizes and types of orders placed, along with the history of their implementation and payment history for the delivery of goods and services. Maintaining your own base of recipients is not always easy, so the value of information can hardly be overestimated because information – although it is often partially available in individual departments – in practice cannot always be accessed comprehensively where it is needed at a specific moment.

The advantages of CRM include (5 Benefits of Using Customer Relationship Management (CRM), 2022, Advantages and Disadvantages of Using Customer Relationship Management Software, 2022):

- cost reduction in customer–supplier activities;
- effective advertising and networking with current and potential customers;
- increased involvement in the search for new business solutions for clients;

- better communication between participants in contact with clients;
- increase in trust from clients and cooperation with them;
- simplified marketing;
- lower selling costs.

The disadvantages of CRM software include (Advantages and Disadvantages of Using Customer Relationship Management Software, 2022):

- incomplete control over customer data;
- relatively high costs related to the development and operation of the system (programmers, system administrator, maintenance personnel);
- decline in face-to-face contact;
- costs related to the training of staff and managers;
- resistance of personnel to the implementation of the system (fear of being made redundant).

5.1.3 Supply Chain Management System

SCM involves IT solutions and enterprise management for supply chain networks. SCM is co-developed by the Global Supply Chain Forum and competes with Supply Chain Operation Reference-Model (SCOR) by being a synchronization tool for work, providing co-operators, and making it easier for the company to adapt to collaboration.

The internal expansion of SCM is related to procurement, production, and distribution. An external SCM company integrates users with service providers (Figure 5.4).

SCM solutions are used primarily in the product design phase, for selecting sources of supply, forecasting the demand for products, and controlling their distribution. They contain specialized tools that enable the supervision of individual logistic activities of the company.

In conclusion, the SCM model is based on eight complementary business processes supported by IT tools (Ciesielski & Długosz, 2010): CRM, customer service management, demand management, order completion, production flow management, supplier relationship management, product development and sale, and complaint management. The SCM system allows the development of transparent rules for cooperation between entities involved in the production and distribution of goods (Majewski, 2008).

The efficiency of the entire enterprise is considered not just from the point of view of the global difference between revenues and costs. The

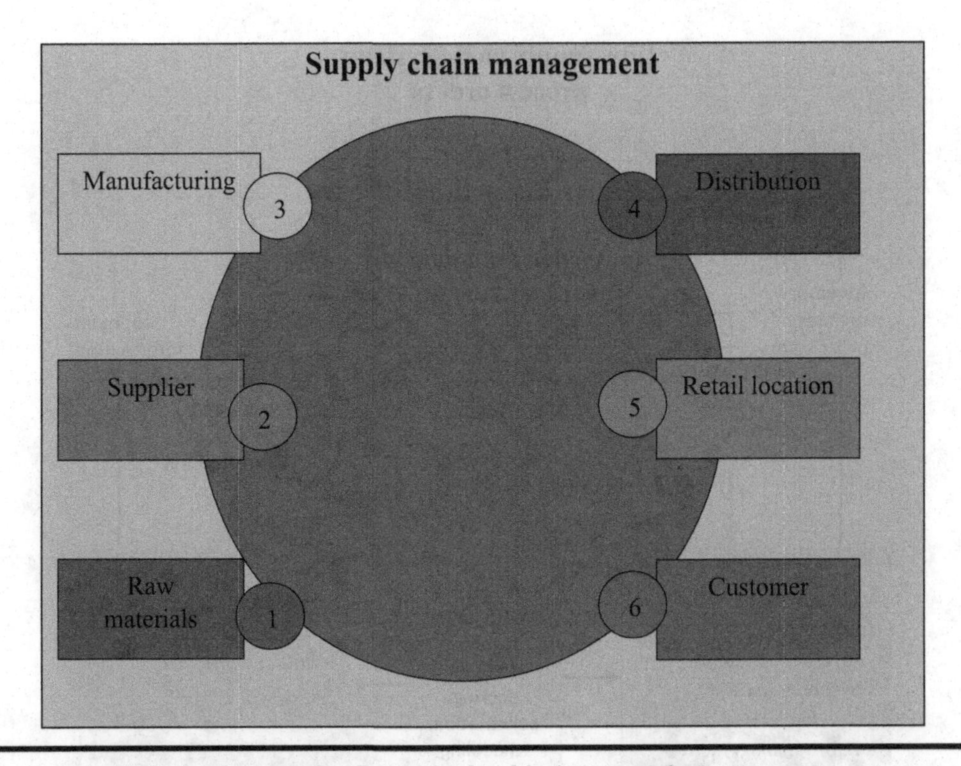

Figure 5.4 Links in the supply chain involved in its operation.

Source: Based on D. Daniel, *Guide to supply chain management,* https://www.techtarget.com/searcherp/definition/supply-chain-management-SCM,28/2/2022.

effectiveness of the production and distribution of each product, possibly the channel of product distribution or supply of materials, is also optimized.

It should be noted that SCM cannot be implemented without mastering production, warehouse management, and the management of own materials and organized transport. The following systems are helpful in the effective functioning of SCM: ERP, WMS, and TMS. With SCM, it is possible to manage not only the processes within the institution itself but also outside it, in the supply chain. The systems that produce a synergistic effect within SCM are ERP, WMS, and TMS, as shown in Figure 5.5.

During the implementation of SCM, the planning and execution functions of the supply chain are performed in more detail. SCM enables the modeling of the entire supply network and all its constraints. Therefore, using this model, you can synchronize activities and plan the flow of materials throughout the supply chain. Based on this, SCM adjusts supply to demand and creates workable plans for procurement, production, inventory, and

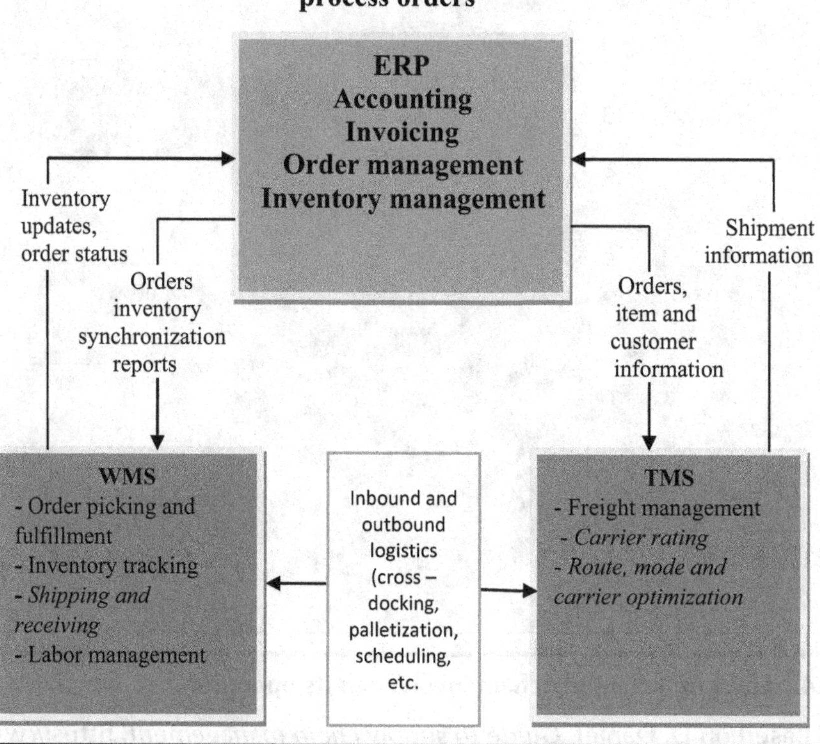

Figure 5.5 Basic subsystems included in the SCM system.

Source: Based on D. Daniel, *Guide to supply chain management,* https://www.techtarget.com/searcherp/definition/supply-chain-management-SCM,28/2/2022.

transportation. Multiple locations, their interdependencies, the global logistics chain, and the company's trading partners are considered in SCM planning. The collaborative process on a global scale is new to larger companies and requires organizational changes. It includes not only implementation but also strategic, tactical, and operational planning. As a result, SCM has an impact on business processes, even at the lowest level.

Real-time planning, advanced simulation methods, and optimization possibilities offered by SCM guarantee a completely new process flow, different from that offered by the ERP system. Therefore, SCM users must become thoroughly familiar with the operation of the entire supply chain. The benefits of SCM systems certainly include (Daniel, 2022; Kurnia & Johnston, 2001):

- improving relationships with suppliers, distributors, and retailers;
- improving the brand image;

- environmental sustainability;
- improving cash flow;
- reducing risk in the supply chain
- making products and services safer;
- reducing overhead costs;
- increasing accountability and compliance; and
- boosting innovation.

5.1.4 Distribution Requirement Planning System

The DRP method is defined as a system determining the demand for inventories in individual distribution centers of the enterprise (Rutkowski, 2001). It collects information on this demand and passes it on to the production and material systems. Forecasting starts from the bottom of the distribution channel, that is, a store or a warehouse. When the needs at the lower level are added up, a quantitative distribution of the demand for links higher up in the structure is obtained. This type of planning makes it possible to obtain fairly accurate demand forecasts, as well as plan the appropriate level of stocks and their storage locations for all links of the integrated chain. An example of a DRP model is presented in Figure 5.6.

DRP is a mirror image of MRP, and it also uses the same operational principles as MRP (Radziejowska, 2001):

- time distribution of demand within the company's distribution system;
- gross needs that result from the demand for the final product;

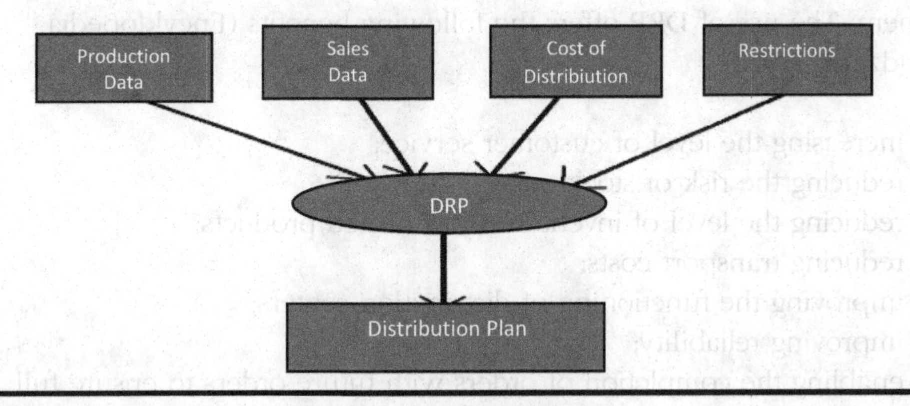

Figure 5.6 Components of DRP model functioning.

Source: **Based on *Distribution Requirement Planning (DRP),* https://www.geeksforgeeks.org/distribution-requirement-planning-drp/, 25/2/2022.**

- net needs for open orders, that is, actual needs over a period of time (after considering stocks and deliveries in transit);
- submitting supplementary orders in the event of a real need (at the level equal to the net needs or specified by the manufacturer);
- synchronization of the demand, which concerns the precise determination of the date of placing an order for a specific quantity of a product (knowing the time of order completion by a given warehouse and the length of the product's production cycle).

The demand data is transferred to the information system that supports the production and to the MRP system(s). Demand forecasting starts at the lowest link in the distribution channel. The needs of the lowest levels are summed up to estimate, in quantitative terms, demand for the links higher in the hierarchy.

The use of the presented system, in addition to considerable precision in forecasting the demand, also makes it possible to plan the appropriate level and location of inventory throughout the entire integrated distribution chain. The aggregated amounts of demand from individual distribution centers, determined independently or by customers for assumed future periods, are used for creating an inventory demand schedule and are transferred to the link in the chain that deals with production. After comparing with the previously prepared forecasts regarding the production volume, the necessary adjustments are made while considering the needs of customers and limited production capacity. On this basis, it is possible to develop production plans and, at the same time, a material requirements plan.

A distribution plan is also developed, showing the distribution of supplies to individual distribution cells in accordance with the demand reported by them. The use of DRP offers the following benefits (Encyklopedia zarządzania, 2022):

- increasing the level of customer service;
- reducing the risk of stock-outs;
- reducing the level of inventories of finished products;
- reducing transport costs;
- improving the functioning of distribution centers;
- improving reliability;
- enabling the completion of orders with future orders to ensure full truckloads;
- enabling demand forecasts at the retailer (customer) level;
- improving the level of customer service and satisfaction.

It is worth mentioning that DRP systems often feature a marketing support module. It enables the creation of databases related to the implementation of the aforementioned function, the management of projects undertaken in this area, and the transfer of relevant information for engaging business partners in selected marketing campaigns.

5.1.5. Warehouse Management System

WMS is an IT program for managing the material flow in warehouses. It supports the implementation and control of the flow through the warehouse and provides information about this flow, and enables the creation of documentation accompanying this flow (Słownik terminologii logistycznej, 2006).

WMS solutions are often modular. They are based on the main program, which is responsible for such aspects as storage management or goods management. In terms of the WMS architecture, the modules that define the storage machines are of special importance. The main modules of the WMS include such elements as (WMS – zarządzanie magazynem, 2022): delivery service; input supervision; handling of shipments; output supervision; support of forwarding; changes inside the warehouse; inventory; reports; packaging; classification of goods according to the ABC and XYZ methods, which allows for the management of the warehouse space and speeds up entry/exit operations.

WMS systems have a number of functions that contribute to their specificity and accurately describe the mechanism of their operation. They include (WMS – zarządzanie magazynem, 2022):

- maximum use of warehouse space;
- reduction of time spent on activities related to the delivery and ordering of goods;
- increasing the turnover of inventories and assets;
- improving the quality of services provided by producers;
- reducing possible errors thanks to advanced control and quick resolution of possible problems between producers and suppliers;
- high flexibility and mobility of data exchange with the system;
- easier access to data;
- complete supervision of orders;
- the ability to manage warehouse traffic;
- facilitating the creation of documentation for preparing goods for shipment and the automation of this process;

- the possibility of using barcodes or RFID labels for marking goods and logistic units;
- the ability to record inventory levels by specific locations, batches, or expiry dates;
- automation of the inventory process.

Contemporary WMS is evolving toward the shared use of a network of cyberspace systems (CPS). They become an intermediary that connects people, objects, and physical processes in the warehouse through (Lee et al., 2018): communication technologies including radio frequency identification/short-range communication (RFID/NFC)[4]; wireless networks of sensors and actuators; Internet of Things (IoT); Big data and cloud computing.

5.1.6 Transportation Management System

TMS is a software category that supports the planning and implementation of the physical flow of goods. It can be used by everyone in the supply chain, from manufacturers to distributors and third-party logistics (3PL) service providers – virtually any party looking to coordinate shipping. Supervising the entire shipping process, the TMS control tower captures data about goods in real time using API or EDI technology (Figure 5.7).

There are two main groups of TMS users: shippers, producers, and distributors; 3PL service providers. The TMS is software that allows carriers from the TSL industry (transport, forwarding, and logistics) to process in electronic form the data necessary for effective transport management.

The TMS system cooperates with the fleet management system (FMS[6]), which is responsible for the processing of data, such as information on the condition of the vehicle, driving and rest times, loading and unloading times, service time, driver behavior on the road or the level and condition of loading or unloading. At the heart of the FMS system is its open database structure. The onboard computer is responsible for collecting the necessary information about the driver, vehicle, and cargo (Szymonik, 2015). The main functions and tasks performed by TMS with the participation of FMS are (Figure 5.8) (TMS Falcon – system do zarządzania transportem, 2022):

- optimization of deliveries through consolidation of orders, transport and delivery planning, management of drivers, the fleet of vehicles and suppliers of transport services, and monitoring of transport events;
- handling of atypical forwarding orders thanks to the function of defining features for various industries, according to individual needs;

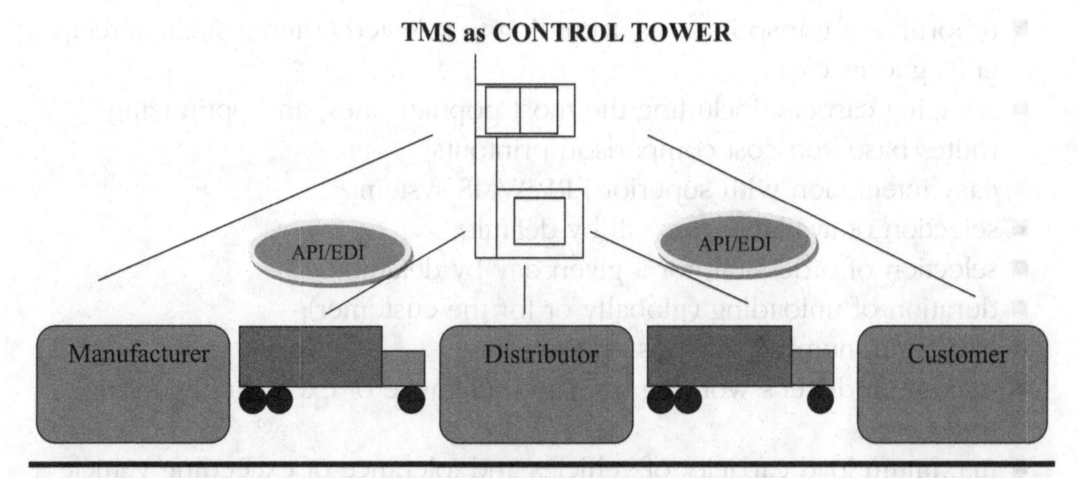

Figure 5.7 Communication between producers and customers using API[5] and EDI.

Source: **Based on *Transportation Management System: Benefits, Features, and Main Providers,* https://www.altexsoft.com/blog/transportation-management-system/, 28.02.2022.**

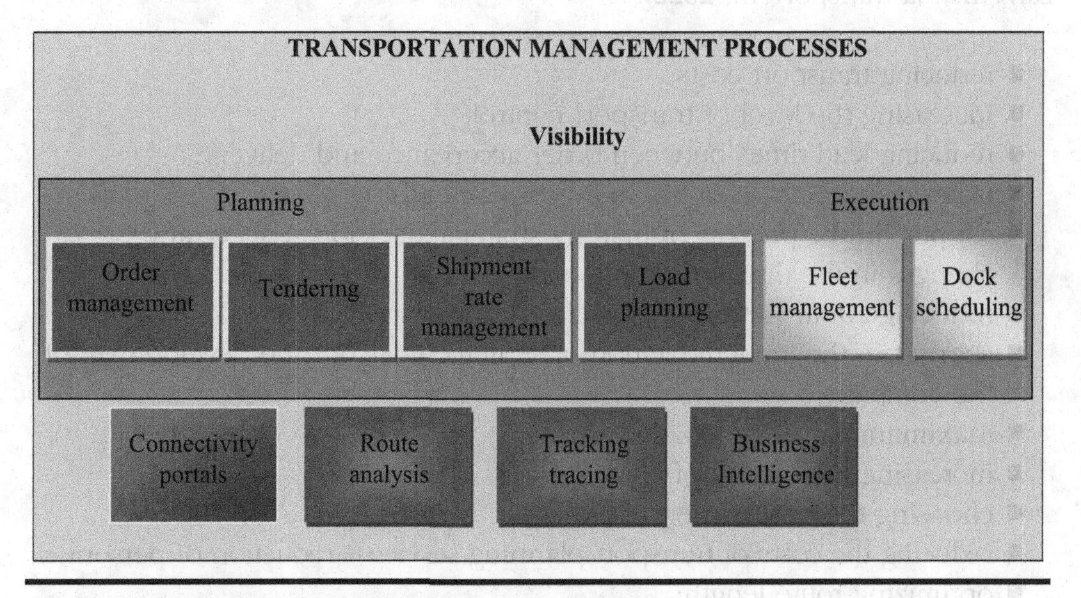

Figure 5.8 The main functions and tasks of the TMS.

Source: **Based on *Transportation Management System: Benefits, Features, and Main Providers,* https://www.altexsoft.com/blog/transportation-management-system/, 28.02.2022.**

- full service of orders in the supply chain;
- handling contracts for transport tasks and the transport fleet, preparation of analyses and reports;
- user-defined price lists for transport services and billing for transport services;

- reporting of transport costs according to selected criteria, such as recipients, goods, etc.;
- selecting carriers, including the most popular ones, and optimizing routes based on cost comparison printouts;
- easy integration with superior ERP/WMS systems;
- selection of available cars (all by default);
- selection of orders (all for a given day by default);
- duration of unloading (globally or for the customer);
- maximum number of stops on the route;
- maximum driver's working time and tolerance of exceeding working time;
- maximum load capacity of vehicles and tolerance of exceeding vehicle load capacity.

The benefits of using the system include (TMS Falcon – system do zarządzania transportem, 2022):

- reducing transport costs;
- increasing the level of transport control;
- reducing lead times between order acceptance and delivery;
- faster response to changes in customer needs;
- support in the process of making strategic decisions concerning changes in the distribution network;
- reducing administrative costs related to transport;
- support in the implementation of strategic goals for the development of the company;
- maximum use of the loading space;
- increasing the quality of customer service;
- choosing the best carrier;
- reducing the costs of transport planning service – reduction of personnel;
- optimizing route length;
- tracking and traceability of shipments
- suitability for any type of enterprise;
- integration with shipping systems;
- settlement of transport invoices in connection with transport orders;
- own fleet management;
- monitoring of transport-related events
- scheduling of own transport;
- planning of drivers' working time;

- integration with fleet supervision systems
- lower "social costs" – reducing the number of trucks, exhaust emissions, and accidents.

The system stores data on, and warns about the expiry of deadlines related to, inter alia:

- collision, comprehensive, third-party, and accident insurance;
- technical and warranty inspections;
- date of tachograph verification;
- incidents, e.g. tire changes, etc.;
- validity of documents.

Shippers, suppliers, and 3PL providers must abandon paper documentation not only to compete but, above all, to survive. And it is not that difficult when the technology is here to enable (*Transportation Management System: Benefits, Features, and Main Providers*, 2022):

- machine-to-machine communication (cyber-physical space) – when logistics companies are connected, better visibility, better efficiency, and lower costs are achieved;
- location technology and RFID – tracking vehicles and shipments enables faster response to disruptions and improves efficiency;
- mobile access to customers – customer satisfaction depends on how much information customers have about their goods.

It must consistently meet these expectations to be able to incorporate truly innovative ideas: robotics, driverless transport, and artificial intelligence.

5.1.7 Enterprise Asset Management System

EAM systems are used to support maintenance in manufacturing companies, as well as managing tenants, contracts, and spaces. Their task is also to help oversee the long-term value of the property, as well as sustainable development or ecological initiatives. Generally speaking, EAM facilitates: keeping records of property, managing the property, and keeping inventories (Figure 5.9).

EAM systems have an advantage over modules that are components of an ERP system, as they make it possible to record assets and generate relevant documents while bypassing such processes as further asset management

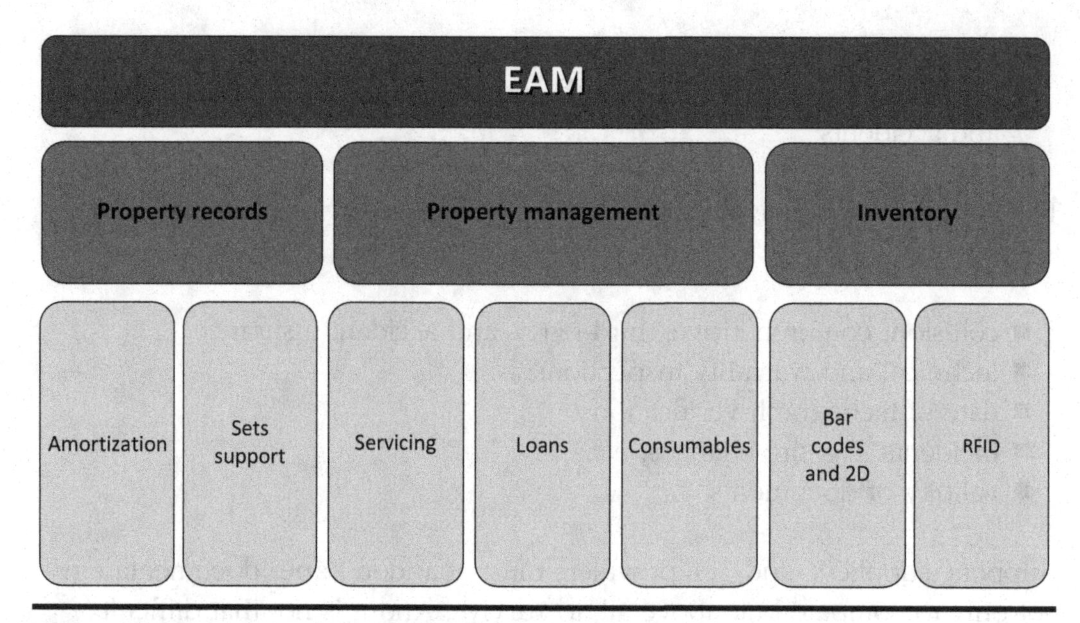

Figure 5.9 Functions of EAM systems.

Source: **Based on Zarządzanie majątkiem przedsiębiorstwa – czy warto rozbudowaćposiadanysystemERP?,http://www.insoftconsulting.pl/,12.01.2022**

and asset inventory. A cursory treatment of the last two elements can often contribute to inappropriate use of the possessed fixed assets and equipment, thus causing losses to the enterprise (Zarządzanie majątkiem przedsiębiorstwa – czy warto rozbudować posiadany system ERP?, 2022).

The best EAM solutions are cloud-based, which means that any data stored by a user in the system is always available when they need it, and updates occur in real time. Cloud software also means it is accessible from anywhere and thanks to a mobile-friendly solution, ManagerPlus, the system can be accessed from any computer, tablet, or smartphone even if it is not connected to the internet because everything will be updated as soon as the connection is restored (Cockerham, 2022).

The most popular EAM systems that have been implemented in companies, for example, from the metal industry, are the systems offered by IFS, SAP, Neuron, and Junisoftex. They are used in the areas of (Efektywne zarządzanie aktywami, 2022):

- purchasing and storage management (to handle purchase requests and access to stock levels, for example, inventories of spare parts or consumables);

- managing movable assets, including fixed assets (register, equipment, costs, locations, inventory numbers);
- space or tenant management (space, allocation of equipment and resources to space, premises, tenants, lease agreements, removals, space optimization);
- handling requests (e.g., incidents, problems, resource reservations);
- vehicle management (i.e., register, technical, registration, insurance data, service, equipment);
- management of planned works (e.g., planned preventive works);
- property organization and maintenance, maintenance work, and service contracts.

5.1.8 Enterprise Resource Planning System

ERP (more commonly referred to by manufacturers as Advanced Resource Management) – defines the class of IT systems supporting enterprise management or the cooperation of a group of enterprises by collecting data and enabling operations on the collected data.

Support offered by ERP may cover all or some management levels and it helps to optimize the use of the company's resources and processes. ERP systems are modular software, that is, they consist of independent, yet cooperating applications and are included in the class of Integrated IT Systems.

ERP systems are an extension of MRP II systems. Their essential element is the database, which is usually common to all other modules. These modules usually cover the following areas (Figure 5.10) (Słupski & Sobiesiński, 2022): informing the management, supporting decisions, protecting data, integrating multimedia, accessing data via web browsers, warehousing, managing inventories, tracking realized deliveries, planning production, supplies, sales, contacts with customers, accounting, finance, managing human resources (payroll, personnel).

ERP systems may also include other modules, such as transport management and control, or project management. ERP systems are quite flexible and allow these modules to be adapted to the specifics of individual enterprises, for example, because individual modules may be independent of other modules (i.e., they can work without their presence). These systems usually also allow you to set access authorizations for individual users. Another characteristic feature of ERP systems is that they allow users to

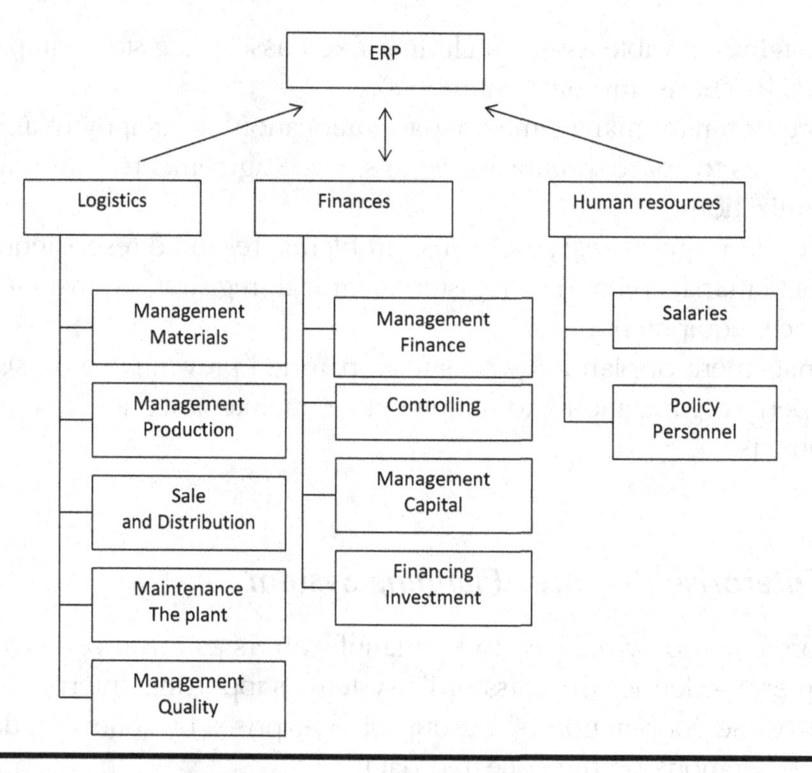

Figure 5.10 Architecture of the integrated ERP system.

Source: **Based on Rokicka-Broniatowska A., *Wstęp do informatyki gospodarczej, SGH,* Warszawa (2006), p. 432.**

carry out the bottom-up replanning process, that is, the possibility of introducing changes (making corrections, considering alternative solutions) in the solutions proposed by the system (e.g., changing the size of a delivery batch).

In the era of a global village and knowledge-based economy, companies need to maintain closer ties with customers and partners than they did a few years ago. The concept of traditional ERP systems ceases to fit modern economic and technological realities. Therefore, companies that want to gain competitiveness are already starting to plan the migration of software from ERP to the needs of Industry 4.0. including **Logistics 4.0.**

The new first-class ERP systems were developed at the end of the last century. They constitute a further development of the idea of integrated systems supporting company management. Changes to the ERP system include advanced planning and scheduling (APS), web-based business solutions, including CRM, and SCM.

Additionally, the following subsystems are offered (Parys, 2022):

- product lifecycle management – a solution enabling the management, tracking, and control of all information related to the product;
- strategic company management – a solution supporting strategic planning (Business Intelligence, data warehouses, and controlling);
- human resource management – solutions for HR and payroll services.

The current ERP systems already work with (Tavana et al., 2022): internet technologies, mobile wireless networks, artificial intelligence, network computing, knowledge management, architecture of internet services, blockchain, IoT, artificial intelligence, machine learning, big data, etc.

Contemporary ERP systems increasingly cooperate with the IoT, which is supported by sensors, actuators, and applications (on mobile or Windows devices). The information collected forms a common structure that allows data to be shared and connected to the cloud via a semantic web. The data is also linked to the IoT application via the cloud (Figure 5.11).

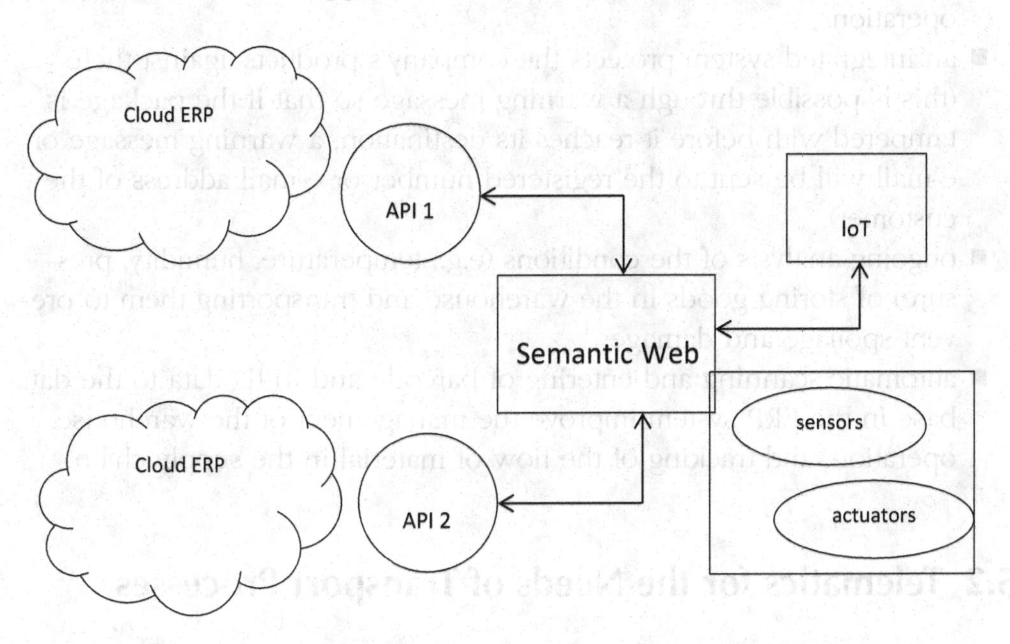

Where: Semantic Web – a project that aims to contribute to the creation and dissemination of standards for describing content on the Internet in a way that will allow machines and programs (e.g. agents) to process information in a manner appropriate to their meaning. API, or application programming interface, is a set of rules that allow data to be transferred between applications.

Figure 5.11 Model of the integration of IoT with ERP in the cloud.

Source: **Based on M. Tavana, V. Hajipour, S. Oveisi, IoT-based enterprise resource planning: Challenges, open issues, applications, architecture, and future research directions, https://doi.org/10.1016/j .iot.2020.100262 2542-6605.**

Where: Semantic Web – a project that aims to contribute to the creation and dissemination of standards for describing content on the internet in a way that will allow machines and programs (e.g., agents) to process information in a manner appropriate to their meaning. API, or application programming interface, is a set of rules that allow data to be transferred between applications.

Integrating IoT and ERP has many advantages, including:

- current, automatic notifications about stocks and missed deliveries by means of sensors and devices connected to the internet;
- IoT enables sending notifications to manufacturers in unplanned situations related to the product;
- ERP and IoT systems provide real-time data that reflect the situation (problem) and propose potential solutions; In fact, IoT will create unnecessary information that can be mined with ERP to improve operations;
- an integrated system protects the company's products against theft (this is possible through a warning message so that if the package is tampered with before it reaches its destination, a warning message or e-mail will be sent to the registered number or e-mail address of the customer);
- ongoing analysis of the conditions (e.g., temperature, humidity, pressure) of storing goods in the warehouse and transporting them to prevent spoilage and damage;
- automatic scanning and entering of barcode and RFID data to the database in the ERP system improve the management of the warehouse, operation, and tracking of the flow of material in the supply chain.

5.2 Telematics for the Needs of Transport Processes

Telematics is intelligent systems that combine the latest discoveries in the fields of telecommunications, IT, and automation. Thanks to them, it is possible to remotely transmit information between devices in real time, collect them using sensors, and process, analyze and transfer them to an IT system. Based on the data obtained, the administrator may take appropriate actions, for example, to increase security or optimize various business processes. Telematics is most often used in the transport, logistics, medical, energy and insurance industries (*Czym jest telematyka i jakie ma znaczenie w transporcie*?, 2022). The basic modules are (Figure 5.12) (Neumann, 2018): system providers, transport – its types, information – road, driver's work, emergency services, etc., databases, positioning systems, geographic information system, user.

Transport telematics is a branch of knowledge about transport, integrating information technology and telecommunications in applications for the needs of traffic management and control in transport systems, stimulating technical and organizational activities that enable increasing the operational efficiency and safety of these systems. Individual telematics solutions cooperate with each other, often under the control of a superior factor. Telematics in transport processes is associated with such concepts as:

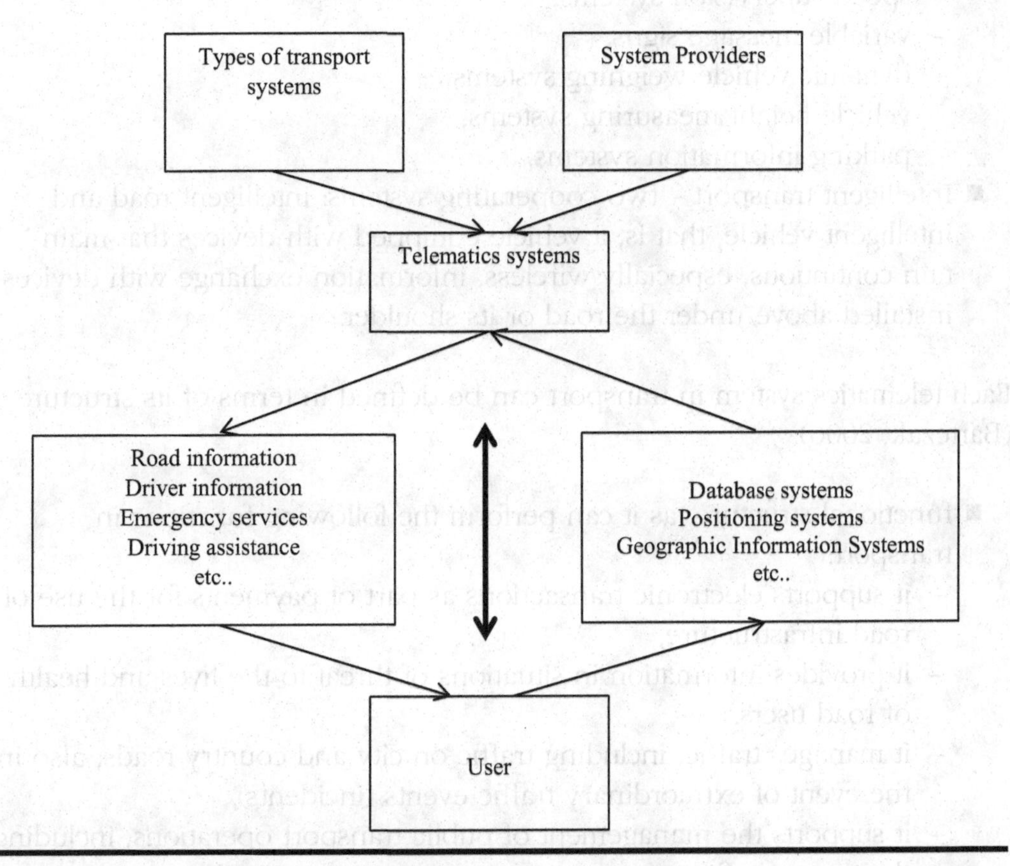

Figure 5.12 Telematics system modules.

Source: **Based on T. Neumann, The Importance of Telematics in the Transport System, [in:] TransNav the International Journal on Marine Navigation and Safety of Sea Transportation, Volume 12, Number 3, September 2018, p. 618.**

- Intelligent Transport Systems (ITS) that cover a wide range of technological solutions aimed at improving transport by increasing mobility and road safety. These systems combine many elements and activities aimed at improving broadly understood transport in terms of communication, prevention, traffic control and management, incident detection, supervision or elimination of traffic violations, etc. The ITS system includes, among others:
  - Traffic Management Centers,
  - integrated traffic management systems,
  - traffic control systems, including traffic light control,
  - public TMSs,
  - CCTV video monitoring systems (Nomad, 2022),[7]
  - ANPR video monitoring systems (Artr, 2022),[8]
  - speed supervision systems,
  - variable message signs,
  - dynamic vehicle weighing systems,
  - vehicle height measuring systems,
  - parking information systems.
- Intelligent transport – two cooperating systems: intelligent road and intelligent vehicle, that is, a vehicle equipped with devices that maintain continuous, especially wireless, information exchange with devices installed above/under the road or its shoulder.

Each telematics system in transport can be defined in terms of its structure (Bartczak, 2006):

- functional structure, as it can perform the following functions in transport:
  - it supports electronic transactions as part of payments for the use of road infrastructure,
  - it provides information in situations of threat to the lives and health of road users,
  - it manages traffic, including traffic on city and country roads, also in the event of extraordinary traffic events (incidents),
  - it supports the management of public transport operations, including the transport fleet,
  - it supports drivers in driving vehicles (navigation),
  - it provides information to passengers before and during the journey,

  - it supports the observance of legal regulations relating to road traffic,
  - it supports the management of transport operations;
- physical structure, which in transport includes, inter alia:
  - system centers, that is, places where data is collected and processed by computers, for example, traffic control centers (TCC), traffic information centers (TIC), cargo and vehicle management centers, etc.,
  - roadsides, that is, places where there are devices for traffic measurement, toll collection, providing information to drivers, etc.,
  - vehicles, that is, means of transport in which appropriate electronic (onboard) systems for the electronic exchange of information with the environment have been installed,
  - personal devices owned by the driver or passenger which enable them to communicate electronically with other elements of the telematics system,
  - devices installed on loading units, for example, containers and semitrailers, which can transmit or receive information electronically with the environment,
  - kiosks, i.e. devices available in public places that allow limited access to information resources stored in databases in the transport system;
- communication structure – individual physical places of the telematic system, where individual functions or groups of functions are performed, which must be electronically interconnected within a specific communication system (creation of an appropriate communication structure of the telematic system in transport requires the selection of appropriate information and telecommunications technologies that are generally available on the commercial market).

5.2.1. Monitoring of Automotive Means of Transport

The growing number of motor vehicles (Table 5.1) and new information and telecommunications technologies enable the introduction of integrated services involving the continuous localization of vehicles and automatic supervision of domestic and international transport.

Growing congestion on roads and railways, variable weather conditions, and various sudden road and rail events significantly affect the quality and safety of transport tasks. Mobile communication is becoming increasingly important in transport and in search and rescue operations.

Table 5.1 Motor vehicles and tractors registered in thousands of items

Description	*2010*	*2015*	*2019*	*2020*
Overall including	23,037	27,409	31,989	2,992
Cars	17,240	20,723	24,360	25,114
Coaches	97	110	123	125
Trucks and tractor units	2,982	3,428	3,883	3,999

Source: Based on *Mały rocznik statystyczny Polski 2021,* Warsaw (2021), p. 326.

Many companies, including Polish ones, produce countless devices which, in combination with other techniques and technologies, constitute a system for determining the position and data of the vehicle, which enables (Fletcher, 2022):

- automatic transmission of information about the route of the means of transport (constant monitoring);
- finding a vehicle, for example, a stolen one;
- remote immobilization of the vehicle, for example, in the event of theft;
- forwarding information related to the transport of hazardous materials to the relevant services to reduce the likelihood of a disaster and prevent its consequences;
- optimization of transport and operating costs (real-time data on speed, working time, and stops, as well as planning routes for safety reasons, that is, traffic intensity, repairs, weather conditions, road surface conditions);
- increasing safety by identifying dangerous road events and easily protecting fleets against claims;
- integration of vehicles with an intelligent camera, which allows visual monitoring of events on the road;
- tracking weather conditions;
- online transport management (elimination of empty runs and unused cargo space, quick reaction in case of unforeseen events, such as accidents or theft);
- effective use of means of transport and human potential (timely preparation of unloading, quick response to disturbances in transport planning).

The monitoring system provides, among other things (Szulc, 2021):

- real-time localization of transport facilities using GPS;
- monitoring of facilities with the use of detailed digital city maps and road maps of Poland and Europe;
- round-the-clock access to current and archival information on the location of facilities;
- cheap and fast data transmission thanks to the use of GPRS packet data transmission;
- activation of the alarm mode by the motion sensor system in the event of an unforeseen tilt or movement of the vehicle;
- effective 24/7 protection against vehicle and cargo theft;
- assembly performed in a way that prevents unauthorized persons from accessing the GPS receiver and ensures its undetectability;
- vehicle fleet management;
- supporting the settlement of the operating costs of means of transport through automated data exchange (this feature is not common in other described systems).

To establish communication with the selected transport object, the monitoring system connects via the Internet or SMS with a GSM station using a special terminal. Then the vehicle (equipped with a location and transmission controller) sends the necessary information to the GSM station via two alternative routes, that is, via GPRS or SMS. The GSM station sends the collected data to the monitoring station (monitoring center).

All data from sensors located in different parts of the means of transport comes to the computer marked as 11, as shown in Figure 5.13. In practice, the following elements can be used:

1. container detection and identification sensor;
2. load stability sensor;
3. authorization reader;
4. accident sensor;
5. temperature sensor;
6. trailer ID;
7. fuel tank opening sensor;
8. GSP module;
9. GSM module;
10. satellites;
11. computer.

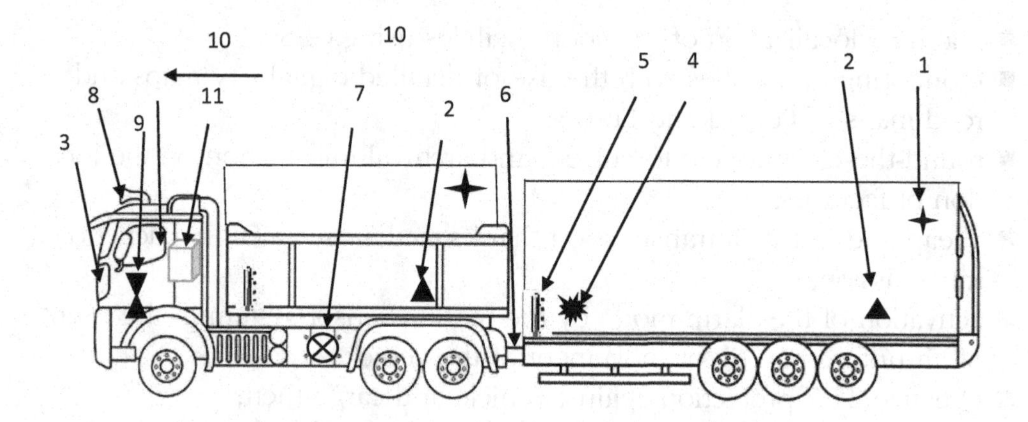

1 - container detection and identification sensor; 2 - load stability sensor; 3 - authorization reader; 4 - accident sensor; 5 - temperature sensor; 6 - trailer ID; 7 - fuel tank opening sensor; 8 - GSP module; 9 - GSM module; 10 - satellites; 11 - computer.

Figure 5.13 Diagram of a satellite vehicle tracking system.

Source: **Based on W. Drewek, *Monitorowanie ładunków niebezpiecznych w transporcie drogowym,* [in:] Logistyka 5/2011, p. 516.**

- Container detection and identification sensor – detection of the presence of a container activates the RFID transponder reader located at the rear of the vehicle cabin. Depending on the method of loading, each container is equipped with one or two RFID transponders. The reader identifies the unique code assigned to each of them. The collected information about the presence (from the presence sensor) and the unique code (transponder reader) of the container are transferred to the central unit (computer), from where, along with the information about the geographical position of the vehicle and time, it is sent to the dispatcher (or driver) (System identyfikacji kontenerów, 2022).
- Load stability sensor (several may be mounted) makes it possible to check whether the load is present on the vehicle and whether the load is in the position in which it was placed during loading. After loading, the container (packaging) is "detected" – waves reflecting from the surface of the packaging confirm its presence and distance from the edge of the walls of the truck box or container. The sensor controls and activates the RFID reader. The reader identifies the code assigned to each sensor (Drewek, 2011).
- Accident sensors send an alarm signal to the GPS/GSM system by providing coordinates. An accident is understood as a collision or rollover

of the vehicle around any axis. Immediately after one of such events, an alarm signal is sent to the central unit, which in turn sends a message to the dispatcher's server and phone number 112.

- Fuel Cap Opening Sensors – fuel cap protection for trucks and machines is a device mounted on fuel filler caps to monitor and control their opening and closing. The device operates based on radio access control (RFID) technology, so any attempts to interfere with it will result in signaling the violation with SMS or e-mail notification. The assembly consists in replacing the existing plug with a special cast permanently attached to the fuel filler (Czujnik zabezpieczający – skuteczne monitorowanie poziomu paliwa, 2022).
- Temperature sensor, for example, in a car refrigerator – the data is transmitted to the system and, together with other information about the monitored vehicle, is a valuable material for analysis. Mounting such a sensor on the refrigerated truck enables continuous temperature control of the transported goods. It additionally enables independent and remote control of the operation of the aggregate, while also protecting against unjustified accusations from contractors claiming that goods have been transported under inappropriate conditions. The use of a digital sensor ensures high measurement accuracy and does not require any additional calibrations.
- Trailer sensor – identifier in the form of a chip, mounted in the socket of the coiled cable coupling the trailer (semi-trailer) with the tractor. Used where interchangeable use of trailers (semi-trailers) is possible. It allows you to create documentation of trailers' work.
- Opening sensor, most often transponder (chip with a unique number read by radio). It allows the control of the opening of flaps, doors, etc.

5.3 Traceability in the Supply Chain

Traceability,[9] or the TTC (Track, Trace and Control) system, enables:

- tracking (tracing) the product, from the moment it is created from raw materials until it reaches the last customer in the supply chain, both at the top and bottom;
- registration of parameters identifying these goods and any location covered by the flow.

The TTC system can be used in the food industry, pharmacy, and cosmetics sectors.

The use of traceability in the above-mentioned areas was enforced by the following regulations of the European Commission:

- 178/2002 and 1935/2004 on materials and articles intended to come into contact with food;
- 852/2004 of April 29, 2004, on the hygiene of foodstuffs.
- 1224/2009 on fish products, the requirements of which apply from January 1, 2013;
- 1223/2009 on cosmetic products, the requirements of which apply from July 11, 2013;
- 995/2010 on timber and timber products, the requirements of which apply from March 3, 2013.

In this regard, national laws have also been issued in Poland, such as:

- the Act of August 25, 2006, on Food and Nutrition Safety (Ustawa z dnia 25 sierpnia 2006 r. o bezpieczeństwie żywności i żywienia);
- the Act of July 28, 2005, amending the Act on Health Conditions of Food and Nutrition and certain other acts (Ustawa z dnia 30 października 2003 r. o zmianie ustawy o warunkach zdrowotnych żywności i żywienia oraz niektórych innych ustaw);
- The Act of January 29, 2004, on Veterinary Requirements for Products of Animal Origin (Ustawa z dnia 29 stycznia 2004 r. o wymaganiach weterynaryjnych dla produktów pochodzenia zwierzęcego).

Traceability makes it possible to precisely identify the processes of the material stream implemented on the market of suppliers and recipients, provided that all participants comply with the same rules and regulations, for example, based on GS1 standards and the requirements of the European Union. The basic GS1 standards include:

- identification of trade items (goods) – GTIN (GTIN-8, GTIN-12, GTIN-13, GTIN-14);
- logistic unit identification (SSCC);
- location identification (GLN);
- description of the standards (barcodes, EPC, eCom[10] electronic messages, etc.).

The above-mentioned standards define and ensure that (Hałas, 2012):

- all tracked goods or loads are recognizable thanks to the use of the same identifiers;
- the identification remains on the goods/cargo throughout its tracking;
- all locations (modal points) are identified with GLNs throughout the supply chain;
- data on products and their physical flow are collected and made available according to rules agreed upon between trading partners (e.g., using GDSN, EDI messages, and EPCIS internet solutions).

The operational model of the traceability system in the supply chain is presented in Figure 5.14.

The basic elements of the model are:

- retailers – points of sale (1A… 1N);
- distribution center (2);
- producer (3);

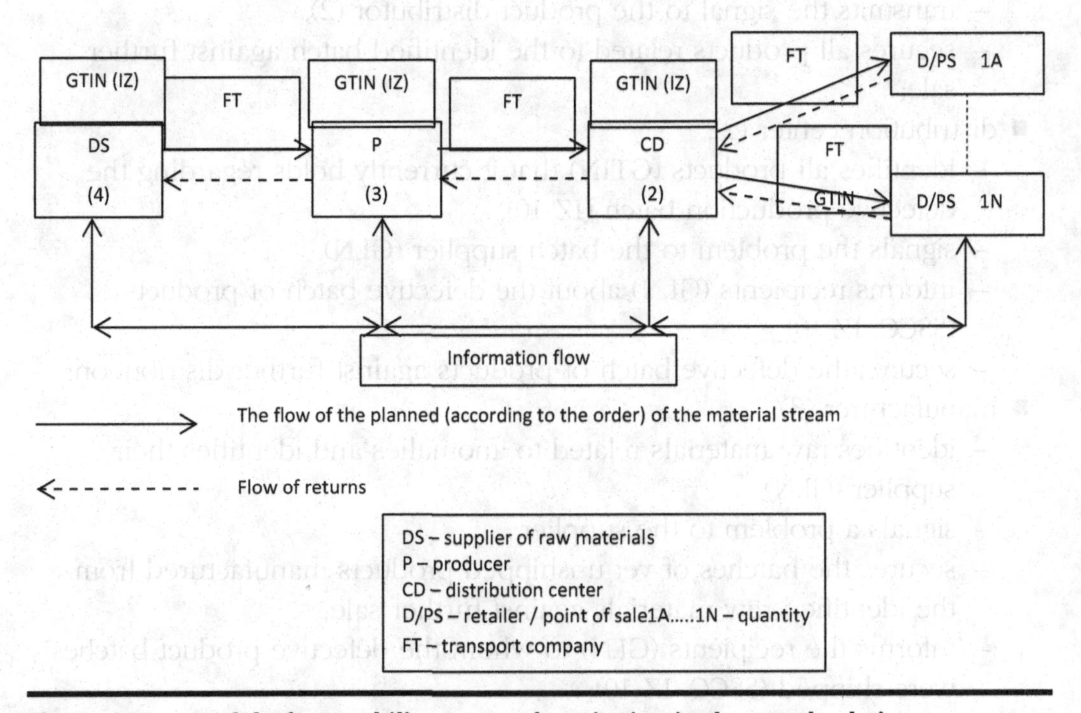

Figure 5.14 Model of traceability system functioning in the supply chain.

***Source:* own elaboration.**

- supplier of raw materials (4);
- suppliers (transport companies) who deliver raw materials and products to the entities;
- an information system ensuring the flow of information between the links in the supply chain.

If the supply chain model works smoothly, the flow of the material stream follows the orders placed successively by retailers/points of sale (1A … 1N) to the distribution center (2), then to the producer (3), and then to the supplier of raw materials (4).

In the event of difficulties with the quality of products, previously developed procedures are launched, which allow for quick action to eliminate the emerging disturbance. Thanks to the applied standards and appropriate IT technologies, in the case of delivering a defective product to the final consumer, actions are taken and (Sokołowski, 2014):

- retailer – point of sale (1A):
  - identifies the name of the defective product, its number (GTIN), supplier (GLN), production batch number (IZ 10),
  - transmits the signal to the product distributor (2),
  - secures all products related to the identified batch against further sale;
- distribution center (2):
  - identifies all products (GTIN) that it currently holds regarding the defective production batch (IZ 10),
  - signals the problem to the batch supplier (GLN),
  - informs recipients (GLN) about the defective batch of products (SSCC, IZ 10),
  - secures the defective batch of products against further distribution;
- manufacturer (3):
  - identifies raw materials related to anomalies and identifies their supplier (GLN),
  - signals a problem to the supplier,
  - secures the batches of yet unshipped products manufactured from the identified raw materials against further sale,
  - informs the recipients (GLN) to whom the defective product batches were shipped (SSCC, IZ 10);
- supplier of raw materials (4):
  - analyzes the cause of the problem – finds and confirms the cause,

  - informs all recipients (GLN) about the essence of the problem and discloses the number of the affected batch of raw materials (IZ 10),
  - identifies all goods shipped from these shipment batches (SSCC),
  - protects the remaining raw materials that belong to these batches against further use;
- producer (3) – based on historical data:
  - finds defective batches of products produced in the past;
  - identifies the SSCC numbers of the boxes and pallets containing the product lots to be delivered
  - withdraws them,
  - identifies the recipients (distribution center 3) of defective products (GLN) and provides them with information about the products to be returned (SSCC, GTIN, IZ 10);
- distribution center – based on additional data received from the manufacturer (3):
  - identifies boxes and pallets (GTIN, SSCC) to be returned,
  - removes and returns defective products from the distribution center (GTIN, SSCC),
  - provides retailers and points of sale (1A… 1N) with SSCC and/or GTINs and batch numbers of shipped items to be removed;
- retailer – point of sale (1A… .1N):
  - retailers identify suspicious products (knowing the GTIN, batch number IZ10) and return them to the supplier–distribution center (2).
- The tracking system is also increasingly used in:
- manufacturing companies from the OEM[11] sector;
- automotive industry (e.g., identification of parts/components used in the automotive sector – led by GS1 Germany);
- the financial sector (e.g., global transaction identification – administered by GS1);
- the catering industry (improving food safety);
- healthcare (e.g., patient service, records of fixed assets).

Traceability is also a system for the automatic tracking of a production batch (Figure 5.15). Using barcode or RFID labels, the system records all operations involving a given batch or product and thus makes it possible to (Szymonik, 2015):

- reconstruct product genealogy (who, when, on which machine, from what raw material, with what process parameters);

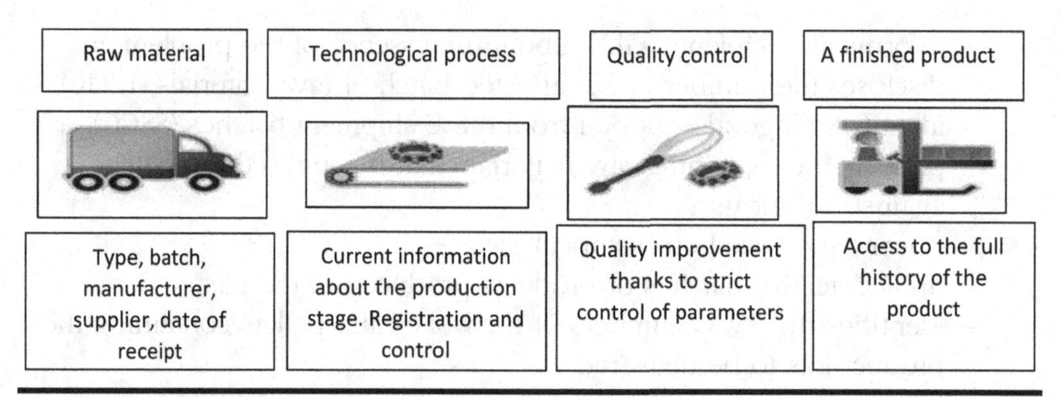

Figure 5.15 Traceability in tracking production batches.
Source: **Based on A.Szymonik, Informatyka dla potrzeb logistyka(i), Difin, Warszawa (2015), p. 127.**

- control the correctness of the course of the process (whether all activities have been performed, in the correct sequence and at the right time intervals);
- search for the numbers of all suspected batches.

In manufacturing companies, MES (Manufacturing Execution Systems) IT systems are used for traceability. These systems use appropriate IT technologies, software, automation components, and data collected directly from production stations. The entire process takes place in real time, which enables the transfer of data to the area of business (Jaworska, 2022).

Thanks to the functionality of the system, it is possible to obtain immediate feedback on the level of production performance, make the right decisions and react to irregularities occurring during the production process on an ongoing basis. The data obtained from the production process enables the analysis of key performance indicators in production and obtaining an accurate picture of the use of production capacity. The functions of the MES system include (Jaworska, 2022):

- flow tracking, production genealogy;
- real-time production tracking and visualization;
- tracking the real-time productivity of machines and people,
- downtime tracking,
- registration of downtime causes,
- planning the execution of production orders and controlling their execution at the operational level,

- updating inventories of materials, semi-finished products, and final products,
- collecting information on the quality of production,
- generating automatic reports, analysis of collected information,
- settlement of production costs.
- Traceability using the global GS1 traceability standard has both its (Visayadamrong, 2013):
- advantages – all traceability partners share a common standard, which makes it easy to share and transfer data throughout the supply chain (tracking is efficient and accurate); and
- disadvantages – all traceability partners must use the same GS1, which requires a large investment in hardware and software (very often small businesses cannot afford such high costs).

5.4. e-Logistics

e-Logistics can be defined as:

- all services supporting the functioning of supply chains, which are not related in any way to the physical movement of goods, nor are they connected with the possession of warehouses or any means of transport (Flis, 2009);
- a system organizing the flow of the material stream with the use of information technology;
- a logistics department that uses the Internet and IT systems for cooperation and integration in supply chains and networks (*Leksykon transportowy*, 2022).

The analysis of these and other definitions leads to the following conclusions:

First. The processes carried out in e-logistics relate[12] to data and information sent between the links in the supply chain and they also relate to the product (e.g., price, warranty, method of delivery, and parameters). The most frequently used communication tool is the internet and mobile devices (e.g., tablets, smartphones, smartwatches, notebooks, laptops, iPads, iPhones, etc.). **Second.** The customer ordering the product bypasses the processes related to storage, distribution, and transport. **Third**. The providers of e-logistics services are production and service companies, including transport companies, electronic markets, wholesalers, warehouses, and logistics centers. **Fourth.** Like any service, it has its positive and negative sides. Always in business transactions, the good and bad sides should be taken into account as well as the fact that one should always manage trust and risk. In practice, e-logistics is often associated with:

- electronic business (e-business) – all (commercial and production) processes are carried out through the exchange of information by electronic means;
- e-commerce (electronic commerce) is defined as a series of activities performed in order to make a transaction by electronic means of communication
- electronic commerce (also known as e-commerce) – part of a business activity involving the purchase/sale of (tangible and intangible) products by specialized enterprises via the Internet (Konopielko et al., 2016).
- online sales – a set of activities that are to persuade a potential customer to purchase the offered goods or services using an online platform (this is one of the parties to the transaction in e-commerce; its basic forms are: online auctions, classified websites, online stores, online shopping malls, electronic markets, and virtual stock exchanges) (*Encyklopedia zarządzania* 2022).

The terms listed above are used interchangeably and this applies to practice and vocabulary used in the literature on the subject. It should be emphasized that e-logistics, can be defined as a branch of logistics involving the use of the latest information technologies (including the internet) to carry out processes related to supply, production, distribution, transport, customer service, information flow in the micro (e.g., a single enterprise) or macro (e.g., by participants in the global supply chain) dimension. Thus, e-logistics includes activities that relate to procurement, production, and distribution in the micro dimension and processes implemented in supply chains in the macro dimension. Coordination of the flow of material with the support of e-logistics may concern:

- production companies (including supply, production, distribution, internal and external transport, and disposal);
- service enterprises;

- intermediaries (e.g. distributors, wholesalers, retailers, dealers, agents);
- transport companies;
- links that are participants in the supply chain;
- government and self-government administration entities;
- other economic systems.

It is in e-logistics that first, all order details (how much, where, when) are agreed upon, most often via the internet or mobile devices, and then the product is physically moved, possibly without storage, from the sender (producer) directly to the recipient (retailer, consumer) by transport companies.

Apart from placing an order, the basic areas which are dealt with by e-logistics include:

- supplying companies with goods necessary for production;
- warehouse management;
- movement of goods and products to consumers;
- organization of internal and external transport;
- after-sales service;
- market research and consumer behavior research.

A component of e-logistics is e-commerce,[13] which includes transactions carried out over networks, based on the IP protocol and over other computer networks. Goods and services are ordered through these networks, but payment and final delivery of the ordered goods or services can be made online or offline. Transactions can be made between businesses, individuals, government agencies, or other private and public organizations.

In the literature on the subject, one can find various forms of e-commerce distribution between:

- B2B (Business-to-Business) companies – business exchange between enterprises, thanks to specialized IT programs;
- the company and the consumer (B2C, Business to Customer), an example are online stores organized by the manufacturer, which are eagerly used by individual recipients;
- C2C (Customer-to-Customer) consumers, for example, individual internet auctions, internet sales;

- the consumer and a C2B (Customer to Business) company, for example, an individual proposes a product (service) that the economic entity is interested in.

In addition, e-commerce facilitates the following solutions:

- B2E (Business-to-Employee) – relations between the employing company and its employees;
- B2G (Business-to-Government) – relations between an economic entity and public administration;
- e-Government (e-Gov) – the market of electronic contacts between the government and government administration institutions and their environment – in the following three combinations:
  - Government-to-Citizen (G2C), also referred to as Government-to Public (G2P) – concerns the contacts of government administration with citizens;
  - Government-to-Government (G2G) – includes contacts between government institutions;
  - Government-to-Business (G2B) – involves streamlining the offer of government administration for companies.

Another typology distinguishes the following types of distribution in e-commerce (e-commerce, 2022):

- direct (also known as the catalog system or e-Procurement) – the entire transaction takes place, in this case, exclusively in the network, based on electronic catalogs and supporting IT systems;
- indirect (also known as auction and tender) – the order is placed and payment is made via the network, but the specific item or service is delivered using the traditional method;
- hybrid – where various transitional forms are used.

5.4.1 Modern Tools to Improve e-Logistics

Distribution support tools include:

- GDSN – Global Data Synchronization Network;
- ERP – enterprise resource management system;
- CRM – customer relationship management system;
- SCM – supply chain management system.

GDSN is (Synchronizacja-danych, 2022):

- a network of compatible electronic catalogs;
- possibility of systematic creation of safe, synchronized, up-to-date data;
- consistent data on a specific unit online.

The Global Data Synchronization Network consists of:

- Global Register that contains identifiers of all goods from certified databases, this register communicates with all certified data catalogs using standard registration and subscription messages;
- certified catalogs that are based on the Global Product Classification (GPC)[14];
- standards for communication between directories.
- The following GS1 identifiers are used under GDS (Synchronizacja-danych, 2022):
- Global Trade Item Numbers (GTINs);
- Global Location Numbers (GLN).

The order of data exchange between the recipient and the supplier in the GDSN network is as follows:

- The supplier enters the product data into their home electronic catalog that is affiliated with GDSN, and the catalog then publishes the information in the GDSN register.
- At the same time, the data recipient (retailer) searches for data in their home directory; this activity is performed by subscription, that is, electronic subscription to data. If the recipient's home directory does not find the requested information, it will automatically direct the subscription to the GDSN Registry. At the same time, the register, upon recognizing the location of the requested information, sends the subscription of the commercial network to the appropriate supplier's directory.
- The supplier directory, when it receives a subscription from the GDSN Registry, establishes a direct connection to the data recipient directory. As a result of this operation, the supplier's catalog sends the requested product information to the home directory of the retail network.
- In order to close all operations, electronic confirmations are returned between the participants of the master data exchange.

5.4.2 e-Commerce – Advantages and Disadvantages

E-logistics is most often associated with e-commerce and includes online sales of physical goods and digital products, online sales of intangible digital products, intellectual property, digital services, real-time auctions, ticket sales, utility bill charges, electronic banking, and internet markets.

Some of the advantages of e-commerce for making transactions include (Figure 5.16) (Dasza, 2022) (Exploring the Advantages and Disadvantages of Ecommerce, 2022):

- Online shopping accelerates the receipt of the desired product and saves customers time and effort. Instead of going from store to store in search of an item, you can check if it is available in a store or not. You can shop anywhere using mobile devices.
- It can provide detailed information about the product (product description with photos).
- Shopping personalization – using cookies, you can collect information about the customer, and then obtain accurate information about who

Figure 5.16 Advantages of e-commerce.

Source: **Based on M. Dasza, *What are Ecommerce Advantages and Disadvantages?*, https: //belvg.com/blog/what-is-advantage-and-disadvantage-of-e-commerce.html, 3/6/2022.**

they are, for example, gender, age, interests, etc. Using this data, you can configure your store to automatically offer customers the products they may be most interested in.

- e-commerce works without space or time constraints. Payment can be made even without a credit card. The online store accepts orders around the clock.
- Running a brick-and-mortar store is a fairly costly activity (facility rental, utility bills, insurance, warehouse maintenance, and staff compensation. There are a large number of operational costs to be aware of, such as repair bills, employee training, advertising costs, and so on. e-commerce sites do not have to pay for a physical location.

The disadvantages of e-commerce at the stage of making transactions include (Ferreira, 2022): no possibility of buying while a site is down, no possibility for customers to test, touch, or try before buying, the possibility

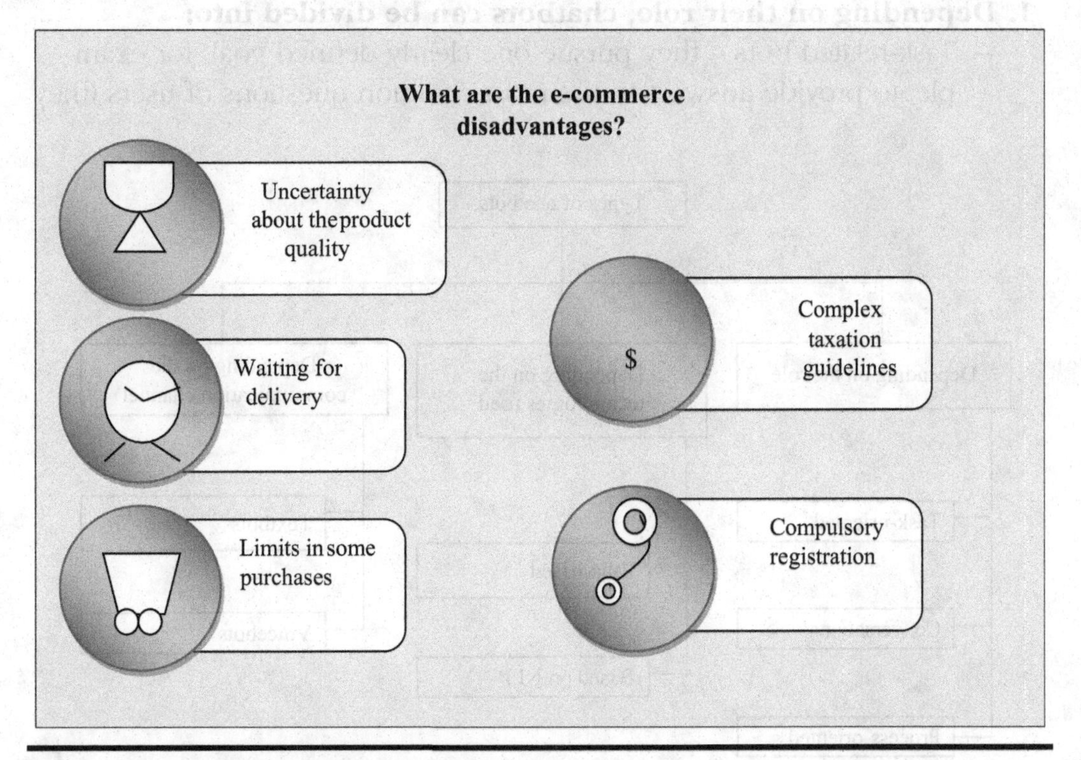

Figure 5.17 Disadvantages of e-commerce.

Source: **Based on M. Dasza, *What are Ecommerce Advantages and Disadvantages?*, https://belvg.com/blog/what-is-advantage-and-disadvantage-of-e-commerce.html, 3/6/2022.**

of some customers becoming impatient, the risk that shipping times may be long, uncertainty about the quality of the product, the need to wait for the product to be delivered, the difficulty for some items to be bought online. See illustration in Figure 5.17.

5.5 Chatbots in the Supply Chain

Chatbot (Bilińska, 2022)[15] is a computer program that interacts with the user through natural (human) language or text. It has become a consultant with whom you can talk, get answers to frequently asked questions, obtain information, book a ticket, or solve any problem related to a product, logistics, or service (Zając & Barabasz, 2022).

Chatbots can be divided into three groups (Figure 5.18) (Rodzaje chatbotów – wirtualnych asystentów, 2022).

1. **Depending on their role, chatbots can be divided into:**
   - Task-related bots – they pursue one clearly defined goal, for example, to provide answers to the most common questions of users (they

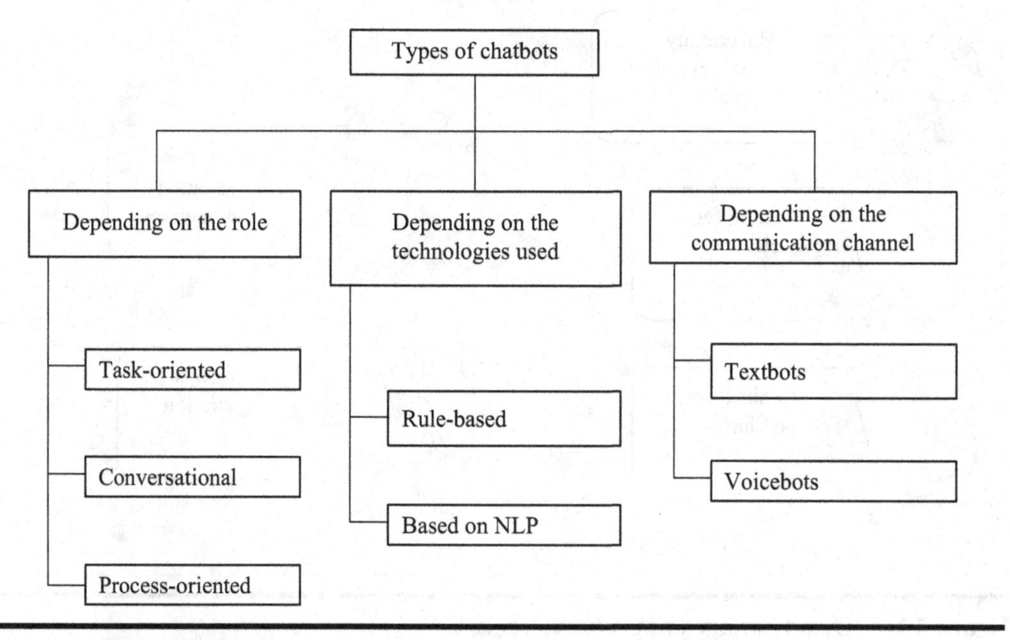

Figure 5.18 Chatbot types.
Source: Based on *Rodzaje chatbotów – wirtualnych asystentów,* https://www.polski-chatbot.pl/rodzaje-chatbotow, 3/20/2022.

are successfully implemented by commands without the support of artificial intelligence).
- Conversational bots – they communicate with users on a level similar to a conversation with a human being. They are developed with the use of artificial intelligence so that they can "learn" based on the conducted conversations. At the same time, it is good practice to introduce certain restrictions using rules that exclude side effects.
- Process-related bots – more and more organizations are trying to create bots that will be able to independently carry out the selected process/processes in the organization. Such a bot does not have to be a master of conversation on every topic; it is rather a variant of a task bot which, however, does not perform just one action but can guide the user through the entire process.

2. **Depending on the type of technology used by bots, they can be divided into:**
   - Rule-based bots – also often referred to as Gen 1 bots – that do not use machine learning (Machine Learning, 2022).[16] The database created for this purpose makes it possible to answer specific questions. A good example is the FAQ.[17]
   - Bots based on NLP[18] – they use natural language processing. NLP is an area of artificial intelligence research, one of the tasks of which is the natural interaction between the computer and humans. This technology helps machines understand human speech and communicate with its use, using, i.a., learning algorithms.
   - Mixed bots – this type of bot is most commonly used nowadays because it combines the advantages of both technologies mentioned above.

3. **Depending on the communication channel, chatbots are divided into:**
   - Textbots – the user, using written text, asks a question in the chatbot window and receives the answer there. They are popular on websites in social media messengers.
   - Voicebots – (also known as voice assistants) are another incarnation of virtual advisers. Voicebot is a computer program dedicated to operating in the voice channel, which allows this specific type of chatbot to move to new fields of use. It is a tool powered by artificial intelligence with great potential to generate business benefits and create new quality in the organization.

The logistics activities are currently based on modern tools and instruments, including automation, robotization, GS1 standards, e-commerce, automatic identification, and IT systems. The analysis of the literature shows that chatbots are widely used in the management of material flows along the supply chain. Whether it is cargo tracking, product inventory management, CRM updates, team coordination, meeting scheduling, or warehouse management, they help the logistics industry and monitor customer performance and experience (Importance of Chatbots for Logistics and Supply-Chain, 2022). Chatbots in logistics services are integrated with other technologies, which include (Lahoti, 2022):

- IoT, which combines sensors, meters, and meters for measuring warehouse temperature, and humidity, selected important elements from warehouse management, transport, and its possibilities in one system. This allows for ongoing monitoring of material flow along the supply chain both in its top and bottom parts. The data obtained from IoT facilitate online control under the physicochemical conditions prevailing in, for example, a warehouse.
- Voice recognition, which makes it easier, for example, for logisticians to perform automatic identification during picking in a warehouse or to communicate with people who carry out logistic processes.
- Big Data – chatbots collect and store all conversations with customers, suppliers, managers, personnel, and drivers, and thus are a source of data that can be used by logistics specialists to analyze them and manage processes carried out within the supply chain.

As practice shows, chatbots are used to improve the following ten logistics processes (Patel, 2022; Rathod, 2022; Shah, 2021):

- **First.** Chatbots facilitate the management of orders from receipt to execution. They make it possible to track the status of deliveries.
- **Second.** Chatbots receive customer inquiries, problems, and complaints and help customers find possible solutions. This increases the value of the basic service that customers expect and keeps them satisfied.
- **Third.** Logistics chatbots can receive delivery terms from customers, send order details and process them. They can issue receipts and invoices for the order. They support shipping space, time booking, and online tracking. For any documentation work, users can provide full details of products that need shipping and pay online.

- **Fourth.** Logistics chatbots facilitate real-time analysis of data related to customer orders.
- **Fifth.** Possibility to send news, promotions, and discounts directly to the messenger of a specific user.
- **Sixth.** Possibility to automate the warehouse with the use of intelligent bots to improve the picking process or finding goods.
- **Seventh.** Chatbots are helpful for planning the delivery of goods in accordance with orders, thanks to the use of IoT devices and sensors. This system can, for example, provide information on changing the delivery date of goods.
- **Eighth.** The integration of chatbots with GPS makes it possible to supervise the route, the operation of the vehicle, and the driver's work in transport.
- **Ninth.** Chatbots in the supply chain can enable the (future) use of driverless vehicles to save costs and improve delivery schedules.
- **Tenth.** Chatbots enable 24/7 customer support in the industry.

Notes

1 Collaborative – cooperation and communication in business.

2 OLAP – tools that enable multidimensional analysis of business data collected in warehouses and personalized access to analysis results using selected communication media (*Encyklopedia zarządzania*, https://mfiles.pl/pl/index.php/Systemy_OLAP, 7/25/2022).

3 Data mining is an analytical process designed to analyze large amounts of data (usually related to economic or market issues) for regular patterns and systematic interrelationships between variables, and then to evaluate the results by applying the detected patterns to new data subsets (Techniki zgłębiania danych (data mining), https://www.statsoft.pl/, 7/25/2022).

4 NFC – short-range, high-frequency communication, allowing for wireless data exchange at a distance of up to 20 centimeters.

5 API stand for Application Programming Interface that enables communication and connection between software components and network applications, as well as data exchange between separate systems (https://xsale.ai/czego-jest-api-i-do- co-you-can-go-use /, 2/28/2022).

6 FMS is a fleet vehicle maintenance management program for ensuring online connectivity between the service, the Euromaster headquarters (vehicle and user database) and the fleet headquarters.

7 CCTV stands for closed circuit television. Generally, a CCTV system is understood as a set of cooperating devices for receiving, processing, transmitting, archiving and displaying video and sound in monitored facilities (Nomad, http://nomad.com.pl/cctv/ 3/17/2022).

8 ANPR is used to recognize and search motor vehicles identified on the basis of registration plate numbers. The system registers the vehicle, along with the time and place of its stay, and automatically recognizes and assigns the vehicle registration numbers to the numbers entered in the system (Artr, http://www.artr.eu/, 3/17/2022).
9 Traceability – another term for tracking.
10 GS1 eCom is a set of standard electronic messages that allow companies to transfer business data quickly, efficiently and accurately between trading partners electronically, in the form of classic Electronic Data Exchange messages – EDI or as XML documents.
11 OEM (Original Equipment Manufacturer) – a company that sells its own brand products made by other companies. The term is misleading because OEM is not always a manufacturer, but sometimes only a seller of end-user equipment, although it also happens to be its designer.
12 Business – a profit-making commercial or production enterprise; colloquially also: the company carrying out this project, (http://sjp.pwn.pl, 2/20/2022).
13 Orders received by phone, fax or e-mail are not part of e-commerce.
14 Identification keys themselves do not provide sufficient information and therefore they have been supplemented with defined attributes, such as: location description, price, size, packaging, name, address, etc. One of the newly developed attributes is the Global Product Classification (GPC). This classification makes it possible to determine what kind of commodity the identified product is and to which group of goods it belongs. GPC plays a key role in the process of searching for goods in the GDS network.
15 In practice, chatbot is often treated as a synonym of bot. However, it should be remembered that bot – short for the word robot; in the world of information technology, it means a program functioning in a space intended for humans and simulating the behavior of a living user. Conversational chatbots and voicebots are a special type of bots, O. Bilińska, *Nie każdy bot to chatbot – poznaj różnice* (https://kodabots.com/blog/nie-kazdy-bot-to-chatbot-poznaj-roznice/, 3/20/2022).
16 Machine Learning is a branch of Artificial Intelligence and Computer Science that focuses on using data and algorithms to mimic the way people learn, gradually improving accuracy, Machine Learning (https://www.ibm.com/pl-pl/cloud/learn/machine-learning, 3/21/2022).
17 FAQ (Frequently Asked Questions) – is a database of questions with answers so that the user can quickly find the answer to their problem.
18 NLP – neuro-linguistic programming, an ordered set of communication techniques and methods of working with images, aimed at creating and modifying humanlike patterns of perception and thinking (https://pl.wikipedia.org/wiki/Programowanie_neurolingwistyczne, 3/20/2022).

Chapter 6

Use of Renewable Energy Sources in Logistics

6.1 Selected Renewable Energy Sources

Modern logistics cannot function without energy, which is used by many devices that allow the movement of the material stream and people from the point of sending to the point of receipt carried out by TFL (transport, forwarding, logistics) companies. A similar situation applies to the flow of information necessary to communicate between participants in the supply chain.

In practice, in logistics companies, renewable energy can be used for lighting, HVAC (heating, ventilation, and air conditioning), loading forklifts and any electrical devices in a traditional warehouse system, charging electric cars, and ensuring transshipment in cross-docking warehouses.

Today, the energy of the future does not harm the environment, is not based on fossil resources, and is obtained from renewable energy sources (RES), also known as green electricity sources. RES can be successfully used in logistics (in storage and transport) because:

- they have an inexhaustible potential;
- they are stable and durable;
- they significantly reduce electricity and heating bills;
- they have a low environmental impact (in principle, they do not emit harmful by-products of combustion to the environment);
- heating buildings with RES is much safer than with most traditional sources, such as boilers (devices using renewable energy for heating are

DOI: 10.4324/9781003372615-7

practically failure-free, most of them have long-term guarantees, and in the event of complications, they do not cause a fire);
- heat pumps and similar devices can be used like air conditioning (for heating and cooling);
- investments in RES, which are energy-saving and environmentally friendly, boost the image and value of TFL companies;
- energy can be stored in moments of its surplus;
- they ensure independence from large commercial or state-owned energy suppliers.

However, it should be remembered that RES cannot provide energy continuously, as the sun is not always shining, the wind is not blowing everywhere, and sometimes we cannot ensure adequate water levels in rivers and streams. Energy shortages in warehouses that require special conditions (e.g., temperature, humidity) to keep stocks, can lead to large financial losses. What should also be considered are the costs of installing RES, which may discourage some investors. Other disadvantages of renewable energy include:

- environmental impact of some types of RES, for example, geothermal energy, the use of which may cause negative gas emissions to the atmosphere or contamination of deep waters;
- impact on the landscape and the natural environment (e.g., photovoltaic (PV) farms and other RES).

The most commonly used RES include wind, liquid biofuel, biogas, heat pumps, solar radiation, water, sun, and geothermal energy. The structure of energy obtained from RES in Poland in 2017–2019 is presented in Table 6.1.

Poland, compared to other countries in the EU, has nothing to boast of when it comes to energy production with regard to three parameters: fossil fuels, nuclear energy, and renewable energy. In 2020, for the first time in history, more energy in the entire European Union came from RES than from fossil fuels (Figure 6.1) (Rogala, 2021).

Wind energy is one of the oldest types of renewable energy used by man. It was the kinetic energy of moving air masses that drove grain mills, sawmill equipment and drainage pumps, and recently wind turbines. The latter, often grouped into so-called farms, produce green electricity that reaches households and businesses. The wind turbine consists of several essential elements (Energia z wiatru, 2021):

Table 6.1 The share of individual renewable energy carriers in total energy from renewable sources in 2017–2019, in% in Poland

Description	*2017*	*2018*	*2019*
Solid biofuels	66.94	68.06	65.56
Wind energy	13.82	12.19	13.72
Liquid biofuels	9.89	10.03	10.36
Biogas	3.02	3.19	3.15
Heat pumps	1.98	2.,37	2.69
Water energy	2.37	1.88	1.78
Solar energy	1.40	0.92	1.40
Municipal waste	1.00	1.09	1.08
Geothermal energy	0.24	0.26	0.26

Source: Based on Statistics Poland, Statistical Publishing Establishment, Warsaw (2020), p. 67.

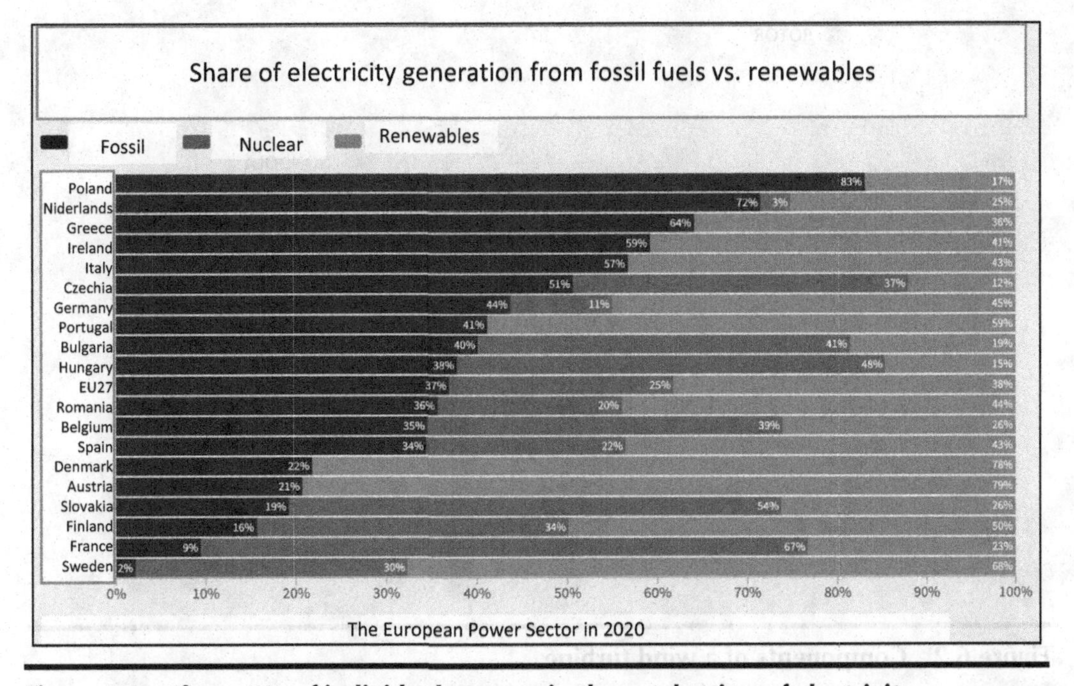

Figure 6.1 Share (%) of individual sources in the production of electricity.

Source: **Based on The European Power Sector in 2020, 25/1/2021**

- A tower enabling the location of the turbine at a significant height, where the gusts of wind are much stronger.
- A movable gondola that makes it possible to set the turbine in the direction of the blowing wind. With the motor and gear installed at the top of the tower, the turbine can be rotated 360 degrees. The nacelle is an element in which the generator and the systems controlling all devices are located;
- A rotor that converts the kinetic energy of the wind into electricity. Typically, three blades are mounted on an axis (although designs with two or more blades are also common).

The elements of the wind turbine are shown below (Figure 6.2).

In practice, wind farms are also used to produce energy on a smaller scale, only for the needs of a single building. Such a wind farm consists of the following elements: wind turbine, meter, cabling, and battery. Small wind

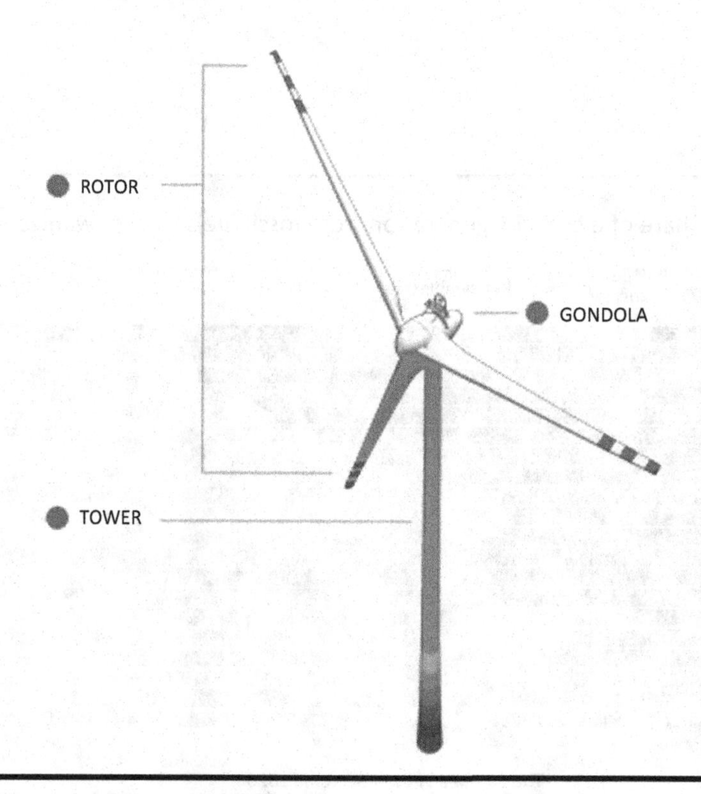

Figure 6.2 Components of a wind turbine.

Source: Based on *Energia z wiatru,* https://pgeeo.pl/Zielona-energia-i-OZE/Energia-z-wiatru, 12/12/2021.

farms generate low power that covers the needs of a single building. Most often, these are devices with a power of approx. 3–5 kW, but there are also power plants generating 10–50 kW, which enable the sale of surplus energy to the power grid. Regardless of the power of the wind farm selected by the investor, the scheme of its operation is always the same and consists of converting kinetic energy into electricity by means of wind turbines, which can then be supplied to all utility devices. The scheme of operation of a wind turbine is as follows (Fodrowska, 2021):

- the rotor blades in the wind turbine move by air movement;
- this movement is then transmitted through the shaft and gearbox to a generator, which produces electricity in a way similar to a generator or alternator;
- the electricity obtained in this way can be stored by the user or fed to the general power grid.

The greater the capacity of the wind farm, the faster the reimbursement of costs. A 50 KW power plant allows to cover the energy demand of the entire building but also allows the sale of its surplus to the power grid. In Poland, wind farms are mostly built to support other sources of electricity. They perfectly complement PV installations that generate better yields on sunny and windless days. Areas where it is worth building wind farms are shown in Figure 6.3.

Low-power plants have their advantages and disadvantages. The advantages include (Fodrowska, 2021):

- free wind energy, which can be used not only to power appliances such as a refrigerator, computer, and TV, but also the building's electric heating system or a boiler for heating domestic hot water (DHW);
- simple and reliable operation;
- the possibility of selling the surplus of produced energy to the power utility, which makes it possible to reduce electricity costs;
- the possibility of constructing them on one's own;
- a vast variety of small wind farm types (a wide range of design variants allows the device to be adapted to individual needs, required power, or the place of installation);
- the fact that they generate energy also at night and in winter, thanks to which they can support other RES (such as, e.g., a PV set) which have lower efficiency at that time;

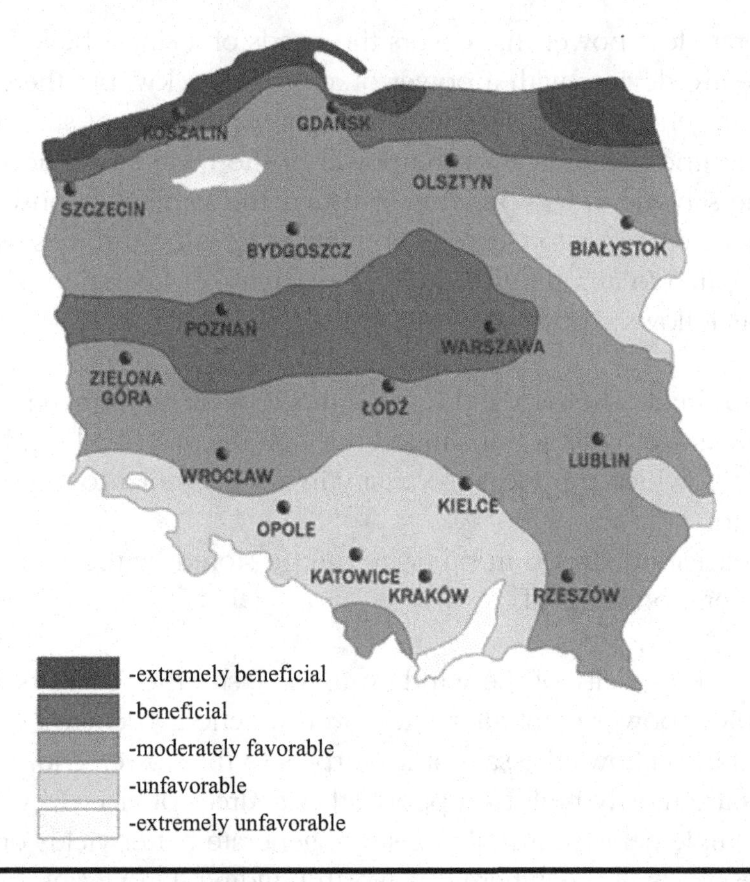

Figure 6.3 Map of wind conditions in Poland.

Source: **Based on *Energia wiatru,* http://www.praze.pl/?a=static&l=pl&id=25, 2/1/2022.**

- solid and esthetic structure and easy assembly;
- environmentally friendly operation, the use of a wind power plant to produce electricity is not burdened with the emission of carbon dioxide and other pollutants into the atmosphere (it also does not generate waste).

The disadvantages of wind farms include:

- investment costs, which will pay off only after a few to a dozen or so years (the cheaper a turbine and the lower its power, the longer it will take to provide a return on investment);
- downtime in energy production due to lack of wind (the power plant will operate only when the wind blows);

- the need to purchase expensive batteries with short life expectancy in which the investor will store electricity (this is typical of off-grid[1] solutions);
- the production process of batteries, which is burdened with the discharge of pollutants and carbon dioxide into the atmosphere;
- lower efficiency in areas with lower wind intensity.

6.1.1 Energy from Biomass

Biomass is defined as the biodegradable fraction of products, waste, or residues of biological origin from agriculture, including plant and animal substances, forestry and fishing, and related industries, including fish farming and aquaculture, as well as the biodegradable fraction of industrial and municipal waste, including from waste management facilities and water and waste-water treatment facilities (Ustawa z dnia 19 lipca 2019 r., 2019). The main types of biomass used for energy purposes are (Biomasa – odnawialne źródło energii, 2021):

- wood and waste from wood processing: wood in pieces, sawdust, shavings, chips, bark, etc.;
- plants from energy crops: fast-growing woody plants (e.g., willow, poplar, eucalyptus);
- dicotyledonous perennials (e.g., Jerusalem artichoke, Virginia mallow, knotweed), perennial grasses (e.g., common reed);
- agricultural products and organic waste from agriculture: for example, straw, hay, sugar beet, sugar cane, potatoes, rape, fruit processing residues;
- animal feces;
- organic fractions of municipal waste and municipal sewage sludge, some industrial waste, for example, from the paper industry.

The use of biomass in obtaining renewable energy has its pros and cons (Biomasa – odnawialne źródło energii, 2021). The advantages of using biomass include the reduction of greenhouse gas emissions, use of local energy resources, decentralization of energy generation, diversification of energy sources, reduction of environmental damage associated with the extraction of fossil fuels, waste management, and support of social and economic development by creating new jobs.

The disadvantages include low energy value compared to fossil fuels, which translates into the need to use more biomass to obtain a similar amount of energy, and low density – it makes the storage, use, and transport of the obtained biomass much more difficult, very wide humidity range – in some conditions, it makes it difficult to process the biomass in such a way as to make it fit for use.

The current share of biomass in meeting global energy needs is 14% and is based mainly on waste from agriculture and forestry and direct use of forests. Depending on the state of matter, biofuels can be divided into (Michalski, 2021):

- solid biofuels – they include, among others, straw pressed into bales, cubes or briquettes, sawdust or straw pellets, wood, hay, as well as a variety of other types of processed plant waste (they are used in the combustion, gasification or pyrolysis processes to produce heat and electricity);
- liquid biofuels – are obtained through the alcoholic fermentation of carbohydrates, butyl fermentation of biomass, or from vegetable oils esterified in biodiesel (plant-derived methyl and ethyl alcohol is also added to traditional fuels that are used in transport);
- gaseous biofuels (so-called biogases) are produced as a result of anaerobic fermentation of agricultural livestock waste, for example, manure (they are used to produce electricity or heat or are supplied to the gas network).

According to the data from Statistics Poland, the breakdown of energy obtained from RES in Poland by energy carriers in 2020 was as follows (Energia ze źródeł odnawialnych w 2020 r., 2022): solid biofuels – 71.61%; wind energy – 10.85%; liquid fuels – 7.15%; biogas – 2.58%; heat pumps – 2.38; solar energy – 1.99; water energy – 1.46; municipal waste – 1.15%; geothermal energy – 0.20%.

6.1.2 Heat Pumps

Heat pumps are a type of RES increasingly often used in our latitude. They enable the use of solar energy stored in the ground, in groundwater, in rock or air, and can be used for heating or cooling. The heat pump technology is based on a very simple and well-known mechanism used, for example, in refrigerators. The most important elements of heat pump construction are (Figure 6.4): compressor, condenser, expansion valve, and evaporator.

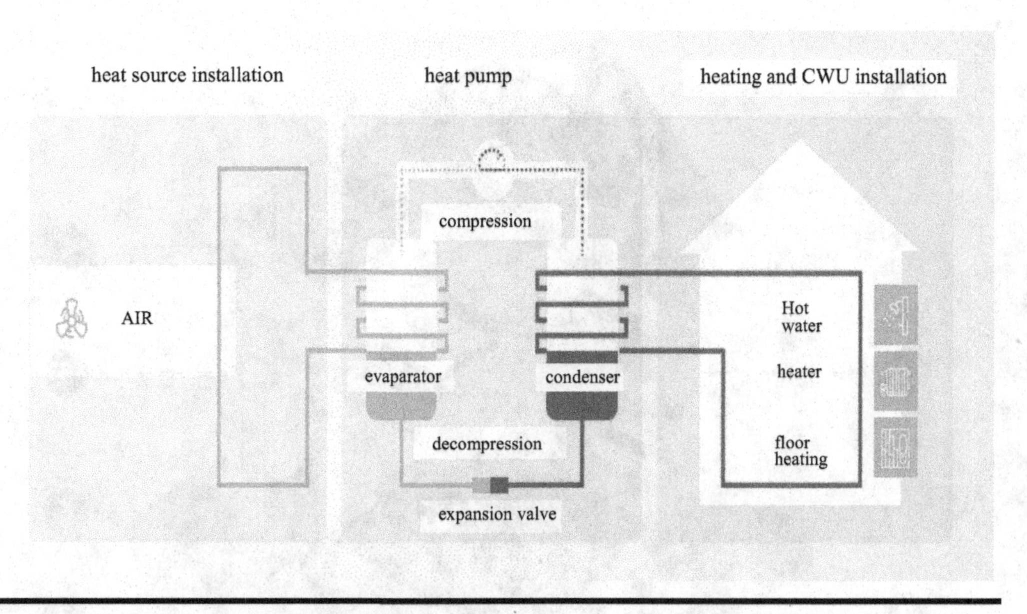

Figure 6.4 Construction of a heat pump.

Source: **Based on S. Lewkowicz, Pompa ciepła powietrze-woda – jak działa? https://columbusenergy.pl/, 12/22/2021.**

However, the pump would not fulfill its function without the working medium. Refrigerant is a liquid that circulates inside the system, boiling at low pressure and extracting heat at low temperatures (outside the building). Thanks to the compressor, the pressure and temperature increase in the system, the refrigerant changes into a gas and then goes to the condenser, where it gives off heat to the installation. After that, the liquid refrigerant passes through the expansion valve, where the pressure and temperature drop, and the cycle starts again (Lewkowicz, 2021).

In practice, there are various versions of heat pumps, for example, air-source heat pumps, or water-source heat pumps. The air source heat pump is quite economical compared to other types of pumps. It does not require significant expansion of the installation and the combination of PVs with an air-source heat pump is an economical and rational solution (Figure 6.5).

Air source heat pumps are highly efficient when it comes to heating a building. The main advantages of this system are (Zalety stosowania pomp ciepła, 2021):

- it is a heating solution of the future (it is possible that in the near future, 100% of energy will be obtained from RES and CO_2 emissions will be completely eliminated);

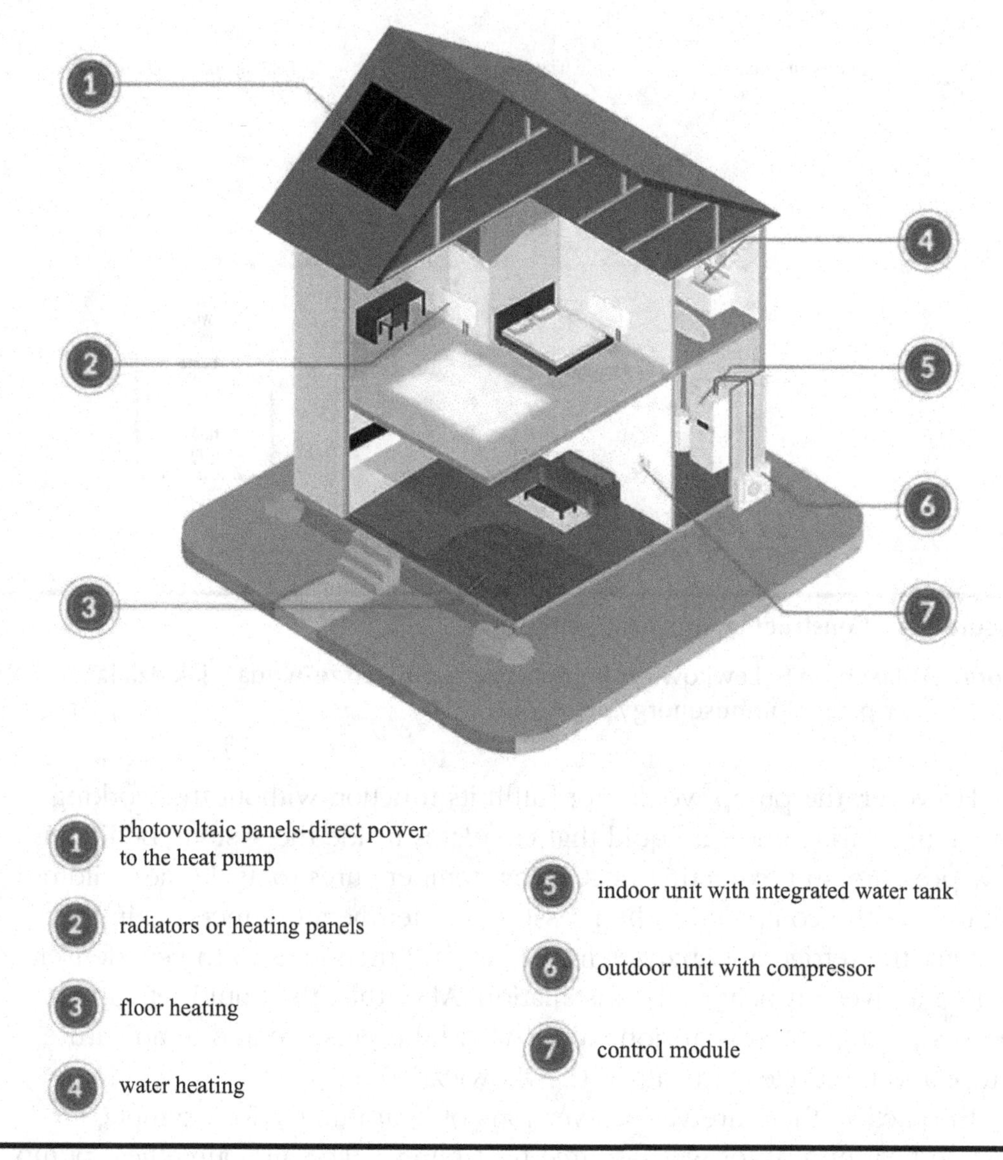

Figure 6.5 Practical use of a heat pump and solar energy source.

Source: **Based on S. Lewkowicz, Pompa ciepła powietrze – woda – jak działa? https://columbusenergy.pl/, 12/22/2021.**

- they can efficiently cool the rooms in the building at a very low cost (so-called passive cooling in the case of ground source heat pumps with a vertical ground-coupled heat exchanger);
- availability and versatility – they can be installed in newly built and existing buildings;

- easy and quick installation – there is no need to drill holes or perform earthworks; an experienced installer will install an air source heat pump in a finished house in about three days;
- multifunctionality – it can be used to heat a house, building, DHW, and in summer to cool rooms;
- safety – with heat pump heating, there is no risk of explosion, smoke, or fire;
- they are maintenance-free and comfortable to use – there is no need for cleaning, lighting the furnace, or filling a fuel tank; the use of the pump is clean, quiet (approx. 39 dB), and completely emission-free;
- ecology – operation does not emit harmful compounds to the environment;
- long service life –the service life of the heat pump is estimated to be even longer than 20 years;
- cheap operation – in combination with PVs, the device works practically without any costs;
- they increase the financial value of the building in which they are installed – it is easier to sell a house or a building with low maintenance costs.

6.1.3 Hydroelectric Power

Hydroelectric power plants are devices that capture some of the energy of flowing water. Depending on the nature of the flow, they are usually divided into the following types (Energia z wody, 2021):

- run-of-river power plants without a reservoir – the amount of energy produced by them depends on the amount of water flowing over the river bed at a given moment;
- flow control (reservoir) power plants – there is a water damming reservoir in front of the power plant;
- power plants where the circulation of water is artificially produced – by successive pumping of water from the lower to the upper reservoir, and then its discharge through the power plant back to the lower reservoir (pumped storage power plants).

In hydroelectric power plants, energy is obtained through a fairly simple process based on the conversion of potential energy into kinetic energy of flowing water. One way to increase the energy potential is the damming of water with erected dams. The water moves a turbine with a generator and thus produces electricity. The most common method of generating hydropower is the use of inland waters, in this case, rivers and permanent water reservoirs.

There are both benefits and shortcomings of high-power hydropower[2] plants (Wady i zalety energetyki wodnej, 2021). The advantages of a high-power plant are that it does not pollute the natural environment with exhaust gases and fluids generated in the process of burning non-RES, such as fossil fuels, it can provide flood protection thanks to the possibility of storing water in appropriate retention reservoirs, it generates electricity more efficiently than conventional power plants, it does not consume non-RES, so they can last longer, generating electricity there is several times cheaper than in the case of traditional power plants, they are modular, they improve navigation conditions, which contributes to the growth of tourism in the vicinity of power plants.

The disadvantages of this type of power plant include (Hydroenergetyka, 2021): interference with the natural environment related mainly to the difficulties in the migration of fish to spawning areas and the elimination of bird breeding sites, which contributes to the reduction in their number, even two to three times higher outlays for investments than in the case of traditional power plants, causing silting of water reservoirs, and thus reduce their capacity, which in periods of heavy rainfall or thaw may lead to flooding, change in the water level contributing to the occurrence of landslides and bank abrasion, generation of noise in the electricity production process, which is burdensome for the inhabitants in the vicinity of the power plant, the need to relocate people in the case of building power plants in previously populated areas that may also contribute to social protests, the possibility of harmful methane emissions from water reservoirs of power plants.

With the development of technology, small hydropower plants (SHPs), which do not exceed 10 MW, are increasingly used. The advantage of SHP is undoubtedly the possibility of using hydro-technical structures from the post-war period or old power plants of mills, forges, and sawmills. Generally, SHPs do not require special maintenance and guarantee constant energy production. They are usually owned by the local community and are very important for water management. The advantage of mini and micro power plants is the ability to connect directly to the low-voltage grid and use electricity production directly. SHPs:

- offer the possibility of improving the hydrological and hydrobiological balance of their surrounding areas;
- can be built on small watercourses that will suffice for their proper functioning;

- can be quickly and efficiently designed and then built within a period not exceeding two years;
- due to their specificity, can be located close to consumers, which reduces the distance of electricity transmission.

6.1.4 Solar Energy

Solar energy is the most common free renewable source of energy. Man has been using solar energy for a long time, either randomly or deliberately. Initially, the sun's rays helped to warm our bodies and dry our clothes, and along with technological progress, new, more effective solutions appeared.

Solar energy can be used in several ways. Here are some of them (Energia słoneczna – czym jest i jak powstaje?, 2021). **First.** PV conversion – it can be used in PV cells, also popularly known as solar cells. These are devices that directly convert the energy of solar radiation into electricity. This conversion is possible thanks to the use of semiconductor p-n junctions. When a photon reaches the silicon wafer, it is absorbed by the silicon, thereby knocking an electron out of its position and setting it in motion. This motion is the flow of electric current. PV cells are used, among others in: installations for the production of electricity, warehouses, companies, single-family houses, calculators, solar lamps, watches, sailing equipment, and telecommunications.

Second. Passive photothermal conversion – direct conversion of solar radiation energy into thermal energy. There are several types of heating systems using this mechanism, such as:

- direct heat acquisition that can be achieved through large, glazed surfaces mounted where the low-operating sun in winter heats the interior of the rooms;
- system with collector and storage walls – heating with storage collectors mounted on walls that face the sun, made of materials with high heat accumulation (such a wall absorbs solar energy, converting it into heat and then storing it);
- greenhouses, orangeries – this system consists of extending the collector and storage wall by moving the transparent cover away from the wall (the space obtained in this way can be used, for example, as an orangery or a winter garden).

Third. Active photothermal conversion that involves converting the energy of solar radiation into another form of energy with the use of specially constructed devices called solar collectors. Popular types of solar collectors are flat collectors and vacuum collectors. This conversion is mainly used for heating water for households and for industrial facilities. An example of such an installation is shown in Figure 6.6.

Where A – solar collector, B – pump, C – auxiliary heater, D – domestic hot water, E – return water

Fourth. Photochemical conversion, that is, conversion of solar radiation energy into chemical energy. So far, it has not been used in technology on a large scale, but it occurs in living organisms and is called photosynthesis. The energy efficiency of this process is 19–34%, calculated based on energy stored in plants (approx. 1%), but there are photoelectrochemical cells that dissociate water when exposed to sunlight (Uzyskiwanie energii z promieniowania słonecznego, 2021). The advantages of solar energy are as follows. Access to this source of energy is unlimited, it is free and available to the public, its generation does not damage the environment, it offers the possibility of selling surplus energy, it allows independence and self-sufficiency, and it saves water – while the operation of gas, coal or nuclear power plants is associated with very high water consumption, PV panels work virtually cost-free and trouble-free, and their lifetime is estimated at a minimum of 30 years or more.

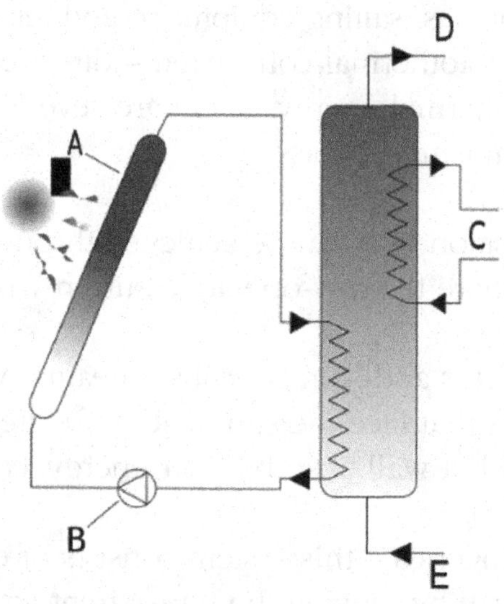

A – solar collector, B – pump, C – auxiliary heater,
D – domestic hot water, E – return water

Figure 6.6 Diagram of a solar installation for obtaining domestic hot water.

Source: Based on *Uzyskiwanie energii z promieniowania słonecznego,* http://www.slonecznydach.pl/, 12/23/2021.

Disadvantages of using solar energy solutions include the fact that the sun does not shine 24 hours a day. Also, toxic chemical elements are used to produce solar panels, which is why the disposal of panels pollutes the environment to some extent. What is more, devices for the generation of solar energy are relatively expensive and PV modules have low efficiency. PV cells can work in three configurations: on-gird, off-gird, and in a hybrid mode combining these two modes (Figure 6.7).

The on-gird configuration is the connection of the PV system with the power grid. Thus, any surplus electricity that cannot be used on an ongoing basis goes to the grid. The advantages of the on-grid system include:

- they solve the problem of electricity surpluses generated by solar cells;
- energy can be claimed back when it is needed, for example, in December when panels provide little electricity and because more electricity is used in the time of Christmas;
- it is a common solution, and most energy suppliers have an offer for prosumers (people involved in the provision of a given product or service, and at the same time in using it);
- the average electricity bill during the year can be reduced, making it easier to control the budget.

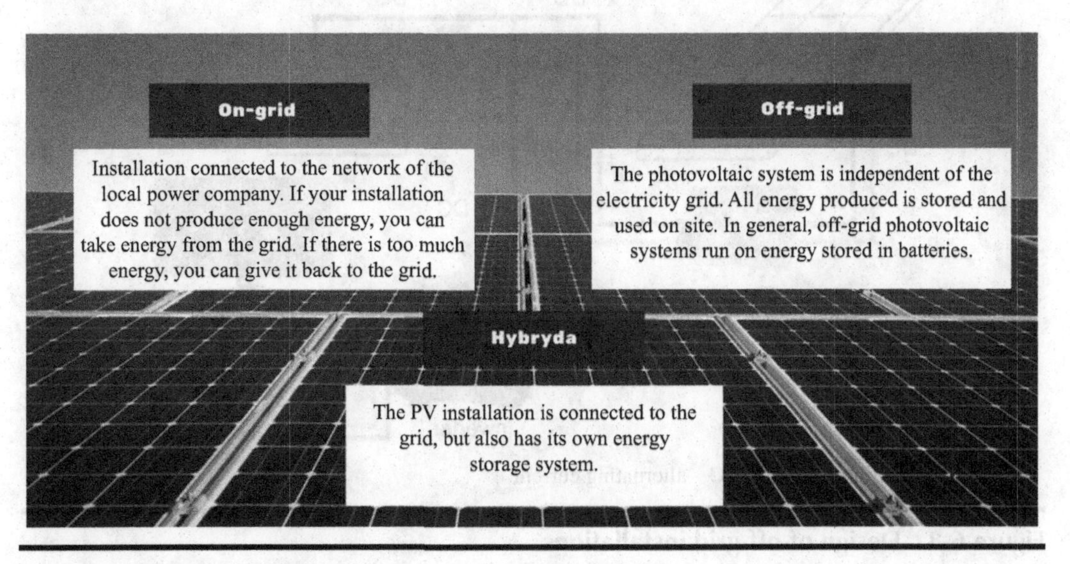

Figure 6.7 Ways of managing energy from photovoltaics.

Source: **Based on Magazynowanie energii z fotowoltaiki – Magazyny energii (e-magazyny.pl), 21.12.2021.**

The off-grid configuration is a PV system in which surplus energy is stored using batteries, most often lithium-ion batteries, installed at the prosumer (Figure 6.8).

Where: DC – direct current, AC – alternating current

A PV installation with energy storage consists of PV panels, a charge regulator, energy storage, an inverter, and a receiver. The off-grid PV system has several important advantages, which include: the possibility of independence from electricity suppliers, an electricity resource that can be used in the event of a network failure, the possibility of using the stored electricity fully, and not just 70–80% of it as in the case of on-grid networks, a particularly valuable solution in places where breakdowns occur often or where it is difficult to supply electricity from the power grid.

6.1.5 Geothermal Energy

Geothermal energy – energy stored in soil, rocks, and fluids filling rock pores and crevices. It is constantly supplemented by the flow of heat transferred from the hot interior of the Earth to the surface, which is why it is

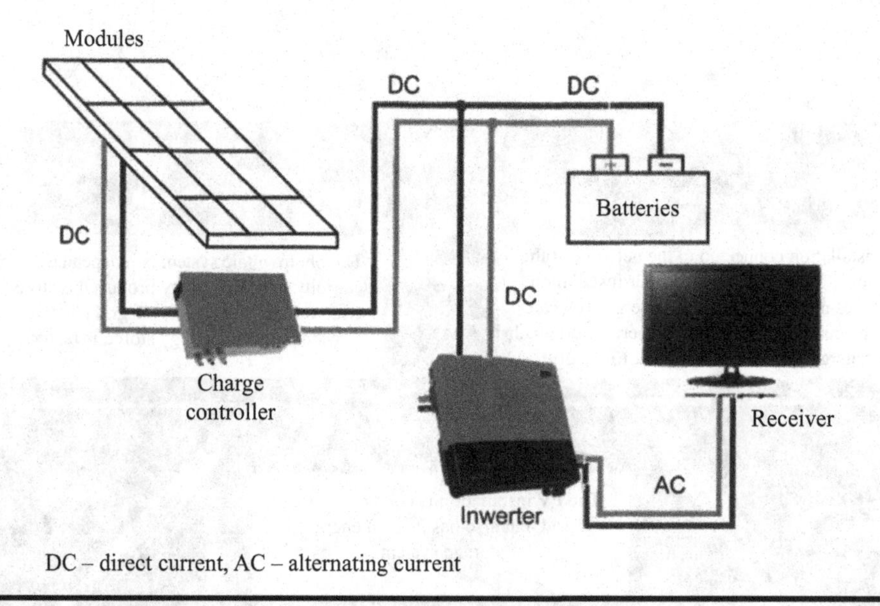

Figure 6.8 Design of off-grid installations.

Source: Prepared on the basis of I. Góralczyk, R. Tytko, *Fotowoltaika. Urządzenia, instalacje fotowoltaiczne i elektryczne,* Wydawnictwo i Drukarnia Towarzystwa Słowaków w Polsce. Kraków 2015, p. 237.

inexhaustible. The heat in the interior of the Earth is partly the primordial heat remaining from the formation of our planet.

The main method of obtaining geothermal energy is to drill boreholes for hot geothermal water reservoirs. At a certain distance from the intake hole, a second hole is made through which geothermal water, after receiving heat from it, is forced back into the bed. As a rule, geothermal waters are highly saline, which is the reason for particularly difficult working conditions for heat exchangers and other elements of geothermal fittings (Energia geotermalna – Wikipedia, 2021).

Depending on the aggregate state of the heat carrier and its temperature, the sources of geothermal energy can be divided into the following groups (Energia geotermalna – baza wiedzy, 2021):

- soil and rocks up to a depth of 2,500 m, from which heat is extracted using heat pumps;
- groundwater as a lower heat source for heating pumps;
- hot water, extracted through deep production boreholes;
- steam released from boreholes for energy production;
- salt beds, from which energy is extracted with brine or salt-neutral liquids;
- hot rocks where pressurized water circulates in a porous rock structure.

6.1.6 Heat Pumps in Geothermal Energy

In recent years, the number of installations that use heat pumps to meet thermal needs has increased. Principle of operation:

- the lower heat source supplies the heat pump evaporator with the energy necessary to change the physical state of the working medium, which evaporates in the evaporator and then is compressed;
- compression increases the pressure and temperature of the working medium;
- subsequently, the medium is condensed (cooled) in the condenser, and useful heat is released (e.g., for space heating);
- the expansion valve then expands the refrigerant, reducing its pressure and temperature, and then the refrigerant is recirculated to the evaporator, closing the circuit.

The rules of functioning of heat pumps in geothermal energy are shown in the picture below (Figure 6.9).

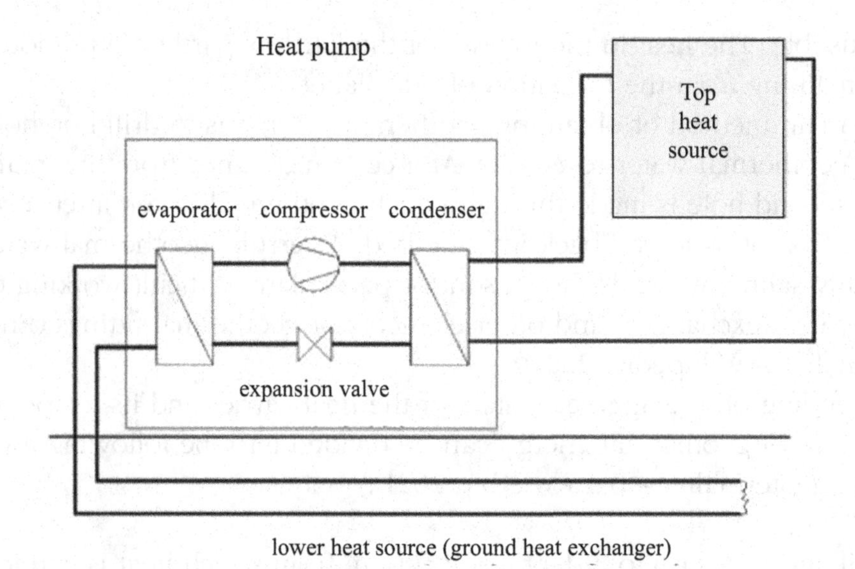

Figure 6.9 Principles of operation of compressor heat pumps.

Source: **Based on *Energia geotermalna,* https://www.mae.com.pl/, 12/26/2021**

6.2 Energy Storage for Logistics

Care for the environment, search for affordable power sources, and the increasing popularity of RES installations have contributed to the storage of electricity when its production is greater than consumption. Energy storage enables independence from the power grid based on RES or balancing the grid as well as energy demand and supply.

In practice, energy storage systems allow for energy collection, storage, and use at a convenient time. This is possible thanks to the cooperation of energy storage systems with information and communication technologies. The methods and technologies of energy storage can be divided into:

- mechanical energy storage – the most frequently used are: pumped storage power plants, flywheels, diabatic compressed air tanks,[3] and adiabatic compressed air tanks (Klonowicz et al., 2022),[4] gravity energy storage;
- electric energy storage – capacitors and supercapacitors are most commonly used in this method;
- electrochemical/chemical energy storage – lead-acid and lithium-ion batteries are most commonly used in this method;

- thermal/thermochemical energy storage – most commonly used hot water storage, steam storage, latent heat storage, and sorption/reversible bonds are most commonly used in this method.

The methods are shown in the figure below (Figure 6.10).

6.2.1 Batteries

In logistics processes, electricity is stored, inter alia, using batteries. Lead-acid batteries are the best known and most commonly used type, in which the electrolyte is an aqueous solution of sulfuric acid in liquid or gelatinous form (in the so-called gel batteries, they are a rejuvenated version of their predecessor) or the electrolyte is trapped in the glass mat between the plates (this was used in AGM – Absorbed Glass Mat batteries). Batteries are used, among others, in internal transport (forklifts) and in sudden power cuts, in

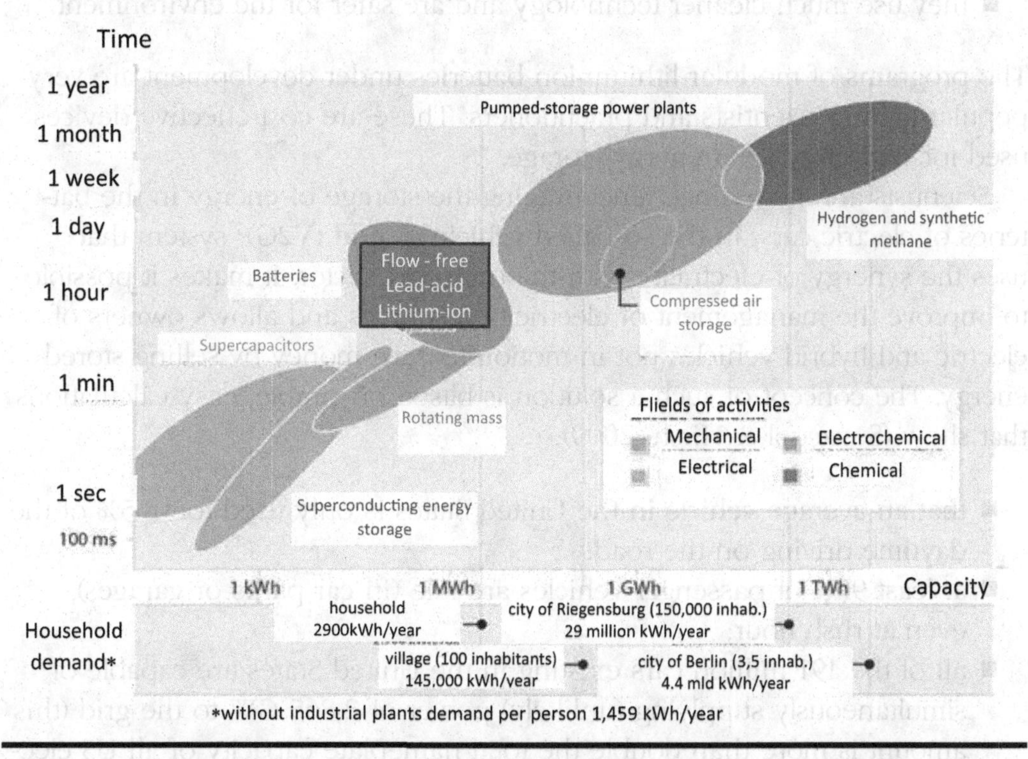

Figure 6.10 Energy storage technologies – installations operating in Germany.

Source: **Based on Murator plus, https://www.muratorplus.pl/technika/elektroenergetyka/magazyny-energii-w-domowych-systemach-pv-aa-b8Lp-yqDe-MKVq.html, 11/22/2021.**

systems such as powering alarms and lighting systems. These types of batteries are also used in off-grid installations.

Another group of batteries used for storage in logistics is lithium-ion batteries, which have many advantages over lead-acid batteries. These advantages include (Adamska, 2021):

- high energy efficiency (while charging, they consume up to 40% less electricity than traditional batteries, e.g., lead batteries);
- much longer lifetime – they can be charged more times (lithium-ion batteries up to 5,000, lead-acid ones 300–500);
- low losses in transmitted energy, which are within 5% in relation to traditional batteries;
- possibility of using and mounting in various positions (e.g., the battery can be turned by 180°);
- they are lighter than traditional ones by almost 70%;
- they are maintenance-free and ready for immediate use;
- they use much cleaner technology and are safer for the environment.

The programs of modular lithium-ion batteries under development are very popular among scientists and practitioners. These are cost-effective devices used for stationary solar energy storage.

Scientists are increasingly encouraging the storage of energy in the batteries of electric cars, in the so-called vehicle-to-grid (V2G)[5] system that uses the synergy of electricity with the transport sector. It makes it possible to improve the management of electricity resources and allows owners of electric and hybrid vehicles not in motion to earn money by selling stored energy. The concept of such a solution is based on simple, easy calculations that show (Sovacool & Hirsh, 2009):

- that an average vehicle in the United States is only used for 4–5% of the daytime driving on the road;
- at least 90% of passenger vehicles are idle (in car parks or garages), even at rush hour;
- all of the 191 million cars existing in the United States are capable of simultaneously supplying (unlikely) power of 2,865 GW to the grid (this amount is more than double the total nameplate capacity of all US electric generators in 2006).

The V2G fleet can replace or supplement energy obtained from hydropower plants and compressed air energy storage.

6.2.3 Supercapacitors

Another solution for storing electricity is supercapacitors (also called ultracapacitors or double-layer capacitors), which can store hundreds of times more energy than a classic capacitor, thanks to the very large surface area of active carbon.

The most characteristic and, at the same time, efficient use of supercapacitors is, among others, in the transport industry (e.g., in hybrid vehicles when starting and when climbing and for energy recovery from braking, in fuel cell vehicles), thanks to their robustness and long service life, mobile and portable devices, thanks to the possibility of cyclical operation, in cranes, where they provide or recover power while lifting or lowering the load, respectively, renewable and alternative energy sources (e.g., wind turbines – the ability to control each rotating airscrew), backup power supplies (e.g., warehouses, factories), alarms and fire protection systems, as well as emergency lighting systems, etc.

6.2.4 Energy Storage – the Flywheel Mechanism

Electricity can also be stored through the use of a flywheel and compressed air (Jak można magazynować energię elektryczną?, 2022). In the first case, with excess energy, an electric motor sets a flywheel with a very high moment of inertia in high-speed motion, and then a special clutch disconnects the motor. The spinning wheel is kept in a special cover in a vacuum (without air resistance), and its bearings ensure minimal friction, so once set in motion, it can spin for many hours. When the moment comes to recover the kinetic energy accumulated in the wheel – the clutch and the drive motor are turned on, with the motor at that moment becoming a generator, returning electricity to the grid. The disadvantage of this method is that it stores a relatively small amount of energy and some energy is lost because there is always some friction associated with the spinning motion, which "steals" energy.

In the second case, energy is stored in tanks placed in specially constructed sites. The tanks store compressed air, which can be kept without energy losses. When there is excess energy in the network, electrically operated compressors compress the air in tanks that can withstand very high pressures (typically 70 atmospheres). As soon as there is an energy deficit in the network, the compressed air can be released into a turbine that generates electricity and the stored energy can be recovered.

6.2.5 Energy Storage – Hydrogen Technology

The use of hydrogen for the needs of RES is a future-proof solution that will revolutionize industry, transport, logistics, and energy. However, this technology is not widely used on the market yet, due to the relatively high implementation costs. Energy storage based on hydrogen is possible because (Rozwiązania wodorowe, 2022): it makes up 75% of the mass of the entire universe – in the form of water and organic elements, it is the lightest and most basic element with the chemical symbol H and atomic number 1, it is a gas at standard temperature and pressure, and can be compressed and liquefied, it is exceptionally clean, lighter than air, odorless and non-toxic, and it can be safely manufactured, stored and transported.

Hydrogen has an advantage over other RESs in terms of energy storage and use because renewable electricity can be converted into hydrogen through electrolysis, consuming excess power.

Hydrogen for energy storage can be obtained in many ways. One of them is the so-called electrochemical technology based on the water electrolysis process (decomposition into H_2 and O) and ensuring that high-purity (99.9%) hydrogen is obtained. In practice, the so-called electrolyzers are run on electricity generated from RES that are ecological and carbon dioxide-free.[6] The basic components of an energy storage system using hydrogen are hydrogen batteries, which contain (Elektroliza i ogniwa paliwowe, 2022): an electrolysis system to which, for example, a hybrid solar inverter and a water supply network are connected via a purification unit, fuel cell power system, and hydrogen-storage system.

An example of the operation and use of a hydrogen battery in practice is a solution offered by Lavo. In this system, renewable energy is connected to the water mains via a purification unit. The hydrogen battery uses the excess energy it absorbs by acting on the principle of electrolysis of water. Then, the resulting hydrogen is stored in a patented Hydride sponge at 30 bar or 435 psi. At times of increased energy demand, this innovative storage system uses a fuel cell to supply energy to the building as well as a small 5 kWh lithium buffer battery. This battery is able to provide an immediate response (Pierwszy domowy akumulator wodorowy, 2022).

Sunlight is often used as a source of renewable energy, and then hydrogen is produced via photoelectrolysis (Burzyński, 2022)[7] in a photo-electrolysis cell (PEC), in which solar energy is converted into electricity used for water electrolysis (Bartosik et al., 2022). Special hydrogen batteries can be used for[8]: providing energy for longer periods compared to lead or lithium-ion batteries, and storing up to three times more energy than, for example, traditional lithium-ion batteries.

Many innovative companies on the market, including international ones, propose various hydrogen technologies that in practice can be used for energy storage. One of the examples is HPS, a company that designed and implemented the Picea system, combining energy storage, supporting heating and ventilation of rooms into one integrated structure (Magazyny wodoru – samowystarczalne budynki, 2022). Picea combines the following components:

- fuel cell (Gis, 2022)[9] – provides electricity from a hydrogen storage facility in winter;
- electrolyzer – converts solar energy collected in summer into hydrogen;
- battery – makes it possible to use the energy of the midday sun in the evening;
- solar charge controller – stores solar energy;
- stand-alone inverter – provides the electricity network;
- hydrogen storage – enables the use of solar energy in winter;
- hot water tank – uses waste heat from the heating system of the building;
- ventilation device – supplies the building with fresh air;
- enthalpy exchanger – supplies heat to the facility through heat recovery;
- energy management – ensures efficient interaction between all components in one solution.

The variants of system use depend on the season and day. Four options are available. **First.** On sunny days, the system stores solar energy in a battery. Excess solar energy is converted into hydrogen by an electrolyzer and stored in a storage unit for later use during the winter. The excess energy can also be used to heat hot water and operate the air conditioning system (Figure 6.11).

Second. In summer, in the evening, after sunset, the electricity stored in the battery is used to power the building and the heat is collected from the hot utility water tank (Figure 6.12).

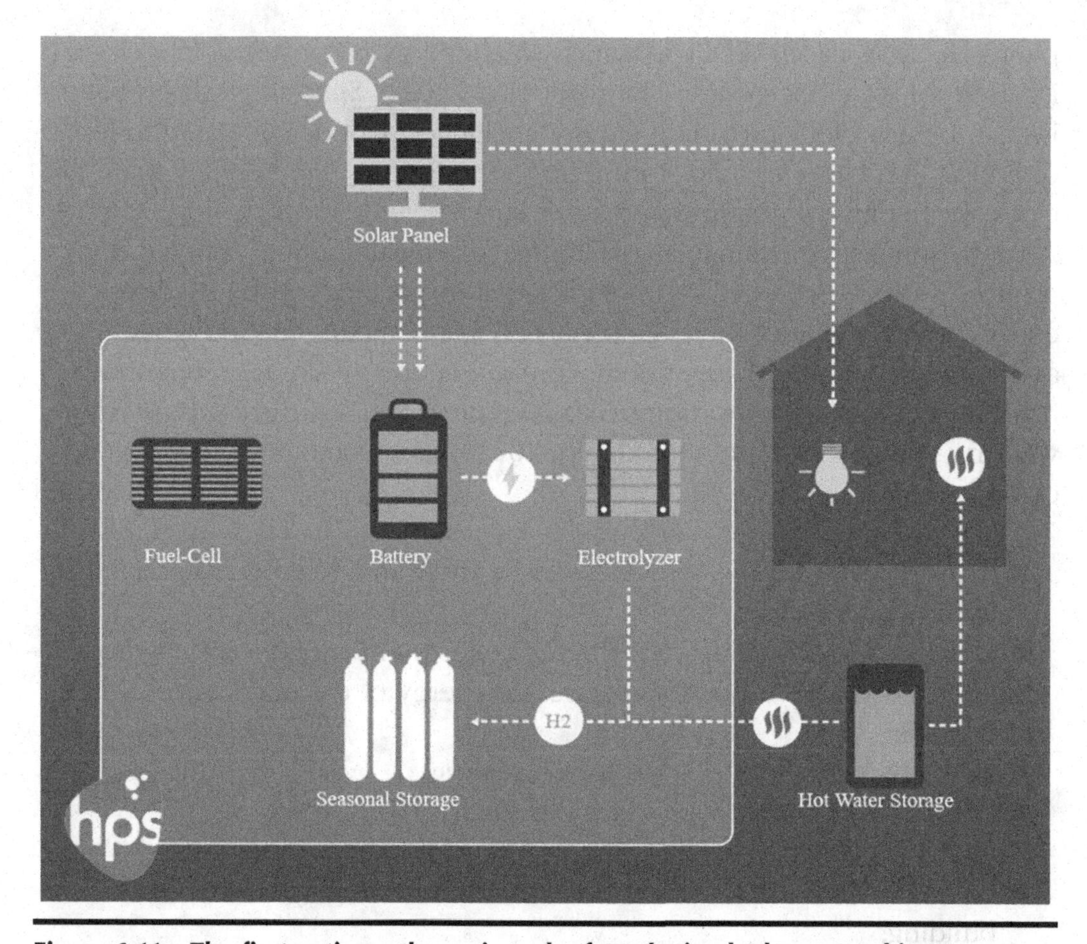

Figure 6.11 The first option – the main task of producing hydrogen and its storage.

Source: Based on *Magazyny wodoru – samowystarczalne budynki,* https://ecoprius.pl/pl/magazyny-wodoru-samowystarczalne-budynki.html, 1/4/2022.

Third. In winter, when there is little solar energy, electricity is obtained from a fuel cell, which also generates heat and acts as an addition to the heating device (Figure 6.13).

Fourth. If solar energy is not available, the building is served by a seasonal storage unit in winter (Figure 6.14). The fuel cell uses hydrogen to produce electricity and heat. Controlled indoor air humidification additionally increases comfort and ensures healthy coziness.

The presented solution is a pilot that is being tested for safety, efficiency, ergonomics, and reliability. The system that is being developed has many advantages, including the fact that: hydrogen is seen as the future of the clean energy sector, the new storage system lasts longer than lithium-ion

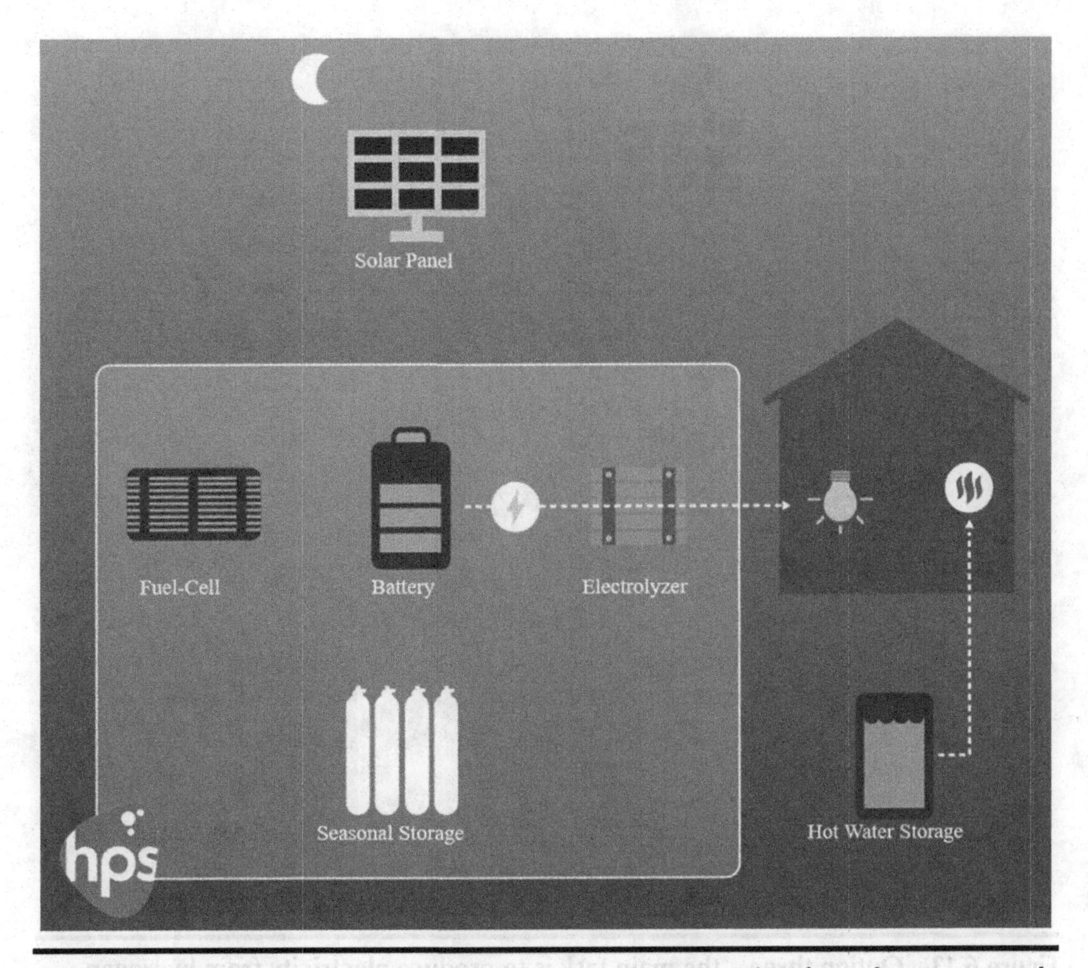

Figure 6.12 Option two – the main task is energy consumption from the storage tank.

Source: **Based on *Magazyny wodoru – samowystarczalne budynki,* https://ecoprius.pl/pl/magazyny-wodoru-samowystarczalne-budynki.html, 1/4/2022.**

because it is based on hydrogen gas and not on chemicals, a hydrogen battery is more environmentally friendly as it does not use as many rare earth metals.

The disadvantage of the system being developed is the low efficiency of the batteries, which barely exceeds 50% compared to that of lithium-ion batteries.

6.2.6 Gravitational Energy Storage

In the technology of gravity energy storage, the surplus electricity is used to lift heavy blocks, and then when the consumer or the energy system

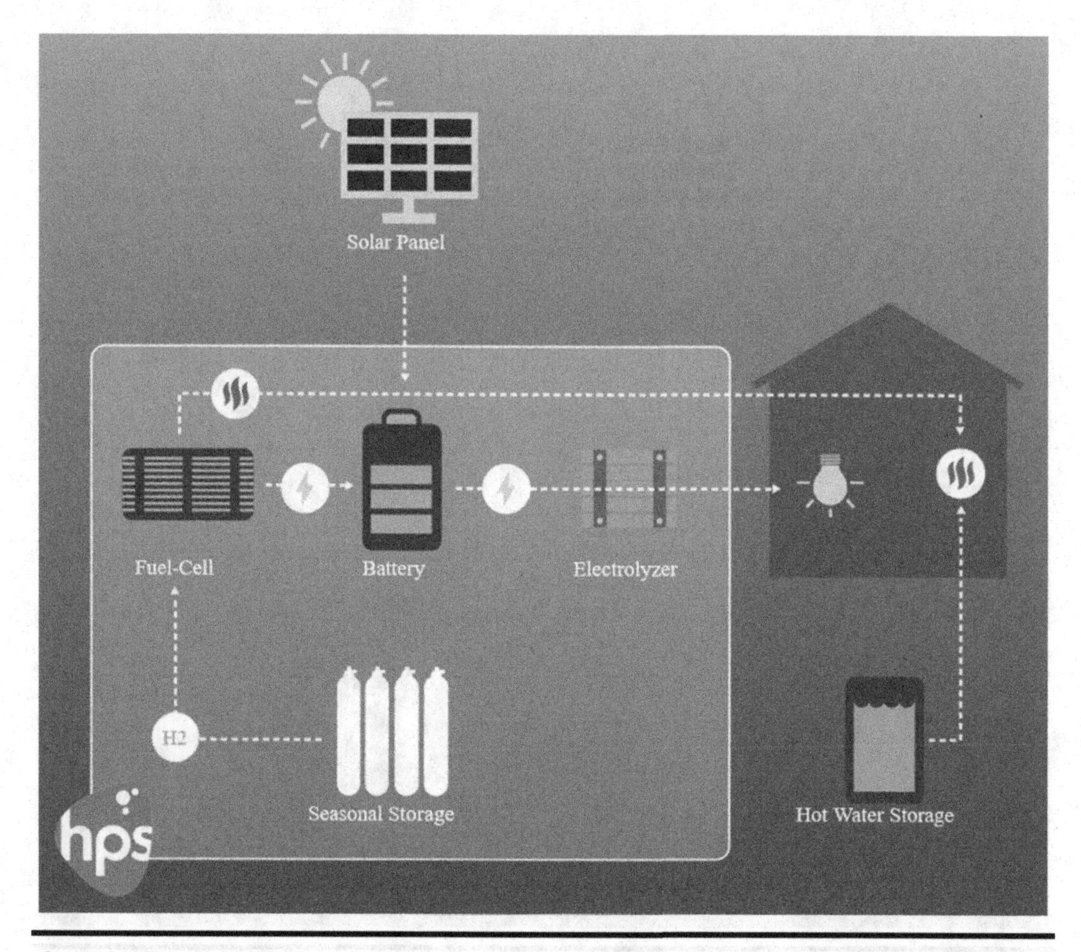

Figure 6.13 Option three – the main task is to produce electricity from hydrogen through a fuel cell.

Source: **Based on *Magazyny wodoru – samowystarczalne budynki,* https://ecoprius.pl/pl/magazyny-wodoru-samowystarczalne-budynki.html, 1/4/2022.**

needs additional power, the blocks are lowered, releasing the stored energy reserves (Figure 6.15).

Gravity energy storage (Grawitacyjne magazyny energii wchodzą na rynek. Duże zamówienie, 2022) uses a mechanism similar to that used in pumped storage power plants and is much cheaper, has no location restrictions, has an efficiency of 80% compared to battery magazines, is more environmentally friendly, and has a service life of up to 30–35 years.

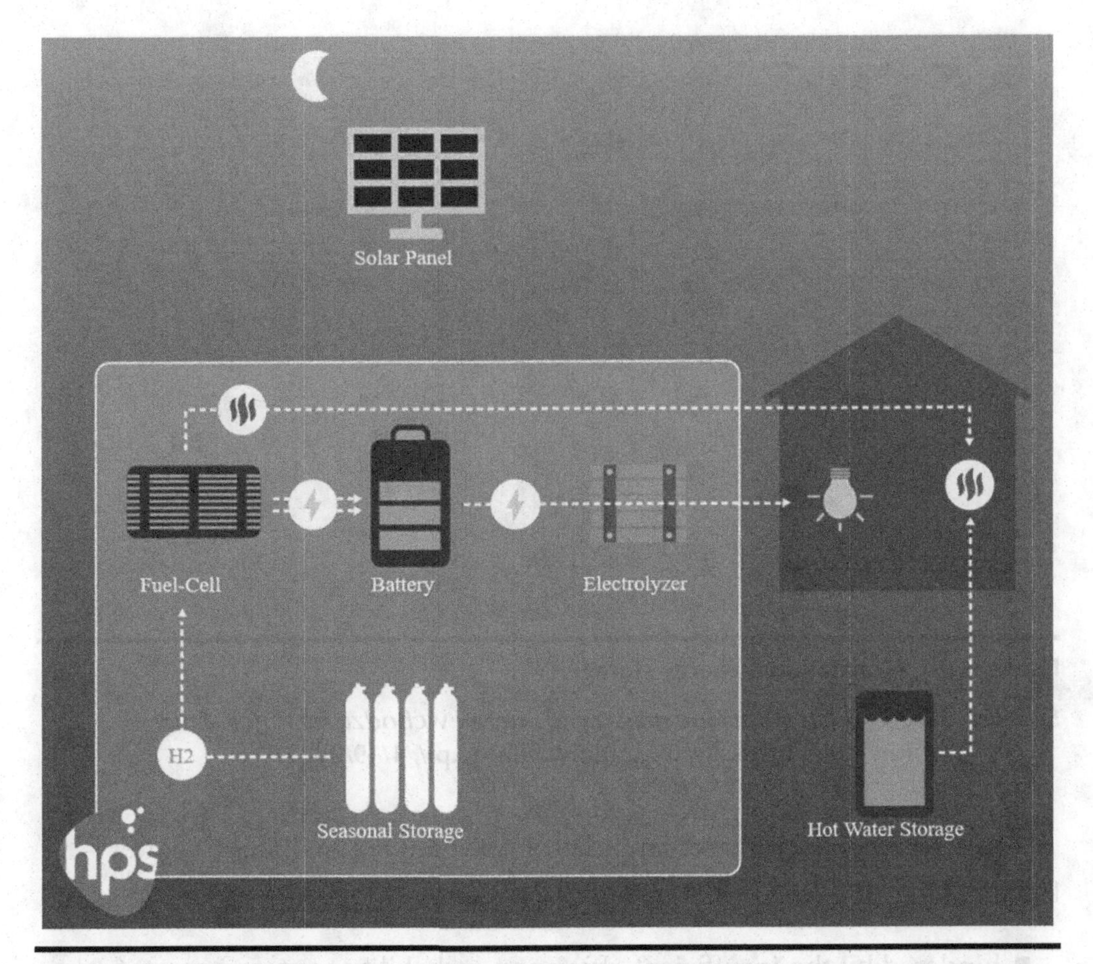

Figure 6.14 The fourth option – Hydrogen storage (seasonal storage) secures the operation of a fuel cell in the production of electricity from hydrogen through a fuel cell.

Source: **Based on *Magazyny wodoru – samowystarczalne budynki,* https://ecoprius.pl/pl/magazyny-wodoru-samowystarczalne-budynki.html, 1/4/2022.**

6.3 Practical Use of Renewable Energy for Logistics

The superiority of electrically powered vehicles (especially trains, trams, trolleys, and forklifts) over traditional vehicles in the context of the environment is widely known and acknowledged. Many research centers in different countries, in cooperation with industry and government administration, are working on the development of technologies that successfully implement "Zero Emission Vehicles" for transport.

Figure 6.15 Gravitational energy storage.

Source: Based on *Grawitacyjne magazyny energii wchodzą na rynek. Duże zamówienie*, https://www.gramwzielone.pl/, 1/19/2022.

The transition from petrol- and diesel-powered automobiles to battery-powered EVs and fuel cell vehicles is:

- hindered by the insufficient efficiency and ability to store energy (gasoline or diesel oil has a high energy density, about 10 kWh per liter, that is, a kilogram of gasoline has about 300 times more energy than a lead battery
- complex, because the production of electricity from RES weighing one kilogram (Knez et al., 2009) cannot be fully forecasted due to changing conditions (sun, wind) and usually does not match the demand curve (e.g., high demand during peak hours);
- difficult when the energy needs are greater than the stored energy resources (e.g., in batteries, hydrogen cells) and do not suffice to fully meet the planned logistics services.

In addition, the use of EVs has other weaknesses, which include (Juan et al., 2016): long EV battery charging times compared to the relatively fast refueling process in ICEVs (internal combustion engine vehicles), and the shortage of public and/or private battery charging stations.

While in larger cities, there is no problem with charging an electric car in a public charger, there is a problem on highways. The number of charging devices with a CCS Combo 2 (Gis, 2022)[10] connector at the end of 2018 in selected EU countries was as follows (Ile jest stacji ładowania CCS w Europie? Na koniec 2018 r. prawie 6 tysięcy sztuk, 2022): Germany – 1,491 charging points, the United Kingdom – 1,106 charging points, Norway – 548 charging points, France – 544 charging points, Sweden – 367 charging points, Austria – 266 charging points, Switzerland – 211 charging points, Denmark – 162 charging points, the Netherlands – 161 charging points, Italy – 152 charging points, Spain – 112 charging points, Belgium – 93 charging points, Finland – 92 charging points, Czech Republic – 89 charging points, Poland – 89 charging points, Latvia – 75 charging points, Portugal – 52 charging points, Ireland – 49 charging points, Slovakia – 41 charging points, Iceland – 41 charging points.

Despite the inconvenience of the use of renewable energy, environmental protection is the reason for the increasing use of PV energy in logistics companies dealing in the distribution of goods, especially in the centers of large cities. Energy from RES is used by public transport companies, at airports for the transport of passengers and luggage, in hospitals for the internal transport of patients, medicines, and waste, and in the handling of warehouse materials (Bernal-Agustin & Dufo-Lopez, 2008).

For the needs of modern logistics, transport uses electric vehicles that can be charged from renewable energy. In practice, there is a whole range of means of transport powered by electricity. They are already in operation or undergoing research and testing. On average, the range of most electric vehicles is estimated to be around 100–150 miles and depends on the type of batteries used, charging speed (fast and slow), load, weather conditions, etc. (Feng & Figliozzi, 2013), (Tredeau, 2009), (Szczepanek, 2009).

Popular electric vehicles are already used to transport people, and electric vans and trucks are used for deliveries (logistic loads). Means of transport for last-mile logistics are a separate category.

6.3.1 Electric Vehicles

In passenger transport, traditional combustion vehicles with various types of electric and hydrogen cars, including (Samochody elektryczne, 2022), (*Rodzaje samochodów elektrycznych i hybrydowych,* 2022):

- BEVs (battery electric vehicles) – they are powered only by a battery, without emitting harmful substances. Their range is from 120 to 200 km, and they are well suited to cities, short- and medium-distance routes when the user has the possibility of regular parking and charging.
- REEV (Range Extended Electric Vehicle) – a second engine – an internal combustion engine – is an additional feature of this type of vehicle. If necessary, it can generate the energy necessary to charge the battery that provides electric propulsion. As a result, the range can be extended to 300–500 km.
- PHEV (Plug-in Hybrid Electric Vehicle) – in the case of this type of vehicle, the electric and internal combustion engines work in parallel. The range of hybrid cars reaches 500–1000 km, making them an ideal means of transport for users regularly traveling long distances. As hybrids can only be propelled by an electric drive for distances of up to 80 km, overall fuel consumption can be significantly reduced.
- HEV (Hybrid Electric Vehicle) – these vehicles are equipped with two engines – a combustion engine and an electric one. The latter is used to start and drive at a speed of up to 50 km/h; hence, it is an interesting choice for a city car because it can be used to enter the green zones of the city. If the load is greater, the internal combustion engine is switched on. These types of hybrids do not have external sockets for charging the electric motor. The batteries are charged with energy while rolling and braking.
- MHEV (Mild Hybrid Electric Vehicle) – although they have the same construction as classic HEVs, there is a significant difference between them in terms of the electric motor used. In mild hybrids, the electric units are much weaker. This engine is used for starting and takes over the function of the alternator. Despite this, fuel consumption can be reduced by up to 15%.
- EREV (Extended Range Electric Vehicle) – a hybrid with an extended range, which is the opposite of an MHEV. The electric motor is the main driving force of this vehicle, while the combustion engine only supports it.
- FCEV (Fuel Cell Electric Vehicle) – a vehicle in which electricity for the battery is generated through a reaction between hydrogen and oxygen. Instead of being provided with electricity, the fuel cells must be refueled with hydrogen.

In urban transport, many solutions for transporting people on buses are gradually being implemented. An example is the MAN city bus with an electric drive tested in Gdańsk (Figure 6.16).

The MAN Lion's City E city bus with electric drive, tested by Gdańsk, is 12.2 m long and equipped with 3 pairs of double doors. It is powered by a 480 kWh battery. The bus guarantees a range of up to 270 km for the lifetime of the battery, and under optimal operating conditions, this range can be much greater. The vehicle can perform its daily transport tasks without being recharged during the day. It is powered by a 160 kW electric motor and charged via a plug at night at the depot. The bus tested by Gdańsk is adapted to the needs of people with disabilities, has fully LED lighting both inside and outside, and has all-vehicle air conditioning. Additionally, it is equipped with ambient interior lighting. The feeling of spaciousness for passengers is provided by large windows, much larger than in other vehicles, and bright-colored elements of equipment. The passengers have at their disposal seats with increased comfort and soft upholstery (Gdańskie Autobusy i Tramwaje testują autobus elektryczny – to MAN Lion's City E, 2022).

Figure 6.16 MAN city bus with electric drive used in Gdańsk.

Source: **Based on *Nowy model autobusu elektrycznego na testach w Gdańsku*, https://sozosfera.pl/, 1/3/2022.**

6.3.2 Delivery Vehicles and Trucks

Due to their environmental, safety, and congestion constraints, cities are forcing companies to change fleets if they want to move their deliveries close to the center, to end suppliers. The number of electric trucks and vans available on the market is increasing. Manufacturers such as Mercedes, Audi, Volvo, VW, Ford, Jaguar, Fiat, and BMW have already announced that in ten years they will have shifted to manufacturing only electric cars. This process is to be carried out evolutionarily.

The main brands that dominate the market of electric vans include (data from 09.10. 2021) (Samochody elektryczne – ciężarowe i dostawcze, 2022):

- Citroen – Berlingo and Partner models (22 kWh battery and 170 km range);
- Nissan – eNV200 (40 kWh battery with a range of up to 300 km), a car that probably does not attract a lot of people, but it offers a large payload and a good range.
- Renault – Kangoo ZE (200 km range), Zoe Van (range up to 395 km with a 52 kWh battery, and Master e-tech with a range of 120 km.

The Volkswagen e-Crafter delivery van (Figure 6.17) is also worth mentioning, as it has the following tactical and technical data (Elektryczna rewolucja w logistyce? Tak, ale pod kilkoma warunkami…, 2022):

- when fully charged, the e-Crafter can travel 174 km (a diesel delivery car covers up to 230 km per day);
- an electric car can carry a payload of less than 1,000 kg of cargo, compared to 1,300 kg in a Crafter with an internal combustion engine;
- the cost of driving the e-Crafter per 100 km is only PLN 15 – while for diesel, it is PLN 34 (the company can save almost PLN 10,000 on fuel per year, assuming that the average mileage is 45,000 km – considering the purchase price of an electric car, the difference in price is returned only after 9 years);
- the simple design of the e-Crafter can largely reduce the risk of more serious damage after the warranty period (such repairs are most often required for the internal combustion engine).

Electric trucks are systematically used in logistics in practice. Here are some examples (Lubczański, 2022):

Figure 6.17 An example of a Volkswagen e-Crafter electric vehicle.

Source: **Based on *Elektryczna rewolucja w logistyce? Tak, ale pod kilkoma warunkami…*, https://biznes.newseria.pl/, 1/30/2022; Ł. Witkowski, Projekt „Misja Zerowa Emisja" – eCrafter w logistyce miejskiej", https://www.vwdostawcze.pl/, 1/30/2022.**

- Volvo Trucks supplements its offer with electric trucks available in Poland and these are the FL and FE models (these are not long-distance vehicles, Volvo FL Electric has a power of approx. 270 HP, and the batteries are based on, depending on the specification, up to 6 modules, each of which has 66 kWh) and the tested Volvo FH Electric (Figure 6.18);
- Mercedes eActros – a battery of maximum 420 kWh giving a range of up to 400 km;
- DAF offers the CF and LF series – the first one has a power of 240 kW and batteries with a capacity of 315 kWh, giving a range of 200 km, and the second model has a power of 370 kW, and a range of up to 280 km.

6.3.3 Hydrogen Vehicles

The next generation of vehicles can increasingly be found on the roads, and these include hydrogen-powered cars. It should be noted that hydrogen

Figure 6.18 An electric truck from Volvo, FH Electric.

Source: **Based on *Volvo FH Electric: bezemisyjny długodystansowiec,* https://nowoczesnaflota.pl, 1/22/2022.**

cars are a type of electric car, and the difference concerns, among others (Figure 6.19) (Samochody elektryczne vs. auta wodorowe – na co się zdecydować?, 2022):

The method of storing energy – in the case of classic electric cars, energy is taken from the battery. On the other hand, cars with hydrogen drives are equipped with a fuel tank containing compressed hydrogen. Hydrogen is passed to the fuel cells, where it is combined with oxygen to produce electricity. For some people, the solution used in hydrogen-powered cars is a very good alternative to batteries used in electric ones. Among the disadvantages of batteries is often mentioned that despite the manufacturers' efforts, they are still too heavy, quite large, and can take very long to recharge – especially when it is done at home (Figure 6.19.).

Efficiency – the key disadvantage of hydrogen cars is their efficiency. As much as 45% of the initial energy is lost at the stage of obtaining hydrogen by electrolysis. Further losses are related to such processes as compression, liquefaction, transport, filling, and energy generation in the fuel cell. The moment a vehicle changes from hydrogen to current, slightly more than half of its remaining energy is lost. This means that in the end, the efficiency of a car using hydrogen may be only about 25–35% (Figure 6.19).

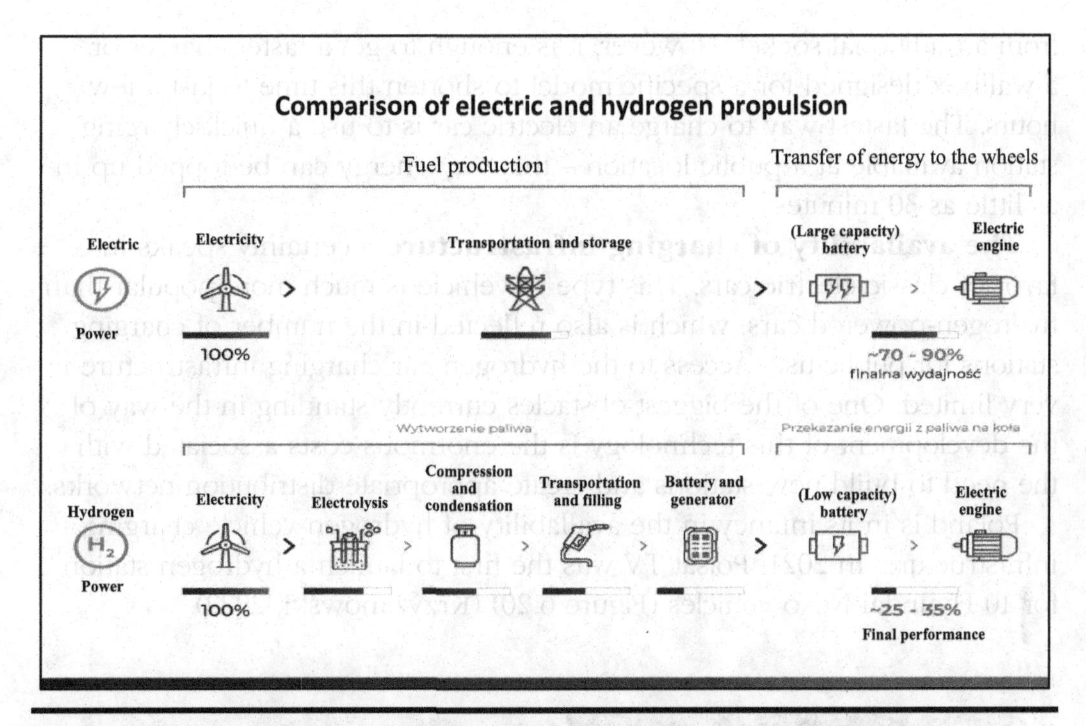

Figure 6.19 A comparison of the electric drive with the hydrogen drive.

Source: Based on *Samochody elektryczne vs. auta wodorowe – na co się zdecydować?*, https://ampergo.pl/, 28.02.2022.

Range – in terms of range, hydrogen cars usually outperform standard electric ones. The large range of hydrogen-powered cars makes such vehicles a good choice for longer journeys. Electric cars, on the other hand, are better for shorter distances, for example, in the city. However, it all depends on the specific car model. Some cars with hydrogen drive offer similar ranges to electric cars with a battery.

Prices and operating costs – when it comes to the costs associated with electric cars and hydrogen cars, the purchase of the former is more profitable. Hydrogen cars are more expensive than electric ones with a battery. The same applies to operating costs. Hydrogen and other e-fuels (synthetic fuels) are more expensive because much more energy is needed to produce them. Electric cars with a battery not only allow for cheaper charging but also offer a much better energy balance compared to hydrogen cars.

Charging – the speed of charging is an issue in which hydrogen cars excel. Their refueling takes only a few minutes. For this reason, for longer routes, they can be a very good alternative to classic electric vehicles. Charging an electric vehicle can take up to 20 hours if it is charged at home from a traditional socket. However, it is enough to get a faster charger or a wallbox designed for a specific model to shorten this time to just a few hours. The fastest way to charge an electric car is to use a quick-charging station available at a public location – this way energy can be topped up in as little as 30 minutes.

The availability of charging infrastructure – certainly speaks in favor of classic electric cars. This type of vehicle is much more popular than hydrogen-powered cars, which is also reflected in the number of charging stations for public use. Access to the hydrogen car charging infrastructure is very limited. One of the biggest obstacles currently standing in the way of the development of this technology is the enormous costs associated with the need to build new stations and create appropriate distribution networks.

Poland is in its infancy in the availability of hydrogen vehicle charging infrastructure. In 2021, Polsat TV was the first to launch a hydrogen station for 10 Hyundai Nexo vehicles (Figure 6.20) (Krzyżanowski, 2022).

Figure 6.20 A hydrogen station for the vehicles used by Polsat TV.

Source: **Based on P. Krzyżanowski, *Powstała pierwsza w Polsce stacja tankowania wodoru. Obsłuży cztery samochody na godzinę,* https://www.auto-swiat.pl/, 2/22/.2022.**

6.3.4 The Last Mile

Particularly noteworthy is the use of electric transport in last-mile logistics, which concerns the delivery of an order from a warehouse or distribution center to the final recipient – a customer, store, or collection point. The last mile is often associated with the logistic activities of the final stage of the supply chain, that is, delivering the cargo regardless of the distance that has to be covered. Most often, in the last mile, the B2C model[11] is used, which is the most complex. It consists in delivering products purchased via the Internet directly to customers who order them (Ostatnia mila, czyli zarządzanie logistyką dostaw zamówień do klientów, 2022). In Figure 6.21, the functioning of the last mile in practice is presented.

The e-commerce market is growing at a crazy pace (this is also the result of the Covid-19 pandemic) and therefore the last mile has to face challenges such as (Marszycki & Waszczuk, 2022):

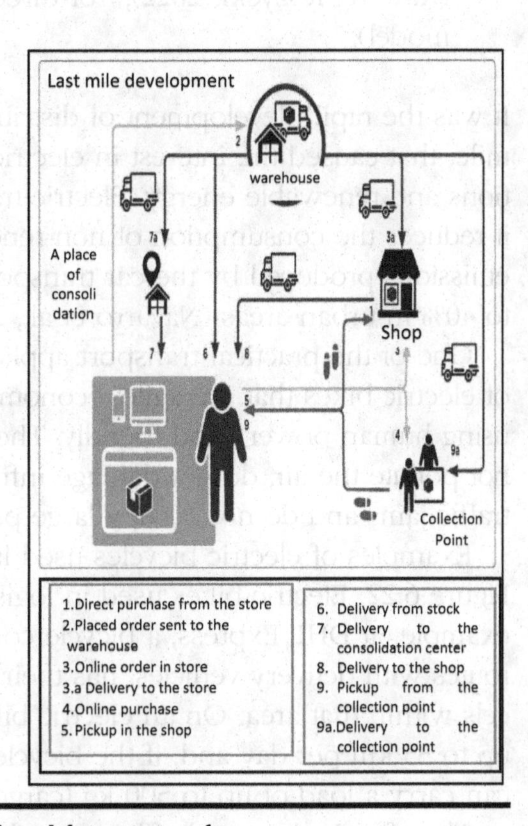

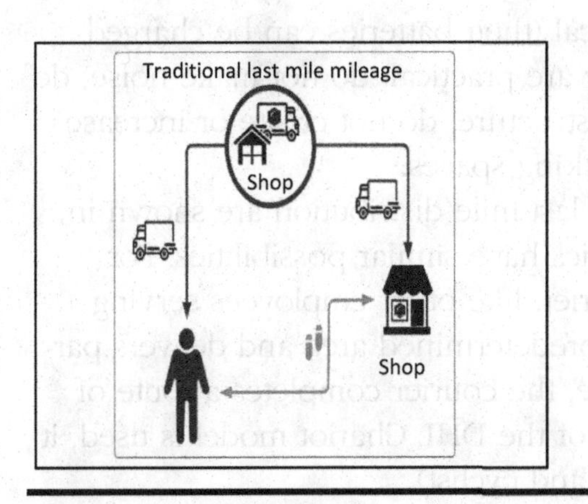

Figure 6.21 Last mile scheme – traditional and future-proof.

Source: **Based on Ostatnia mila, *czyli zarządzanie logistyką dostaw zamówień do klientów,* https://www.mecalux.pl/, 2/2/2022.**

- a significant increase in the number of orders delivered;
- intensification of road traffic in urban areas – transport in the city is associated with additional regulations that must be followed by transport companies (e.g., traffic in certain urban areas only at certain times);
- seasonality of supplies – a sharp increase in demand during holidays or periodic sales;
- greater number of priority deliveries and goods with differing characteristics – perishable loads with a short shelf life (e.g., food or pharmaceuticals) require a reduction in the duration of their stay both in warehouses and in means of transport;
- increase in the number of delivery addresses – a larger number of order recipients means a more complicated and demanding process of planning optimal delivery routes;
- large fragmentation of collection points – customers want to collect parcels at home, from parcel lockers and collection points (PUDO) (Kawa & Różycki, 2022),[12] or directly in the store (Click & Collect model).

It was the rapid development of distribution logistics, including the last mile, that caused the interest in electric transport based on innovative solutions and renewable energy. Electric transport is environmentally friendly; it reduces the consumption of non-renewable energy and carbon dioxide emissions produced by the car transport sector in the EU by 30%, and by up to 40% in urban areas (Navarro et al., 2022).

One of the practical transport applications for last-mile logistics is the use of electric bikes that are agile, economical (their batteries can be charged using human power), and friendly. They are practical: do not make noise, do not pollute the air, do not damage infrastructure, do not create or increase traffic jams and do not occupy large parking spaces.

Examples of electric bicycles used in last-mile distribution are shown in Figure 6.22. Electric bikes used in logistics have similar possibilities. For example, at DHL Express, a bicycle courier, like other employees serving routes with delivery vehicles, has their predetermined area and delivers parcels within that area. On an electric bike, the courier completes a route of up to 35 km per day and, if the bicycle of the DHL Chariot model is used, it can carry a load of up to 500 kg (cargo and cyclist).

The effectiveness and efficiency of the use of transport in last-mile logistics depend, among other things, on:

Figure 6.22 Electric bikes used in last-mile logistics.

Source: **Based on C. Navarro, M. Roca-Riu, S. Furió, M. Estrada, Designing new models for energy efficiency in urban freight transport for smart cities and its application to the Spanish case, [in:] The 9th International Conference on City Logistics, Tenerife, Canary Islands (Spain), 17–19 June, 2015, https://www.researchgate.net, 1/20/2022. DHL Express wprowadza pierwszy w Polsce elektryczny rower kurierski, https://www.logistyka.net.pl/, 1/23/2021**

- the number of reloading terminals that facilitate the safe storage of logistic cargo and sorting, and also provide a social mini base for couriers;
- the density of the network of multi-functional car parks and mini transshipment platforms in the districts from which goods can be delivered using carts, electric vehicles, and tricycles/cargo bicycles;
- the number of charging stations available, both for standard electric vehicles and for hydrogen vehicles;
- the integration of last-mile transport with the transport network in terms of the number and type of stations, location, capacity, etc.

Figure 6.23 Charging electric trucks using solar energy.

Source: **Based on Toyota. https://toyota-forklifts.pl/o-toyocie/pr-and-news/energia-sloneczna-wozki-widlowe-toyota/,11/29/2021.**

6.3.5 The Use of Renewable Energy in Warehouses

A warehouse is a facility that has in its infrastructure technical means of handling and transport, warehouse devices, and IT systems supporting warehouse management. All of them, depending on the power of the installation and the obtained renewable energy, can be connected to renewable energy. An example is an electric truck used in internal transport, in which the batteries are charged thanks to the energy obtained from PVs (Figure 6.23).

In warehouses, renewable energy can also be supplied by: equipment installed in social rooms (fridge, microwave oven, dishwasher, induction hobs, RTV equipment), heat pumps that can heat or cool buildings, alarm and fire protection systems, emergency power supply systems, etc.

Notes

1 An off-grid photovoltaic system is a system in which the surplus energy instead of being returned to the grid is stored independently in batteries.

2 Hydroelectric power plants can be divided according to their capacity into large hydropower plants with a capacity above 10 MW; small hydropower plants (SHP) with a capacity of 1MW–10 MW; mini hydropower plants with a capacity of up to 1 MW; and micro hydropower plants with a capacity of less than 200 kW.

3 Diabatic solution – the thermal energy obtained from the compression process is transferred to the environment, and the temperature increases at the turbine inlet due to the use of an additional heat source.
4 In the adiabatic solution, the heat obtained from the compression process is transferred to the energy storage unit, (P. Klonowicz, Ł. Witanowski, Ł. Jędrzejewski, T. Suchocki, J. Surwiło, D. Stępniak, *Wstępna analiza potencjału zasobników energii typu UWCAES w Zatoce Gdańskiej*, https://www.cire.pl/, 1/29/2022).
5 V2G (vehicle-to-grid) is the free version of the vehicle-to-grid interface. It allows two-way communication with the electrical network. This means more or less that the electricity can not only be taken from the socket, but also transferred to it. Of course, communication is controlled by a special driver and it is up to the driver to decide when the charging will take place. Thus, the car can be charged, for example, whenever the load on the electric network is lower, or when lower night tariff energy rates apply. In other words, the car then is used for storing energy that can be transferred to the grid when the need arises.
6 Electrolyser – a device in which electrolysis is carried out, that is, the decomposition of the electrolyte under the influence of an external source of electric current.
7 Photoelectrolysis – a method of obtaining hydrogen. In this case, sunlight captured by photovoltaic cells is used to break down water into hydrogen and oxygen (R. Burzyński, Magazynowanie energii – czy ostatecznie wygra wodór?, https://www.polskiinstalator.com.pl/, 1/5/2022).
8 Hydrogen energy storage systems are very expensive today. In Australia, they cost around $ 26,900 per unit, which is three times the price of Tesla's Powerwall batteries. Nevertheless, Lavo is not giving up and has announced that the price will drop to approximately $ 22,800 when this product becomes available worldwide. This is to take place in the last quarter of 2022. *Pierwszy domowy akumulator wodorowy*, https://e-magazyny.pl/, 1/6/2022.
9 Fuel cells are electrochemical devices that generate useful energy (electricity, heat) as a result of a chemical reaction between hydrogen and oxygen. The by-product is water. The process begins with the supply of hydrogen from a high-pressure tank to the cell (M. Gis, *Ogniowo wodorowe - jak to działa?* https://e.autokult.pl/, 1/6/2022).
10 CCS Combo 2 – a plug for electric cars that was invented in Germany. It is considered the standard plug for European countries – opted for by the European Commission. Most manufacturers offering their electric models on the Old Continent equip them with this standard (M. Gis, *Rodzaje wtyczek do samochodów elektrycznych, Rodzaje wtyczek do samochodów elektrycznych*, https://e.autokult.pl/,1/21/2022).
11 B2C – a type of business relationship between a company and an individual customer.

12 PUDO (Pick Up Drop Off) locations are places where access for customers is relatively easy. This service is derived from the click & collect concept, which was initially developed by companies trading mainly in brick-and-mortar stores (e.g., retail chains), but gradually transferring some of their sales to the Internet. Thanks to it, customers did not have to wait for the courier and pay for delivery (A. Kawa, M. Różycki, *PUDO, czyli jak ułatwić klientom nadawanie i odbieranie przesyłek?*, https://www.magazyn-ecommerce.pl/,2/20/2022).

Chapter 7

Environmental Protection Illustrated with the Example of Storage Management – Own Research

7.1 Research Methodology

The research methodology in this monograph concerned quantitative research and was related to the development of a series of research tasks forming closed sequentially ordered sets. Determining these tasks and arranging them in the correct order is referred to as the research procedure (Czakon, 2014). According to Czakon, several important tasks can be distinguished that make up this procedure, including defining the current state of affairs, identifying research gaps, selecting the subject of research, sampling, collecting and analyzing empirical data, and drawing conclusions. Distinguishing these tasks made it possible to divide them into two main stages: preparation for research and actual research. Based on this list, a research procedure scheme was developed for this monograph (Figure 7.1).

In the first stage, the literature was analyzed (using the method of critical literature review) in order to define the research problem and its originality as compared to other research problems described in the literature. In addition, the analysis of the literature made it possible to determine the current state of research on the use of renewable energy sources in warehouses and measures taken to protect the environment. The analysis of the literature

DOI: 10.4324/9781003372615-8

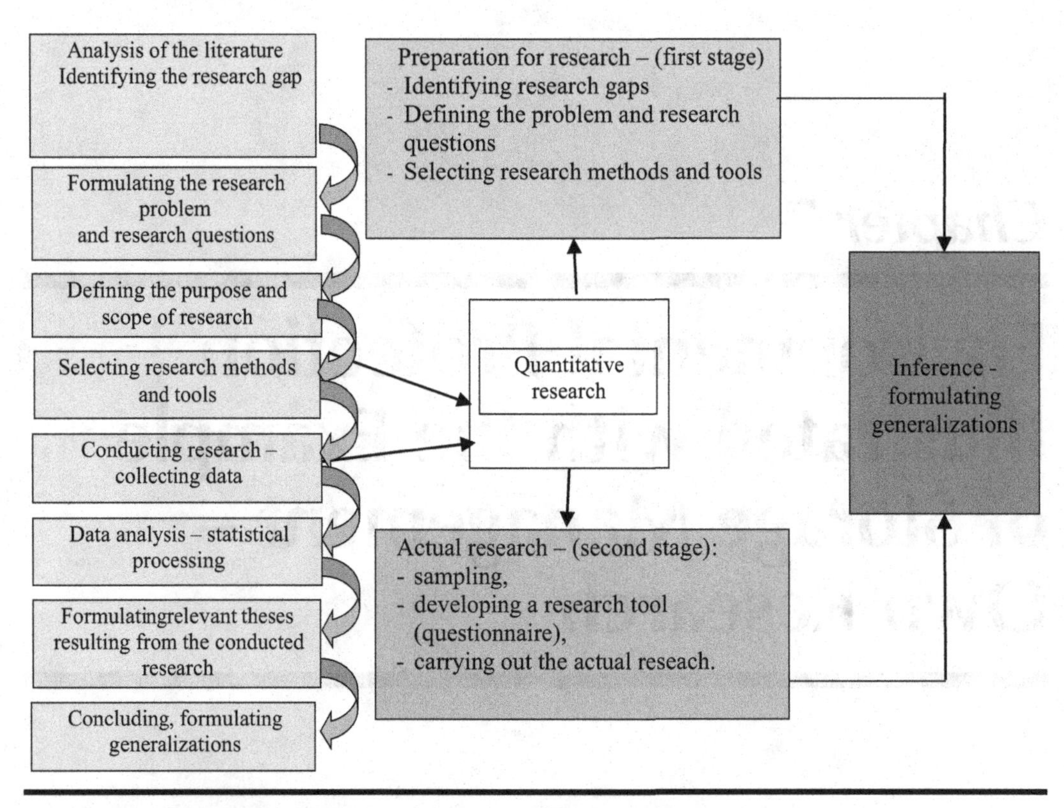

Figure 7.1 Simplified diagram of the research procedure.

Source: **Own elaboration based on R. Stanisławski, Open innovation a rozwój innowacyjny mikro, małych i średnich przedsiębiorstw, Monographs, Wydawnictwo Politechniki Łódzkiej, Łodź (2018).**

therefore makes it possible to determine the research gap concerning the discussed issues. It turned out that the issues related to the implementation of new solutions in warehouses in Poland are relatively recent and require thorough research. Based on such observations, a general research gap was identified regarding the assessment of the relevance of these solutions for energy saving and environmental protection. More specifically, several research gaps have been distinguished, the first of which is **a theoretical gap** that reveals a lack of model attitudes for the use of modern solutions focused on environmental protection in Polish warehouses. The second, **empirical gap**, is related to the shortage of research on the application of these solutions and the assessment of their importance in warehouse management. Finally, the third, **practical gap**, concerns a shortage of recommendations for the rational use of natural resources and their savings through implementations aimed at improving energy efficiency.

As part of the first stage, research methods and tools were selected in accordance with the specified research purpose. In this research, the purpose was formulated as follows: **to identify and classify eco-friendly practices that are implemented in storage companies.** The research was carried out using surveys (a questionnaire specially prepared for this purpose). To obtain reliable results, the study was based on a high level of methodological rigor. This rigor concerned the assessment of four key areas (Rowley, 2002; Stanisławski, 2018):

- **assessment of internal validity** – based on the analysis of cause and effect relationships between variables and the results obtained,
- **assessment of external validity** – concerning generalizing and verifying the current state of affairs against specific judgments, opinions, theories, etc. Negative verification does not mean a lack of external validity and is not perceived as a negative phenomenon. According to many scientists, negative verification is a "motor of progress" in science (Czakon, 2014),
- **assessment of the accuracy of measures** – consisting of the selection of appropriate methods of measuring specific phenomena while maintaining the highest possible level of their compliance with the surrounding reality (the study used a properly selected Likert scale to measure the assessment levels),
- **assessment of reliability** – that is, the possibility to repeat the results obtained – this is the result of questionnaire surveys.

Research reliability means properly formulated research questions (adjusted to the needs of the research), properly developed research procedures, the use of specific standards and rules of conduct adapted to the scientific discipline, and the creation of databases and their proper storage. It is also important to combine the theoretical and practical dimensions, that is, refer the obtained results to the theory and draw conclusions on this basis.

The second stage focused on conducting the actual research, in which three elements were distinguished: selection of the research sample, development of the research tool, and conducting the actual research. The selection of the sample was random and purposeful. The need for targeted selection (the first stage of sample selection) resulted from the need to identify enterprises conducting storage activities (this was done based on PKD – Polish Classification of Activities). As a result, approx. 1,000 enterprises were selected at this stage, of which a population of approx. 300 entities were surveyed. This number was the result of random sampling. As a result of the research, feedback was received from 163 enterprises (warehouses) broken down by size and voivodeship, with 124 of them carrying out activities for ecology and environmental protection. Purposefulness has been limited to this essential sampling criterion. The answers were provided by business owners or (competent) employees indicated by them (in the case of smaller entities) or by senior managers (in the case of larger entities). In turn, with regard to the second element (development of a research tool), it should be mentioned that the study used an original questionnaire with closed-ended questions. The questions in the questionnaire were formulated based solely on the author's own knowledge in the area of the discussed issues and experience in conducting this type of research. As for the third element (actual research), the research was carried out using the CAWI (Computer-Assisted Web Interview) technique, which was intended to provide easier access to the respondents and provide them with greater comfort of the survey consisting in the lack of restrictions and time frames. The advantages of this technique include: **access to selected groups of respondents** with strictly defined predispositions and properties (e.g., warehouses operating 24 hours a day), a **quick research procedure** – preliminary results are available even after 2–3 days from their start, **it generates relatively low costs** (compared to other techniques), which results from no need of hiring interviewers and remunerating them, no need to print and send materials or perform other additional work indirectly related to research, **interactivity**, which gives the possibility of modifying questions, and their order depending on the answers provided, which allows for questions to be directed to respondents with greater precision (Stanisławski, 2017). Therefore, the choice of this technique for these studies was fully justified and adapted to the target group, which, as mentioned earlier, comprised enterprises that have warehouses.

7.2 Description of the Research Sample

Research for this monograph was conducted in 2022. The entities that participated in the study were companies that own and/or manage warehouses. Such enterprises could be production, trade, or service entities with their own warehouses or entities whose activity is directly related to warehouse management, for example, logistics and distribution centers. As is generally known, these centers provide a wide range of services that go far beyond the scope of warehousing and storage of goods. They also (or perhaps above all) focus on customer service, packing, and sorting products to ensure maximum satisfaction to their recipients, for example, through "just-in-time" or "just-in-place" deliveries.

Companies of various sizes participated in the study. The largest number of entities was in the SME group (approx. 70%). The remaining part was large entities, that is, entities employing more than 250 people (30%). Among SMEs, there was the largest number of small enterprises (34.7%), and the smallest number of "micro", which was 8.9%. Medium-sized enterprises constituted 27.4% of the SME group.

The study was conducted throughout Poland. The data below indicates that the largest number of enterprises participating in this study came from three voivodeships: Łódzkie (22.6%), Kujawsko-Pomorskie (16.9%) and Pomorskie (12.1%), and the least from Podkarpackie (0.8%) and Podlaskie (0.8%). Such a distribution of the research sample resulted directly from the willingness of the randomly selected companies to participate in the research. The breakdown by voivodeships (16 voivodeships) is presented in the table below (Table 7.1).

Table 7.1 Division of enterprises participating in the study by location

	Companies participating in the study	
Voivodeship	*Number*	*Share (in%)*
Dolnośląskie	5	4.0
Kujawsko-Pomorskie	21	16.9
Lubelskie	6	4.8
Lubuskie	4	3.2
Łódzkie	28	22.6
Małopolskie	4	3.2
Mazowieckie	11	8.9
Opolskie	7	5.6
Podkarpackie	1	0.8
Podlaskie	1	0.8
Pomorskie	15	12.1
Śląskie	2	1.6

(Continued)

Table 7.1 (Continued)

Voivodeship	*Companies participating in the study*	
	Number	*Share (in%)*
Świętokrzyskie	3	2.4
Warmińsko-Mazurskie	2	1.6
Wielkopolskie	8	6.5
Zachodniopomorskie	6	4.8

Source: Own elaboration

Another characteristic of the surveyed enterprises is the reach of the warehouse. Warehouses with national (33.1%), regional (within the province) (32.3%), and international reach (20.2%) had the largest share in the study. Companies in which the scope of the magazine's impact was local (8.1%) and global (intercontinental) (6.5%) constituted the smallest group in this study. Generally speaking, warehouses focus their activities on serving regional and international recipients within the same continent (Figure 7.2).

Such a division in the surveyed sample of entities (warehouses) proves that the greatest demand from service recipients' "necessitates" such a range of warehouses in Poland. This is because the market (customer) is the dominant feature determining the reach of services provided.

The next (extremely important) characteristic of the research sample is the type of services offered by the analyzed enterprises. Its importance stems from the fact that, as mentioned above, the activity of warehouses (enterprises operating based on warehouse management) is not only the storage of finished products. They usually provide a wide range of "support" services to their clients. The most frequently mentioned services offered by these entities include the following: production (25% of respondents), reloading (25% of respondents), and commercial (25%) services (Table 7.2).

The above set of data confirms the thesis about the high level of diversification of the types of services provided by warehouses in Poland. Also, in this case, it should be noted that this is an effect directly shaped by the market, where the recipients of services have a significant impact on the nature of the business activity conducted by these entities.

The next characteristic of the research sample is undoubtedly its division according to the type of warehouse. Enterprises have been divided according to two basic criteria: the scope of activities and racking height in the warehouse (Table 7.3).

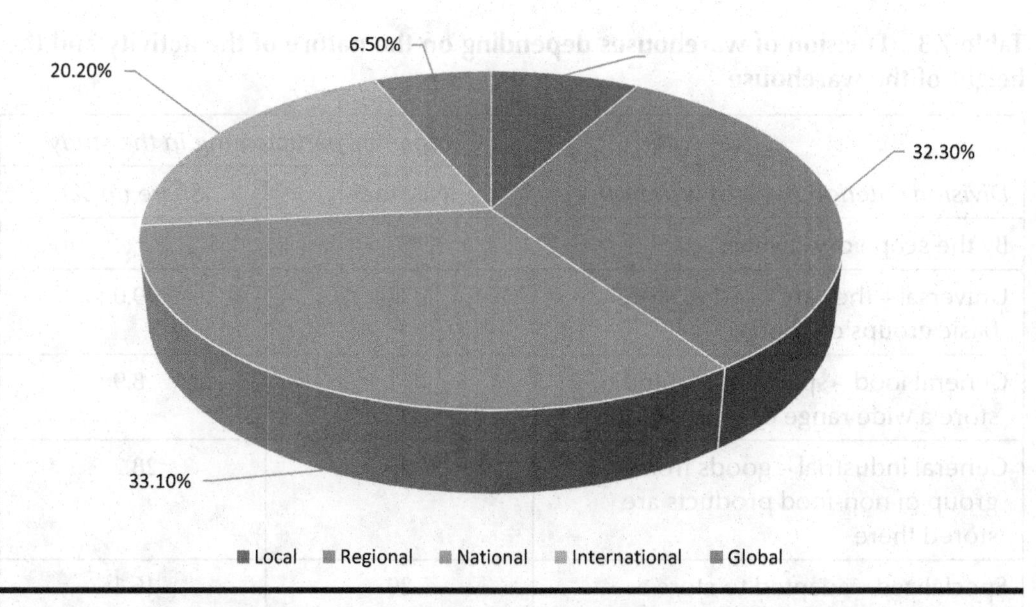

Figure 7.2 Division of the research sample (warehouses) according to the range of impact.
Source: **Own elaboration.**

Table 7.2 Types of services provided by the surveyed enterprises

	Companies participating in the study	
Type of services provided	*Number*	*Share (in %)*
Production	31	25.0
Reloading	31	25.0
Distribution (e-distribution)	16	12.9
Commercial	28	22.6
Customs services	4	3.2
Consignment	3	2.4
Container handling	4	3.2
Packaging of goods	7	5.6

Source: Own elaboration

The above data indicate that universal (29%) and general-industrial warehouses (28.2%) were owned or managed by the largest number of entities participating in the study. "Narrowly specialized" warehouses, where activities involve one product range (17.7%) also accounted for a large share. This indicates that the three above-mentioned groups of warehouses play

Table 7.3 Division of warehouses depending on the nature of the activity and the height of the warehouse

Division criterion (type of warehouse)	Companies participating in the study	
	Number	*Share (in %)*
By the scope of activities		
Universal – they are used to store basic groups of goods	36	29.0
General food – specially adapted to store a wide range of food products	11	8.9
General industrial – goods from the group of non-food products are stored there	35	28.2
Specialized – adapted to store a specific group of products that require special storage conditions	20	16.1
Narrowly specialized – they store only one type of goods with a simple assortment	22	17.7
By racking height		
Low storage	28	22.6
Medium-height storage	58	46.8
High storage	38	30.6

Source: Own elaboration

a significant role in customer service and are among the most "popular" in Poland. The second criterion of division, in turn, is dominated by warehouses from the "medium-height storage" group (46.8%). Their height is between 4.2 m and 7.2 m. It seems that they are among the most universal and thus most commonly built warehouses in Poland.

The last characteristic describing the research sample is the level of mechanization (automation) of warehouses. Most of them are mechanized or automated entities (39.5–34.7%), that is, modern ones – in accordance with the assumptions of "Industry 4.0". Only some of them (14.5–7.3%) have no features of technological advancement, which results from the fact that they were built in the previous century. What is common to them is that most activities are performed manually and their nature is limited to the storage

Table 7.4 The level of technological advancement of warehouses in Poland (based on the research sample)

Level of technological advancement of warehouses	*Companies participating in the study*	
	Number	*Share (in %)*
Unmechanized	18	14.5
Mechanized	49	39.5
Not automated	9	7.3
Automated	43	34.7
Not mechanized and not automated	5	4.0

Source: Own elaboration

of products, that is, the traditional scope of activities. However, the share of these entities is relatively low compared to the "mechanized" or "automated" group, which proves that the level of technological advancement of warehouse management (as a whole) in Poland is relatively high. Figures reflecting the level of advancement in this regard in the research sample are presented in the table below (Table 7.4).

The thesis about the relatively high level of technological advancement of warehouses in Poland is confirmed by the data in the table above. Only 4.0% of respondents indicated that their warehouses were "non-mechanized and non-automated". The rest of the respondents marked at least one element of technological advancement (mechanized or automated). It can therefore be concluded that the warehouses operating in Poland are based on technologically advanced solutions in accordance with the assumptions of "Logistics 4.0" and "Industry 4.0". This is extremely important from the perspective of the use of systems based on renewable energy sources.

7.3 Situation in Poland in Terms of Pro-ecological Practices and Their Impact on Environmental Protection in Warehouse Management

When assessing and identifying the pro-ecological practices of enterprises (warehouses) in Poland, attention will be drawn to three basic elements. The first is the indication of the sources of renewable energy most frequently used by warehouses to protect the environment. The next element concerns the identification of a variety of solutions employed by entities to save energy, and thus also protect the environment. The last element is the assessment of willingness to implement a building management system (BMS). Its role is to eliminate energy losses and make better use of energy. These three elements described above will not only make it possible to briefly describe, but also to determine the importance of, individual renewable energy sources as well as various solutions used in warehouses in Poland for environmental protection. This is undoubtedly an attempt to assess pro-ecological attitudes among Polish entrepreneurs.

The first of the above-mentioned elements concerns the identification of the sources of renewable energy most frequently used by warehouses in Poland. This process will consist of determining the difference between the total number of answers provided by entities using various renewable energy sources (in each case, 124 answers) and indications of "none", that is, entities that do not use any specific solutions. The data in the table below shows that the most frequently used sources include: photovoltaic cells (85.5%), solar collectors (68.5%), and air-source heat pumps (62.3%). The least frequently used solutions are: water turbines (44.2%), wind turbines (50.0%), and biomass (50.0%) (Table 7.5).

The popularity of these sources, as indicated above, is essentially motivated by objective reasons. First of all, the first two solutions are the most easily available in Poland and widely advertised among the public. Secondly, there are widely promoted programs of direct financial support for these sources (reliefs and co-financing of investments). Thirdly, recently (last few years), there have been many entities dealing with the consulting and installation of this type of solutions both in households and enterprises (including warehouses). Fourthly, this support, to a large extent financed by EU funds, encourages the installation of such solutions. In addition, it is worth noting that the current government in Poland, under a law introduced in 2016, effectively discouraged the creation of wind farms and the use of turbines, arguing that it has a negative impact on human health. Quite a tricky "puzzle" is the relatively small share of biomass in total renewable energy production. This is probably due to its low availability or relatively high costs of recovery (processing, sorting, or giving it the final form that allows it to be used – e.g., pellets). The sun is the cleanest source of energy that is easiest to obtain, where the only condition is to have the right installation – with a usable life of even several dozen years. Hence, the great popularity of this type of solution.

Table 7.5 Identification and importance of renewable energy sources

Source of energy	*Importance*													
	Of no importance		*Of very little importance*		*Of little importance*		*Of medium importance*		*Important*		*Very important*		*Total*	
	N	*%**	*N*	*%*	*N*	*%*	*N*	*%*	*N*	*%*	*N*	*%*	*N*	*%*
Solar panels	39	31.5	9	7.3	11	8.9	20	16.1	38	30.6	7	5.6	124	100
Photovoltaic cells	18	14.5	4	3.2	8	6.5	18	14.5	49	39.5	27	21.8	124	100
Wind turbines	62	50.0	5	4.0	8	6.5	17	13.7	23	18.5	9	7.3	124	100
Water turbines	68	54.8	3	2.4	4	3.2	23	18.5	22	17.7	4	3.2	124	100
Biomass	62	50.0	7	5.6	4	3.2	29	23.4	18	14.5	4	3.2	124	100
Heat pumps	51	41.1	5	4.0	8	6.5	15	12.1	35	28.2	10	8.1	124	100
Air source heat pumps	48	38.7	1	0.8	7	5.6	25	20.2	33	26.6	10	8.1	124	100
Kinetic plates	63	50.8	9	7.3	8	6.5	22	17.7	20	16.1	2	1.6	124	100

Source: Own elaboration

The widespread use of such solutions in Poland is also evidenced by the respondents' assessment of the importance of individual renewable energy sources. In their opinion, all the most often used sources are very important from the point of view of their usefulness. Among the most frequently used sources, that is, photovoltaic cells and solar collectors, over 60% of respondents indicated the great importance of these solutions from the point of view of generated savings ("important solution" – 39.5% of respondents and "very important solution" – 21.8% of respondents). It should therefore be assumed that they provide the expected benefits, which is clearly emphasized by the respondents in this study. The least positive ratings concern "kinetic slabs" (17.7% of "important" and "very important" ratings), which may (probably) result from the low popularity" of this solution among Polish entrepreneurs.

Another element regarding the pro-ecological approaches among Polish enterprises is the indication of solutions that have been used in warehouses to save energy and protect the environment. It turns out that in most cases (over 90% of respondents) such simple solutions as: LED lighting, motion sensors, or better use of natural lighting are commonly used. Measures such as thermal imaging tests (64% implement this measure), heat recovery from machines (60% implement this measure), or systematic replacement of devices with energy-saving ones (70% implement this measure) are much less frequent in warehouses (Table 7.6).

The relatively lower propensity to use these solutions is undoubtedly related to the need of considerable outlays, which limits their popularity among the surveyed entities. However, it should be noted that these solutions are not "foreign" in most enterprises, which is undoubtedly the effect of the increase in the "pro-ecological" awareness of Polish entrepreneurs.

Then, analyzing the assessment of individual solutions implemented in warehouses for environmental protection, it should be noted that the simple ones are rated the best, both in terms of the importance of environmental impact and in the context of the generated energy savings (approx. 41% of respondents consider these measures as important, and 29–33% as very important). In contrast, solutions that are more "advanced" and, at the same time, more "capital-intensive" are rated slightly worse (considered "important" by 28–34% and "very important" by 9–15%). Similarly, it is the result of "higher expectations with higher expenditures", which in practice means that enterprises investing in new technologies and undertaking new activities with relatively high expenditures expect to obtain good or very good results, usually in a short period of time – which is not always possible.

Table 7.6 Solutions for energy saving and environmental protection in warehouses in Poland

	Importance													
	Of no importance		*Of very little importance*		*Of little importance*		*Of medium importance*		*Important*		*Very important*		*Total*	
Solutions	*N*	*%**	*N*	*%*	*N*	*%*	*N*	*%*	*N*	*%*	*N*	*%*	*N*	*%*
Energy-saving lighting systems	11	8.9	6	4.8	7	5.6	25	20.2	49	39.5	26	21.0	124	100
LED lighting	5	4.0	2	1.6	7	5.6	23	18.9	51	41.1	36	29.0	124	100
Motion detectors	8	6.5	1	0.8	8	6.5	22	17.7	52	41.9	33	26.6	124	100
Natural light	3	2.4	2	1.6	5	4.0	21	16.9	51	41.1	42	33.9	124	100
Rainwater tanks	32	25.8	6	4.8	9	7.3	27	21.8	37	29.8	13	10.5	124	100
Energy saving campaign	16	12.9	2	1.6	11	8.9	35	28.2	48	38.7	12	9.7	124	100
Thermal imaging tests	36	29.0	4	3.2	9	7.3	29	25.4	35	28.2	11	8.9	124	100
Heat recovery from machines	40	32.3	4	3.2	12	9.7	27	21.8	29	23.4	12	9.7	124	100
Faucet aerators	25	20.2	5	4.0	9	7.3	29	25.4	43	34.7	13	10.5	124	100
Replacement of energy-consuming devices	30	24.2	3	2.4	7	5.6	22	17.7	43	34.7	19	15.3	124	100
Installing destratificators	45	36.3	5	4.0	11	8.9	23	18.5	31	25.0	9	7.3	124	100

Source: Own elaboration

The third (last) element to be identified and assessed is the use of systems for energy saving and environmental protection. Such a system is BMS focused on automatic solutions to reduce resource consumption and minimize the negative impact on the environment (intelligent building). The study conducted shows that only a small part of entrepreneurs use this system (about 30% of the respondents). Much more respondents who were aware of the existence of such a system did not implement it in their enterprises (approx. 40% of respondents). Also, a significant part of the respondents indicated that they are not aware and have no knowledge of whether such a system functions in their warehouses (approx. 30% of respondents) (Figure 7.3). It should therefore be concluded that the popularity of these systems among enterprises in Poland is not very high, which may be due to the limited knowledge of entrepreneurs about the existence of such solutions (on the one hand), and the high expenditures related to their implementation in practice (on the other). There is one more important aspect – entrepreneurs are not always sure when the investment will pay off, which may result in uncertainty and lack of decision about making it. There is a need to conduct a campaign for greater public awareness of the cost-effectiveness of pro-ecological solutions and their positive impact on the environment. The lack of such actions will delay "useful" implementations to the detriment of both enterprises and their environment.

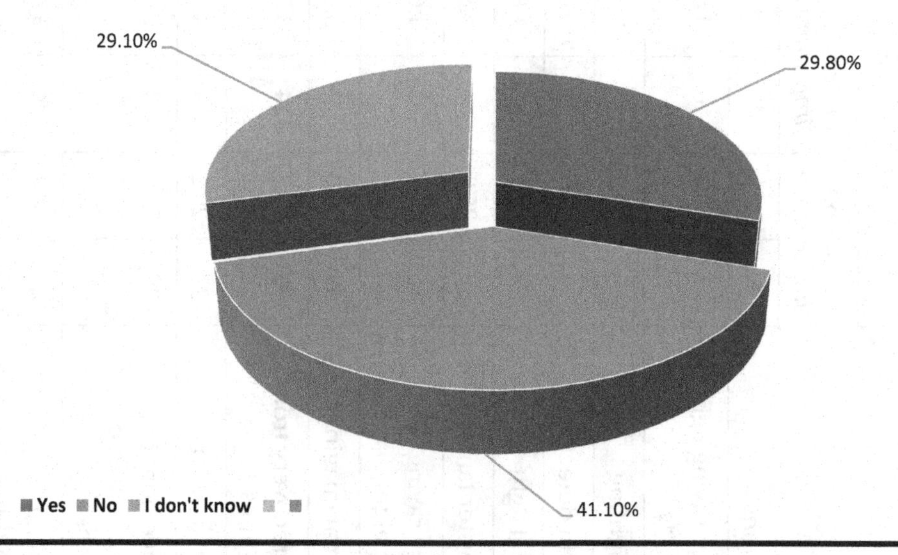

Figure 7.3 The level of BMS implementation among warehouses in Poland.

Source: Own elaboration.

Table 7.7 Evaluation of the usefulness of individual systems within the BMS

	Importance – usefulness													
	Of no importance		*Of very little importance*		*Of little importance*		*Of medium importance*		*Important*		*Very important*		*Total*	
System	*N*	*%**	*N*	*%*	*N*	*%*	*N*	*%*	*N*	*%*	*N*	*%*	*N*	*%*
System for managing and optimizing the distribution and consumption of energy and utilities	1	2.7	1	2.7	4	10.8	5	13.5	23	62.2	3	8.1	37	100
Energy and utilities consumption monitoring system	1	2.7	0	0	2	5.4	8	21.6	21	56.8	5	13.5	37	100
Uninterruptible power supply system	4	10.8	0	0	2	5.4	13	35.1	16	43.2	2	5.4	37	100
Power and electricity consumption management system	1	2.7	0	0	0	0	9	24.3	22	59.5	5	13.5	37	100

Source: Own elaboration.

The importance of individual BMS systems in the group of entities implementing BMS is evidenced by the following data (Table 7.7). Overall, this assessment is very positive. With regard to the three systems, the respondents assessed their usefulness as above 70% ("important" and "very important"). This applies to the management of power and electricity consumption (73% of respondents); energy and utilities consumption management and optimization system (70.3%) and energy and utilities consumption monitoring system (70.3%). This proves that entrepreneurs appreciate such solutions, mainly from the point of view of usability and savings they achieve from these systems. This confirms the earlier thesis about the usefulness of these solutions and the lack of awareness of a large part of entrepreneurs not only as to the pro-ecological but, above all, the economic importance of these systems.

The importance of the systems used within the BMS in terms of their usefulness is also evidenced by very few ratings "of very little importance" and "of little importance" assigned by the respondents using these solutions. In most cases, these were "zero" ratings, which means that, in principle, the respondents did not speak negatively about the systems used. This clearly shows that it is worth using them despite the high initial outlay.

7.4 Identification and Assessment of the Importance of Practices and Activities for Environmental Protection in Warehouse Management in Poland

Another element discussed in this chapter is the identification and assessment of practical actions taken to protect the environment. The first of them is **ESG** (Environmental, Social, and Corporate Governance) practices covering some areas where actions are most often undertaken to improve the current state of affairs in the context of environmental protection. The analysis of the obtained research results shows that the assumptions of ESG practices were implemented only in approx. 30% of warehouses, for the most part, that is, over 36%, they were not implemented, while approx. 32% are unable to answer the question about taking ESG measures (Figure 7.4).

It seems that the share of enterprises (warehouses) implementing ESG, that is, approx. 30%, is not very high. This is because the increase in social awareness among the management staff in Poland is still slow. However, fortunately, running a business in the spirit of sustainable development and

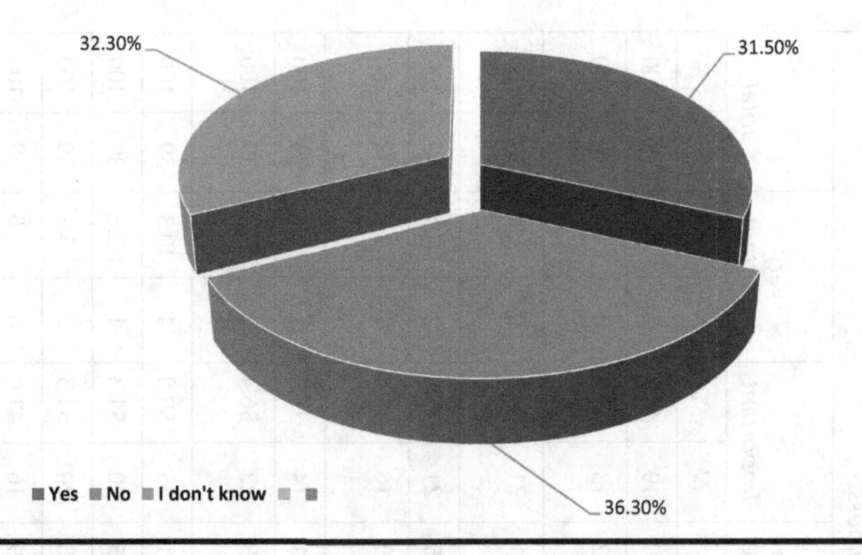

Figure 7.4 The level of implementation of ESG assumptions in the surveyed enterprises (warehouses) in Poland.

Source: **Own elaboration.**

maintaining environmental protection standards in Polish realities is becoming a priority for a growing group of entrepreneurs, especially from the younger, pro-ecologically oriented generation.

The next step is to identify and evaluate the areas where ESG practices are being undertaken. The most frequently indicated areas related to ESG practices are: packaging and waste (approx. 95% of respondents), renewable energy (approx. 88% of respondents), and water management (approx. 84% of respondents). The smallest share of ESG implementations is carried out in areas related to emissions, that is, reducing the carbon footprint (approx. 67% of respondents) or the supply of raw materials (approx. 67%) (Table 7.8).

The analysis of the above data also shows that ESG is most positively evaluated in such areas as renewable energy (as indicated by 61.5% of respondents), clean technologies (56.4%), emission of toxins and waste (61.5%), electronic waste (53.9%), and vulnerability to climate change (53.8%). Water management (in the context of ESG) (5.8%) and the supply of raw materials (35.9%) are rated the lowest by the respondents. Summing up, it should be concluded that the assumptions of ESG practice are known and applied in Poland to a moderate extent, and only in a few selected areas.

At this point, it is also worth looking at the activities that have been undertaken so far in enterprises (warehouses) and, in the opinion of the respondents, had the greatest positive impact on environmental protection.

Table 7.8 Areas of ESG practices

	Importance – usefulness													
	Of no importance		*Of very little importance*		*Of little importance*		*Of medium importance*		*Important*		*Very important*		*Total*	
Area	*N*	*%**	*N*	*%*	*N*	*%*	*N*	*%*	*N*	*%*	*N*	*%*	*N*	*%*
Co_2 emissions	9	23.1	0	0	2	5.1	7	17.9	19	48.7	2	5.1	39	100
Product carbon footprint	13	33.3	0	0	2	5.1	11	28.2	13	33.3	0	0	39	100
Vulnerability to climate change	7	17.9	0	0	2	5.1	9	23.1	21	53.8	0	0	39	100
Water management	6	15.4	1	2.6	1	2.6	8	20.5	21	5.8	2	5.1	39	100
Biodiversity and land management	10	25.6	1	2.6	4	10.3	7	17.9	16	41.0	1	2.6	39	100
Raw material supply	13	33.3	1	2.6	1	2.6	9	23.1	14	35.9	1	2.6	39	100
Emission of toxins and waste	7	17.9	1	2.6	0	0	7	17.9	22	56.4	2	5.1	39	100
Packaging and waste	2	5.1	0	0	1	2.6	9	23.1	23	59.0	4	10.3	39	100
Electronic waste	7	17.9	2	5.1	1	2.6	8	10.5	20	51.3	1	2.6	39	100
Clean technologies	9	25.1	1	2.6	2	5.1	5	12.8	20	51.3	2	5.1	39	100
Green construction	11	28.2	2	5.1	3	7.7	7	17.9	16	41.0	0	0	39	100
Renewable energy	5	12.8	2	5.1	0	0	8	20.5	24	61.5	0	0	39	100

Source: Own elaboration.

Table 7.9 Identification of activities that have had the greatest impact on environmental protection so far

	Importance – usefulness													
	Of no importance		*Of very little importance*		*Of little importance*		*Of medium importance*		*Important*		*Very important*		*Total*	
Activities	*N*	*%**	*N*	*%*	*N*	*%*	*N*	*%*	*N*	*%*	*N*	*%*	*N*	*%*
Waste minimization	21	16.9	4	33.2	10	8.1	24	19.4	55	44.4	10	8.1	124	100
Ecological handling of packaging	21	16.9	3	2.4	10	8.1	28	22.6	44	35.5	18	14.5	124	100
Ecological transport	24	19.4	4	3.2	12	9.7	27	21.8	49	39.5	8	6.5	124	100
Energy-saving construction (lighting, heating system, humidity, water consumption)	7	5.6	3	2.4	8	6.5	23	18.5	64	51.6	19	15.3	124	100
Energy-saving reloading and storage devices	22	17.7	3	2.4	13	10.5	23	18.5	48	38.7	15	12.1	124	100
Obtaining renewable energy	5	4.0	5	4.0	10	8.1	32	25.8	50	40.3	22	17.7	124	100
Ergonomics of warehouse infrastructure	23	18.5	4	3.2	11	8.9	35	28.2	43	34.7	8	6.5	124	100

(*Continued*)

Table 7.9 (Continued)

	Importance – usefulness													
	Of no importance		*Of very little importance*		*Of little importance*		*Of medium importance*		*Important*		*Very important*		*Total*	
Activities	*N*	*%**	*N*	*%*	*N*	*%*	*N*	*%*	*N*	*%*	*N*	*%*	*N*	*%*
Changing management systems, including personnel management systems	14	11.3	7	5.6	18	14.5	41	33.1	36	29.0	8	6.5	124	100
Change in the attitude of the management and staff toward ecology as a result of activities taken by the social/business/ regulatory environment (e.g., European Union)	9	7.3	11	8.9	16	12.9	37	29.8	45	36.3	6	4.8	124	100
Carrying out activities to raise environmental awareness, e.g., training	8	6.5	10	8.1	17	13.7	39	31.5	39	31.5	11	8.9	124	100

Source: Own elaboration.

Most of the activities undertaken by entrepreneurs concerned: the use of renewable energy (96% of respondents), the use of energy-saving construction (94.4% of respondents), changing the management's attitude to ecology (92.7% of respondents), and improving environmental awareness by organizing training or courses among the staff (94.5% of respondents) (Table 7.9).

In the opinion of the respondents – to the greatest extent so far (defined as important or very important) "hard" measures, such as energy-saving implementations in construction (lighting, heating), which allowed to reduce energy consumption (quantity/value) (66.9% of respondents), the use of ecological packaging (approx. 50% of respondents), and greater use of ecological transport (approx. 46% of respondents) were of the greatest importance for environmental protection in warehouses. "Soft" measures, such as changing management systems or training, were assessed as less "useful" from the point of view of ecology (25.5% and approx. 40%, respectively). This is also evidenced by the ratings of "of very little importance", which were at the level of 5.6–8.9% – by way of comparison, in the case of "hard" measures, these ratings were in the range of 2.4–3.2%. Undoubtedly, this is the effect of greater "tangibility and directness" of hard measures. In the case of "soft" measures, the effects are indirect and usually spread over time.

7.5 Evaluation of Resources Enabling Environmental Protection in Warehouse Management in Poland

Another question that is important from the point of view of these studies is whether warehouses in Poland have the necessary resources to implement pro-environmental solutions. The data presented in the table below indicate that the biggest problem is the lack of financial and material resources (proper equipment) (Table 7.10).

About 9% of respondents indicate that they have deficiencies in terms of financial resources and 2.4% indicate deficiencies in material resources. The problem with human resources in the context of the number of employees (shortages affect only 0.8% of respondents) is of the lowest importance. This means that in practice, approximately 90% (or more) of warehouses have resources that enable them to implement various types of solutions, systems or take measures to save energy and protect the environment. Therefore, it is likely that the relatively low level of implementation of pro-ecological solutions has two main reasons. First of all, too short a period for warehouses

Table 7.10 Resources for environmental protection (identification and assessment) at the disposal of warehouses

	Importance – usefulness													
	Of no importance		*Of very little importance*		*Of little importance*		*Of medium importance*		*Important*		*Very important*		*Total*	
Resources	*N*	*%**	*N*	*%*	*N*	*%*	*N*	*%*	*N*	*%*	*N*	*%*	*N*	*%*
Financial	11	8.9	6	4.8	7	5.6	28	22.6	59	47.6	13	10.5	124	100
Human (adequate number of staff)	1	0.8	7	5.6	7	5.6	25	20.2	61	49.2	23	18.5	124	100
Tangible (equipment)	3	2.4	8	6.5	10	8.1	28	22.6	61	49.2	14	11.3	124	100
Intangible: knowledge, competence, skill of the staff	2	1.6	8	6.5	6	4.8	32	25.8	50	40.3	26	21.0	124	100

Source: Own elaboration.

to prepare for the rapidly changing business environment (expansive development of Logistics 4.0 and Industry 4.0) and still low social awareness in terms of environmental protection and energy savings. Of course, the new situation, shaped by the rapidly changing circumstances (high costs of energy carriers, climate change) will make pro-ecological attitude a priority among all entrepreneurs (investors) in Poland. There is one more important element here – more and more customers, when purchasing goods or services, are guided by ecological criteria and choose those entities that take ecological assumptions into account in their business activities.

Respondents assessing the importance of these resources clearly indicate that three of them are of key importance for the process of environmental protection. These are material resources (about 60% of respondents) and human resources (both the number of employees and the knowledge and skills of employees) (over 61% of respondents). Interestingly, the respondents do not mention financial resources as the most important in the first place. This may be the result of relatively easy access to these resources (despite indicating that they are a serious problem) for the creation of storage infrastructure in Poland. In fact, many foreign investors in this area are particularly interested in the expansion of logistics centers. After all, Poland is at the crossroads of numerous transport routes in the east-west and north-south directions. Hence, financial resources are one of the elements of lower importance in the discussed process. Human factors take the lead in terms of the number of suitably qualified employees.

7.6 Identification of Determinants and Barriers Affecting Environmental Protection in Warehouse Management in Poland

This section offers an interpretation of the main determinants (stimulants) indicated by the respondents as important in taking action to save energy and protect the environment. This analysis will be carried out separately for two groups of stimulants: internal (resulting from the conditions inside the organizations – warehouses) and external (considering the conditions of the environment's regulatory directly or indirectly influencing the actions of the company). Among the former, the most important include: the search for savings (only 0.8% indicated that this element was of no importance), ensuring greater stability of the company (6.5% indicated the lack of this factor) and the desire to supplement pro-ecological knowledge and greater rationalization of the use of natural resources (12.1% of responses indicating "of no importance" each). It is worth noting that the last three elements are market-driven, which means that warehouses "can see" the internal need to adapt to the requirements of the environment's regulatory (Table 7.11).

This confirms the earlier thesis that an environment that "necessitates" specific market behavior is an excellent stimulator. Of course, financial criteria are also important here, as exemplified by the "rationalization of the use of natural resources", which has not only an "adaptive", but also an economic context. Rationalization is reduced to better use, that is, savings in the consumption of natural resources.

When assessing the importance of individual determinants (stimulators) in the field of environmental protection, it should be emphasized that in the first place, the respondents indicated "savings" (over 75% of responses concerned this factor). Ecology should therefore also be treated as a "tool", that is, it should contribute to lower consumption of resources – mainly energy. Nothing stimulates better than reducing expenses and improving financial standing. Among other stimulators, respondents indicate market-oriented factors. These are: promoting own services through ecology (approx. 63%) and ensuring greater stability in the environment (approx. 55%). This undoubtedly proves the role of the environment's regulatory in shaping the ecological attitudes of warehouses in Poland.

The above thesis is confirmed by the example of external stimulants. The first place among them is occupied by "improvement of the company's image in the social/business environment…" (11.3% indicate that this determinant is of no importance). Business entities are aware of the need to adapt to the "ecological" environment. Among other determinants, they also mention "availability of resources for future generations" (with 12.1% indicating "of no importance"), which proves forward thinking. In turn, "the exchange of mutual experiences and establishing partnerships" prove openness to cooperation with the business environment. This is undoubtedly a very positive signal proving that these enterprises promote "open attitudes" aimed at exchanging ideas and technologies related to more effective ways of protecting the environment and saving energy (Table 7.12).

When it comes to assessing the importance of the determinants mentioned above, enterprises generally indicate "competitiveness" (approx. 51%). That is, the market (social/business environment) determines actions in this area, "necessitating" the implementation of pro-ecological solutions and promotion of attitudes fostering the protection of natural resources by economic entities.

Table 7.11 Internal determinants of taking actions for environmental protection

	Importance – usefulness													
	Of no importance		*Of very little importance*		*Of little importance*		*Of medium importance*		*Important*		*Very important*		*Total*	
Internal determinant	N	%*	N	%	N	%	N	%	N	%	N	%	N	%
Seeking to increase the scale of operations – considering the pro-ecological attitudes of customers	23	18.5	6	4.8	21	16.9	26	21.0	39	31.5	9	7.3	124	100
Seeking to disseminate own achievements of pro-ecological implementations in the surroundings	19	15.3	6	4.8	10	8.1	40	32.3	39	31.5	10	8.2	124	100
Seeking to supplement knowledge about new pro-ecological solutions	15	12.1	7	5.6	16	12.9	32	25.8	44	35.5	10	8.2	124	100
Promotion of own pro-ecological services	20	16.1	5	4.0	9	7.3	36	29.0	41	53.1	13	10.5	124	100
Search for savings	1	0.8	2	1.6	9	7.3	18	14.5	60	48.4	34	27.4	124	100

(Continued)

Table 7.11 (Continued)

	Importance – usefulness													
	Of no importance		*Of very little importance*		*Of little importance*		*Of medium importance*		*Important*		*Very important*		*Total*	
Internal determinant	*N*	%*	*N*	%	*N*	%	*N*	%	*N*	%	*N*	%	*N*	%
Ensuring greater stability of the company in the environment through ecology	8	6.5	4	3.2	10	8.1	33	26.6	53	42.7	16	12.9	124	100
The need to create new, more competitive pro-ecological products (technologies)	22	17.7	7	5.6	6	4.8	27	21.8	48	38.7	14	11.3	124	100
Necessity to change the current strategy to a pro-ecological one (necessitated by the environment's regulatory)	16	12.9	8	6.5	13	10.5	35	28.2	42	33.9	10	8.1	124	100
Rationalization of the use of natural resources necessary for business or production	15	12.1	6	4.8	8	6.5	34	27.4	49	39.5	12	9.7	124	100

Source: Own elaboration.

Table 7.12 External determinants of taking actions for environmental protection

	Importance – weight													
	Of no importance		*Of very little importance*		*Of little importance*		*Of medium importance*		*Important*		*Very important*		*Total*	
External determinants	N	%*	N	%	N	%	N	%	N	%	N	%	N	%
Seeking to use EU programs	19	15.3	6	4.8	11	8.9	27	21.8	46	37.1	15	12.1	124	
Opportunities to exchange mutual experiences and establish partnerships in the field of ecology	16	12.9	10	8.1	13	10.5	32	25.8	45	36.3	8	6.3	124	100
The need to improve competitiveness on the existing market through ecology	20	16.1	4	5.2	8	6.5	30	24.2	52	41.9	10	8.1	124	100
The need to expand own sales markets (acquiring new customers with a pro-ecological attitude)	20	16.1	9	7.3	8	6.5	32	25.8	40	32.3	15	12.1	124	100

(Continued)

Table 7.12 (Continued)

	Importance – weight													
	Of no importance		*Of very little importance*		*Of little importance*		*Of medium importance*		*Important*		*Very important*		*Total*	
External determinants	N	%*	N	%	N	%	N	%	N	%	N	%	N	%
Improvement of the company's image in the social/business environment through pro-ecological implementations	14	11.3	6	4.3	9	7.3	34	27.4	46	37.1	15	12.1	124	100
Ensuring the protection of resources and their availability for future generations	15	12.1	7	5.6	9	7.3	36	29.0	42	33.9	15	12.1	124	100

Source: Own elaboration.

Another element analyzed is the barriers that prevent or hinder the implementation of pro-ecological solutions in warehouses. The barriers indicated in this section of the study confirmed the thesis that financial resources are less important than human and material resources which limits the positive impact on ecology (referred to in point 7.5). Human and material resources were indicated as more destructive (2.4% of nonexistence of such barriers) than financial ones. Among other barriers, "uncertainty as to the final effects" resulting from pro-ecological implementations was indicated (7.3% of the existence of such barriers). This proves that entrepreneurs are not able to predict whether the outlays incurred in terms of investments for savings will pay off in specific cases. Indeed, what is typical of environmental investments is that they are highly personalized and difficult to predict. What is profitable for one entrepreneur does not have to be profitable for another – it depends on many conditions, for example, scale and scope of business activity and implemented pro-ecological activities. An interesting fact is also that the "lack of a proper pro-ecological development strategy" is indicated at the level of "of no importance" by about 10% (i.e., about 90% claim that this barrier exists) (Table 7.13). This confirms the earlier thesis that social awareness of the importance of ecology and environmental protection among entrepreneurs is quite poor and is constantly evolving.

In the assessment of the importance of barriers, the largest negative impact, according to the respondents, was attributed to two factors: uncertainty as to the final effects (approx. 40%) and difficulties in overcoming old management methods and mental habits (approx. 37%). Thus, summarizing this fragment, it can be said with certainty that the limitations are of a "human" and technical nature, the former being the "effect" of historical background because ecology was not treated as a priority in the past. The change of attitude is currently necessitated by the massive degradation of the natural environment (climate change) as well as the need to limit the consumption of natural resources (economic and financial factor) and the increasing difficulty in accessing them.

The last element discussed in this section is the benefits that warehouses achieve from the use of a pro-ecological approach related to environmental protection. In the first place, the respondents pointed to the reduction of costs related to the use of various types of utilities (only 0.8% of respondents said that they did not notice any benefits from this – over 99% claim that such benefits exist). Another benefit indicated by the respondents is "reducing warehouse operating costs" (only 3.2% of the respondents stated that there is no such benefit) (Table 7.14). These two benefits clearly prove

Table 7.13 Barriers in taking action to protect the environment

	Importance – usefulness													
	Of no importance		*Of very little importance*		*Of little importance*		*Of medium importance*		*Important*		*Very important*		*Total*	
Barriers	*N*	*%**	*N*	*%*	*N*	*%*	*N*	*%*	*N*	*%*	*N*	*%*	*N*	*%*
Lack of a proper pro-ecological development strategy	12	9.8	18	14.6	26	21.1	28	22.8	33	26.8	6	4.9	123	100
Different expectations of company management and staff as to pro-ecological implementations	10	8.1	15	12.2	19	15.4	35	28.5	33	26.8	4	3.3	116	100
Lack of interest in pro-ecology on the part of top management	18	14.6	14	11.4	12	9.8	32	26.0	34	27.6	6	4.9	116	100
Lack of proper technical infrastructure	7	5.7	11	8.9	20	16.3	35	28.5	36	29.3	7	5.7	116	100
Difficulties in overcoming old management methods and mental habits	14	11.4	10	8.1	10	8.1	36	29.3	41	33.3	5	4.1	116	100

(Continued)

Table 7.13 (Continued)

	Importance – usefulness													
	Of no importance		*Of very little importance*		*Of little importance*		*Of medium importance*		*Important*		*Very important*		*Total*	
Barriers	*N*	*%**	*N*	*%*	*N*	*%*	*N*	*%*	*N*	*%*	*N*	*%*	*N*	*%*
Too much uncertainty about the final effects of pro-ecological implementations	9	7.3	10	8.1	11	8.9	36	29.3	43	35.0	6	4.9	115	100
Lack of adequate financial resources	4	3.3	9	7.3	8	6.5	33	26.8	29	23.6	6	4.9	89	100
Lack of adequate human resources (inadequate number of staff)	3	2.4	8	6.5	18	14.6	31	25.2	26	21.1	4	3.3	90	100
Lack of appropriate material resources (lack of proper equipment)	3	2.4	10	8.1	12	9.8	31	25.2	31	25.2	3	2.4	90	100
Lack of appropriate intangible resources: knowledge, competences, staff skills	2	1.6	10	8.1	11	8.9	35	28.5	27	22.0	3	2.4	88	100

Source: Own elaboration.

Table 7.14 Benefits achieved by warehouses in connection with the implementation of environmental protection measures

	Importance – weight													
	Of no importance		*Of very little importance*		*Of little importance*		*Of medium importance*		*Important*		*Very important*		*Total*	
Benefits	*N*	*%**	*N*	*%*	*N*	*%*	*N*	*%*	*N*	*%*	*N*	*%*	*N*	*%*
Reduction of costs resulting from the consumption of utilities (electricity, gas, water)	1	0.8	6	4.8	12	9.7	16	12.9	66	53.2	23	18.5	124	100
Increased competitiveness on the markets thanks to ecology	22	17.7	4	3.2	10	8.1	31	25.0	46	37.1	11	8.9	124	100
Acquisition of new customers	22	17.7	7	5.6	9	7.3	24	19.4	47	37.9	15	12.1	124	100
Better access to information	22	17.7	7	5.6	12	9.7	30	24.2	41	33.1	12	9.7	124	100
Mitigating the effects of the economic crisis on the warehouse	8	6.5	7	5.6	11	8.9	31	25.0	55	44.4	12	9.7	124	100
Reduction of customer service time	21	16.9	4	3.2	16	12.9	28	22.6	42	33.9	13	10.5	124	100

(*Continued*)

Table 7.14 (Continued)

	Importance – weight													
	Of no importance		*Of very little importance*		*Of little importance*		*Of medium importance*		*Important*		*Very important*		*Total*	
Benefits	*N*	*%**	*N*	*%*	*N*	*%*	*N*	*%*	*N*	*%*	*N*	*%*	*N*	*%*
Providing customers with innovative forms of services focused on ecology	20	16.1	5	4.0	12	9.7	30	24.2	49	39.5	8	6.5	124	100
Improving the quality and comprehensiveness of services	20	16.1	7	5.6	10	8.1	23	18.5	47	37.5	17	13.7	124	100
Reducing warehouse operating costs	4	3.2	4	3.2	7	5.6	24	19.4	58	46.8	27	21.8	124	100
Improving contact with customers (including those with pro-ecological attitudes)	19	15.3	9	7.3	7	5.6	32	25.8	44	35.5	13	10.5	124	100

Source: Own elaboration.

that the pro-ecological attitude of enterprises results in significant savings in the use of utilities and consumption of resources. There is one more benefit, which is a "consequence" of the last two – "mitigating the effects of the economic crisis" (6.5% of respondents indicated that it does not occur) (Table 7.14). This reduction is the result of a better and more rational use of resources. As it is commonly known, their more economical management in the long run reduces capital intensity, and thus improves efficiency and reduces production inputs. The end result is reducing the consumption of energy and raw materials, which is not without significance in times of crises (the current energy crisis).

The above thesis is confirmed by data on the importance (weights) of these benefits. As "important" and "very important", the respondents indicated "reducing the costs of media consumption" (over 70% of respondents in total) in the first place. The second place was taken by "reducing warehouse operating costs" (a total of approx. 67% of respondents). In third place (approx. 54% of the respondents), the respondents marked "mitigating the effects of the crisis". As stated above, these three elements are interconnected and emphasize the implementation of capital savings. Less spending on resources means greater efficiency and the ability to survive in a difficult period, that is, the energy crisis. Therefore, the benefits from the implementation of environmental protection measures are direct and translate into the functioning of enterprises in a measurable way. Other benefits (apart from the three referred to above) were also perceived by the respondents, but at a slightly lower level – approx. 50%, which should also be seen in a positive light – they encourage the implementation of pro-ecological solutions in warehouses.

7.7 Plans for the Future – Implementation of Pro-ecological Solutions

Another task undertaken in this monograph is to answer the question about the next plans of enterprises (warehouses) for future pro-ecological implementations. The data presented in the table below (Table 7.15) show that only 46% of the respondents declare pro-ecological implementations in their enterprises.

Table 7.15 Willingness of the surveyed entities to implement further pro-ecological solutions in warehouses

Answers	*Answers*	*Answers*
Yes	57	46.0%
No	31	25.0%
I don't know	36	29.0%
Total	124	100

Source: Own elaboration.

Of course, the answer to the question of whether that is a lot or a little is a matter of opinion. Despite the obvious benefits resulting from the implementation of pro-environmental activities (Table 7.14), enterprises are hesitant about further investments in environmental protection. There can be many reasons, but the most likely is the "uncertainty of tomorrow". This is a continuation of the idea of limiting expenses (introducing savings) driven mainly by economic reasons, not necessarily by environmental concerns. This is confirmed by the data in the table below (Table 7.16).

The data in this table indicate that, as in the case of "benefits", "reduction of the use of utilities" is also in the first place here (1.8% of respondents indicate that they will not introduce such measures). On the other hand, only 5.3% say that they do not intend to invest in new pro-ecological management methods in the future (i.e., approx. 95% intend to undertake such actions). In the assessment of the importance of these two activities (taking into account the "important" and "very important" ratings), over 60–70% indicate them as important from their point of view. However, the key action that 93% of respondents intend to introduce is the implementation of a new technology. The weight rating is also very high, reaching the level of approx. 83%. Of course, a secondary issue is the question of what technologies we are talking about. Are they modern solutions in the field of Industry 4.0 or other types of technologies aimed at more effective environmental protection? The answers to these questions will be to some extent provided by data in the next subsection of this monograph.

Table 7.16 Future environmental protection activities

Future environmental protection	*Importance – weight*													
	Of no importance		*Of very little importance*		*Of little importance*		*Of medium importance*		*Important*		*Very important*		*Total*	
	N	*%**	*N*	*%*	*N*	*%*	*N*	*%*	*N*	*%*	*N*	*%*	*N*	*%*
Introduction of new technology	4	7.0	0	0	1	1.8	4	7.0	37	64.9	11	19.3	57	100
Obtaining ecological certificates for the warehouse (BREEAM, LEED, etc.)	6	10.5	0	0	4	7.0	10	17.5	28	49.1	9	15.8	57	100
Use of rainwater or gray water	4	7.0	0	0	4	7.0	11	19.3	21	36.8	17	29.8	57	100
Arrangement of green areas around the building (decorative plantings, flower meadows, insect boxes, etc.)	4	7.0	2	3.5	3	5.3	10	17.3	23	40.4	15	16.3	57	100
Addition of sensors for lighting, heating and cooling	5	8.8	1	1.8	3	5.3	10	17.3	26	45.6	12	21.1	57	100
Installation of photovoltaic panels	4	7.0	0	0	0	0	9	15.8	23	40.4	21	36.8	57	100

(*Continued*)

Table 7.16 (Continued)

Future environmental protection	*Importance – weight*													
	Of no importance		*Of very little importance*		*Of little importance*		*Of medium importance*		*Important*		*Very important*		*Total*	
	N	*%**	*N*	*%*	*N*	*%*	*N*	*%*	*N*	*%*	*N*	*%*	*N*	*%*
Replacement of lighting with LED	4	7.0	0	0	1	1.8	7	12.3	24	42.1	21	36.8	57	100
Segregation of waste	4	7.0	0	0	1	1.8	5	8.8	25	43.9	22	38.6	57	100
Organization of collective transport for employees	4	7.0	3	5.3	8	14.0	9	15.8	18	31.6	15	26.3	57	100
Use of biodegradable packaging in warehouses	5	8.8	1	1.8	3	5.3	13	22.8	22	38.6	13	22.8	57	100
Introduction of new management methods	3	5.3	1	1.8	4	7.0	15	26.3	24	42.1	10	17.5	57	100
Reduction of the consumption of utilities	1	1.8	0	0	1	1.8	13	22.8	26	45.6	16	28.1	57	100

Source: Own elaboration.

7.8 Current Status and Plans for the Future – Implementation of Modern Pro-ecological Solutions as Part of Industry 4.0

At this point, the analysis will focus on two important elements. First, what pro-environmental solutions within the Industry 4.0 concept have already been implemented in warehouses in Poland? Second, what kind of solutions do entrepreneurs intend to implement in their enterprises?

By way of an answer to the first of the questions, it should be noted that the most "popular" solutions implemented so far among warehouses in Poland are: broadly understood "robotization" (implemented by 75% of respondents) and "autonomous systems for storage, picking and internal transport inside the warehouse" (implemented by approx. 74%). Systems such as cloud computing (approx. 70%) and the Internet of Things (IoT) (implemented by 69% of respondents) were slightly less common (Table 7.17).

These solutions are very popular among entrepreneurs in Poland. The level of 60–70% of implementation of such solutions is quite high, especially considering the fact that they are not particularly affordable. This confirms the earlier thesis that despite the lack of financial resources, the respondents did not consider this type of resource to be the most important in the process of implementing pro-ecological solutions (Table 7.10). In assessing the importance of the solutions implemented so far in warehouses in Poland, the most important were "robotization" (approx. 39%) and "autonomous storage systems…" (approx. 35%). This confirms the thesis about the use and relatively high level of importance of these solutions for pro-ecological measures. Entrepreneurs also use such technologies (systems) as IoT and Big Data, although to a slightly lesser extent (approx. 66–69% of respondents). Their importance is also rated quite high, as about 33–34% of respondents rate these systems as "important" and "very important". Therefore, modern solutions within the Industry 4.0 concept are used in warehouses in Poland in connection with the implementation of pro-ecological assumptions.

Another issue concerns plans for the future regarding the implementation of new pro-ecological solutions as part of Industry 4.0. A total of 1.8% of respondents declare the lack of implementation of "robotization" in the future, so, it approx. 98% of them say that they will undertake such actions. Also, a high level of declarations concerns "autonomous storage systems…" or Big Data, where over 90% of respondents expressed their interest in implementing such solutions in the future. The respondents are

Table 7.17 The level of implementation and assessment of modern solutions (Industry 4.0) in warehouses in Poland – current state

Modern solutions (Industry 4.0)	*Importance – weight*													
	Of no importance		*Of very little importance*		*Of little importance*		*Of medium importance*		*Important*		*Very important*		*Total*	
	N	*%**	*N*	*%*	*N*	*%*	*N*	*%*	*N*	*%*	*N*	*%*	*N*	*%*
Internet of Things (IoT)	39	31.5	2	1.6	14	11.3	27	21.8	36	29.0	6	4.8	124	100
Big Data	42	33.9	4	3.2	8	6.5	27	21.8	37	29.8	6	4.8	124	100
Cloud Computing	38	30.6	5	4.0	12	9.7	26	21.0	33	26.6	10	8.1	124	100
Blockchain	53	42.7	5	4.0	12	9.7	29	23.4	21	16.9	4	3.2	124	100
SMAC	59	47.6	5	4.0	12	9.7	24	19.4	18	14.5	6	4.8	124	100
SCADA	56	45.2	9	7.3	15	12.1	21	16.9	21	16.9	2	1.6	124	100
Autonomous storage, picking, and transport systems inside the warehouse	33	26.6	8	6.5	14	11.3	25	20.1	38	30.6	6	4.8	124	100
Robotization	31	25.0	9	7.3	16	12.9	20	16.1	41	33.1	7	5.6	124	100

Source: Own elaboration.

Table 7.18 Modern solutions in connection with the implementation of pro-ecological assumptions for the future as part of Industry 4.0

Modern solutions (Industry 4.0)	*Importance – weight*													
	Of no importance		*Of very little importance*		*Of little importance*		*Of medium importance*		*Important*		*Very important*		*Total*	
	N	%*	N	%	N	%	N	%	N	%	N	%	N	%
Internet of Things (IoT)	10	17.5	0	0	3	5.3	10	17.5	25	43.9	9	15.8	57	100
Big Data	6	10.5	1	1.8	4	7.0	12	21.1	27	47.4	7	12.3	57	100
Cloud Computing	8	14.0	1	1.8	5	8.8	11	19.3	25	43.9	7	12.3	57	100
Blockchain	9	15.8	1	1.8	8	14.0	14	24.6	21	36.8	4	7.0	57	100
SMAC	14	24.6	3	5.3	4	7.0	12	21.1	22	38.6	2	3.5	57	100
SCADA	13	22.8	2	3.5	4	7.0	10	17.5	25	43.9	3	5.3	57	100
Autonomous storage, picking, and transport systems inside the warehouse	5	8.8	0	0	6	10.5	12	21.1	27	47.4	7	12.3	57	100
Robotization	1	1.8	1	1.8	3	5.3	8	14.0	35	61.4	9	15.8	57	100

Source: Own elaboration.

least interested in such systems as SMAC and SCADA (approx. 22–24% of respondents), probably due to their specificity and application mainly in manufacturing companies (Table 7.18). Nevertheless, it should be noted that entrepreneurs have plans to modernize warehouses through new solutions, the use of which may be of considerable importance in connection with the implementation of pro-ecological assumptions under the Industry 4.0 concept.

The popularity of using such solutions is also correlated with the assessment of their importance. Entrepreneurs consider them "important" or "very important", and in the case of "robotization", the importance of this solution for pro-ecological attitudes in the future was estimated at almost 80%. In practice, this means that it will be prioritized compared to other solutions implemented in the context of Industry 4.0. "Autonomous storage systems..." were also rated highly. Almost 60% of the respondents pointed to the "important" and "very important" role of these systems in the implementation of pro-ecological assumptions, which means a declaration in favor of their further implementation. As in Table 7.17 – also here, the SMAC system is assessed the lowest in terms of importance (approx. 41% of respondents in total confirmed it to be "important" and "very important") and Blockchain (approx. 44% of respondents expressed approval for this solution), which may be a consequence of relatively low "popularity" and knowledge of this system among enterprises in Poland.

7.9 Research Conclusions

The research carried out and presented in this monograph allows us to draw a number of important conclusions. **First**, warehouses in Poland are very diverse in terms of services provided and business activities. In addition to activities typical for warehouses, such as storage of products or raw materials, these companies conduct regular production, handling (sorting), or commercial activities. **Second**, warehouses in Poland are predominantly universal warehouses (used to store basic commodity groups), general industrial warehouses (related to the storage of non-food goods), and highly specialized warehouses (oriented to handling one type of goods). In terms of raking height, in turn, the largest number of warehouses provides "medium-height storage", whose height is between 4.2 and 7.2 m. In terms of technological advancement, both mechanized and automated warehouses have the largest share of the total number. This proves a relatively high level of technological advancement in warehouse management in Poland. **Third**, the conclusions pertain to the assessment of the renewable energy sources most frequently used (in warehouses) in Poland, which include: photovoltaic cells, solar collectors, and air-source heat pumps. Wind and water turbines or biomass are much less frequently used. The widespread use is the result of widely disseminated direct and indirect forms of support programs. In turn, the low "popularity" of the latter three results from the unfavorable policy of the state government, which discourages their use (wind turbines), and the relatively high costs of biomass recovery and low availability of raw material for biomass production. **Fourth**, the research presented in this chapter points to other types of solutions that are used in warehouses to protect the environment. Most often, simple solutions are used, such as LED lighting, motion sensors, or better use of natural light. Complex measures, such as thermal imaging tests, heat recovery from machines, or systematic replacement of devices with energy-saving ones are introduced less frequently. An example of the latter is the implementation of the BMS (intelligent building) system. However, due to many reasons, its popularity is not very high. This is mainly due to the entities' limited knowledge of the existence of such solutions, as well as the high expenditures related to their implementation. In addition, entrepreneurs are not always sure when the investment will pay off, which may result in uncertainty and a lack of decision about making it. **Fifth,** ESG practices aimed at improving the current state of affairs in the context of environmental protection were assessed. It turns out that only a small proportion of enterprises apply the solutions provided for in the ESG framework, and only in a few selected areas. Among them, one can mention, for example, packaging and waste, renewable energy, and water management. The least frequent ESG implementations are in areas related to emissions, that is, reducing the carbon footprint or the supply of raw materials. **Sixth,** the assessment of resources is rather good. In practice, approximately 90% (or more) of warehouses have resources that enable them to implement various types of solutions and systems or take measures to save energy and protect the environment. The greatest deficiencies in this area concern financial resources, and the smallest pertain to human resources in the context of the number of employees. Since the level of resources is so high, it seems necessary to find an answer to the question about the relatively low level of pro-ecological implementations in warehouses in Poland. This is attributed to two main reasons: too short a period of preparation of warehouses for the rapidly changing environment and still low social awareness in terms of greater focus on environmental protection and energy savings. **Seventh,** the stimulants for pro-ecological implementations in warehouses in Poland were analyzed and it turned out that they are market-driven, which means that these entities strive to adapt to the requirements of the environment's regulatory and introduce solutions that allow savings. In many cases, ecology is therefore treated as a "tool", which means that it should contribute to lower consumption of resources – mainly energy. In turn, considering the requirements of the environment's regulatory (apart from market orientation) has one more important aspect. It proves that these entities promote "open attitudes" focused on the exchange of ideas and technologies related to more effective ways of protecting the environment and saving energy. **Eighth**, an in-depth analysis of barriers indicated that the lack of adequate human and material resources is more destructive than the lack of financial resources. Worth noting is the uncertainty of entrepreneurs as to the final effects of the outlays incurred for pro-ecological implementations. An important barrier is also the "lack of a pro-ecological development strategy", which in turn proves the existence of limitations in terms of awareness of the importance of ecology and environmental protection among entrepreneurs. It can therefore be concluded that the barriers are mainly of a "human" and technical nature, with the former being the "effect" of historical background, because ecology was not treated as a priority in the past. **Ninth**, warehouses that implement pro-ecological solutions benefit from this. Among the benefits, in the first place, are those related to savings in the consumption of utilities and lower costs of warehouse operation. As a consequence, the effects of the economic crisis can be mitigated. Therefore, the benefits from the implementation of environmental protection measures are direct and translate into the functioning of enterprises in a measurable way. The "environmental" dimension of the benefits achieved is mainly "instrumental" in nature and is not an effect in itself. Entities practice "ecology" because it brings them economic (financial) benefits. Ecology is therefore a tool for achieving goals that are not necessarily pro-ecological (environmental). **Tenth**, respondents answered questions about their intentions for the future, almost half of them declaring pro-ecological implementations in their enterprises. The main reasons for such declarations are savings and the willingness to implement new technologies. To a large extent, it is about solutions in the field of Industry 4.0. Among them, "robotization" and the use of "autonomous storage systems" are in the first place. To a slightly lesser extent, respondents indicate other systems such as "Big Data", "SMAC", or "SCADA". This may be due to the limited familiarity with these systems in Poland.

To sum up, it should be concluded that warehouses in Poland apply pro-ecological solutions, although in this respect, they are guided by a variety of considerations. These are not always ecological reasons related to care for the natural environment. In most cases, the practical aspect, which is the ability to save key resources for the company, is of great importance. 90% of warehouses indicate there is an access to and use of these resources without any problems. Declarations concerning the implementation of new pro-ecological solutions also pointed to a relatively positive trend. Therefore, it seems that the reasons for the not very high pro-ecological standards should be attributed to three aspects: the continuous and systematic development of the discussed entities in Poland, the short implementation period, lack of certainty as to the return on pro-environmental outlays, and relatively low public awareness of the importance of such solutions in the context of environmental protection.

Conclusion

This monograph covers important issues related to "modern logistics", with particular emphasis on reverse logistics, which has an impact on reducing the negative impact of humans on the ecosystem. The material, gathered in seven chapters, shows that the raised problems, related to the functioning of the supply chain in reverse logistics are up-to-date and developing. Such chapters as *Modern Logistics, Supply Chain Management, Logistics and IT Systems, The use of Renewable Energy Sources in Logistics* confirm that the subject is embedded in the issues of environmental protection. Moreover, it should be noted that the presented considerations concern the 21st century and that they are multi-stage and prospective.

The material presented in the monograph suggests that the subject matter requires further theoretical and empirical research that will allow to improve the functioning of reverse logistics in the context of environmental protection. These considerations should address issues such as:

1. Automation, robotization in reverse logistics.
2. The use of the Internet of Things in supply chains in reverse logistics.
3. The use of Cloud Computing and Big Data for reverse logistics.
4. Energy storage for reverse logistics and its practical use.
5. Sustainable logistics as an effective tool for the pro-ecological use of resources in order to reduce the adverse impact of activities on the environment and society.
6. Using advanced analytics to improve the efficiency of processes in reverse logistics.

DOI: 10.4324/9781003372615-9

7. Safety of implemented logistic processes in unplanned situations and occurring threats.
8. Cybersecurity in the context of the functioning of the supply chain in reverse logistics.

The presented research areas are only selected elements that, according to the authors of this monograph, are important for the proper functioning of the supply chain in reverse logistics. It should be remembered that the implementation of new solutions in logistics can minimize the carbon footprint left by the business.

Chapter 7 (empirical) deals with the importance of new solutions in reverse logistics. Based on the analysis of data obtained in research and concerning companies managing warehouses in Poland, several important conclusions can be drawn. **Firstly,** entrepreneurs in Poland are aware of the importance of "innovation" for environmental protection. Therefore, the use of renewable energy sources such as photovoltaic cells, solar collectors or air-source heat pumps is quite popular. Other solutions used in practice include: LED lighting, motion sensors, or better use of natural light. Less often, complex measures are introduced, which include: thermal imaging tests, heat recovery from machines, or systematic replacement of devices with energy-saving ones. **Secondly,** a serious barrier limiting the use of these solutions is the lack of certainty of their profitability and return on investment. In practice, this means that "ecology" is used as a tool, bringing specific (measurable) benefits (e.g., reduction of energy consumption). **Thirdly,** ecological activities are largely "steered" by the market. Here, we can talk about the influence of the environment on the decisions of entrepreneurs. They are guided by the opinions and trends that are "popular" among potential customers. It should therefore be emphasized that the environment becomes a key stimulator of decisions made in enterprises, forcing, in many cases, a pro-ecological attitude in the field of final products and services provided (including logistics), or the technologies used. **Fourthly,** in the field of reverse logistics, "openness to the environment" plays a huge role. This allows for an effective exchange of ideas and innovative solutions for environmental protection and energy saving. The flow of knowledge in this area is much more "free" than in other areas of the economy, which means that "environmental awareness" is constantly being developed. Unfortunately, research in this area shows that the level of this awareness is still insufficient. **Fifthly,** the dimensions of "Logistics 4.0" and "Industry 4.0" are becoming more and more important, in which the pro-ecological idea occupies a key place. Also, in this context, entrepreneurs will look for savings resulting from this type of implementation. This applies to more efficient use of resources, and thus lower inputs and lower costs.

Summing up, as indicated above, this monograph is a contribution to further research in the field of reverse logistics and its impact on the natural environment. It is particularly important at the moment, where ecological aspects are becoming not so much a "fashion" as a necessity resulting from care for the environment in the context of future generations. Lack of progress in this area will lead to its irreversible degradation and will make life on Earth impossible.

References

5 Benefits of Using Customer Relationship Management (CRM). (2022), available at: https://www.webfx.com/martech/learn/benefits-of-crm, 28.02.2022.

5 Key Factors to Measure Proven Logistics Service Quality. (2022), available at: https://www-scmdojo-com.translate.goog/logistics-service-quality/?, 22.05.2022.

5 Top Internet of Things Startups Impacting Logistics & Supply Chain. (2022), available at: https://www.startus-insights.com/innovators-guide/5-top-internet-of-things-startups-impacting-logistics-supply-chain/ 01.05.2022.

6 Ways Technology Reduces the Environmental Impact of Supply Chains. (2022), available at: https://www.blumeglobal.com/learning/environmental-impact-supply-chains/, 22.07.2022.

8 kluczowych wskaźników dla efektywnej obsługi klienta, available at: https://systell.pl/blog/mierniki-obslugi-klienta/, 15.02.2022.

8 typów marnotrawstwa, available at: http://techmine.pl/, 10.02.2022.

Adamczyk W. (2004), *Ekologia wyrobów – jakość, cykl życia, projektowanie*, PWE, Warszawa.

Adamska B. (2021), *Akumulator litowo-jonowy Vs kwasowo-ołowiowy, Magazyny energii w budynkach mieszkalnych i zakładach przemysłowych – użyteczne rozwiązanie czy zbędny gadżet*, available at: www.muratorplus.pl, 22.11.2021.

Adonisa A. (2022), *The 10 Major Threats to Global Supply Chains*, available at: www.whispir.com/en-us/blog/the-10-major-threats-to-global-supply-chains/, 01,10,2022.

Advantages and Disadvantages of Using Customer Relationship Management Software, available at: https://infinigeek-com.translate.goog/8-advantages-disadvantages-using-customer-relationship-management-software/?, 28.02.2022.

Analiza cyklu życia, available at: coin.wne.uw.edu.pl/tzylicz/1105AURA, 12.04.2022.

ARTR. (2022), available at: http://www.artr.eu/, 17.03.2022.

Banomyong R. (2008), Logistics Development in the Greater Mekong Subregion: A Study of the North-South Economic Corridor, *Journal of Greater Mekong Subregion Development Studies*, 4(44), 43–57.

Baraniecka A. (2004), *ECR Efficient Consumer Response, Łańcuch dostaw zorientowany na klienta*, IliM, Poznań.

Bartczak K. (2006), *Technologie informatyczne i telekomunikacyjne jako podstawa tworzenia systemów telematycznych w transporcie*, [in:] *Współczesne procesy i zjawiska w transporcie*, [ed.] E. Załoga, Uniwersytet Szczeciński, Szczecin.

Bartosik M., Kamrat W., Kaźmierkowski M., Lewandowski W. Pawlik M., Peryt T., Skoczkowski T., Strupczewski A., Szeląg A. (2022), *Magazynowanie energii elektrycznej i gospodarka wodorowa,* available at: http://pe.org.pl/articles/2016/12/78.pdf, 04.01.2022.

Bernal-Agustin J.L., Dufo-Lopez R. (2008), Hourly Energy Management for Grid-Connected Wind-Hydrogen, *International Journal of Hydrogen Energy*, 33(22), 6401–6413.

Biała Księga Bezpieczeństwa Narodowego Rzeczypospolitej Polskiej. (2013), Warszawa.

Big Data – czym jest i w jaki sposób funkcjonuje? (2022), available at: https://poradnikprzedsiebiorcy.pl/, 29.05.2022.

Big data: definicja, korzyści, wyzwania (infografika). (2022), available at: https://www.europarl.europa.eu/news/pl/headlines/society/20210211STO97614/big-data-definicja-korzysci-wyzwania-infografika, 05.05.2022.

Bilińska O. (2022), *Nie każdy bot to chatbot – poznaj różnice*, available at: https://kodabots.com/blog/nie-kazdy-bot-to-chatbot-poznaj-roznice/, 20.03.2022.

Biodiversity, available at: https://www.eea.europa.eu/pl/themes/biodiversity/intro, 29.04.2022.

Biomasa – odnawialne źródło energii. (2021), available at: https://www.instalacjebudowlane.pl/4263-23-40-biomasa--odnawialne-zrodlo-energii-.html, 28.12.2021.

Blaik P. (2001), *Logistyka*, PWE, Warszawa.

Blockchain in Logistics and Transportation: Transformation Ahead. (2022), available at: https://www.iotworldtoday.com/2017/10/05/blockchain-logistics-and-transportation-transformation-ahead/, 29.03.2022.

Blumenthal K. (2011), Generation and Treatment of Municipal Waste, *Statistics in Focus, Eurostat*, available at: https://op.europa.eu/en/publication-detail/-/publication/bd8a43dc-8076-4134-987d-c3081c8311e8, 21.03.2011.

Bozarth C., Handfield R.B. (2007), *Wprowadzenie do zarządzania operacjami i łańcuchem dostaw, Kompletny podręcznik logistyki i zarządzania dostawami*, Helion, Gliwice.

Bradley S. (2021), *Futuristic Underground Cargo Project Moves a Step Closer to Reality*, available at: https://www.swissinfo.ch/eng/culture/futuristic-underground-cargo-project-moves-a-step-closer-to-reality/46674218, 04.06.2021

Buczacki A. (2022), *Inne przyczyny powstawania zapasów*, available at: https://notatek.pl/, 10.02.2022.

Budynki pasywne. (2022), available at: https://budowlaneabc.gov.pl/charakterystyka-energetyczna-budynkow/informacje-poradnik/okreslenie-oplacalnych-sposobow-poprawy-efektywnosci-energetycznej-wlasciwych-dla-typow-budynkow/budynki-pasywne/, 27.04.2022.

Bujak A., Gębczyńska A., Miler R. (2014), *Współczesna logistyka - obszary i kierunki przekształceń*, Logistyka, 3, 868–880.

Christopher M. (1996), *Strategia zarządzania dystrybucją*, Placet, Warszawa.
Christopher M. (2000), *Logistyka i zarządzanie łańcuchem dostaw*, Polskie Centrum Doradztwa Logistycznego, Warszawa.
Ciesielski M., Długosz J. (2010), *Strategie łańcuchów dostaw*, PWE, Warszawa.
Circular Economy: Definition, Principles, Benefits and Barriers. (2022), available at: https://youmatter.world/en/definition/definitions-circular-economy-meaning-definition-benefits-barriers/, 02.04.2022.
Cleaner Production: What Is It? (2022), available at: https://www-cprac-org.translate.goog/en/sustainable/production/cleaner?, 28.04.2022.
Co to jest budownictwo pasywne? (2022*)*, available at: https://www.products.pcc.eu/pl/blog/co-to-jest-budownictwo-pasywne/, 23.04.2022.
Co to jest hash? (2022), available at: https://bezpieczny.blog/co-to-jest-hash/, 28.03.2022.
Cockerham J. (2022), *The Biggest Benefits of EAM Software*, available at: https://managerplus.iofficecorp.com/blog/benefits-eam-software, 01.03.2022.
Czakon W. (2014), Kryteria oceny rygoru metodologicznego badań w naukach o zarządzaniu, *Organizacja i Kierowanie*, 1, 51–62.
Czujnik zabezpieczający – skuteczne monitorowanie poziomu paliwa. (2022), available at: http://www.monitoringgps.eu, 29.03.2022.
Czym jest intralogistyka? Trendy w optymalizacji procesów intralogistycznych. (2022), available at: https://www.mecalux.pl, 05.02.2022.
Czym jest technologia blockchain? (2022), available at: https://www.ibm.com/pl-pl/topics/what-is-blockchain, 28.03.2022.
Czym jest telematyka i jakie ma znaczenie w transporcie? (2022), available at: https://www.efl.pl/pl/biznes-i-ty/artykuly/telematyka-w-transporcie, 12.03.2022.
Czym właściwie jest logistyka? Poznaj zasadę 7W. (2022), available at: https://wortale.net, 12.07.2022.
Daniel D. (2022), *Guide to Supply Chain Management*, available at: https://www.techtarget.com/searcherp/definition/supply-chain-management-SCM, 28.02.2022.
Dasza M. (2022), *What are Ecommerce Advantages and Disadvantages*?, available at: https://belvg.com/blog/what-is-advantage-and-disadvantage-of-e-commerce.html, 08.03.2022.
Deyglio W. (2022), *Supply Chain Logistics – Agility and Flexibility*, available at: https://loginstitute-ca.translate.goog/2020/05/27/supply-chain-logistics-agility-and-flexibility/?, 11.05.2022.
Disrupting and Redefining Fulfillment, AI Cloud Software and Robotic Automation That Keeps Inventory in Motion. (2022), *GreyOrange*, Robotics Solution for Automated Warehouse Picking, available at: www.greyorange.com. 02.05.2022.
Distribution Requirement Planning (DRP). (2022), available at: https://www.geeksforgeeks.org/distribution-requirement-planning-drp/, 25.02.2022.
Dobrostan, available at:https://encyklopedia.pwn.pl/haslo/dobrostan;3893293.html, 04.29.2022.

Donovan A. (2020), *The Top 5 Challenges in Retail Supply Chains*, available at: https://www.adecesg.com/resources/blog/the-top-5-challenges-in-retail-supply-chains/, 28.01.2020

Drewek W. (2011), *Monitorowanie ładunków niebezpiecznych w transporcie drogowym*, Logistyka, 5, 499–512.

Ducrot L. (2022), *The Essence of Supply Chain Management (IMHO)*, available at: https://www-linkedin-com.translate.goog/pulse/essence-supply-chain-management-imho-léo-ducrot?, 06.06.2022.

Dutka W. (2022), *Logistics and Supply Chain in the Cloud: Capabilities and Migration Strategies*, available at: https://intellias-com.translate.goog/logistics-and-supply-chain-in-the-cloud-capabilities-and-migration-strategies/?, 03.05.2022.

Dutka W. (2022), Logistics and Supply Chain in the Cloud: Capabilities and Migration Strategies, available at: https://intellias.com/logistics-and-supply-chain-in-the-cloud-capabilities-and-migration-strategies/, 04.05.2020.

Dyché J. (2002), *CRM. Relacje z klientami*, Helion, Gliwice.

Dziennik Ustaw Rzeczypospolitej Polskiej Warszawa, z dnia 7 października 2019 r. w sprawie ogłoszenia jednolitego tekstu rozporządzenia Ministra Środowiska w sprawie szczegółowego sposobu selektywnego zbierania wybranych frakcji odpadów (Dz.U. 2019 poz. 2028).

Dziurdzińska N. (2022), *35 lat temu doszło do katastrofy w Czarnobylu*, available at: https://dzieje.pl/wiadomosci/35-lat-temu-doszlo-do-katastrofy-w-czarnobylu, 03.04.2022.

e-commerce, available at: http://www.heuristic.pl/blog/e-commerce/106.html, 15.02.2022.

Efektywne zarządzanie aktywami. (2022), available at: http://www.4metal.pl/?a=3&id=23307, 18.01.2022.

Efficient Consumer Response (ECR): Adding Customer Value to the Supply Chain using Collaboration. (2022), available at: https://www.globaltranz.com/efficient-consumer-response/, 28.03.2022.

Ekologia[PL] Wiedza. (2022), available at: https://www.ekologia.pl/wiedza/slowniki/leksykon-ekologii-i-ochrony-srodowiska/ochrona-srodowiska, 02.04.2022.

Elektroliza i ogniwa paliwowe. (2022), available at: https://ecoprius.pl/, 06.01.2022.

Elektryczna rewolucja w logistyce? Tak, ale pod kilkoma warunkami… (2022), available at: https://biznes.newseria.pl/, 30.01.2022.

Ellen MacArthur Foundation, available at: https://ellenmacarthurfoundation.org/circular-economy-diagram

EMAS, available at: https://www.mos.gov.pl, 22.04.2022.

Encyklopedia naukowa. (2022), available at: http://encyklopedia.naukowy.pl/, 19.01.2022.

Encyklopedia PWN. (2022), available at: https://encyklopedia.pwn.pl/haslo/dobrostan;3893293.html, 29.04.2022.

Encyklopedia zarządzania, available at: http://mfiles.pl/, 22.02.2022.

Energia geotermalna. (2021), available at: https://pl.wikipedia.org/wiki/Energia_geotermalna, 26.12.2021.

Energia geotermalna. (2021), available at: https://www.mae.com.pl/oferta-mae/baza-wiedzy/odnawialne-zrodla-energii/energia-geotermalna, 26.12.2021.

Energia słoneczna – czym jest I jak powstaje? (2021), available at: https://www.esoleo.pl/, 20.12.2021.

Energia z wiatru. (2021), available at: https://pgeeo.pl/Zielona-energia-i-OZE/Energia-z-wiatru, 12.12.2021.

Energia z wody. (2021), available at: https://pgeeo.pl/Zielona-energia-i-OZE/Energia-z-wody, 18.12.2021.

Energia ze źródeł odnawialnych w 2020 r. (2022), available at: https://stat.gov.pl, 20.02.2022.

Essex D. (2022), *Reverse Logistics*, available at: https://www-techtarget-com.translate.goog/searcherp/definition/reverse-logistics?, 23.04.2022.

Evans G. (1994), *Współpraca dla pokoju. Agenda globalna na lata dziewięćdziesiąte i następne*, Polski Instytut Spraw Międzynarodowych, Warszawa.

Exploring the Advantages and Disadvantages of Ecommerce. (2022), available at: https://www.lightspeedhq.com/blog/advantages-and-disadvantages-of-ecommerce/, 08.03.2022.

Feng W., Figliozzi M.A. (2013), An Economic and Technological Analysis of the Key Factors Affecting the Competitiveness of Electric Commercial Vehicles: A Case Study from the USA Market. *Transportation Research Part C Emerging Technologies*. 26, 135–145, DOI:10.1016/j.trc.2012.06.007

Ferreira N.M. (2022), *20 Advantages and Disadvantages of Ecommerce/Oberlo*, available at: https://www.oberlo.com/blog/20-ecommerce-advantages-and-disadvantages, 08.03.2022.

Fertsch M. (2006), *Słownik terminologii logistycznej*, Instytut *Logistyki* i Magazynowania, Poznań.

Ficoń K. (2021), *Procesy logistyczne w przedsiębiorstwie*, Impuls Plus Consulting, Gdynia.

Five Business Benefits of Using Cloud Logistics. (2022), available at: https://blog-gravitysupplychain-com.translate.goog/5-business-benefits-of-using-cloud-logistics?, 03.05.2022.

Fletcher L. (2022), *Top 14 Benefits of Telematics Beyond Tracking*, available at: https://www.worktruckonline.com/10144040/top-14-benefits-of-telematics-benefits-beyond-tracking, 17.03.2022.

Flis R. (2009), *E-usługi – definicja i przykłady*, Polska Agencja Rozwoju Przedsiębiorczości (PARP), Warszawa.

Fodrowska K. (2021), *Przydomowa elektrownia wiatrowa – cena, jak działa?*, Przydomowa elektrownia wiatrowa – cena, jak działa? | enerad.pl, 25.12.2021.

Foodlogistics. (2022), available at: https://www.foodlogistics.com/safety/blog/21070106/food-safety-traceability-and-transparency-by-way-of-blockchain, 20.04.2022.

Gdańskie Autobusy i Tramwaje testują autobus elektryczny – to MAN Lion's City E. (2022), available at: https://www.gdansk.pl/27.01.2022.

Gdzie najczystsze powietrze na świecie? (2021), available at: http://www.administrator24.info, 05.12.2021

Geoffrion A. (2022), *5 Ways to Boost Sustainable Innovation in Packaging Operations*, available at: https://www-sdcexec-com.translate.goog/sustainability/packaging/article/21772176/dhl-5-ways-to-boost-sustainable-innovation-in-packaging-operations? 10.07.2022.

Gil K.G. (2022), *Advantages and Disadvantages of the Circular Economy*, available at: *https*://www.bbva.ch/en/news/advantages-and-disadvantages-of-the-circular-economy/, 28.04.2022.

Gilb O. (2022), *Big Data in Logistics: Key Benefits & 3 Real Use Cases*, available at: https://acropolium-com.translate.goog/blog/big-data-in-logistics-key-benefits-3-real-use-cases/?, 02.05.2022.

Gis M. (2022), Rodzaje *wtyczek do samochodów elektrycznych, Rodzaje wtyczek do samochodów elektrycznych,* available at: https://e.autokult.pl/, 21.01.2022.

Gladek E. (2022), *The Seven Pillars of the Circular Economy*, available at: https://www-metabolic-nl.translate.goog/news/the-seven-pillars-of-the-circular-economy/?, 20.04.2022.

Główny Urząd Statyczny. (2020), Zakład Wydawnictw Statystycznych, Warszawa.

Gołembska E. (2001), *Kompendium wiedzy o logistyce*, PWN Warszawa – Poznań.

Góralczyk I., Tytko R. (2015), *Fotowoltaika. Urządzenia, instalacje fotowoltaiczne i elektryczne*, Wydawnictwo i Drukarnia Towarzystwa Słowaków w Polsce. Kraków.

Grawitacyjne magazyny energii wchodzą na rynek. Duże zamówienie, available at: https://www.gramwzielone.pl/, 19.01.2022.

Groims M. (2022), *Autonomous Vehicles in Logistics Part 1: Opportunities and Risks*, available at: https://www.allthingssupplychain.com/autonomous-vehicles-in-logistics-part-1-opportunities-and-risks/, 09.05.2022.

Halbmaier R. (2022), *Flexible Logistics 101: What Is Fixed and Flexible Logistics?*, available at: https://www-flexe-com.translate.goog/articles/flexible-logistics-101-fixed-flexible-logistics-omnichannel-strategy?, 06.05.2022.

Hoey B. (2022), *How Cloud Computing Could Impact Logistics 4.0,* available at: https://blog-flexis-com.translate.goog/how-cloud-computing-could-impact-logistics-4.0?, 11.05.2022.

How to Effectively Reduce Waste in Manufacturing. (2022), available at: https://www-hashmicro-com.translate.goog/blog/how-to-reduce-waste-in-manufacturing/?, 24.04.2022.

Hydroenergetyka. (2021), available at: http://fundacjaenergia.pl/, 25.12.2021.

IBM. (2022), available at: https://www.ibm.com/pl-pl/cloud/learn/machine-learning, 21.03.2022.

Ile jest stacji ładowania CCS w Europie? Na koniec 2018 r. prawie 6 tysięcy sztuk. (2022), available at: https://elektrowoz.pl/, 30.01.2022.

Importance of Chatbots for Logistics And Supply-Chain. (2022), available at: https://locobuzz.com/blogs/importance-of-chatbots-for-logistics-and-supply-chain/, 20.03.2022.

ISO 14001: 2015 Certification Process, available at: https://www.dekra-certification.com.pl, 13.01.2022, M. Hammer, 6 Key Benefits of ISO 14001, available at: https://advisera-com.translate.goog/14001academy/ knowledgebase/6-key-benefits-of-iso-14001/?, 13.01.2022.

Israni N. (2022), *CRM Database: Overview, Structure, Strategies & Maintenance Tips*, available at: https://www-engagebay-com.translate.goog/blog/what-is-a-crm-database/?, 25.07.2022.

Jak można magazynować energię elektryczną? (2022), available at: https://www.rp.pl/nowe-technologie/art9080721-jak-mozna-magazynowac-energie-elektryczna, 04.01.2022.

Jaką chmurę obliczeniową wybrać? Typy i rodzaje chmur obliczeniowych, available at: https://www.beyond.pl/baza-wiedzy/poradniki/jaka-chmure-obliczeniowa-wybrac-typy-i-rodzaje-chmur-obliczeniowych/, 03.05.2022.

Jaworska M. (2022), *MES, czyli jak wskoczyć na wyższy poziom*, available at: http://automatykab2b.pl, 09.03.2022.

Jędrak J. (2022), *Ile ofiar pochłonęła katastrofa w Fukushimie? Tysiące, ale z nieoczywistego powodu*, available at: https://smoglab.pl/fukushima-ofiary-wplyw-na-srodowisko/, 03.04.2022.

Jędrzejak A., Mazur A., Piotrowska M. (2014), *Praktyczne aspekty wdrażania metody 5-S*, [in:] Zeszyty naukowe Politechniki Poznańskiej, nr 62 Organizacja i Zarządzanie, p. 63.

Jenkins A. (2022), *A Guide to Reverse Logistics: How It Works, Types and Strategies*, available at: https://www-netsuite-com.translate.goog/portal/resource/articles/inventory-management/reverse-logistics.shtml?, 02.04.2022.

Jones M.D. (2022), *A New Economic Model for People and Planet*, available at: https://www-metabolic-nl.translate.goog/what-we-do/circular-economy/?, 30.04.2022.

Juan A.A., Mendez C.A., Javier J. Faulin, J. de Armas, Grasman S.E. (2016), *Electric Vehicles in Logistics and Transportation: A Survey on Emerging Environmental, Strategic, and Operational Challenges*, Energis, 9/7, 547, DOI:10.3390/en9020086.

Kalicka E. (2022), *Oświetlenie LED Wady i Zalety*, available at: http://www.e--instalacje.pl/, 23.01.2022.

Kazojć K. (2014), *Koncepcja społecznej odpowiedzialności i jej obszary w organizacjach*, Studia i Prace Wydziału Nauk Ekonomicznych i Zarządzania, Wydawnictwo Naukowe Uniwersytetu Szczecińskiego, 38, Szczecin.

Kiperska-Moroń D., Krzyżaniak S. (2009), *Logistyka*, Biblioteka Logistyka, Poznań.

Knez M., Rosi B., Sternad M., Bajor P. (2009), *Positive Impact of Electrical Energy Resources on the Implementation of Logistics Operations*, The Second BH Congres on Road, Sarajevo.

Kołodziński E. (2015), *Modelowanie systemów bezpieczeństwa*, [in:] Inżynieria systemów bezpieczeństwa, [ed.] P. Sienkiewicz, PWE, Warszawa.

Kondraciuk J. (2022), *CSR to skrót coraz częściej spotykany w świecie biznesu. Co oznacza i dlaczego często bywa źle rozumiany?*, available at: http://info.mergeto.pl, 28.02.2022.

Konopielko E., Wołoszyn M., Wytrębowicz J. (2016), *Handel elektroniczny Rewolucja, Perspektywy*, Oficyna Wydawnicza Uczelni Łazarskiego, Warszawa.

Kortschuk B.H. (1992), *Was ist logistyk*, Instytut Wspierania Rozwoju Gospodarczego, Austria–Kraków.

Korzeń Z. (2001), *Ekologistyka*, Biblioteka Logistyka, Poznań.

Kost E. (2022), Największe zagrożenia w Twoim łańcuchu dostaw w 2022, available at: https://www-upguard-com.translate.goog/blog/biggest-supply-chain-security-risks?, 26.05.2022.

Krzyżanowski P. (2022), *Powstała pierwsza w Polsce stacja tankowania wodoru. Obsłuży cztery samochody na godzinę*, available at: https://www.auto-swiat.pl/, 22.02.2022.

Kulułka J. (1982), *Międzynarodowe stosunki polityczne*, Państwowe Wydawnictwo Naukowe, Warszawa.

Kurnia |S., Johnston R. (2001), Adoption of Efficient Consumer Response: The Issue of Mutuality, *Supply Chain Management: an International Journal*, 6(5), 230–241, DOI:10.1108/13598540110407778

Lahoti N. (2022), *Big Data & Its Revolutionary Impact On Logistics & Supply Chain Management*, available at: https://mobisoftinfotech-com.translate.goog/resources/blog/big-data-in-logistics/?, 05.05.2022.

Lahoti N. (2022), *The Role of Chatbots in Logistics and Supply Chain Industry*, https://mytruckpulse-com.translate.goog/blog/role-of-chatbots-in-logistics-and-supply-chain-industry.html?, 22.03.2022.

Learn the 4 Principles of Sustainable Packaging Logistics, available at: https://rotom.co.uk/services/packing-recover, 07/10/2022.

Lee C.K.M., Yaqiong Lv, Ng K.K.H., Ho W., Choy K.L. (2017), *Design and Application of Internet of ThingsBased Warehouse Management System for Smart Logistics*, [in:] International Journal of Production Research, 1–16, DOI: 10.1080/00207543.2017.1394592

Leksykon transportowy. (2022), available at: https://www.timocom.pl/lexicon/leksykon-transportowy/e-logistyka, 04.03.2022.

Leończuk D. (2012), Możliwości zastosowania technologii cloud computing w logistyce, *Logistyka*, 5, 627–634.

Levy G. (2022), *CAPA Management,* available at: https://support.tulip.co/en/articles/4840558-capa-management, 19.05.2022.

Lewandowska J., Januszewski F. (2013), Przyczyny i miejsca powstawania strat w łańcuchu dostaw, *Logistyka*, 5,133–136.

Lewkowicz S. (2012), *Pompa ciepła powietrze – woda – jak działa?* available at: https://columbusenergy.pl/, 22.12.2021.

Logistyczna obsługa klienta – definicja, elementy, strategii, available at: https://www.templatka.pl, 26.02.2022.

Logistyka w przedsiębiorstwie, przewodnik do ćwiczeń, (ed.), G. Radziejowskiej, Gliwice 2001, p. 53.

Lont M. (2022), *Budownictwo energooszczędne i pasywne*, available at: https://horyzont.com/budownictwo/budownictwo-energooszczedne-i-pasywne, 30.04.2022.

Lotko A. (2003), *Zarządzanie relacjami z klientem*, Politechnika Radomska, Radom, 2003.

Lubczański M. (2022), *Elektryczne ciężarówki wjeżdżają do Polski. Volvo Trucks wprowadza modele FL i FE*, available at: https://e.autokult.pl/, 23.01.2022.

Lutkevich B. (2022), *Supply Chain*, available at: https://www-techtarget-com.translate.goog/whatis/definition/supply-chain?, 04.07.2022.

M&A, available at: https://rpms.pl/ma- transaction-mergers-acquisitions, 20.06.2022.

Magazynowanie energii z fotowoltaiki – Magazyny energii. (2021), available at: http. www.e-magazyny.pl, 21.12.2021.

Magazyny wodoru – samowystarczalne budynki. (2022), available at: https://ecoprius.pl/pl/magazyny-wodoru-samowystarczalne-budynki.html, 04.01.2022.

Maihold G., Mühlhöfer F. (2022), *Supply Chain Instability Threatens Security of Supplies,* available at: https://www-swp--berlin-org.translate.goog/en/publication/supply-chain-instability-threatens-security-of-supplies?, 09.07.2022.

Majer P. (2012), W poszukiwaniu uniwersalnej definicji bezpieczeństwa wewnętrznego, *Przegląd bezpieczeństwa wewnętrznego*, 7(4), 11–19.

Majewski J. (2008), *Informatyka dla logistyki*, Instytut Logistyki i Magazynowania, Poznań, 60.

Malczan N. (2022), *CRM Database: Overview, Structure, Strategies & Maintenance Tips*, available at: https://www-engagebay-com.translate.goog/blog/what-is-a-crm-database/?, 20.07.2022

Mały rocznik statystyczny Polski 2021, Warszawa.

Marszycki M., Waszczuk P. (2022), *Ostatnia mila w logistyce to już nie tylko dostawa*, available at: https://itwiz.pl/ostatnia-mila-w-logistyce-to-juz-nie-tylko-dostawa/, 19.01.2022.

Mecalux. (2021), *Jak wdrożyć elastyczną logistykę? 4 kluczowe trendy.* (2021), available at: https://www.mecalux.pl/blog/elastyczna-logistyka, 21.11.2021.

Michalik J., Budzik R., *Procesy magazynowe w przedsiębiorstwie produkcyjnym*, [in:] Logistyce 2/2011, p. 427.

Michalski M. (2021), *Biopaliwa*, available at: https://www.viessmann.edu.pl, 22.12.2021.

Modelowanie ryzyka gospodarczego przedsiębiorstwa produkcyjnego, available at: http://ksiegarnia.iknt.pl/, 29.01.2022.

Monnappa A. (2022), *Top 10 Reasons to do a SMAC Certification*, available at: https://www-simplilearn-com.translate.goog/10-reasons-to-do-smac-certification-article?, 07.06.2022.

Murator plus. (2021), available at: https://www.muratorplus.pl/technika/elektroenergetyka/ magazyny-energii-w-domowych-systemach-pv-aa-b8Lp-yqDe-MKVq.html, 22.11.2021

Nadaj SMAC swojemu biznesowi, available at: https://www.erp-view.pl/artykuly-it-solutions/26191-nadaj-smac-swojemu-biznesowi.html, 05.06.2022.

Navarro C., Roca-Riu M., Furió S., Estrada M. (2016), Designing New Models for Energy Efficiency in Urban Freight Transport for Smart Cities and Its Application to the Spanish Case, *Transportation Research Procedia*, 12(3), 314–324.

Nelson J. (2022), Managing the 21st Century Supply Chain, available at: https://www-sdcexec-com.translate.goog/professional-development/article/21081387/the-hackett-group-inc-managing-the-21st-century-supply-chain?, 04.06.2022.

Neumann T. (2018), The Importance of Telematics in the Transport System, [in:] *TransNav the International Journal on Marine Navigation and Safety of Sea Transportation*, 12/3, 618.

Nomad. (2022), available at: http://nomad.com.pl/cctv/ 17.03.2022.

Nowy Model autobusu elektrycznego na testach w Gdańsku. (2022), available at: https://sozosfera.pl/, 30.01.2022.

Ocena ryzyka na potrzeby zarządzania kryzysowego, Raport o zagrożeniach bezpieczeństwa narodowego. (2013), RCB, Warszawa.

Ochrona środowiska 2014 Environment. (2014), Zakład wydawnictw statystycznych, Warszawa.

Ochrona środowiska 2017 Environment. (2017), Zakład wydawnictw statystycznych, Warszawa.

Ochrona środowiska 2018 Environment. (2018), Zakład wydawnictw statystycznych, Warszawa.

Ochrona środowiska 2019 Environment. (2019), Zakład Wydawnictw Statystycznych, Warszawa.

Ochrona środowiska 2020 Environment. (2020), Zakład Wydawnictw Statystycznych, Warszawa.

Ochrona środowiska 2021 Environment. (2021), Zakład wydawnictw statystycznych, Warszawa.

Olczak U. (2022), Dom energooszczędny a pasywny – czym się od siebie różnią?, available at: https://obido.pl/odkrywaj/dom-energooszczedny-a-pasywny-czym-sie-od-siebie-roznia.html,2, 9.04.2022.

Ostatnia mila w logistyce to już nie tylko dostawa. (2022), available at: https://itwiz.pl/ostatnia-mila-w-logistyce-to-juz-nie-tylko-dostawa/, 05.05.2022.

Ostatnia mila, czyli zarządzanie logistyką dostaw zamówień do klientów, available at: https://www.mecalux.pl/, 02.02.2022.

Parys T. (2022), *Bariery wdrożeniowe systemu zintegrowanego klasy ERP i ich postrzeganie przez użytkowników*, available at: https://www.researchgate.net/, 28.02.2022.

Patel U. (2022), *AI Chatbot Development for Supply Chain & Logistics Industry*, available at: https://www.tristatetechnology.com/blog/ai-chatbot-development-for-supply-chain-logistics-industry, 18.09.2019.

Pierwszy domowy akumulator wodorowy, available at: https://e-magazyny.pl/, 06.01.2022.

Podrecznik https://www.instrukcjaobslugipdf.pl/yealink/sip-t26p/instrukcja. available at: http://www.4ip.pl › file 27.02.2022.

Pół tony odpadów komunalnych wytworzono na jedną osobę w UE; Polska na końcu zestawienia. (2022), available at: https://samorzad.pap.pl/, 10.02.2022.

Polcikiewicz Z. (2012), *Teoria bezpieczeństwa*, WSOWL, Wrocław.

Poradnik Przedsiębiorcy, available at: https://poradnikprzedsiebiorcy.pl/-czego-jest-big -date, 02/03/2022.

Powódź w obliczu zagrożenia. (2013), Wydział analiz RCB, Warszawa.

Poznaj 4 zasady zrównoważonej logistyki opakowań. (2022), available at: https://rotom.pl/articles/post/poznaj-4-zasady-zrownowazonej-logistyki-opakowan, 10.07.2022.

Prabhat S., Albright D. (2022), Food Safety: Traceability and Transparency by Way of Blockchain, available at: https://www.foodlogistics.com/safety/blog/21070106/food-safety-traceability-and-transparency-by-way-of-blockchain, 4/20/2022.

Problem ostatniej mili. Czym jest i jak go rozwiązać?, available at: https://log24.pl/news/problem-ostatniej-mili-czym-jest-i-jak-go-rozwiazac/, 02.05.2022.

Procedura opracowania raportu cząstkowego do *Raportu o zagrożeniach bezpieczeństwa narodowego*. (2010), RCB Rządowe Centrum Bezpieczeństwa, Warszawa.

Procesy logistyczne w przedsiębiorstwie - etapy przygotowania, wykorzystanie nowoczesnych technologii, available at: https://inzynieria.com/budownictwo/wiadomosci/61109,procesy-logistyczne-w-przedsiebiorstwie-etapy-przygotowania-wykorzystanie-nowoczesnych-technologii,jak-planuje-sie-procesy-logistyczne-w-firmie, 29.01.2022.

Pros and Cons of Big Data: Solutions to Empower Your Business. (2022), available at: https://innovecs-com.translate.goog/blog/pros-and-cons-of-big-data/?, 06.05.2022.

Pruziński A., *Na czym polega dobra obsługa klienta?*, available at: https://www2.deloitte.com/pl/, 28.02.2022.

Rączkowski B. (2010), *BHP w praktyce*, ODiDK, Gdańsk.

Radomska-Deutsch E. (2010), Nowoczesny magazyn: zrównoważony znaczy zielony, *Logistyka*, 4, 26–29.

Ransomware, available at: https://www.avast.com/en-pl/c-ransomware, 28.07.2022.

Rathod A. (2022), *Chatbots: How Can they Transform Logistics and Supply Chain Management?*, available at: https://knowledgehubmedia-com.translate.goog/chatbots-transform-logistics-supply-chain-management/?, 20.03.2022.

Reduce Costs with Returnable Packaging Management in Supply Chain, available at: https://www2-novacura-com.translate.goog/blog/reduce-costs-with-returnable-packaging?, 7/20/2022.

Responsible Business Alliance. (2022), available at: https://www-responsiblebusiness-org.translate.goog/?, 07.07.2022.

Rinkesh A. (2022), *Passive House Design: How It Works and Misconceptions Explained*, available at: https://www-conserve--energy--future-com.translate.goog/passive-house-design-works.php?, 29.04.2022.

Rodríguez A., Fernández-Medina E, Piattini M.M. (2022), *A BPMN Extension for the Modeling of Security Requirements in Business Processes*, available at: https://www.researchgate.net, 20.02.2022.

Rodzaje chatbotów – wirtualnych asystentów. (2022), available at: https://www.polski-chatbot.pl/rodzaje-chatbotow, 20.03.2022.

Rodzaje samochodów elektrycznych i hybrydowych. (2022), available at: https://www.autobaza.pl, 23.01.2022.

Rogala B. (2021), *Po raz pierwszy w historii Unii Europejskiej OZE dostarczyły więcej energii niż węgiel, available at:* https://300gospodarka.pl/, 27.12.2021.

Rokicka-Broniatowska A. (2006), *Wstęp do informatyki gospodarczej*, SGH, Warszawa.

Rokicka-Broniatowska A. (2006), *Wstęp do informatyki gospodarczej*, SGH, Warszawa, p. 129.

Rosenberg J., Mateos A. (2011), *Chmura obliczeniowa. Rozwiązania dla biznesu*, Helion, Gliwice.

Rowley J. (2202), Using Case Studies in Research, *Management Research News*, 25/1, 16–27.

Rozporządzenie Ministra Infrastruktury z dnia 26 października 2005 r. w sprawie warunków technicznych, jakim powinny odpowiadać telekomunikacyjne obiekty budowlane i ich usytuowanie, (Dz.U. 2005 nr 219 poz. 1864).

Rozporządzenie ministra środowiska z dnia 27 września 2001 r. w sprawie katalogu odpadów, (Dz.U. 2001 nr 112 poz. 1206).

Rozporządzenie Ministra Środowiska z dnia 6 lutego 2015 r. w sprawie komunalnych osadów ściekowych, (Dz.U. 2015 poz. 257).

Rozporządzenie Ministra Środowiska z dnia 7 października 2016 r. w sprawie szczegółowych wymagań dla transportu odpadów, (Dz.U. 2016 poz. 1742).

Rozporządzenie Ministra Środowiska z dnia 9 grudnia 2014 r. w sprawie katalogu odpadów, (Dz.U. 2014 poz. 1923).

Rozporządzeniem Ministra Środowiska z dnia 11 maja 2015 r. w sprawie odzysku odpadów poza instalacjami i urządzeniami, (Dz.U. 2015 poz. 796).

Rozwiązania wodorowe, available at: https://www.virtud.pl/h2-wodor/, 02.01.2022.

Rutkowski K. (2001), *Logistyka dystrybucji*, Difin, Warszawa.

Sahiner O. (2022), *Cloud in Logistics*, available at: https://www-morethanshipping-com.translate.goog/cloud-in-logistics/?, 03.05.2022.

Salesforce. (2022), available at: https://www.salesforce.com, 24.02.2022.

Samochody elektryczne – ciężarowe i dostawcze. (2022), available at: https://samochody.pl, 26.01.2022.

Samochody elektryczne. (2022), available at: https://mlodytechnik.pl, 23.01.2022.

Samochody elektryczne vs. auta wodorowe – na co się zdecydować? (2022), available at: https://ampergo.pl/, 28.02.2022.

Scherf J. (2022), *What Is Logistics 4.0? Everything You Need to Know about Digitization & Logistics*, available at: https://www.maschinenmarkt.international, 09.02.2022.

Shah P. (2021), *AI Chatbot in Supply Chain and Logistics Industry*, available at: https://yourstory.com/mystory/ai-chatbot-supply-chain-logistics-industry/amp, 08.04.2021

Sikorska M., Józefiak J. (2022), *10 porad, jak nie przyczyniać się do ocieplania klimatu*, available at: https://www.ogrzewnictwo.pl/aktualnosci/10-porad-jak-nie-przyczyniac-sie-do-ocieplania-klimatu, 05.04.2022.

Skłodowska M., Elżbieciak T. (2022), *Śmieci zamiast węgla i gazu. Przybywa spalarni*, available at: https://wysokienapiecie.pl, 18.02.2022.
Skorżepo M. (2022), *Dom pasywny. Czym jest i jak powstaje? – poradnik*, available at: https://www.expondo.pl/inspiracje/dom-pasywny-czym-jest-i-jak-powstaje/, 29.04.2022.
Skowronek Cz., Sarjusz-Wolski Z. (2007), *Logistyka w przedsiębiorstwie*, PWE, Warszawa.
Śladkowski S. (2004), *Bezpieczeństwo ekologiczne Rzeczpospolitej Polskiej*, Akademia Obrony Narodowej, Warszawa.
Słowiński B. (2008), *Podstawy sprawnego działania*, Wydawnictwo Uczelniane Politechniki Koszalińskiej, Koszalin.
Słownik biznesowy. (2022), available at: http://www.biznesowe.edu.pl, 09.06.2022.
Słownik biznesu i ekonomii. (2022), available at: http://www.biznesowe.edu.pl, 20.01.2022.
Słownik języka polskiego. (2022), PWE, available at: http://sjp.pwn.pl/, 10.02.2022.
Słownik logistyczny, available at: https://www.logistyka.net.pl/, 28.02.2022.
Słownik pojęć. (2022), available at: https://systell.pl/slownik-pojec/ivr/, 20.02.2022.
Słownik terminologii logistycznej. (2006), ILiM, Poznań.
Słupski M., Sobiesiński K. (2022), *Systemy informatyczne wspomagające zarządzanie*, available at: https://present5.com/systemy-informatyczne-wspomagajace-zarzadzanie-michal-slupski-krzysztof-sobiesinski, 03.03.2022.
SMAC Net: The Digital Platform of the Future? (2022), available at: https://www-sifytechnologies-com.translate.goog/blog/smac-net-the-digital-platform-of-the-future/?, 05.06.2022.
Smid W. (2012), *Boss Leksykon*, Dr Lex, Kraków.
Sojka M. (2022), *Co to jest automatyzacja magazynu? Definicja i dlaczego warto*, available at: https://www.bekuplast.com/pl/blog/co-to-jest-aco to jest automatyzacja mautomatyzacja-magazynu-definicja-i-dlaczego-warto/, 02.05.2022.
Sokołowski G. (2014), *Traceability – bezpieczeństwo i śledzenie przepływu produktów w łańcuchach dostaw, w oparciu o standardy GS1 i wymagania UE*, ILiM, Poznań.
Sołtysik M. (2000), *Zarządzanie logistyczne*, Akademia Ekonomiczna, Katowice.
Sovacool B.K., Hirsh R.F. (2009), Beyond Batteries: An Examination of the Benefits and Barriers to Plug-in Hybrid Electric Vehicles (PHEVs) and a Vehicle-to-Grid (V2G) Transition, *Energy Policy*, 37, 1095–1103.
Sprawdzili najbardziej zanieczyszczone państwa świata. Polska w połowie stawki. (2022), available at: https://www.tokfm.pl/, 15.02.2022.
Stanisławski R. (2017), Triangulacja technik badawczych w naukach o zarządzaniu, "Organizacja i Kierowanie", 4/178, 103–119.
Stappen R.K. (2006), *A Sustainable World is Possible. Der Wise Consensus: Problemlösungen für das 21 Jahrhundert. Impuls* - dokument Manuskript, 1.2.
Statistics Poland (2020), Statistical Publishing Establishment, Warsaw.
Stefanowicz J. (1984), *Bezpieczeństwo współczesnych państw*, Wydawnictwo Pax, Warszawa.

Stoner J.A.F., Freeman E.R., Gilbert Jr D.R. (2001), *Kierowanie,* PWE, Warszawa.

Supply Chain Sustainability, available at: https://www-gep-com.translate.goog/supply-chain-sustainability?, 19.06.2022.

Supply Chain, available at: https://corporatefinanceinstitute-com.translate.goog/resources/knowledge/strategy/supply-chain/?, 06/08/2022.

Synchronizacja-danych, available at: http://www.gs1pl.org/system-gs1/standardy-gs1/synchronizacja-danych, 16.02.2022.

System identyfikacji kontenerów. (2022), available at: http://www.eltegps.pl, 10.03.2022.

Szczepanek, A. (2009), Fast Charging vs. Slow Charging: *Pros and Cons for the New Age of Electric Vehicles.* In *Proceedings of the EVS24 International Battery, Hybrid and Fuel Cell Electric Vehicle Symposium*, Stavanger, Norway, 13–16 May 2009.

Szekalska E. (2022), *Wiele odpadów niebezpiecznych można i warto odzyskiwać*, available at: https://www.teraz-srodowisko.pl, 12.02.2022.

Szulc W. (2021), *Elektroniczne metody monitorowania ruchomych środków transportowych*, available at: http://www.zabezpieczenia.com.pl/, 17.07.2021.

Szymonik A. (2010), *Logistyka i zarządzanie łańcuchem dostaw*, część 1, Difin, Warszawa.

Szymonik A. (2010), *Logistyka w bezpieczeństwie*, Difin, Warszawa, p. 107.

Szymonik A. (2010), *Technologie informatyczne w logistyce*, Placet, Warszawa.

Szymonik A. (2015), *Informatyka dla potrzeb logistyka(i)*, Difin, Warszawa.

Szymonik A. (2016), *Zarządzanie bezpieczeństwem gospodarczym w systemie bezpieczeństwa narodowego Aspekt logistyczny*, Politechnika Łódzka, Łódź.

Szymonik A. (2016), *Zarządzanie bezpieczeństwem gospodarczym w systemie bezpieczeństwa narodowego Aspekt logistyczny*, Politechnika Łódzka, Łódź, pp. 55–58.

Szymonik A. (2018), *Ekologistyka Teoria i Praktyka,* Difin, Warszawa 2018, p. 120.

Szymonik A. (2018), *Ekologistyka, Teoria Praktyka,* Difin, Warszawa.

Szymonik A., Stanisławski R., Błaszczyk A. (2021), *Nowoczesna koncepcja ekologistyki*, Difin, Warszawa.

Tavana M., Hajipour V., Oveisi S. (2022), *IoT-based Enterprise Resource Planning: Challenges, Open Issues, Applications, Architecture, and Future Research Directions*, available at: https://doi.org/10.1016/j.iot.2020.100262.

Techmine, available at: http://techmine.pl/, 10.02.2022.

Techniki zgłębiania danych (data mining). (2022), available at: https://www.statsoft.pl/, 25.07.2022.

Technologia Blockchain – czym jest? (2022); available at: https://tokeneo.com/pl/technologia-blockchain-co-to-jest/, 28.03.2022.

The Carbon Disclosure Project, available at: https://climatestrategiespoland.pl/blog/carbon-disclosure-project/, 07.07.2022.

The European Power Sector in 2020. (2021), available at: https://www.agora-energiewende.de/en/publications/the-european-power-sector-in-2020/, 25.01.2021.

The Supply Chain and Blockchain. I: Pros and Cons. (2022), available at: https://www.blocktac.com/en/newness/the-supply-chain-and-blockchain-i-pros-and-cons/, 28.03.2022.

TMS Falcon – system do zarządzania transportem. (2022), available at: http://www.optidata.pl/, 09.01.2022.

Top 10 Logistics Industry Trends & Innovations in 2022. (2022), available at: https://www-startus--insights-com.translate.goog/innovators-guide/top-10-logistics-industry-trends-innovations-in-2021/?, 20.04.2022.

Top 5 Out Of 600 Robotics Startups In Logistics. (2022), available at: https://www-startus--insights-com.translate.goog/innovators-guide/top-5-out-of-600-robotics-startups-in-logistics/?, 05.01.2022.

Toyota. (2021), available at: https://toyota-forklifts.pl/o-toyocie/pr-and-news/energia-sloneczna-wozki-widlowe-toyota/, 29.11.2021.

TPM – *Total Productive Maintenance.* (2022), available at: https://queris.pl/baza-wiedzy/tpm-total-productive-maintenance/, 22.05.2022.

Transportation Management System: Benefits, Features, and Main Providers, available at: https://www.altexsoft.com/blog/transportation-management-system/, 28.02.2022.

Tredeau F.P. Salameh Z.M. (2009), Evaluation of Lithium Iron Phosphate Batteries for Electric Vehicles Application. In *Proceedings of the IEEE Vehicle Power and Propulsion Conference*, Dearborn, MI, USA.

Uchwała Nr 39/2010 Rady Ministrów z dnia 15 marca 2010 r. zmieniająca uchwałę w sprawie ustanowienia programu wieloletniego pod nazwą „Program Oczyszczania Kraju z Azbestu na lata 2009 – 2032".

Uchwała nr 67 Rady Ministrów z dnia 6 maja 2021 r. w sprawie Krajowego planu gospodarki odpadami 2022, Warszawa, dnia 11 sierpnia 2016 r. poz. 784, zmieniająca uchwałę w sprawie Krajowego planu gospodarki odpadami.

Uchwała nr 88 Rady Ministrów z dnia 1 lipca 2016 r. w sprawie Krajowego planu gospodarki odpadami 2022, Warszawa, dnia 11 sierpnia 2016 r.

UN Global Compact, available at: https://ungc.org.pl/o-nas/, 07.07.2022.

Under F. (2022), *Autonomous Vehicles in logistics: Everything you Need to Know*, available at: https://businesspartnermagazine-com.translate.goog/autonomous-vehicles-logistics-everything-need-know/?, 11.05.2022.

Ustawa o odpadach medycznych z dnia 27 kwietnia 2001 roku, (Dz.U. 2001 nr 62 poz. 628).

Ustawa o odpadach z dnia 27 kwietnia 2001 roku.

Ustawa z dnia 10 lipca 2008 r. o odpadach wydobywczych, (Dz. U. 2008 Nr 138 poz. 865).

Ustawa z dnia 12 września 2002 r. o normalizacji, (Dz.U. 2002 nr 169 poz. 1386).

Ustawa z dnia 13 czerwca 2013 r. o gospodarce opakowaniami i odpadami opakowaniowymi, (Dz.U. 2013 poz. 888).

Ustawa z dnia 14 grudnia 2012 r. o odpadach, (Dz.U. 2013 poz. 21).

Ustawa z dnia 18 lipca 2001 r. *Prawo wodne*, (Dz.U. 2001 Nr 115 poz. 1229).

Ustawa z dnia 19 lipca 2019 r. o zmianie ustawy o biokomponentach i biopaliwach ciekłych oraz niektórych innych ustaw, (Dz.U. 2019 poz. 1527).

Ustawa z dnia 20 stycznia 2005 r. o recyklingu pojazdów wycofanych z eksploatacji, (Dz. U. 2005 Nr 25 poz. 202).

Ustawa z dnia 24 kwietnia 2009 r. o bateriach i akumulatorach, (Dz. U. Nr 79, poz. 666, z późn. zm.)

Ustawa z dnia 26 kwietnia 2007 r. o zarządzaniu kryzysowym, (Dz.U. 2007 nr 89 poz. 590)

Ustawa z dnia 26 kwietnia 2007 r. o zarządzaniu kryzysowym, (Dz.U. 2007 nr 89 poz. 590).

Ustawa z dnia 27 kwietnia 2001 r. art.3. prawo ochrony środowiska, (Dz. U. 2001 Nr 62 poz. 627).

Ustawa z dnia 9 czerwca 2011 r. – Prawo geologiczne i górnicze, (Dz.U. 2011 nr 163 poz. 981).

Ustawia z dnia 11 września 2015 r. o zużytym sprzęcie elektrycznym i elektronicznym, (Dz.U. 2015 poz. 1688).

Uzyskiwanie energii z promieniowania słonecznego. (2021), available at: http://www.slonecznydach.pl/, 23.12.2021.

Vademecum logistyki. (2020), (ed.). S. Kauf, Difin, Warszawa, p. 26.

Vademecum teleinformatyka II. (2002), IDG, Warszawa.

Vilko J., Karandassov B., Myller E. (2011), Logistic Infrastructure and Its Effects on Economic Development, *China-USA Business Review*, 11(11), 1152–1167.

Villena V.H., Gioia D.A., More M. (2022), *Sustainable Supply Chain*, available at: https://hbr-org.translate.goog/2020/03/a-more-sustainable-supply-chain?, 18.06.2022.

Visayadamrong Ch., Sooksmarn S., Anussornnitisarn P. (2013), *Supply Chain Traceability – A Market Driven Approach*, International conference, Zadar Croatia.

Volvo FH Electric: bezemisyjny długodystansowiec. (2022), available at: https://nowoczesnaflota.pl, 22.01.2022.

Wady i zalety energetyki wodnej. (2021), available at: https://www.esoleo.pl/baza-wiedzy/poradnik-fotowoltaika-esoleo/oze-i-ekologia/jakie-wady-i-zalety-ma-energia-wodna/, 25.12.2021.

Wasylko M. (1999), *Logistyka w gospodarce narodowej, Podstawowe problemy makrologistyki*, Wydawnictwo Naukowe Wyższej Szkoły Kupieckiej w Łodzi, Łódź.

What Are the Main Supply Chain Challenges? (2022), available at: https://www-blumeglobal-com.translate.goog/learning/supply-chain-challenges/?, 07.07.2022.

What Does the Design Process Look Like?, available at: https://rotom.pl/uslugi/projektowanie-opakowan, 20.07./2022.

What Is a Passive House? (2022), available at: https://passipedia-org.translate.goog/basics/what_is_a_passive_house?, 28.04.2022.

What Is a Transportation Management System: Benefits, Features, and Main Providers. (2022), available at: https://www.altexsoft.com/blog/transportation-management-system/, 28.02.2022.

What Is Customer Service: Definition, Types, Benefits, Stats.

What Is Customer Service?, Definition & Tips, available at: https//www.salesforce.com, 24.02.2022.

What Is It? available at: https://www-cprac-org.translate.goog/en/sustainable/production/cleaner?, 28.04.2020.

What Is Reverse Logistics and How Is It Different than Traditional Logistics. (2022), https://www.globaltranz.com/what-is-reverse-logistics/, 20.04.2022.

What is the CRM Process? 5 key Steps, What Is the CRM Process? 5 key steps.

Why Is Quality Assurance Important in the Logistics Sector?

Why Quality Assurance Is Vital in the Logistics Sector? (2022), available at: https://www-logmore-com.translate.goog/post/logistics-quality-assurance?, 22.05.2022.

Wiąckowski S. (2008), *Ekologia ogólna*. Oficyna Wydawnicza Branta, Bydgoszcz.

Witkowski J. (2003), *Zarządzanie łańcuchem dostaw*, PWE, Warszawa.

WMS – zarządzanie magazynem. (2022), available at: http://www.programyerp.com/wms, 19.01.2022.

Wolański N. (2008), *Ekologia człowieka. Ewolucja i dostosowanie biokulturowe*, PWN, Warszawa.

Zagrożenia okresowe występujące w Polsce. (2013), Wydział analiz RCB, Warszawa.

Zając M., Barabasz Sz. (2022), *Co to jest Chatbot?*, available at: https://greenparrot.pl/nasza-oferta/chatbot/, 16.03.2022.

Zalety stosowania pomp ciepła (2021), available at: https://dombezrachunkow.com/dom-bez-rachunkow/zalety-stosowania-pomp-ciepla/, 24.12.2021;

Zarządzanie majątkiem przedsiębiorstwa – czy warto rozbudować posiadany system ERP? (2022), available at: http://www.insoftconsulting.pl/, 12.01.2022.

Zarzycki R., Imbierowicz M., Stelmachowski M. (2007), *Wprowadzenie do inżynierii ochrony środowiska. Ochrona środowiska naturalnego*, WNT, Warszawa.

Zeszyty naukowe Politechniki Poznańskiej, nr 62 Organizacja i Zarządzanie 2014.

Żółtowski B., Kwiatkowski K. (2012), *Zagrożone środowisko*, Wydawnictwa Uczelniane Uniwersytetu Technologiczno–Przyrodniczego w Bydgoszczy, Bydgoszcz.

Appendices

Appendix 3.1 Classification of maximum wind speeds in Poland and their effects

No class	*Wind speed in m/s at a height of 10m*	*Wind speed in km/h at a height of 10 m*	*Characteristic wind*	*Consequences actions*
I	17.2–20.7	62–74	violent wind	the wind breaks tree branches, walking against the wind is difficult
II	20.8–24.4	75–88	gale	the wind damages buildings, tears off tiles, and breaks whole trees
III	24.5–28.4	89–102	strong gale	the wind tears up trees by their roots, causes great damage to buildings (tearing off roofs, breaking towers and power poles)
IV	28.5–32.6	103–117	violent gale	the wind causes extensive damage, danger to life
V	≥ 32.7	≥ 118	hurricane or whirlwind	the wind causes destruction and havoc, possible fatal accidents
V-1	35.1–50.1	126–180	strong	
V-2	50.2–70.2	181–253	devastating	
V-3	≥ 70.3	≥ 254	devastating	

Source: Based on: A. Szymonik, ***Zarzadzanie bez.pieczeństwem gospodarczym w systemie bezpieczeństwa narodowego Aspekty logistyczne,*** Politechnika Łódzka, Łódź (2016), p. 362.

Appendix 3.2 Severity levels depending on the criteria for issuing a weather alert for winds

The degree of danger	*Conditions*	*Possible losses/ recommendations*
The degree of danger	54 km/h <Vavg ≤ 72 km/h	Damage to buildings, roofs; damage to the stand, breaking branches and trees; communication difficulties. Caution recommended, need to follow news and weather developments.
1 (yellow)	i.e., 15 m/s <Vavg ≤ 20 m/s	
	or in gusts	
	72 km/h <V ≤ 90 km/h	
	i.e., 20 m/s <V ≤ 25 m/s	
The degree of danger	72 km/h <Vavg ≤ 90 km/h	Damage to buildings, roofs; breaking and uprooting trees by roots; communication difficulties; damage to overhead lines. Caution recommended, need to follow news and weather developments.
2 (orange)	i.e., 20 m/s <Vavg ≤ 25 m/s	
	or in gusts	
	90 km/h <V ≤ 115 km/h	
	i.e., 25 m/s <V ≤ 32 m/s	
The degree of danger	Vavg> 90 km/h	Destruction of buildings, removal of roofs; destruction of overhead lines; large damage to the stand; significant difficulties in communication; danger to life.
3 (red)	i.e., Vavg> 25 m/s	
	or in gusts	
	V> 115 km/h	
	i.e., V> 32 m/s	

where:

Vavg – mean wind speed (in the warning text in km/h)
V – gust wind speed (warning text in km/h)

Source: Based on: A. Szymonik, *Zarzadzanie bezpieczeństwem gospodarczym w systemie bezpieczeństwa narodowego Aspekty logistyczne, Politechnika* Łódzka, Łódź (2016), p. 363.

Appendix 3.3 Severity levels depending on the criteria for issuing a meteorological warning for severe frosts

The degree of danger	*Criteria*	*Consequences*
The degree of danger 1 (yellow)	–25 ° C <Tmin ≤ –20 ° C Tmax> –10 ° C Duration, at least two days	The risk of cooling down organisms, frostbite, frostbite.
The degree of danger 2 (orange)	–25 ° C> T min ≤–20 ° C Tmax <–10 ° C Duration, at least two days.	High risk of organisms cooling down, frostbite, freezing, freezing of hydrotechnical installations and devices.
The degree of danger 3 (red)	T min ≤ –25 ° C Duration, at least two days.	Very large in a large area the risk of cooling down organisms, frostbite, freezing, freezing of hydrotechnical installations and devices, danger to life.

Source: Based on: *Zagrożenia okresowe występujące w Polsce,* aktualizacja, Wydział analiz RCB, styczeń (2013), p. 11.

Appendix 3.4 Severity levels depending on the meteorological warning criteria for heavy snowfall

The degree of danger	*Criteria*	*Consequences*
The degree of danger 1 (yellow)	Increase of snow cover over 15 cm in 24 hours.	Traffic problems, slippery roads.
The degree of danger 2 (orange)	Increase of snow cover over 25 cm in 24 hours. in lowlands or more than 40 cm within 24 hours. in areas located above 600 m above sea level.	Communication difficulties, impassability of local roads.
The degree of danger 3 (red)	Increase of snow cover over 35 cm in 24 hours. in lowlands or more than 50 cm within 24 hours in areas located above 600 m above sea level.	Major communication difficulties, road impassability, damage to the forest stand, damage to roofs, danger to life.

Source: Based on: *Zagrożenia okresowe występujące w Polsce,* aktualizacja, Wydział analiz RCB, styczeń (2013), p. 11.

Appendix 3.5 Severity levels depending on the criteria for issuing a meteorological alert for blizzards

The degree of danger	*Criteria*	*Consequences*
The degree of danger	Unstable snow cover or light or moderate snowfall and wind of:	The formation of snowdrifts, communication difficulties.
1 (yellow)	Vavg> 6 m/s	
	Vavg – average wind speed	
The degree of danger	a) Unstable snow cover or light or moderate snowfall and wind of:	Rapid formation of snowdrifts, communication difficulties.
2 (orange)	Vavg> 10 m/s	
	b) heavy snowfall and wind by:	
	Vavg> 6 m/s	
	Vavg – average wind speed	
The degree of danger	Heavy snowfall and wind about:	Numerous rapidly growing drifts in large areas, difficulties in communication, impassability of roads.
3 (red)	Vavg> 10 m/s	
	Vavg – average wind speed	

Source: Based on: *Zagrożenia okresowe występujące w Polsce*, aktualizacja, Wydział analiz RCB, styczeń (2013), p. 11.

Appendix 3.6 Severity levels depending on the criteria for issuing a meteorological alert for freezing rainfall

The degree of danger	*Criteria*	*Possible losses/recommendations*
The degree of danger 1 (yellow)	Freezing drizzle or rainfall lasting up to 12 hours in one place	Glaze; slippery roads, roads and sidewalks; communication difficulties.
The degree of danger 2 (orange)	Freezing drizzle or rainfall lasting 12 to 24 hours in one place	Glaze; communication difficulties; icing of roads, obstruction to pedestrian traffic; damage to the stand and overhead lines
The degree of danger 3 (red)	Freezing drizzle or rainfall lasting more than 12 hours in one place	Glaze; fast icing of roads; great difficulties in communication and in pedestrian traffic; damage to the stand and overhead lines.

Source: Based on: *Stopnie zagrożenia w zależności od kryteriów wydawania ostrzeżenia meteorologicznego dla poszczególnych zjawisk meteorologicznych,* https://prudnik.pl/, 20.06.2022.

Index

Note: **Bold** page numbers refer to tables; *italic* page numbers refer to figures and page numbers followed by "n" denote endnotes.

Printed in the United States
by Baker & Taylor Publisher Services

Printed in the United States
by Baker & Taylor Publisher Services